This Book is dedicated to the memory of Bernie (1954-2001).

BRENTFORD FOOTBALL CLUB PREMIER YEARS VOLUME ONE

1935-36

Compiled and Produced by Mark Chapman

Published by Brentford Football Club

ACKNOWLEDGMENTS

Thank you to Steve Smith, Peter Gilham and David Harrison, who kindly lent programmes to be used for the book, and to Dave Tuffney for the Cover design.

Mark Chapman October 2001

First Published 2001 by:

Brentford FC Limited
Griffin Park, Braemar Road, Brentford, Middlesex,
TW8 0NT www.brentfordfc.co.uk

Copyright 2001 Mark Chapman and Brentford FC Limited

British Library Cataloguing-in-Publication Data
A catalogue record for this book is available
from the British Library

ISBN: 0-9541630-0-1

Book Design & Production by:

Oxygen 3, 12 First Cross Road, Twickenham,
Middlesex TW2 5QA www.oxygen3.tv

Cover Jacket Design:

Suparama Supermonkey Ltd, 4th Floor, 20-22 Elsley Court,
Great Titchfield Street, London, W1W 8BE www.suparama.com

Printed and bound by The Bath Press

THE PROGRAMMES

Trial Matches

21st August 1935 Stripes vs Whites
24th August 1935 Stripes vs Whites

Football League Division One

5th September 1935 vs Blackburn Rovers
7th September 1935 vs Huddersfield Town
21st September 1935 vs Aston Villa
5th October 1935 vs Sheffield Wednesday
19th October 1935 vs Stoke City
2nd November 1935 vs Arsenal
16th November 1935 vs Sunderland
30th November 1935 vs Leeds United
14th December 1935 vs Liverpool
25th December 1935 vs Preston North End
28th December 1935 vs Bolton Wanderers
18th January 1936 vs Middlesbrough
1st February 1936 vs Wolverhampton Wanderers
29th February 1936 vs Birmingham
14th March 1936 vs Manchester City
25th March 1936 vs Portsmouth
28th March vs Chelsea
11th April 1936 vs Grimsby Town
13th April 1936 vs Everton
25th April 1936 vs West Bromwich Albion
2nd May 1936 vs Derby County

Foreword

Halcyon days indeed. For anyone who saw Brentford in their first epic journey to the top flight in 1935, a dream had indeed come true. The Bees had completed a whirlwind sequence from the lowly reaches of the Third Division South to the First Division in just two years and the right to play Chelsea, Arsenal and as it turns out, a division above Manchester United!

For anyone who has supported Brentford after the loved 'Royal Oak' end was demolished in 1986 will probably miss how big a ground Griffin Park actually was, and to think it could hold nearly 40,000 spectators, but it did and these programmes faithfully record those moments when it was packed to the rafters.

Look out for the fixture lists at the start of the season and then check the end. Notice anything different? The 1935-36 season was the start of the "pools war" where the scheduled fixture list was torn up to stop the Pools companies making money on the Saturday football scores. Changing them at short notice created havoc, disrupting all Football League Clubs, the players, and not to mention programme printers.

For reasons of tedium, the covers have not been reproduced as they were the same throughout Brentford's 21 issued programmes. Or should that be 22? Eagle eyed readers will spot a gap where issue number 14 is missing.

Brentford's scheduled match against Portsmouth was called off on the day of the game. And, as the programme editor of the time announced they did not go into circulation, but if someone out there has a copy, they have in their possession a true collectors item.

Mark Chapman

Brentford Football Club

Registered Office :

GRIFFIN PARK,

BRAEMAR ROAD,

BRENTFORD.

Ground :

GRIFFIN PARK,

EALING ROAD,

BRENTFORD.

Official Programme

SEASON 1935-36

TRIAL GAME

Wednesday, August 21st, 1935

Kick-off 6-15 p.m.

ONE PENNY   *[Copyright]*

TEANS

STRIPES

1—MATHIESON

2—BATEMAN   3—POYSER

4—McKENZIE   5—JAMES   6—WATSON

8—ROBSON   10—SCOTT

7—HOPKINS   9—HOLLIDAY   11—FLETCHER

Referee—Mr. F. T. BARTON. O Linesmen—Messrs. W. Casling and J. A. Harding.

12—SULLIVAN   14—DUNN   16—FENTON

13—MUTTITT   15—BROWN

17—SMITH   18—WILSON   19—J. BRIDDON

20—METCALF   21—ASTLEY

22—LYNCH

WHITES.   —1st Half

12—L. SMITH   14—A. BATCHELOR   16—BROWN

13—GIBBONS   15—McALOON

17—MARLEY   18—SCOTT   19—RAVEN

20—METCALF   21—DUMBRELL

22—NICHOLS

WHITES.   —2nd Half

Notes from the Hive

Season 1935-36 is about to commence, and in this, our first public trial, we take the opportunity of extending to our supporters a very hearty welcome, with the sincere hope that they will all enjoy the games at Griffin Park.

$*$ $*$ $*$

We also extend a hearty welcome to our new players, viz. :— Tom Lynch (Yeovil), Joe Wilson (Southend), Horace Marley (Leyton), Billy Dunn (Celtic), and Leslie Sullivan (Rochdale). We trust that they will have a happy and successful time at Brentford.

$*$ $*$ $*$

Included in the Whites' team, is a young 19-year-old amateur— S. Briddon—who comes from Nottingham district.

$*$ $*$ $*$

Jackie Burns, our popular amateur, is on holiday.

$*$ $*$ $*$

The prices for admission for season 1935-36 will be as follows :—

Reserve Games.

Admission **6d.**, Boys **3d.** New Enclosure (Brook Road), **1/-**, Boys **6d.** Enclosure **1/-**, Boys **6d.** Stands, **1/6.**

League Games.

Admission **1/-**, Boys **6d.**

New Enclosure (Brook Road) **1/6**, Boys **9d.**

Enclosure **2/-**, Boys **1/-**.

Stands—

Wing Stands, ...	**2/6**
Blocks A and G ...	**3/-**
Block F	**3/6**
Block B	**4/-**

Block B. seats can be booked in advance for League Games. Numbered and reserved seats at 4/-. Applications by post must be accompanied by a remittance and stamped addressed envelope.

With reference to this evening's trial, may I appeal to our supporters to appreciate the fact that it is a trial game, and the players are playing under definite instructions.

* * *

We apologise to any of our supporters who may experience any inconvenience owing to the work on the ground not yet being completed. Much has yet to be done before the season opens officially on August 31st, 1935, but I am very confident that everything will be completed in time.

* * *

There are still a few Season Tickets left in Block E at £4 5s. (only).

* * *

The kick-off in the final Public Trial Game on Saturday next, August 24th, is at 3.30 p.m.

* * *

All the proceeds from the Trial Games are allocated to charity.

* * *

I have an interesting letter from a supporter, Mr. Charles W. Garrard, of 106, Uxbridge Road, West Ealing, W.13, who informs me that he. has been in communication with the L.M.S. Railway Company *re* an excursion to Bolton to witness the opening game on August 31st. The Company has agreed to issue a cheap ticket for the return fare of 16/-, providing the party is 30 or over. Any supporter interested should please get in touch with Mr. Garrard direct.

* * *

Supporters should note that a new 24-page Programme will be issued for our League games. It will contain many interesting items and will be well worth the 2d. charged.

* * *

We offer sincere thanks for the valuable support accorded to the Club during past seasons, with the hope that during the coming season the game at Griffin Park will receive further encouragement and increased support.

H.C.C.

The Brentford Printing and Publishing Co., Ltd

Brentford Football Club

Registered Office :

GRIFFIN PARK,

BRAEMAR ROAD,

BRENTFORD.

Ground :

GRIFFIN PARK,

EALING ROAD,

BRENTFORD.

Official Programme

SEASON 1935-36

TRIAL GAME

Saturday, August 24th, 1935

Kick-off 3-30 p.m.

ONE PENNY   [*Copyright*]

TEAMS

PROBABLES

1—NICHOLS

2—BATEMAN   3—POYSER

4—McKENZIE   5—JAMES   6—WATSON

8—ROBSON   10—SCOTT

7—HOPKINS   9—HOLLIDAY   11—FLETCHER

| Referee— | O | Linesmen—Messrs. L. Brown |
| Mr. W. J. LEWINGTON | | and E. S. Harris. |

12—SULLIVAN   14—DUNN   16—FENTON

13—CIBBONS   15—McALOON

17—RAVEN   18—WILSON   19—MARLEY

20—METCALF   21—ASTLEY

22—LYNCH

POSSIBLES

XXXXXXXXXXXXXXXXXXXX   XXXXXXXXXXXXXXXXX

Saturday Next, August 31st, 1935.

BRENTFORD v. CHARLTON
ATHLETIC

(London Combination.)   Kick-off 3-30 p.m.

Notes from the Hive

To-day is our final Public Trial.

* * *

We again apologise to our supporters who may experience any inconvenience owing to the work on the ground not yet being completed. It is anticipated that all will be completed by Saturday next, August 31st, 1935.

* * *

Seats can now be booked for the games versus Blackburn Rovers on Thursday, September 5th, kick-off at 6.15 p.m., and versus Huddersfield Town on Saturday, September 7th, kick-off at 3.30 p.m. Numbered and reserved seats in Block B at 4/- each, all other Stand seats will be **unreserved.** Applications by post must be accompanied with remittance and stamped addressed envelope.

* * *

The prices for admission for season 1935-36 will be as follows :—

Reserve Games.

Admission **6d.,** Boys **3d.** New Enclosure (Brook Road), **1/-,** Boys **6d.** Enclosure **1/-,** Boys **6d.** Stands, **1/6.**

League Games.

Admission **1/-,** Boys **6d.** New Enclosure (Brook Road) **1/6,** Boys **9d.** Enclosure **2/-,** Boys **1/-.**

Stands—

Wing Stands, ...	**2/6**
Blocks A and G ...	**3/-**
Block F	**3/6**
Block B	**4/-**

(numbered and reserved)

There are still a few Season Tickets left in Block E at £4 5s. 0d. (only).

All the proceeds from the Trial Games are allocated to charity.

* * *

We are represented at the White City Stadium this afternoon in a Six-a-Side Competition, our team being : Mathieson (capt.), Scott (A.), Smith, Muttitt, Brown and M. Batchelor.

* * *

I have an interesting letter from a supporter, Mr. Charles W. Garrard, of 106, Uxbridge Road, West Ealing, W.13, who informs me that he has been in communication with the L.M.S. Railway Company *re* an Excursion to Bolton to witness the opening game on August 31st. The Company has agreed to issue a cheap ticket for the Return Fare of 16/-, providing the party is 30 or over. Any supporter interested should please get in touch with Mr. Garrard direct.

* * *

Supporters should note that a new 24-page Programme will be issued for our League games. It will contain many interesting items and will be worth the 2d. charged.

* * *

Charlie Walsh will not be available for the opening games as the injured knee that gave him so much trouble last season was again injured during training. Charlie was examined by a specialist who ordered him three weeks' special treatment.

Our sympathy is with this player who has had more than his share of bad luck since coming to Brentford. We wish him better luck for the future.

* * *

Sam Briddon, the young amateur from Nottingham, who played in the trial on Wednesday last, has been signed on as a professional. Age 19, height 6ft. 0½ins. and weight over 11 stone, he is a young player of much promise.

* * *

If Jackie Burns returns from his holidays in time, he will take part in to-day's game in the second half.

H.C.C.

The Brentford Printing and Publishing Co., Ltd

BRENTFORD FOOTBALL AND SPORTS CLUB, LIMITED.

Registered Office :—GRIFFIN PARK, BRAEMAR ROAD, BRENTFORD.

President and Chairman :
MR. L. P. SIMON. •

ALDERMAN W. FLEWITT, J.P.   MR. H. W. DODGE.
MR. H. N. BLUNDELL.   MR. C. L. SIMON.
MR. H. J. SAUNDERS.

Hon. Treasurer :
ALDERMAN W. FLEWITT, J.P.
Club Medical Officer ; DR. A. D. GOWANS.

Telephones :
GROUND : EALING 1744.
PRIVATE HOUSE : EALING 1183.

Vice-Chairman :
MR. F. A. DAVIS.

MR. F. W. BARTON.
ALDERMAN H. F. DAVIS.
MR. J. R. HUGHES, J.P., C.C.

Secretary-Manager ;
MR. H. C. CURTIS,
" DORINCOURT," BOSTON GARDENS, BRENTFORD.

Telegraphic Address ;
CURTIS, FOOTBALL, BRENTFORD.
Ground ; GRIFFIN PARK, EALING ROAD, BRENTFORD.

No. 1.   **Thursday, September 5th, 1935.**

Notes from the Hive.

*T*HE writer has been contributing notes to the Brentford Programme for a number of years, yet during a comparatively short period how things have changed !

Not so long ago the Bees could be placed in the category of just an ordinary Third Division Club with hopes of promotion not very great. Then came the upward swing. The Bees began to sting with a vengeance and being no respecter of persons, or rather in this instance clubs, Brentford forced their way into the limelight in no uncertain manner. The first step, promotion to the Second Division, came in due course and the next hurdle, a more difficult one, was accomplished in the short space of two years. With just a little luck it might have been bridged in one, but we are not bemoaning our fate in having to wait two years to realise the ambition of every club outside the highest circle —a place in the First Division.

The Bees did the trick last season and few will deny that the prize was well earned. In passing I take this opportunity of congratulating the Brentford players on winning a place in the First Division. My congratulations are, of necessity, mingled with the start of a new campaign and a warm welcome into the top class for the Bees.

SAME OLD FACES.

Rightly, and I think the majority of enthusiasts will agree with the decision, the Brentford Manager has decided to give the team that won promotion a chance to carry on the good work in a higher sphere. It remains to be seen whether the successful Bees of the Second Division are good enough to hold their own in the next class. I think they will prove their worth in no uncertain manner providing undue injuries do not peg our boys back.

The Club Management evidently think in a like strain for very few new players have been engaged. But should changes be necessary they will be made, and if needed further new players secured. In any case I sincerely hope that supporters of the Club will give every encouragement to the players. It may take a while for the Bees to find their bearings in the First Division, for the change of status often has a psychological effect which requires time for players to become normal in their play. There is no keener set of players in the Football League than those who will represent Brentford in this great new adventure of First Division football at Griffin Park, while the club spirit at the Bees' headquarters is a joy to behold.

OUR NEW CHUMS.

I feel that the opportunity should be taken of introducing the new players who have been signed. It will be remembered that the directors decided at the end of last season to re-sign every professional on the books of the Club. A very nice gesture which was duly accomplished. Since then Bert Stephens, a utility wingman, has been transferred to Brighton, where we wish him the very best of luck.

Naturally it was felt that a few new players might become a necessity if only to more strongly duplicate the different departments. That is why T. J. Lynch, goalkeeper from Yeovil was secured. This young man has a brilliant future I think. H. J. Marley, the promising Leyton half back, has now become a professional, and another newcomer to this department is Joe Wilson, from Southend United. New players in attack are Billy Dunn from Glasgow Celtic, and Leslie Sullivan, outside left from Rochdale. In the first public practice game a trial was given to S. Briddon, a tall young half back from the Nottingham district. He only played in the first half but showed such good form that he was fixed up as a professional after the game. I wish every one of these new chums a happy and successful sojourn at Griffin Park.

A GREAT START.

The Bees opened a new season in great style with a two clear goals win at Bolton. The game aroused great interest, over 30,000 being present, for this first line-up between the two clubs which gained promotion last season. That Brentford were well worthy of their success no one can doubt, for practically every critic on the game reviews the game in the same strain. In a nutshell—" Brentford were too clever, too fast and much better together." The team work of our boys was a delight to watch. The margin might have been considerably wider for the ball was in the Bolton net four, and probably five, times. Much surprise was occasioned among the onlookers when the referee decided against awarding a goal to Brentford on the two occasions the ball was definitely in the net. It is all the luck of the game and the fact that the Bees eventually won so well is really all that matters. It might have, of course, been otherwise. Jack Holliday scored both goals. I mention that fact in passing—for individual mention would be out of place so well did every man pull his weight.

RESERVES' HOME VICTORY.

It was a very good game at Griffin Park on Saturday last, when our second string just finished ahead of Charlton Reserves by the odd goal in three. Gibbons and Dunn were the scorers.

BLACKBURN ROVERS HERE TO-DAY.

The honour of being the first club to figure in a First Division game at Griffin Park falls to Blackburn Rovers, to whom we extend a very cordial welcome. The Rovers were famous when Brentford were only small fry in the football world, but the two clubs meet in the same sphere this evening. Like ourselves Blackburn commenced the season with a win, scoring the only goal in their home game with Grimsby Town. The Bees anticipate a hard struggle and they are not likely to be disappointed, for the Rovers play a forceful type of football which should ensure few, if any, dull moments during the whole ninety minutes.

HUDDERSFIELD HERE ON SATURDAY.

Huddersfield Town provide the opposition at Griffin Park on Saturday next, and the popularity of this Yorkshire club should mean something approaching a full house at the Bees' headquarters.

" BUSY BEE."

Jottings from the Board Room.

Mr. L. P. Simon has again been unanimously elected Chairman of the Board of Directors.

It is difficult to estimate what Mr. Simon has done for this Club behind the scenes, but without doubt the Club's rise is in no small measure due to him. He is respected by all; may he enjoy the best of good health and long remain connected with the Bees.

Mr. F. A. Davis has also been unanimously re-elected as Vice-Chairman. Like the Chairman, Mr. Davis has done a lot for the Bees; may he also enjoy the best of good health and long remain with the Bees.

At the conclusion of our game v. Bolton Wanderers, on Saturday last, our Players and Officials spent a very pleasant evening with the home team Players and Officials. Splendid tribute was paid to our boys' display during the afternoon, and it was unanimously agreed that they fully merited their splendid victory.

The function gave ample proof that the Bolton Wanderers F.C. possess a Board of Directors who are great sportsmen.

We extend sincere thanks to them for the splendid gesture that prompted them to invite us to dinner with them to celebrate the advance of us both to the First Division. We enjoyed the AFTERNOON and the EVENING.

The Draw for the 1st Round of the London Challenge Cup resulted as follows :

BRENTFORD v. METROPOLITAN POLICE

to be played on this ground on Monday, October 7th, 1935. Kick-off at 3.30 p.m.

There are still a few Season Tickets (Block " E ") left at £4 5s. each.

Maurice Batchelor, who with Leslie Smith, are assisting the Hayes F.C. this season, scored the two goals that enabled his side to defeat Redhill F.C. by 2—1 on Saturday last in the Athenian League.

Numbered and Reserved Seats can be booked for our game v. Huddersfield on Saturday next, September 7th, 1935. Kick-off 3.15 p.m.

Block " B " at 4/- each. All other Stand Seats are unreserved.

Applications by post must be accompanied by a remittance and a stamped addressed envelope.

The 2nd Division Championship Flag, presented to the Club by Messrs. F. A. and H. F. Davis, will be unfurled by the President and Chairman, Mr. L. P. Simon, before the kick-off of this evening's game.

The Southern Railway announce the issue of cheap day tickets at approximately single fare for the return journey from about 70 of their stations to Brentford for our " Home " Fixtures.

BRENTFORD v. BLACKBURN ROVERS,

THURSDAY, SEPT. 5TH. K.O. 6.15 P.M.

Trains will leave Brentford Station (S.R.) at 8.5 and 8.25 p.m. for Twickenham and intermediates, and for Waterloo and intermediates at 8.15 p.m.

BRENTFORD v. HUDDERSFIELD TOWN,

SATURDAY, SEPT. 7TH. K.O. 3.15 P.M.

Southern Railway will run a special service with trains every few minutes from Waterloo to Brentford from 1.50 p.m. to 2.39 p.m., the cheap day return fare being 9d., with equivalent cheap tickets from stations en route, return services leaving Brentford for Waterloo and intermediates at 5.3, 5.8 and 5.15 p.m. From Hounslow at 2.37, 2.45 and 3.7 p.m., calling at Isleworth and Syon Lane, returning at 5.4, 5.18 and 5.28 for Twickenham, etc. A special train will be run from Reading, Staines, Feltham and intermediate stations direct to Brentford and back on September 7th, 21st and October 5th and 19th and November 2nd, at a return fare of 2/6 from stations Reading to Ascot inclusive, with reduced fares from the other stations en route.

For full particulars see Railway Company's announcements at stations.

RE GEORGE ROBSON

I desire to contradict the press report that stated that our inside forward was likely to be transferred to the Scottish Club, Hearts. The Hearts Club approached this Club for Robson's transfer about nine months ago and were then informed that the player was not for transfer. Since then no further negotiations have taken place. Even if there were, the matter would not receive a moment's consideration. To sum it up, George Robson is not for transfer.

WEAR YOUR " BEE "

A young supporter has had a very neat and attractive—and subtle—little " Bee " badge made, and these will be on sale to-day from the Chocolate Boys at the price of two pence.

If you have any difficulty in purchasing one, please write to the Club.

H.C.C.

Shots from the Spot.

By "Rambler"

Despite the fact that the close season had been notable for an absence of sensations, an air of tense excitement heralded the opening of the football season on Saturday—with the result that about 800,000 people watched the League matches, and the receipts amounted to more than £50,000—figures which I believe constitute a record and which give some idea of the gates that will come later on in the season when the activities of summer have been finally forgotten.

* * *

Brentford is naturally not only a centre for local excitement but for national interest as well. The meteoric quality of the Club's rise has awakened the wonder of the footballing world, and the question, "How will the Bees do in the First Division?" is being debated whenever fans foregather.

* * *

I wish you could all have been with me at Bolton to see the cool, deliberate, masterly fashion in which the Bees set about their task. You know the result; but that is not the only thing about the game which matters. More important even than that to my mind was the standard of football the Bees served up, and the complete lack of nervousness they displayed. It was a fine start for the season—and fully justified the management's policy of playing the players who won promotion for the club last season. As long as that form is maintained, there will be no reason to do anything else—and the more credit will reflect on Club and players alike.

* * *

I also wish that I had had with me at Burnden Park all the scaremongers who write and talk so glibly about the increase in foul and reckless play which is apparent to them (if to no one else) in modern football.

It was a hardly-fought game, with a good deal depending on it for both sides, and I personally never wish to see a game fought in a cleaner, more healthy spirit. Robust? Yes. Vigorous? Yes. Dirty? Emphatically No.

* * *

There is no one who loathes "dirty" football more than I do, but I do wish that people who write about it would expose specific instances rather than talking in vague generalities which merely reflect very unjustly on a body of honourable and sportsmanlike men.

* * *

It is dangerous to take too much notice of a sensational success at the beginning of a season, I know, but the implications of that success can be reckoned up by the experienced fairly properly. Bolton, according to most critics, would prove more fitted to First Division football than Brentford. That remains to be seen, but the outstanding fact is that Brentford, after gaining promotion with a five-point lead, beat their nearest rivals on their own ground —and beat them comfortably. Without making the mistake of underestimating their opponents, they were confident enough in their own ability to get on with the job in so workmanlike a fashion that they astounded the critics and the football world alike.

* * *

We hope that those of you who are reading the Brentford Football Club Programme for the first time will like it and that the old and faithful supporters will appreciate the change.

If you have any suggestions, comments or criticisms, we shall be pleased to hear about them.

OUR VISITORS TO-DAY.
HOW THEY MAY LINE UP.

Although in recent seasons they have been rather in the doldrums Blackburn Rovers, our visitors to-day, have a distinguished record. With Aston Villa they share the distinction of having won the F.A. Cup more times than any other club—six. In 1886 they won it for the third time in succession and were awarded a special trophy. Though they have not had so many successes in the League, they have held the Division I. championship on two occasions.

The club was founded in 1874-5.

Brief biographies of the team, as expected to turn out, follow :—

Binns, Clifford (goalkeeper).— Came to the fore with Halifax Town, joining Rovers in 1930 at a fee of £1,500. During the next three seasons he played in 93 League matches and in one campaign did not miss a single match. Then in May, 1933, he was not re-engaged and went to Workington, North Eastern League. A serious injury to Gormlie, who had superseded him, led to his return in October, 1933. Missed only five matches last campaign.

Gorman, James (right back).— Born at Liverpool. Height, 5ft. 9in. Weight, 11st. 2½lb. Graduated with Burscough Rangers and Skelmersdale United, two Merseyside clubs. Joined Blackburn at an early age and made his first appearances with the League side in season 1930-31. In 1932 he superseded the burly Jock Hutton. Very fast. Also plays baseball and cricket.

Crook, Walter (left or right back) —Born at Blackburn. Height, 5ft. 9½ins. Weight, 10st. 6lb. A local product who came to the fore last season. Was with Blackburn Nomads before going to Ewood Park. He is a strong tackler and kicks well.

Whiteside, Arnold (right half).— Born at Calder Vale, Lancashire. Height, 5ft. 5½ins. Weight, 9st. Was playing with Woodplumpton Village Juniors, near Preston, when spotted by Blackburn. He was called from the mill where he worked to sign on. That was in January, 1932, and by the following November he had appeared in the League side. Shines particularly in constructive work.

Christie, Norman (centre half).— Born at Jarrow. Height, 5ft. 10ins. Weight, 11st. 7lb. Had considerable first-team experience with Huddersfield Town before joining Blackburn last season. Was immediately appointed captain of the Ewood Park club. Is a fine pivot, but can also play a useful game on the flank. A schoolmaster, he had experience with Bishop Auckland.

Pryde, Robert (left half).—Born at Methil, Fifeshire. Height, 6ft. Weight, 12st. A centre half who developed with St. Johnstone and Brechin City. On joining Blackburn however, he showed an aptitude for the flank position and came into the League side during season 1933-4. Well-built, but has many dainty touches.

Bruton, Jack (outside right).— Born at Westhoughton, Lancs. Height, 5ft. 7in. Weight, 11st. 1lb. Brought out by Horwich and Wigan Borough. Burnley secured him in May, 1925, the forms actually being signed on an upturned pit tub. After being capped he moved to the Rovers in December, 1929, and became their captain. Has scored over 100 League goals. Also plays cricket and billiards with more than average skill.

BRENTFORD *v.* BI

BRE

1—M

2—BATEMAN
Right Back

4—McKENZIE
Right Half

5—
Ce

7—HOPKINS
Outside Right

8—ROBSON
Inside Right

9—H
Centr

Referee—Mr. W. P. HARPER

12—TURNER
Outside Left

13—TALBOT
Inside Left

14—Tl
Centr

17—PRYDE
Left Half

18—
Co

20—CROOK
Left Back

22

BLACKBU

HERBERT WATS(
Left Half and Captain

Came to Brentford in 1932-33, as part contingent. Now captains the side, and is a field as he is on. Was born at Springwel 1908, and joined Middlesbrough in 1926. F Division Championship Medals, as well as he won before coming to Brentford. For where team work counts most of all, he is sportsman for whom the club comes firs shoulder responsibility. Is a good cricket an hour's gardening, and is one of the footballers playing to-day.

Bert Stephens, our last season's reserve outs forward, was in the Brighton & Hove Albion Lea team on Saturday, and is reported to have done w He failed with a penalty kick.

Cyril Smith, our young half back, won the La Tennis Championship amongst the Professional Foot Players, and is the holder of the Silver Cup.

CKBURN ROVERS

ORD

ESON
per

3—POYSER
Left Back

6—WATSON
Left Half

ES
lf

AY
rd

10—SCOTT
Inside Left

11—FLETCHER
Outside Left

Linesmen—Rev. C. V. Clibbon (Blue Flag),
and Mr. H. Joel (Red Flag).

SON
ard

15—BEATTIE
Inside Right

16—BRUTON
Outside Right

STIE
alf

19—WHITESIDE
Right Half

21—GORMAN
Right Back

NS
er

ROVERS

Middlesbrough
l at that off the
o. Durham, in
ird and Second
other trophies
like Brentford,
deal captain; a
one who can
ys golf, enjoys
conscientious

Tommy Adamson, our late full back, is now Team
nager of Ards F.C. (Ireland). One of his first signa-
s was Alex Stevenson.
Cars can be garaged, opposite the ground in Ealing
d, at Mr. George Davis, Ealing Road Garage. Room
200 cars. Garage Fees are: Motor Cars 1/-, Motor
les, 6d.; Cycles 2d.

Beattie, John Murdoch (inside right).—Born at Aberdeen. Height, 5ft. 8in. Weight, 11st. After only one season in junior football with Hall Russells F.C., he was secured by Aberdeen. Wolverhampton Wanderers paid a big fee for his transfer in September, 1933, and he played for their first team regularly until transferred to Blackburn in December, 1934. Plays a crafty game in typical Scottish style.

Thompson, John Ernest (centre forward). — Born at Newbiggin, Northumberland. Height, 5ft. 11in. Weight, 11st. At the age of 17 he played trials for Ashington, Bradford and Carlisle, all within a week and in three different positions. Was a utility man with Bristol City. Then moved to Bath where he built up a reputation as a goal-scorer, being secured by Blackburn in 1931. Very fast and an accurate shot.

Broke a leg in November, 1933, but has shaken off the effects.

Talbot, Leslie (inside forward). —Born at Hednesford, Staffs. Brother of " Alec " the ex-Villa centre half now with Bradford. Has been at Blackburn for six years, but it was only last season that he became a recognised first-team man. Originally an inside right, he played principally at inside left following the signing of Beattie last season. Has also played centre forward.

Turner, Thomas Stuart (outside left). Born at Glasgow. Height, 5ft. 5in. Weight, 8st. 10lb. Tiny but good. He was partner to Alex James at Raith Rovers while only a youngster. Blackburn secured him in 1929 and he came to the fore when Cunliffe left for Aston Villa in April, 1933. Considering his stature he is a rare bustler and always in the thick of the fray.

OFFICIAL NOTICE

NOTICE IS HEREBY GIVEN that the transfer books of the Preference and Ordinary Shares of the Company will be closed from the 9th to the 30th September next both days inclusive, for the preparation of dividend letters. Dividends will be posted on or about the 21st September next to the shareholders registered in the books of the Company on the 8th September, 1935.

By Order of the Board,

5th September, 1935.

H. C. CURTIS,
Secretary.

Do You Know ?

The biggest wins in recognised International football were recorded by England. In 1882 England beat Ireland 13—0 in their first meeting and in 1901, they beat Germany by 12—0 at Tottenham.

* * *

Joe Reader, last of the long-trousered players and famous West Bromwich Albion goalkeeper, completed 50 years' connection with the club last season.

* * *

Hulme and Bastin got 53 goals for the Arsenal during season 1928-29.

* * *

Only four clubs outside Glasgow have won the Scottish League championship. They are Dumbarton, Hibernian, Motherwell and Hearts.

* * *

Sheffield Wednesday, last year's Cup winners, first took the cup to Yorkshire in 1895-96.

* * *

Cup and League success do not always go together. West Bromwich Albion won the Cup in 1890-91, but that very season they went from October 25th to March 7th without winning a League game.

* * *

Mortimer, red-haired winger, once with Brentford, is now on Accrington's books.

NAMES IN THE GAME.
No. 1

MR. GEORGE ALLISON.

Mr. George Frederick Allison, as secretary-manager of the Arsenal, gets included in this series as " No. 1," not only for that reason, but alphabetically as well. Born on October 24th, 1883, at Harworth-on-Tees, in Co. Durham. He was a director of the Arsenal for ten years before he became secretary-manager in 1934, after the death of the great Herbert Chapman. Was connected with Middlesbrough for a time. He first became the idol he is with the footballing public to-day through his broadcasting commentaries, which revealed him as having not only a complete and thorough knowledge of the game but an ideal microphone personality as well. Has been called football's " C. B. Cochran "; at any rate both give the public what it wants. Came to Brentford's celebration dinner last season, and was given a great welcome.

NEW CAPITAL

The new capital being raised by the Club takes the form of 6 per cent. Debentures of £50 each, and at the Annual General Meeting held in July last, several shareholders expressed the desire to increase their holdings of shares. The Management have also received many letters from supporters who desire to acquire shares. As the share capital of the Club is fully subscribed, it is not possible to satisfy applicants unless any existing shareholder desires to realise, in which case the shareholder should advise the Secretary *in writing* of the number of shares he desires to sell and the price he is willing to accept. Particulars regarding the new issue of Debentures will be forwarded on request.

FIXTURES, SEASON 1935-36.

FIRST TEAM

Date. 1935.	Opponents.	Ground.	GOALS F.	A.
Aug. 31	Bolton Wanderers ...	A	2	0
Sept. 5	Blackburn Rovers ...	H		
,, 7	Huddersfield Town ...	H		
,, 14	Middlesbrough	A		
,, 18	Derby County ...	A		
,, 21	Aston Villa	H		
,, 28	Wolverhampton Wdrs.	A		
Oct. 5	Sheffield Wednesday ..	H		
,, 12	Portsmouth	A		
,, 19	Stoke City ...	H		
,, 26	Manchester City ...	A		
Nov. 2	Arsenal	H		
,, 9	Birmingham	A		
,, 16	Sunderland ...	H		
,, 23	Chelsea	A		
,, 30	Leeds United ...	H		
Dec. 7	Grimsby Town ...	A		
,, 14	Liverpool	H		
,, 21	West Bromwich Albion	A		
,, 25	Preston North End ...	H		
,, 26	Preston North End ...	A		
,, 28	Bolton Wanderers ...	H		
1936.				
Jan. 1	Blackburn Rovers ...	A		
,, 4	Huddersfield Town ...	A		
,, 11	(3)			
,, 18	Middlesbrough ...	H		
,, 25	(4) Aston Villa ...	A		
Feb. 1	Wolverhampton Wdrs.	H		
,, 8	(5) Portsmouth ...	H		
,, 15	Sheffield Wednesday ...	A		
,, 22	Stoke City	A		
,, 29	(6) Manchester City ...	H		
Mar. 7	Arsenal	A		
,, 14	(S.-F.) Birmingham ...	H		
,, 21	Sunderland	A		
,, 28	Chelsea	H		
April 4	Leeds United ...	A		
,, 10	Everton	A		
,, 11	Grimsby Town ...	H		
,, 13	Everton	H		
,, 18	Liverpool	A		
,, 25	(F.) West Brom. Alb.	H		
May 2	Derby County ...	H		

SECOND TEAM

Date. 1935.	Opponents.	Ground.	GOALS F.	A.
Aug. 31	Charlton Athletic ...	H	2	1
Sept. 4	Watford ...	A		
,, 7	Clapton Orient ...	A		
,, 12	Watford	H		
,, 14	Southend United ...	H		
,, 21	Northampton Town ...	A		
,, 25	Luton Town	A		
,, 28	Crystal Palace ...	H		
Oct. 3	Luton Town	H		
,, 5	Reading	A		
,, 12	Tottenham Hotspur ......H			
,, 19	Bristol City	A		
,, 26	Millwall	H		
Nov. 2	West Ham United ...	A		
,, 9	Swansea Town ...	H		
,, 16	Leicester City ...	A		
,, 23	Coventry City ...	H		
,, 30	Arsenal	A		
Dec. 7	Southampton ...	H		
,, 14	Brighton & Hove A.	A		
,, 21	Queen's Park Rgrs. ..	H		
,, 25	Chelsea	A		
,, 26	Chelsea	H		
,, 28	Charlton Athletic ...	A		
1936.				
Jan. 4	Clapton Orient ...	H		
,, 11	Fulham	H		
,, 18	Southend United ...	A		
,, 25	Northampton Town ...	H		
Feb. 1	Crystal Palace ...	A		
,, 8	Reading	H		
,, 15	Tottenham Hotspur ...	A		
,, 22	Bristol City	H		
,, 29	Millwall	A		
Mar. 7	West Ham United ...	H		
,, 14	Swansea Town ...	A		
,, 21	Leicester City ...	H		
,, 28	Coventry City ...	A		
April 4	Arsenal	H		
,, 10	Portsmouth	A		
,, 11	Southampton	A		
,, 13	Portsmouth	H		
,, 18	Brighton & Hove A.	H		
,, 25	Queen's Park Rgrs. ..	A		
May 2	Fulham	A		
†Bournemouth & Bos. .		H		
†Bournemouth & Bos. .		A		
† To be arranged.				

PRICES OF ADMISSION

The prices for admission for Season 1935-36 will be as follows :—

Reserve Games.
     Admission 6d., Boys 3d.
     Enclosure 1/-, Boys 6d.
     Stands, 1/6.

League Games.
     Admission 1/-, Boys 6d.
     New Enclosure (Brook Road) 1/6, Boys 9d.
     Enclosure 2/-, Boys 1/-.
     Stands—

Wing Stands	2/6
Blocks A and G	3/-
Block F	3/6
Block B	4/-

(numbered and reserved)

There are still a few Season Tickets left in Block E. at £4 5s. only

The Next Game.

On Saturday we shall have the pleasure of entertaining Huddersfield Town, who have become one of the most famous clubs in the League in a comparatively short career. Last season they did not produce the football expected of them, and for a time appeared in danger of relegation, and they finished up in the lower half of the League table.

They began this season with a 1—0 win over Preston North End, at home, Richardson, who has played for England, scoring the only goal of the match.

Their League record is a remarkable one, and they play, even in times of adversity, the attractive, thoughtful football that should bring the best out of the Bees. Whatever the result then, Griffin Park fans may be assured of an afternoon's football that cannot fail to be good to watch.

It is an important game, too. Huddersfield will be anxious to snatch every point they can away from home, to cut a better figure in the League this season, and the Bees will naturally be keen to prove that they are worthy of the First Division status they have so recently won.

We expect a big gate for this game—so it will be as well if you get here just as early as you can—and remember that the other fellow will want to see as well.

The Reserves, who once again promise to be a real force in the London Combination this season, are away to Clapton Orient on Saturday, and hope for a point or even two from these old and friendly rivals.

BRENTFORD FOOTBALL AND SPORTS CLUB, LIMITED.

Registered Office :—GRIFFIN PARK, BRAEMAR ROAD, BRENTFORD.

President and Chairman :
MR. L. P. SIMON.

Vice-Chairman :
MR. F. A. DAVIS.

ALDERMAN W. FLEWITT, J.P.
MR. H. N. BLUNDELL.
MR. H. J. SAUNDERS.

MR. H. W. DODGE.
MR. C. L. SIMON.

MR. F. W. BARTON.
ALDERMAN H. F. DAVIS.
MR. J. R. HUGHES, J.P., C.C.

Hon. Treasurer :
ALDERMAN W. FLEWITT, J.P.
Club Medical Officer : DR. A. D. GOWANS.

Secretary-Manager :
MR. H. C. CURTIS,
" DORINCOURT," BOSTON GARDENS, BRENTFORD.

Telephones :
GROUND : EALING 1744.
PRIVATE HOUSE : EALING 1183.

Telegraphic Address :
CURTIS, FOOTBALL, BRENTFORD.
Ground : GRIFFIN PARK, EALING ROAD, BRENTFORD.

No. 2.   **Saturday, September 7th, 1935.**

Notes from the Hive.

EVERYBODY quite happy! I guess you all are with Brentford taking all four points from their first two First Division games. A great opening win at Bolton, where the Wanderers were beaten by two clear goals, followed by a well-won 3—1 victory over Blackburn Rovers, at Griffin Park on Thursday last. There was a record mid-week attendance to see the Bees' home debut in the First Division.

A HARD KEEN CONTEST

I fully prepared my readers for a keenly fought game and hard contest to be provided by the visit of Blackburn Rovers in the initial First Division game at Griffin Park. Well all those who were present will, I think, agree that it was one of the most strenuous games we have seen at Griffin Park during the last season or two. It was indeed all that, and what a cracker the pace was. The opening half was a real speedy affair and it was hardly expected that such a pace would continue. But continue it did almost up to the last minute.

Brentford won a great victory after losing first goal, which just goes to show that our boys are real fighters all the way.

LEVEL AT THE INTERVAL

Either side might have scored long before the first goal came. The visitors were particularly lively during the early stages around Mathieson, but once the Bees settled down the thrills were much more frequent at the other end. Among the narrow escapes which the Rovers' goal had can be cited the occasion when Holliday hit the underside of the crossbar. Then Scott failed at close quarters after Holliday had allowed the ball to " come through," while later Hopkins shot over the crossbar when an untenanted net was staring him in the face.

Still, these things do happen in football, but those missed chances caused a bit of a cold shiver when the Rovers took the lead at the end of 32 minutes' play. Six minutes later a tremendous shout rent the air—Brentford had equalised., but not without some palpitation, let it be said. The equalising goal came indirectly from a penalty kick which Robson missed—Binns pushing the ball out. Fletcher secured possession and headed a smart goal before the Rovers' goalkeeper could recover position.

BEES' FINE SECOND HALF DISPLAY

Equality at the interval was hardly a fair reflection of first half happenings, but after the change of ends there could be no two opinions that Brentford were the better side. Attacks became persistent and soon our boys were in front. This very important goal was scored by Holliday—a perfect header following a well-placed centre by Hopkins. Later our lead was consolidated by Fletcher, who scored a brilliant, if rather unusual goal. A free kick had been awarded to Brentford 25 yards from goal. Fletcher simply drove a low ball between the defenders lined up in front of him, and the ball went by Binns, the Rovers' goalkeeper, at an alarming pace. Thus Brentford won a meritorious victory by three goals to one.

TO-DAY'S VISITORS.

Most of the First Division Clubs have a history and feats behind them that make them more or less famous, but for attractive opponents few clubs excel Huddersfield Town in the matter of popularity.

That is why this Yorkshire club is so assured of a wonderful welcome on their first visit to Griffin Park in League football.

As clubs go, Huddersfield are comparatively modern making, but during their shorter history they have left their mark in the game and taken quite a big share of the honours. They won promotion to the First Division—along with Tottenham Hotspur—in 1920, and they soon gave conclusive evidence that the Yorkshire " Babes " as they were then rightly known, were quite fitted in every respect for a place in the top class; in fact Huddersfield astounded the football

world by winning the championship of the First Division three years in succession — seasons 1923-24, 1924-25, 1925-26. That wonderful feat had never been previously accomplished, but since the Arsenal have equalled this record and have a chance of beating it. To do that the Highbury club must finish at the head of affairs this season.

But Huddersfield have nothing like the resources of the Arsenal club and the support accorded the two clubs does not bear comparison. Furthermore, Huddersfield have done big things in the F.A. Cup during the post-war period and although they have only succeeded in actually winning the trophy on one occasion it is worth recording that our visitors of to-day have figured in the last stage four times.

Last season Huddersfield did not meet with their usual measure of success in League football, but that was probably due to the fact that it was a kind of transition period for the Club. There were many transfers from and to the Leeds Road ground, which is the Huddersfield headquarters, and this big change in personnel rather pegged the club back.

It is generally believed, however, that the fruits of the changes made will be gathered in this season. In any case Huddersfield have commenced quite well with three points out of a possible four—a Home win against Preston North End and a division on Wolverhampton's ground.

To-day's game should be a real football treat for our supporters. We are expecting a very large crowd and express the hope that you will all be more than satisfied with the fare provided—and the result.

" BUSY BEE."

Jottings from the Board Room.

Seats can be booked for our Home games in Block B at 4/- each. Applications by post must be accompanied by a remittance and a stamped addressed envelope. All other Stand seats will be unreserved.

Owing to the great demand for tickets for our game v. the Arsenal, on this ground on November 2nd, seats in other parts of the Stand will be bookable at 3/6 and 4/-. These tickets will not be available until next week.

———

A bunch of keys in a leather case was picked up on this ground on Thursday last. Will owner please apply for same at Secretary's Office.

———

We were honoured by the presence of many great football personalities at our game on Thursday last, including Mr. John McKenna, President of the Football League; Mr. H. J. Huband, Hon. Treasurer of the F.A.; Mr. F. S. Rous, Secretary of the F.A.; Mr. M. F. Cadman, of the Football League Management Committee, and Mr. George F. Allison, and many Managers and representatives of other clubs.

———

The Hanwell Silver Band will again play on this ground on match days during season 1935—36. We are indeed fortunate to have such a great Band to entertain our patrons before the game and during the interval.

———

Our Reserves play Watford Reserves (London Combination) on Thursday next, September 12th, 1935, on this ground. Kick-off at 6 p.m.

———

On Saturday next, September 14th, 1935, our League Team visit Middlesbrough. This will be an interesting game in many respects.

———

The catering rights on this ground are again in the capable hands of Mr. J. Lynch. Tea and light refreshments can be obtained at the Brook Road end of the ground, and at Braemar Road for the Stand patrons, and also at the Brook Road new Enclosure—all at popular prices.

———

Bert Watson has slightly injured his leg and, in consequence, will be rested for to-day's game. We therefore welcome Jackie Burns, who will deputise.

———

The Draw for the 1st Round of the London Challenge Cup resulted as follows :

BRENTFORD v. METROPOLITAN POLICE

to be played on this ground on Monday, October 7th, 1935. Kick-off at 3.30 p.m.

———

The Southern Railway announce the issue of cheap day tickets at approximately single fare for the return journey from about 70 of their stations to Brentford for our " Home " Fixtures.

———

A special train will be run from Reading, Staines, Feltham and intermediate stations direct to Brentford and back on September 21st and October 5th and 19th and November 2nd, at a return fare of 2/6 from stations Reading to Ascot inclusive, with reduced fares from the other stations en route.

For full particulars see Railway Company's announcements at stations, which also deal with other facilities.

———

Cars can be garaged opposite the ground in Ealing Road, at Mr. George Davis, Ealing Road Garage. Room for 200 cars. Garage Fees are, Motor Cars, 1/-; Motor Cycles, 6d.; Cycles 2d.

WEAR YOUR " BEE "

A young supporter has had a very neat and attractive—and subtle—little " Bee " badge made, and these will be on sale to-day from the Chocolate Boys at the price of two pence.

If you have any difficulty in purchasing one, please write to the Club.

H.C.C.

Shots from the Spot.

By "Rambler"

Two ordeals are over. The first away and the first home game are won, and four points—more than some critics would have us believe we should accumulate during the season—are safely in our locker.

* * *

I watched both games with care. I talked to eminent critics about them, and I can say that the general—and my own—opinion is, that as long as the same team spirit exists as there has in those two games, the Bees need not fear disgrace in any football company. The talent is there: it is nurtured by mutual understanding.

* * *

The Press heralded both our victories with kind and encouraging words. (It has not always been so . . .).

* * *

"Old International," writing of Brentford's game with Bolton, in the "Manchester Guardian," said: "Brentford won handsomely. The referee allowed them two goals: the press-box four; and a fifth was only withheld in sympathy with Jones, the Bolton goalkeeper, who acrobatically scooped a ball off the line and spared Finney the disgrace of scoring against his own side."

* * *

I think, too, that most people will agree that the Bees might have been five or six up on Thursday night without having treated Blackburn with an undue severity.

* * *

Football form is notoriously an evil thing to study, but the fact that Sheffield Wednesday only drew at Burnden Park seems a fair indicator to Brentford's potential First Division strength. It does not, of course, mean all it would appear, but it is a straw in the wind—and a very encouraging one at that.

* * *

As I walked from the ground on Thursday night it was obvious how delighted Brentford fans were with their team's display. If they show the same tolerant and understanding spirit when things are not going so well as they have in the past, they will prove one of the greatest assets a club can have.

* * *

I was glad to see that Ralph Allen opened his Second Division career with Charlton by getting a hat-trick —the first of the season. He has a great affection for Brentford, has Ralph, and one of his ambitions was to play against his old club—but when they got the promotion that denied him that he was as pleased as anyone.

* * *

To-day we have Huddersfield with us: another great game for the fans who can assist the club, themselves and each other by packing as neatly and closely as possible into the ground.

* * *

May I repeat my note in Thursday's programme to the effect that if you like the Club's journal in its new guise, tell your friends; and if you don't, tell us.

OUR VISITORS TO-DAY.
HOW THEY MAY LINE UP.

Since the war no club can boast a more glittering or consistent record than Huddersfield Town, our visitors to-day. Yet it is one of the youngest clubs in the Football League, and was not formed until 1908. The next year the Town gained admission to the Second Division, but there was so little support that in 1919 it looked as if its existence would be curtailed. However, a band of enthusiastic people rallied round and so wholehearted was the support that the club received that, from that year onwards, the Town astounded the football world with a sequence of remarkable triumphs.

The first blow struck in the fight for fame and fortune was when the club won promotion to the First Division soon after the war. Round about this time, too, the Town made their first appearance in a Cup Final when, at Stamford Bridge, they were beaten by Aston Villa by 1—0 after extra time. This was in 1920. Two years later they again figured in the final and this time beat Preston North End after extra time by the only goal of the game. Although the Town made two more Cup Final appearances—both at Wembley—they were not destined to carry off the coveted trophy. When, in 1928, they faced Blackburn Rovers, they were beaten 3—1.

It is when we turn to their League exploits that we see them in all their glory. In 1925-26 they created a record by winning the League Championship for the third year in succession. In 1926-27 they finished second to Newcastle United and in 1927-28 to Everton. On June 4th, 1928, the League presented Huddersfield with a Commemoration Shield in honour of their triple success.

Turner, Hugh (goalkeeper).— Born at Wigan. Height, 5ft. 10in. Weight, 13st. 10lb. Played with Felling Colliery and High Fell, two Tyneside clubs, before coming to the notice of Huddersfield. Signed for the Town in 1925-26 season at the age of 19. Was given his chance with the League side in September, 1926, and made 26 appearances that season. Has been a regular ever since. Agile despite his bulk.

Craig, Benjamin (right back).— Born at Leadgate, Co. Durham. Height, 5ft. 8in. Weight, 10st. 8lb. Went to Leeds Road as a junior and has maintained the tradition of Huddesfield full-backs. Coming into the side last year when the club were having some trouble with their defence, he played brilliantly and kept his place. Made 16 League appearances. Previously with Eden Colliery Welfare.

Mountford, Reginald (left back). —Height, 5ft. 9in. Weight, 11st. Learned his football at Darlington Secondary School. Assisted Darlington, his birthplace, as an amateur while working at a colliery. Joined Huddersfield in 1929, at the age of 19. Son of a Darlington councillor, he plays a good game of golf.

Willingham, Kenneth Charles (right half).—Born at Sheffield. Height, 5ft. 7½in. Weight, 10st. 7lb. Had a rapid rise. Huddersfield secured him from Worksop Town in 1932 when he was just old enough to sign professional. By December that year he was in the first team and twelve months later was chosen to represent England against France, injury robbing him of his cap. Has played for the English League, but not for a full international side. Captained Yorkshire Schools; a schoolboy international; and international runner.

BRENTFORD *v.* H

BRE
Red

1—M

2—BATEMAN
Right Back

4—McKENZIE   5-
Right Half   C

7—HOPKINS   8—ROBSON   9—H
Outside Right   Inside Right   Centr

Referee—Mr. E. R. WESTWOOD

12—LANG 13—RICHARDSON 14—
Outside Left   Inside Left   Cent

17—WIGHTMAN   18
Left Half   C

20—MOUNTFORD
Left Back

22-

Blue

HUDDERS

ARTHUR BATEM

Right Back and Vice-Ca

Played football for Grimsby, the tow
before joining Southend in 1933. There
Brentford, and was secured by Mr. Harr
defence, a job he has done with remarkal
With his friend George Poyser, he has stru
that makes these two as steady a pair o
the country. Coolness and accuracy are
Hobbies include cricket, golf, table-tennis
and music. Made 41 appearances for the

PRICES C

League Games.
Admission 1/-, Boys 6d.
New Enclosure (Brook Road) 1/6, Boys 9d.
Enclosure 2/-, Boys 1/-.

Wing Stands ... ...
Blocks A and G ... ...
There are still a few Season T

DERSFIELD TOWN

ORD

Stripes
ESON
per

3—POYSER
Left Back

ES
lf

6—J. C. BURNS
Left Half

DAY
rd

10—SCOTT
Inside Left

11—FLETCHER
Outside Left

Linesmen—Mr. F. E. Hawkes (blue flag),
Mr. E. H. Jones (red flag).

GOE
ard

15—BUTT
Inside Right

16—LUKE
Outside Right

UNG
alf

19—WILLINGHAM
Right Half

21—CRAIG
Right Back

NER
er

Stripes

LD TOWN

he was born,
" spotted " by
s to stiffen the
cess ever since.
n understanding
as there is in
s of his play.
Club champion),
ast season.

DMISSION

Reserve Games.
Admission **6d.**, Boys **3d.**
Enclosure **1/-**, Boys **6d.**
Stands, **1/6.**

Block F **3/6**
Block B (Numbered and Reserved) **4/-**
left in Block E. at £4 5s. only

Young, Alfred (centre half).— Born at Sunderland. Height, 5ft. 11½in. Weight, 12st 12lb. Signed for Hudderfield in 1926, but had to wait until season 1929-30 for his regular place in the first team. Soon made a name for himself and was capped for England in 1933.

Wightman, J. R. (left half).— Born at Duns, Berwickshire. Height, 5ft. 8in. Weight, 11st 9lb. Was secured from Bradford midway through last season and quickly established himself. Bradford took him from York City during the 1933-4 campaign.

Luke, Charles (outside right).— Born at Esh Winning, Co. Durham. Height, 5ft. 7¼in. Weight, 10st. 3lb. Was signed from Bishop Auckland in 1931 as an inside right. Secured his first team place in season 1932-3 as a winger and has proved a versatile forward, playing on both wings as well as at inside.

Butt (inside right).—A young forward who has been recently signed on from Macclesfield, and for whom a big future is prophecied. Mr. Clem Stephenson's reputation as a juvenile talent discoverer may well go up even more over him.

Lythgoe, Alfred P. (centre forward).—Born at Crewe. Height, 5ft. 7½in. Weight, 11st. After playing for several Cheshire League clubs he reached Stockport County in the summer of 1932 from Ashton National. In 1933-4 broke the Northern Section individual scoring record with 46 goals in 39 matches. In the face of great competition Huddersfield secured his signature last October and in 31 games he scored 22 goals. Makes up in football brains what he lacks in inches.

Richardson, James R (inside left). —Born at Ashington, Northumberland. Height, 5ft. 9½in. Weight, 11st. Joining Newcastle United from Blyth Spartans in season 1927-8, he made well over 100 first team appearances before going to Huddersfield in October last year. While with the North-Eastern club he played for England against Italy and Switzerland and also won a Cup medal. Plays inside right or left.

Lang, Thomas (outside left).— Born at Larkhall, Lanarkshire. Height, 5ft. 7in. Weight, 10st. 7lb. Joined Newcastle United from Larkhall Thistle in October, 1926. Moved to Huddersfield last December in exchange for Bott. Clever and elusive. Used to work on his father's fruit farm.

OFFICIAL NOTICE

NOTICE IS HEREBY GIVEN that the transfer books of the Preference and Ordinary Shares of the Company will be closed from the 9th to the 30th September next both days inclusive, for the preparation of dividend letters. Dividends will be posted on or about the 21st September next to the shareholders registered in the books of the Company on the 8th September, 1935.

By Order of the Board,

H. C. CURTIS,

5th September, 1935.   Secretary.

NAMES IN THE GAME.

No. 2

MR. CLEM STEPHENSON

As Huddersfield are our visitors to-day, it is appropriate that we should chat about Mr. Clem Stephenson, their famous manager. Was taken from Aston Villa to Huddersfield by the late Herbert Chapman, and was the inspiration and genius of the club's amazing League and Cup success. Officially playing inside left, he was actually all over the field, sending out passes that had the opposing defence completely at sea. Others in brilliant forward line were Jackson, Kelly and Smith. In 1920 he got a Cup-winner's medal with the Villa and the following year went to Huddersfield, where he has been ever since. Became manager in 1927.

NEW CAPITAL

The new capital being raised by the Club takes the form of 6 per cent. Debentures of £50 each, and at the Annual General Meeting held in July last, several shareholders expressed the desire to increase their holdings of shares. The Management have also received many letters from supporters who desire to acquire shares. As the share capital of the Club is fully subscribed, it is not possible to satisfy applicants unless any existing shareholder desires to realise, in which case the shareholder should advise the Secretary *in writing* of the number of shares he desires to sell and the price he is willing to accept. Particulars regarding the new issue of Debentures will be forwarded on request.

The Southern Railway are running special trains to cope with the crowds attending the Bees' home games.

* * *

A young supporters' enterprise has resulted in " Bee " badges being on sale at 2d. each. We hope he sells out.

Brentford's 1929-30 performance of winning every one of the 21 home games in Division III. (Southern Section) remains unique.

* * *

Arsenal's 66 points in season 1930-31 remains a record. The same season they got 33 points away from home.

FIXTURES, SEASON 1935-36.

FIRST TEAM

Date. 1935.	Opponents.	Ground.	F.	A.
Aug. 31	Bolton Wanderers	A	2	0
Sept. 5	Blackburn Rovers	H	3	1
,, 7	Huddersfield Town	H		
,, 14	Middlesbrough	A		
,, 18	Derby County	A		
,, 21	Aston Villa	H		
,, 28	Wolverhampton Wdrs.	A		
Oct. 5	Sheffield Wednesday	H		
,, 12	Portsmouth	A		
,, 19	Stoke City	H		
,, 26	Manchester City	A		
Nov. 2	Arsenal	H		
,, 9	Birmingham	A		
,, 16	Sunderland	H		
,, 23	Chelsea	A		
,, 30	Leeds United	H		
Dec. 7	Grimsby Town	A		
,, 14	Liverpool	H		
,, 21	West Bromwich Albion	A		
,, 25	Preston North End	H		
,, 26	Preston North End	A		
,, 28	Bolton Wanderers	H		
1936.				
Jan. 1	Blackburn Rovers	A		
,, 4	Huddersfield Town	A		
,, 11	(3)			
,, 18	Middlesbrough	H		
,, 25	(4) Aston Villa	A		
Feb. 1	Wolverhampton Wdrs.	H		
,, 8	Sheffield Wednesday	A		
,, 15	(5) Portsmouth	H		
,, 22	Stoke City	A		
,, 29	(6) Manchester City	H		
Mar. 7	Arsenal	A		
,, 14	(S.-F.) Birmingham	H		
,, 21	Sunderland	A		
,, 28	Chelsea	H		
April 4	Leeds United	A		
,, 10	Everton	A		
,, 11	Grimsby Town	H		
,, 13	Everton	H		
,, 18	Liverpool	A		
,, 25	(F.) West Brom. Alb.	H		
May 2	Derby County	H		

SECOND TEAM

Date. 1935.	Opponents.	Ground.	F.	A.
Aug. 31	Charlton Athletic	H	2	1
Sept. 4	Watford	A	1	3
,, 7	Clapton Orient	A		
,, 12	Watford	H		
,, 14	Southend United	H		
,, 21	Northampton Town	A		
,, 25	Luton Town	A		
,, 28	Crystal Palace	H		
Oct. 3	Luton Town	H		
,, 5	Reading	A		
,, 9	Bournemouth & Bos.	H		
,, 12	Tottenham Hotspur	H		
,, 19	Bristol City	A		
,, 26	Millwall	H		
Nov. 2	West Ham United	A		
,, 9	Swansea Town	H		
,, 16	Leicester City	H		
,, 23	Coventry City	H		
,, 30	Arsenal	A		
Dec. 7	Southampton	H		
,, 14	Brighton & Hove A.	A		
,, 21	Queen's Park Rgrs.	H		
,, 25	Chelsea	A		
,, 26	Chelsea	H		
,, 28	Charlton Athletic	A		
1936.				
Jan. 4	Clapton Orient	H		
,, 11	Fulham	H		
,, 18	Southend United	A		
,, 25	Northampton Town	H		
Feb. 1	Crystal Palace	A		
,, 8	Reading	H		
,, 15	Tottenham Hotspur	A		
,, 22	Bristol City	H		
,, 29	Millwall	A		
Mar. 7	West Ham United	H		
,, 14	Swansea Town	A		
,, 21	Leicester City	A		
,, 28	Coventry City	A		
April 4	Arsenal	H		
,, 10	Portsmouth	A		
,, 11	Southampton	A		
,, 13	Portsmouth	A		
,, 18	Brighton & Hove A.	H		
,, 25	Queen's Park Rgrs.	A		
May 2	Fulham	A		

Half Time Scores.

	F.	A.
A—Birmingham v. Arsenal	......	......
B—Derby County v. Bolton W.	......	......
C—Grimsby v. Chelsea	......	......
D—Leeds v. Blackburn	......	......
E—Liverpool v. Everton	......	......
F—Portsmouth v. Aston Villa	......	......
G—P.N.E. v. Middlesbrough	......	......
H—Sheffield W. v. Wolves	......	......
J—Sunderland v. Man. City	......	......
K—West Bromwich v. Stoke	......	......
L—Doncaster v. Charlton	......	......
M—Fulham v. Barnsley	......	......
N—'Spurs v. Newcastle	......	......
O—West Ham v. Notts Forest	......	......
P—Notts County v. Clapton O.	......	......
R—Torquay v. Q.P.R.	......	......

The Next Games.

Next Saturday the Bees are away at Middlesbrough, and it is revealing no secret to say that the Bees will be all out for a win.

It is an irony of fate that several of the men who have played so big a part in lifting the Bees to their present fine position were discarded by Middlesbrough — who only escaped relegation by a point the very season that Brentford reached the First Division !

When Holliday and his colleagues run out on to the ground at Ayresome Park, they'll get a great reception—and they'll be all out for goals. The Middlesbrough fans, we know, are looking forward to this game a good deal.

On the following Wednesday, the Bees face what is probably the stiffest hurdle of their First Division career to date—an away game with Derby County.

The Reserves are away to-day to Clapton Orient, and next Thursday they entertain Watford Reserves, who beat them 3—1 during the past week.

On September 14th they are at home to Southend United.

The next First Division game at Griffin Park is on September 21st, when Aston Villa pay us a visit. That'll be a great game . . .

BRENTFORD FOOTBALL AND SPORTS CLUB, LIMITED.

Registered Office :—GRIFFIN PARK, BRAEMAR ROAD, BRENTFORD.

President and Chairman :
MR. L. P. SIMON.

ALDERMAN W. FLEWITT, J.P.
MR. H. N. BLUNDELL.
MR. H. J. SAUNDERS.

MR. H. W. DODGE.
MR. C. L. SIMON.

Vice-Chairman :
MR. F. A. DAVIS.

MR. F. W. BARTON.
ALDERMAN H. F. DAVIS.
MR. J. R. HUGHES, J.P., C.C.

Hon. Treasurer ;
ALDERMAN W. FLEWITT, J.P.
Club Medical Officer ; DR. A. D. GOWANS.

Telephones :
GROUND : EALING 1744.
PRIVATE HOUSE : EALING 1183.

Secretary-Manager ;
MR. H. C. CURTIS,
" DORINCOURT," BOSTON GARDENS, BRENTFORD.

Telegraphic Address ;
CURTIS, FOOTBALL, BRENTFORD.
Ground ; GRIFFIN PARK, EALING ROAD, BRENTFORD.

Saturday, September 21st, 1935.

No. 3.

Notes from the Hive.

Brentford have not maintained the great start made in the First Division. No one really expected our boys would. To keep winning First Division games without a break is more than more fancied clubs than Brentford can do. The " Bees " commenced in grand style with two fine victories, fell at the next hurdle against Huddersfield—at Griffin Park too !—then went to Middlesbrough and played a goalless draw with a club which had scored a dozen goals in two away games. Not a bad performance that ! At the next outing just failed by the odd goal in three at Derby—the " Bees " being the first club to score at Derby this season. Well done " Bees," and I mean it.

" BEES " STUNG—AT HOME.

Brentford's first home defeat came sooner than most expected, and a long time before many of us had hoped. But these things do happen in football sometimes when they are least deserved. I think the general opinion of the large crowd present was that Brentford were decidedly unfortunate to be beaten by Huddersfield Town at Griffin Park. It was a fine game, with plenty of good football, and by the time the interval arrived Brentford should have built up a three goals lead. It did not work out quite like that for our boys had to be content with a 1—0 advantage at the breather. That goal was scored by Hopkins. Huddersfield had been quite over-run in the opening " forty-five," and it did seem a pity that the " Bees " did not get a lead which would have almost ensured success.

A BAD FIFTEEN MINUTES.

This fact was vividly brought home to us all immediately after ends were changed. For a period of about fifteen minutes the "Bees" were out of the hunt altogether. It was a very costly business, too, for Huddersfield took advantage of the turn of the tide to score two goals and gain a victory. It was not too late for the "Bees" to pull the game out of the fire, but when our boys came again they found the Town defence tightened up and not a goal could be got. But, to their credit, Jack Holliday & co. did try all they knew to retrieve the lost lead. It was just grand to see the "Bees" fighting their hardest to prevent a home defeat, but all to no avail, nothing could stave off defeat in the circumstances—it was definitely not our day ! Brentford will finish on the winning side and enjoy much less of the play than they did in the great duel with Huddersfield Town. Make no mistake about that !

NO GOALS AT MIDDLESBROUGH.

If there was one game Middlesbrough enthusiasts really wanted to see this season it was the visit of Brentford. One need not ask why. In the Brentford team were four ex-Middlesbrough players. They had helped to put our club into the First Division and the habitues of Ayresome Park were anxious to get another look at their old favourites. Interest was added by the fact that Middlesbrough had actually scored twelve goals in two successive away games. The whole town went football mad last week-end. The biggest attendance since 1927 was housed at Ayresome Park. Let me here pay tribute to the fine sportsmanship of those present. Surely no club has ever had a greater reception than was accorded Brentford in this game. It was truly magnificent; in fact it seemed to rather upset the equilibrium of both teams, who from the start seemed to be suffering from over excitement. Furthermore the strong wind made it rather difficult in the matter of ball control, so taking everything into consideration it must be admitted that the play was not of such a high standard as in normal circumstances it might have been. The opinion among the Middlesbrough people seemed to strongly favour Brentford who were considered unfortunate not to have won. Well, that may be correct, but looking at the thing from all angles a draw was not a bad result in justice to both teams.

THE GAME AT DERBY.

As Mr. Frank M. Carruthers ("Arbiter" of the "Daily Mail") says, "It was not a lucky match for Brentford." The game was a brilliant one to watch, each side served up some good football. At half time the home team had a two-goal lead but our boys did not give up, and an early goal directly after the interval (and a good one) by Fletcher helped to enthuse our boys, and for the last part of the remainder of the game we held the upper hand. Our luck was completely out not to have scored on a number of occasions, Although we obtained no points I am certain our team left a fine impression of their standard of play at Derby.

RESERVES' REVIEW.

Without being as convincing as some might like, our Reserves have been collecting London Combination points of late—five out of a possible six. The game with Clapton Orient, at Lea Bridge, finished goalless, and this was followed by an odd goal in three win over Watford at Griffin Park. Dunn scored both goals in this game.

On Saturday last another close contest was seen at the "Bees" headquarters, where Southend United were beaten by the only goal of the game, scored by Sullivan.

FAMOUS VISITORS TO-DAY.

Aston Villa, what great deeds such a name conjures up in the minds of the older enthusiasts of the game, are our visitors to-day. Extended to this famous Midland club is the most cordial of all welcomes on their first visit to Griffin Park. All games now are "tit-bits" as far as Brentford are concerned, but some clubs will have greater drawing power than others. Aston Villa are surely one in this category and I shall be greatly surprised if Griffin Park will be able to house all the people who will want to see the game this afternoon.

Aston Villa may have lost some of their former greatness in the matter of team strength, but they still remain one of the greatest draws on the fixture list of all clubs.

" BUSY BEE."

Jottings from the Board Room.

Supporters are asked to kindly reserve the space railed off behind the Ealing Road goal for boys only, and thus prevent the risk of their being injured through the pressure of the crowd.

A special appeal is also made to the early arrivals to assist the management by packing together, and to keep the gangways clear to enable spectators to take up positions to see the game. Please oblige.

Will the spectators endeavour to assist the stewards inside the playing pitch by packing?

At our game v. Huddersfield, on Saturday, September 7th, our young enthusiasts were allowed inside the playing area. Unfortunately this is not permitted and therefore cannot be allowed in future games.

EXCURSION TO WOLVERHAMPTON.

In connection with the League Match between Wolverhampton Wanderers and Brentford, on Saturday, September 28th, the Great Western Railway Company is running a half-day excursion to Wolverhampton as follows:—

Forward—
Paddington, dep. 11.5 a.m.
Wolverhampton (Low Level) arr. 1.35 p.m.

Return—
Wolverhampton (Low Level), dep. 7.20 p.m.
Paddington, arr. 10.5 p.m.
Return fare 7/-.

Congratulations to our Band, the Hanwell Silver Band, on their, for the ninth year in succession, winning the championship of the London and Home Counties Amateur Bands Association.

OUR BAND CHAMPIONS AGAIN.

For the ninth successive year the Hanwell Silver Band has won the championship of the London and Home Counties Association, which comprises over 70 bands, a wonderful record of consistency.

The band has now been associated with the Club for ten years, during which time patrons of the Club have enjoyed the entertainment provided, and old supporters have watched the progress of the Band with interest. Visiting patrons particularly are impressed with the entertainment we provide at Griffin Park, and envy the Club their band.

The Management request patrons to BEWARE OF PICKPOCKETS.

The Southern Railway announce the issue of cheap day tickets at approximately single fare for the return journey from about 70 of their stations to Brentford for our " Home " Fixtures.

A special train will be run from Reading, Staines, Feltham and intermediate stations direct to Brentford and back on October 5th and 19th and November 2nd, at a return fare of 2/6 from stations Reading to Ascot inclusive, with reduced fares from the other stations en route.

For full particulars see Railway Company's announcements at stations, which also deal with other facilities.

Cars can be garaged opposite the ground in Ealing Road, at Mr. George Davis, Ealing Road Garage. Room for 200 cars. Garage Fees are, Motor Cars, 1/-; Motor Cycles, 6d.; Cycles, 2d. On Reserve Match days, Cars 6d., Motor Cycles 4d.

WEAR YOUR " BEE "

A young supporter has had a very neat and attractive—and subtle—little " Bee " badge made, and these will be on sale to-day from the Chocolate Boys at the price of two pence.

v. ARSENAL.

I have received numerous complaints from supporters at their being unable to purchase tickets for reserved seats for our game v. Arsenal, on Saturday, November 2nd. The position is that we had about 2,000 tickets to dispose of, and have received applications for nearly three times that number. Our difficulty is to oblige everyone. In the Director's efforts to do so, it has been decided to reserve the seats in the wings of the stand at 3/6 each.

It is our desire that our own supporters should have the first option to purchase these, and in consequence no further applications will be considered BY POST. Applications must be made personally at the Booking Box in Braemar Road to-day. There are about 400 for sale.

Please do not send any applications by POST.

With reference to our game versus Sheffield Wednesday on this ground on Saturday, October 5th, kick-off at 3.30 p.m., seats numbered and reserved in Block B can be purchased at 4/- each. Applications by post will not be considered unless accompanied with remittance and stamped addressed envelope.

H.C.C.

Shots from the Spot.

By "Rambler"

I drove 250 miles to see Brentford's game with Derby. The journey back was completed in blinding rain, behind failing headlights and a singularly inefficient windscreen wiper.

It was **worth** every bit of it to see Brentford's magnificent second-half rally. It was one of the finest I have ever seen them stage—and their reputation as 90-minute men you all know.

* * *

It was not just that they fought back against a two-goal deficit. That's their habit. What was so gratifying to me was the coolness and precision of their play. Their "carpet passes" and deliberate positioning might have come from a team comfortable in the knowledge of a big lead. There was no wildness, no flustered kick-and-rush stuff.

* * *

They failed to get the goal that would have given them a point : but most people agreed they deserved one, and they gave the County the most severe test they have had on their ground this season—and that's not bad going for the League babes.

* * *

Football form continues to be extremely baffling to the sort of mind that works out football like a problem in algebra. (If A beats B and loses to C, C should beat B).

But surely it is significant that Huddersfield, now top of the League, should have been completely over-run during the first half of their game against Brentford at Griffin Park a fortnight ago?

* * *

I did not see the game against Middlesbrough as Steve Buxton, the old Brentford footballer, was covering that match for the "County of Middlesex Independent," but from all accounts that long-awaited encounter provided as hectic a drama as anyone could have desired.

* * *

In a well-known and fashionable restaurant in town the other day I sat at the next table to a man wearing what is rapidly becoming a familiar emblem in this part of the world—the "Bee" badge!

* * *

Caught a glimpse at Derby of John Clough, Brentford's old 'keeper, now with Rotherham United. He, like others of whom you may have heard, was once on Middlesbrough's books. It's good to see the way old players retain their interest in the Club's doings.

* * *

To the many supporters who have written praising our new programme, we offer our thanks, and will endeavour to fall in with their suggestions whenever practicable.

BEWARE.

It has come to the Management's knowledge that a person or persons are offering tickets for our game v. Arsenal F.C. on November 2nd, for admission to the ground at 1/3 each. These tickets are a fraud and supporters are requested not to purchase them but to give information to the police as the club are anxious to prosecute the individual or individuals concerned. The usual admission arrangements will be in force on November 2nd, being by payment of 1/- through the turnstiles and 1/6 and 2/- enclosure turnstiles.

BRITISH LEGION DOG SHOW

The above show will be held in the Sports Ground of Jantzen Knitting Mills, Ltd., on Saturday, September 28th, 1935. Admission, 2 p.m. Judging 3 till 5. All dogs are eligible and will be judged as to condition and cleanliness only. Silver Challenge Cup will be awarded to the best dog in the Show. For further particulars and entry forms, apply Secretary, Dog Show, Inverness Lodge, Brentford. The Show will be followed by a Concert and Dance at Inverness Lodge.

OUR VISITORS TO-DAY.
HOW THEY MAY LINE UP.

Aston Villa, our visitors to-day, were formed in 1874 by the youths connected with a chapel, and though they have one of the most distinguished records of any club, have been rather a disappointment in recent years, despite their fine playing strength, which includes many names famous wherever football is known, several of whom are expected to turn out to-day.

Original members of the Football League, they have never suffered the ignominy of relegation. They have six times carried off the Championship, but the last time was as long ago as 1910. In the Cup they hold a record equalled by only one other club—Blackburn Rovers—having carried off the trophy on six occasions. Their last success in this competition was in 1920.

They lost their first two home engagements this season, but atoned with a 5—1 victory over Preston last Saturday. They shared four goals with Sunderland a. home on Monday. One of their problems has been the possession of two very famous centre forwards—Waring and Astley—both of who are internationals.

Morton, Harry (goalkeeper).—Born at Oldham, Lancs. Height, 5ft. 10in. Weight, 11st. Joined the Aston club after a brilliant display for the Army at Villa Park in November, 1930. Played as an amateur during his Christmas leave and left the Service to turn professional the following March. Had previously played for Middleton Road Primitives, an Oldham side. Also played Rugger. Clean in his catching and almost uncanny in anticipation.

Beeson, George (right back).—Born at Clay Cross, Derbyshire. Height, 5ft. 10in. Weight, 12s.. 2lb. Developed with Clay Cross and Chesterfield. Joined Sheffield Wednesday in 1929 and gained his regular first team place in 1932-3. Was quickly to the fore and played for the English League in 1933. Joined Villa in 1934 close season, immediately gaining a place with the League side. Very powerful. Used to be a miner.

Young, Norman J. (left back).—Born at Hay Mills, Birmingham. Height, 5ft. 9½in. Weight, 11st. 1lb. Had to wait ten years for his First Division chance. Joined the Villa staff from Redditch (Birmingham Combination) in April, 1925.

Played regularly with Reserves as full back and half back, but did not turn out with seniors until last Saturday against Preston.

Gibson, James D. (right half).—International son of an international father, Gibson was born in Larkhall, Lanarkshire and played for Glasgow Ashfield and Partick Thistle before joining Aston Villa in 1927 for £7,500 fee. Made 27 League appearances last season. Height 6ft. 2½in. Weight, 12st. 3lb.

Allen, James (centre half).—Born at Poole. Height, 6ft. 1in. Weight, 12st. 10lb. Cost Villa a record fee when secured from Portsmouth in June, 1934. At first was a disappointment for he took a considerable time to settle down at Villa Park. Was later appointed captain. Was spotted by Pompey while playing for Poole Town in the Southern League. After gaining a first team place he soon came to the fore and won several caps.

Kingdon, William (half back).—Born at Worcester. Height, 5ft. 9½in. Weight, 11st. 11lb. After experience with Kepex (Worcestershire minor side) and Kidderminster Harriers (Birmingham League) he signed professional for Villa in March, 1926. Originally a full

BRENTFORD

BRE

Ree

1—

2—BATEMAN
Right Back

4—McKENZIE
Right Half

7—HOPKINS   8—ROBSON   9—
Outside Right   Inside Right   Cen

Referee—Mr. H. HARTLEY

12—HOUGHTON   13—DIX   14—
Outside Left   Inside Left   Ce

17—KINGDON
Left Half

20—YOUNG
Left Back

22

Clar

ASTO

THE LEAGUE—DIVISION I.

	P.	W.	D.	L.	F.	A.	P.
Huddersfield T. ...	6	4	2	0	11	5	10
Middlesbrough	6	4	1	1	20	8	9
Sunderland	6	4	1	1	16	7	9
Manchester City ...	5	4	0	1	12	3	8
Blackburn R.	5	4	0	1	10	5	8
Arsenal	6	2	3	1	13	6	7
Liverpool	6	3	1	2	17	12	7
Derby County	6	3	1	2	9	7	7
Stoke City	6	3	0	3	11	10	6
Sheffield Wed.	6	1	4	1	8	8	6
Wolverhampton W. .	6	2	2	2	9	10	6
BRENTFORD	5	2	1	2	7	5	5
Aston Villa	6	2	1	3	12	16	5
Chelsea	6	2	1	3	9	12	5
Everton	6	2	1	3	9	12	5
Birmingham	6	1	3	2	5	7	5
Portsmouth	5	2	0	3	7	8	4
Bolton W.	5	1	2	2	5	9	4
West Brom. A.	6	1	1	4	5	13	3
Preston N.E.	6	1	1	4	4	15	3
Leeds United	6	0	2	4	3	11	2
Grimsby Town	5	1	0	4	4	17	2

ASTON VILLA

...RD
...ipes
...ON

3—POYSER
Left Back

6—WATSON
Left Half

10—SCOTT
Inside Left

11—FLETCHER
Outside Left

Linesmen—Messrs. A. L. R. Bellion (blue flag), and C. Kearse (Red flag).

15—WARING
Inside Right

16—BROOME
Outside Right

19—GIBSON
Right Half

21—BEESON
Right Back

...ON

...ue

...ILLA

LONDON COMBINATION
(Up to, and including, last Saturday's games.)

	P.	W.	D.	L.	F.	A.	P.
Portsmouth	4	3	1	0	12	5	7
Tottenham H.	5	3	1	1	23	10	7
Luton Town	5	3	1	1	18	9	7
BRENTFORD	**5**	**3**	**1**	**1**	**6**	**5**	**7**
Queen's Park R.	5	3	0	2	11	7	6
West Ham U.	5	2	2	1	9	6	6
Chelsea	5	2	2	1	8	6	6
Arsenal	5	3	0	2	8	7	6
Swansea Town	5	2	2	1	5	5	6
Watford	5	2	1	2	15	9	5
Charlton	5	2	1	2	12	12	5
Bournemouth	5	2	1	2	7	9	5
Coventry City	5	2	0	3	9	6	4
Leicester	3	2	0	1	7	3	4
Northampton	5	2	0	3	12	12	4
Southend United	5	2	0	3	9	12	4
Southampton	5	1	2	2	6	9	4
Bristol City	5	2	0	3	6	14	4
Clapton Orient	6	1	2	3	3	15	4
Millwall	4	1	1	2	7	9	3
Brighton & Hove A.	4	1	1	2	4	7	3
Crystal Palace	4	1	1	2	8	19	3
Fulham	5	1	0	4	8	11	2
Reading	4	1	0	3	6	12	2

INDEPENDENT—STEVE BUXTON at M'SBRO!

back, he has proved a great utility half, playing a whole-hearted game in any of the three intermediate positions. Former carpenter.

Broome (outside right). — This will be a big occasion for him, a young winger for whom Aston Villa have high hopes. He first attracted attention by his sterling displays as an amateur for Berkhampsted.

Waring, Thomas (centre forward or inside right).—Born at Birkenhead. Height, 6ft. 1¾in. Weight, 12st. 4lb. Used to sell chocolates on Tranmere Rovers' ground. When "Dixie" Dean moved to Everton, Tom soon became his successor. Went to Villa in February, 1928. In season 1930-1 he scored 49 goals, helping the Aston club to set up the record aggregate of 128. In recent seasons has shared the position with Astley, operating at inside right on several occasions this season. English international v. Scotland, Ireland, Wales, France and Belgium.

Astley, David (centre or inside forward).—Born at Dowlais, South Wales. Height, 5ft. 11½in. Weight, 11st. 11lb. Played for his school side at the age of nine and played for Welsh schoolboys against Scotland in 1923. Started professional career with Merthyr Town at the age of 17. Moved to Charlton Athletic in 1927 and then to Aston three years later. Has a string of caps for Wales.

Dix, Ronald (inside left).—Born at Bristol. Height, 5ft. 9in. Weight 12st. 7lb. Captained English schoolboys against Wales in 1927 and immediately afterwards was secured by Bristol Rovers as an amateur. By the time he 'reached 17 and turned professional he was attracting widespread attention. Blackburn secured him in the face of much competition in 1932. Moved to Villa after one season. Clever dribbler with powerful shot.

Houghton, William Eric (outside right or left). ⸏Born at Billingboro', Lincs. Height, 5ft. 7¾in. Weight, 11st. 6lb. Went to Villa Park in August, 1927, from Boston Town. Previously played with Donnington Grammar School. Before reaching his majority he gained international and inter-League caps. Plays on either wing or at inside forward. Terrific hitter of a dead ball at Soccer or the moving ball at cricket. Plays the latter game for Lincolnshire.

OFFICIAL NOTICE

NAMES IN THE GAME.

No. 3

MR. JAMES McMULLAN.

Aston Villa's team manager and coach, Mr. James McMullan joined our visitors to-day in May, 1934.

He was a brilliant player; probably one of the finest half backs the game has seen. Twice he played for Manchester City in the Cup Final, and he has been capped for Scotland against England, Ireland and Wales on many occasions between 1920 and 1929, while turning out for Partick Thistle and, after 1926, Manchester City.

This record, of course, is of tremendous assistance to him in his dealings with players, and it is hoped that the effect of his team-building will be felt this season. Under his guidance the Villa may well regain their former glory.

NEW CAPITAL

The new capital being raised by the Club takes the form of 6 per cent. Debentures of £50 each, and at the Annual General Meeting held in July last, several shareholders expressed the desire to increase their holdings of shares. The Management have also received many letters from supporters who desire to acquire shares. As the share capital of the Club is fully subscribed, it is not possible to satisfy applicants unless any existing shareholder desires to realise, in which case the shareholder should advise the Secretary *in writing* of the number of shares he desires to sell and the price he is willing to accept. Particulars regarding the new issue of Debentures will be forwarded on request.

JACK HOLLIDAY
Centre Forward

Born at Cockfield, Co. Durham, Jack Holliday has played a big part in Brentford's rise from Third to First Division football. One of the Middlesbrough contingent, he has an amazing record not only as a goal-scorer but for consistency. Made 42 appearances for the club last season, and this year he hopes to reach the " century of goals " mark. At the moment he has 91 to his credit for Brentford. Played for the English XI. v. the Anglo-Scots XI. in Jubilee game last season.

FIXTURES, SEASON 1935-36.

FIRST TEAM

Date. 1935.	Opponents.	Ground.	GOALS F.	A.
Aug. 31	Bolton Wanderers ...	A	2	0
Sept. 5	Blackburn Rovers ...	H	3	1
,, 7	Huddersfield Town ...	H	1	2
,, 14	Middlesbrough ...	A	0	0
,, 18	Derby County ...	A	1	2
,, 21	Aston Villa	H		
,, 28	Wolverhampton Wdrs.	A		
Oct. 5	Sheffield Wednesday ..	H		
,, 12	Portsmouth	A		
,, 19	Stoke City	H		
,, 26	Manchester City ...	A		
Nov. 2	Arsenal	H		
,, 9	Birmingham	A		
,, 16	Sunderland	H		
,, 23	Chelsea	A		
,, 30	Leeds United ...	H		
Dec. 7	Grimsby Town ...	A		
,, 14	Liverpool	H		
,, 21	West Bromwich Albion	A		
,, 25	Preston North End ...	H		
,, 26	Preston North End ...	A		
,, 28	Bolton Wanderers ...	H		
1936.				
Jan. 1	Blackburn Rovers ...	A		
,, 4	Huddersfield Town ...	A		
,, 11	(3)			
,, 18	Middlesbrough ...	H		
,, 25	(4) Aston Villa ...	A		
Feb. 1	Wolverhampton Wdrs.	H		
,, 8	Sheffield Wednesday ...	A		
,, 15	(5) Portsmouth ...	H		
,, 22	Stoke City	A		
,, 29	(6) Manchester City ...	H		
Mar. 7	Arsenal	A		
,, 14	(S.-F.) Birmingham ...	H		
,, 21	Sunderland	A		
,, 28	Chelsea	H		
April 4	Leeds United ...	A		
,, 10	Everton	A		
,, 11	Grimsby Town ...	H		
,, 13	Everton	H		
,, 18	Liverpool	A		
,, 25	(F.) West Brom. Alb.	H		
May 2	Derby County ...	H		

SECOND TEAM

Date. 1935.	Opponents.	Ground.	GOALS F.	A.
Aug. 31	Charlton Athletic ...	H	2	1
Sept. 4	Watford	A	1	3
,, 7	Clapton Orient ...	A	0	0
,, 12	Watford	H	2	1
,, 14	Southend United ...	H	1	0
,, 21	Northampton Town ...	A		
,, 25	Luton Town	A		
,, 28	Crystal Palace ...	H		
Oct. 3	Luton Town	H		
,, 5	Reading	A		
,, 9	Bournemouth & Bos. .	H		
,, 12	Tottenham Hotspur ......H			
,, 19	Bristol City	A		
,, 26	Millwall	H		
Nov. 2	West Ham United ...	A		
,, 9	Swansea Town ...	H		
,, 16	Leicester City ...	A		
,, 23	Coventry City ...	H		
,, 30	Arsenal	A		
Dec. 7	Southampton ...	H		
,, 14	Brighton & Hove A.	A		
,, 21	Queen's Park Rgrs. ..	H		
,, 25	Chelsea	A		
,, 26	Chelsea	H		
,, 28	Charlton Athletic ...	A		
1936.				
Jan. 4	Clapton Orient ...	H		
,, 11	Fulham	H		
,, 18	Southend United ...	A		
,, 25	Northampton Town ...	H		
Feb. 1	Crystal Palace ...	A		
,, 8	Reading	H		
,, 15	Tottenham Hotspur ...	A		
,, 22	Bristol City	H		
,, 29	Millwall	A		
Mar. 7	West Ham United ...	H		
,, 14	Swansea Town ...	A		
,, 21	Leicester City ...	H		
,, 25	Bournemouth & Bos. .	A		
,, 28	Coventry City ...	A		
April 4	Arsenal	H		
,, 10	Portsmouth ...	H		
,, 11	Southampton ...	A		
,, 13	Portsmouth ...	H		
,, 18	Brighton & Hove A.	H		
,, 25	Queen's Park Rgrs. ..	A		
May 2	Fulham	A		

Half Time Scores.

	F.	A.
A—Arsenal v. Manchester C.		
B—Birmingham v. Stoke City		
C—Derby C. v. Middlesbrough		
D—Everton v. Huddersfield T.		
E—Grimsby T. v. Bolton W.		
F—Leeds U. v. Liverpool		
G—Portsmouth v. Sheffield W.		

H—Preston N.E. v. Wolves		
J—Sunderland v. Blackburn R.		
K—West Brom. A. v. Chelsea		
L—Charlton A. v. Barnsley		
M—Fulham v. Bradford City		
N—Manchester U. v. 'Spurs		
O—West Ham v. Doncaster R.		
P—Bournemouth v. Reading		
R—Swindon v. Q.P.R.		

S P I K E D !

The Next Games.

After to-day we settle down to the ordinary one-game a week programme, which eases our players' task considerably. Strenuous mid-week matches that involve a lot of travelling, can be held responsible for a lot of the vagaries of football form that occur at the beginning of every season—and this season more than most!

Next Saturday our first team are away to Wolverhampton Wanderers. They are a fast, virile side, and likely, on the Molineux ground at any rate, to hold their own with any club in the country. Last season it will be remembered, they secured "Boy" Martin and Brown from Ireland, neither of whom quite lived up to their reputations. That may be different this season.

The Reserves entertain old friends and rivals in Crystal Palace, and on the following Thursday are at home to Luton Town.

The next First Division game at Griffin Park is on October 5th, and it is one that readily captures the imagination—Sheffield Wednesday.

They are, besides being the holders of the F.A. Cup, one of the most entertaining and unorthodox sides in the Division. Their form this year has been erratic, to say the least of it, but it will be yet another stern test for the Bees to see how they shape against the unusual style of Ronnie Starling and his men.

It will also be interesting to see whether the Wednesday find Brentford's style to their taste!

BRENTFORD FOOTBALL AND SPORTS CLUB, LIMITED.

Registered Office :—GRIFFIN PARK, BRAEMAR ROAD, BRENTFORD.

President and Chairman :
MR. L. P. SIMON.

Vice-Chairman:
MR. F. A. DAVIS.

ALDERMAN W. FLEWITT, J.P.
MR. H. N. BLUNDELL.
MR. H. J. SAUNDERS.

MR. H. W. DODGE.
MR. C. L. SIMON.

MR. F. W. BARTON.
ALDERMAN H. F. DAVIS.
MR. J. R. HUGHES, J.P., C.C.

Hon. Treasurer:
ALDERMAN W. FLEWITT, J.P.

Club Medical Officer; DR. A. D. GOWANS.

Telephones:
GROUND : EALING 1744.
PRIVATE HOUSE : EALING 1183.

Secretary-Manager;
MR. H. C. CURTIS,
"DORINCOURT," BOSTON GARDENS, BRENTFORD.

Telegraphic Address:
CURTIS, FOOTBALL, BRENTFORD.
Ground; GRIFFIN PARK, EALING ROAD, BRENTFORD.

No. 4.   Saturday, October 5th, 1935.

Notes from the Hive.

THE "Bees'" bright beginning in the First Division has not been maintained, at least not so far as actual results are concerned. In the quality of their football our boys have proved beyond all doubt that they are worthy members of the top class, but results alone count and in this respect the "Bees" have not been delivering the goods in recent games. Three successive defeats have been sustained, four in all in seven games, and each have been by the narrowest of margins—a single goal difference in the scores. Brentford have not deserved defeat in at least three of these games, but the cold facts have to be faced. While Brentford are playing as well as they are there is no need to get panicky, for luck will not continue indefinitely to run against our team. The law of averages would not permit that and the only thing which causes any worry at all is the possibility that if reverses continue for any length of time our boys may lose their confidence and the quality of their play suffer accordingly. That is where the human element figures so strongly where football is concerned. Still, that has not happened yet, so why stress the fact?

VILLA VICTORY.

The first visit of the famous Aston Villa club attracted a large crowd to Griffin Park a fortnight ago, and once again disappointment fell to our lot, for the visitors won by the odd goal in three after having by far the worst of the actual exchanges.

It was a thrilling encounter with all the goals coming before the interval. As usual, Brentford scored first, Holliday netting in the sixth minute of the game. It was a great movement, probably the best in the game, which produced that goal, for besides the scorer, Watson, McKenzie, Scott and Robson all had an indirect interest in this early success. Thus the onlookers were on good terms with themselves very early in the game. Storming raids by the "Bees" following this success should have brought at least two more goals before the first quarter of an hour had passed. But goals which should have accrued, did not, and the Villa got on terms following a "throw down" by the referee, the ball going direct to Waring, who scored easily. The goal which gave the visitors victory was a speculative effort by Astley following a throw-in.

Even after the Villa got in front there was plenty of time and numerous opportunities for Brentford to win the match. One of our

forwards (no names—no C.B.!) missed a veritable "sitter," other almost gilt-edged chances were neglected; in fact nothing would go right in front of goal. Even when the Villa goalkeeper was away from his charge and the ball was sailing into an empty net, another Villa defender came from out of the blue and headed away. It was indeed an unhappy day for our boys.

DEVOURING "WOLVES."

It takes a lot to get the spirit of the "Bees" down; in fact our boys simply refuse to let the unlucky rebuffs they have recently sustained make one iota of difference. They simply come up smiling, like a big-hearted boxer, for the next round.

At Wolverhampton on Saturday last, Brentford commenced like champions. Shocks for the home supporters were early in evidence. Brentford were two goals up inside fifteen minutes and throughout the first half played wonderful football. Holliday and Scott were our scorers and how, or why, others did not follow before the interval was indeed mystifying. It was a very different story after the change of ends. The hungry Wolves appeared to find so much extra speed after the breather that they resembled something of a whirlwind—and they kept it up right to the end. To score three goals after being two down was a fine retrievement, but even so there could be no other opinion than that Brentford were unlucky to be beaten after that great first half show. One good feature about the game which left pleasant reflections as far as Brentford were concerned was the great improvement shown in first-time shooting of our forwards. They had evidently learned their lesson from previous games which should never have been lost.

Even so, there were one or two bad Brentford misses near goal, even in the second half, which the Wolves would claim as their very own in view of the strong pressure exerted. It might be mentioned that Poyser had to stand down at the last minute owing to injury, and Metcalf was drafted into the side, while Jacky Burns resumed in place of McKenzie, who was also indisposed. Both played well and could in no way be blamed for the defeat sustained.

RESERVES' REVIEW.

Our Reserves won a welcome away game at Northampton, where Brown scored the only goal of the game.

A rather unexpected heavy reverse was sustained at Luton (1—4), the "Bees'" goal being scored by Dunn.

On Saturday last Crystal Palace were beaten at Griffin Park by four clear goals. Muttitt (2), Sullivan, and Brown were the successful marksmen.

WELCOME WEDNESDAY!

We have another ultra attraction to offer our patrons to-day. Sheffield Wednesday, to whom we offer a most cordial welcome on their initial visit to Griffin Park, are in the first flight of English clubs. They have a very "even" record to date for eight points have been collected from eight goals, eleven goals have been scored and a like number conceded, while two games have been won, two lost and the remaining four drawn. William Walker, the former English international and Aston Villa star, is manager of the Wednesday club, which has, by comparison, really done better away from home than on their own ground. In "out" matches the Wednesday have beaten Aston Villa 2—1, drawn at Highbury 2—2, at Bolton 1—1, and lost by the odd goal in five at Portsmouth. Very good results these, which pointedly suggests that the "Bees" have a stiff task on hand to-day. They know it too! **"BUSY BEE."**

Jottings from the Board Room.

The Southern Railway Company announce that they are running a special Corridor and Restaurant Car Excursion to Fratton and Portsmouth for the Brentford match v. Portsmouth, on Saturday, October 12th.

The train leaves Brentford at 12.22 p.m. and Kew Bridge at 12.17 p.m. The fare from these stations, and most of the neighbouring ones is 5/9, whilst from Waterloo, where it leaves at 12 o'clock, it is 6/6.

It leaves Fratton, which adjoins the ground, at 6.31 p.m., and supper (2/6) and light refreshments are obtainable. Tickets can be booked in advance.

It is with regret that we have to announce that the injury to Charlie Walsh has proved more serious than anticipated. The report of the specialist who examined him gives doubts to his being able to play again. Charlie is only 24 years of age and his injury is an over-stretched ligament of the knee.

Both McKenzie and Poyser have been declared fit to play.

Patrons are asked to purchase Programmes only from those wearing the Official Badge, as recently a number of unofficial ones have been disposed of.

Our Reserves play the Metropolitan Police in the First Round of the London Challenge Cup on this ground on Monday next, the 7th inst., kick-off at 3.30 p.m.

On Wednesday next, October 9th, Bournemouth and Boscombe will meet our Reserves (London Combination), on this ground, kick-off at 3.30 p.m.

Complaints have been received that at our Reserves' game on Saturday last one or two members of the crowd (we will not term them supporters) caused inconvenience to a number of our supporters by using disgusting language until the police finally put them out of the ground.

The Management do not intend to tolerate such conduct, and do not desire the support of such persons. The police have been given instructions that such persons must be immediately removed from the ground if such conduct is repeated.

The Reserves defeated Luton Town Reserves in the return London Combination game played on this ground on Thursday, by four goals to three. Our goals were scored by Sullivan, Smith, Dunn and Fenton.

Both Metcalf and Dunn were injured in this game and are unfit to play to-day.

The sudden death of Mr. J. Mears, popular vice-chairman of the Chelsea F.C., came as a great shock. To the relatives and to the Chelsea F.C. officials we extend the deepest sympathy from all connected with this club.

Tickets, numbered and reserved, for our game v. Stoke City, on Saturday, October 19th (kick-off at 3.15 p.m.) can be purchased to-day at the Box Hut in Braemar Road, at 4s. each, Block B. Applications by post will not be considered unless accompanied with a remittance and a stamped addressed envelope.

The sum of £259 16s. 0d. has been distributed to various charity organisations, this being the amount received from our Trial Games.

Shots from the Spot.

By "Rambler"

There are only four First Division sides with less goals against them than Brentford—a great tribute to their defence.

Despite the recent defeats, I think that this shows that once the Bees' forwards settle down to get the goals in their old style—and that cannot be long now—the Club will live up to its splendid promise of the early games.

* * *

After all, this business of getting beaten by the odd goal cannot go on for ever. It may be worrying, but it's certainly nothing to get panic-stricken about.

* * *

By the way, several enthusiastic supporters (who apparently keep goal-charts of every game the Bees play) have put me right about Jack Holliday's goal-scoring record to which I referred a fortnight ago.

His total now for Brentford is 94—well on the way to his century.

* * *

I have had a chance of seeing the Reserves once or twice lately—a thing I always like to do to enable me to assess the strength of the Club in the event of injuries.

They have not been remarkably consistent, nor have they—until last Saturday at any rate—been very impressive in front of goal, but you can never judge a player's first team potentialities properly until he gets his chance.

My own opinion is that there are several in the Reserve team capable of seizing that chance when it is presented, and making good.

* * *

Thus Walter Metcalf came into the first team against the Wolves—a big ordeal from which he merged with credit.

Glad to see Ralph Allen and Bert Stephens, old favourites now with Charlton and Brighton respectively, are getting amongst the goals.

Ralph, who is top scorer in the Second Division, has attracted the attention of a First Division Club, but I doubt if Charlton are likely to let him go.

* * *

Letters continue to come in about the programme, and we are all very grateful to the spectators who show their enthusiasm in this way. When making suggestions, though, they might bear in mind that it only contains 24 pages !

* * *

As you probably noticed we had special packers on duty for the game against Aston Villa.

If these gentlemen's instructions are carried out properly, it will mean that both you and the next chap to you will be able to see better and more comfortably.

Our spectators have co-operated splendidly with us in making the best of the new ground improvements.

Without their help the most elaborate arrangements are useless.

* * *

I would like to add my word of sympathy to Charlie Walsh, a cheery sportsman and a good footballer. Through a wretched stroke of ill-luck—coming at the end of a chain of misfortunes—he will probably never kick a ball again.

The game in general and Griffin Park in particular will be the sadder for his absence . . .

OUR VISITORS TO-DAY.

HOW THEY MAY LINE UP.

•

Holders of the English Cup for the third time in their career, Sheffield Wednesday are attractive visitors to Griffin Park.

The famous football club was founded in 1866, but prior to that the club had existed as a cricket organisation. The cricket club played on Sheffield's half-day off (Wednesday) which explains why a football club that plays nearly all its games on a Saturday bears the title of " The Wednesday."

They have carried off the championship of the First Division on four occasions, the two most recent being in 1929 and 1930, while they have also finished at the head of affairs in the Second Division twice.

They are a fascinating side to watch, unorthodox yet extremely effective; the stamp of Manager Billy Walker can be seen in the finesse and polish of their football which may often be disapproved of by critics, but which certainly gets results.

Brown, John H. (goalkeeper).— Born at Worksop, Notts. Height, 5ft. 10¾in. Weight, 12st. 6lb. Product of a pit lads' team at Manton Colliery (Worksop). He graduated with Worksop Town and moved on to Hillsborough in 1923, assisting the Wednesday to gain promotion three years later. Has two League championship medals, a Cup-winner's medal and several caps.

Nibloe, Joseph (right back).— Born at Cockerhill, Lanarkshire. Height, 5ft. 9¾in. Weight, 12st. 8lb. Used to play with Mr. W. H. Walker, his present manager, while with Aston Villa. Went to Sheffield in exchange for Beeson in the summer of 1934. Played with several Scottish junior clubs before gaining recognition with Kilmarnock. Won a Scottish Cup medal in 1930 and an English one this year.

Catlin, Edward (left back).— Born at Middlesbrough. Height, 5ft. 10in. Weight, 10st. 11lb. Was missed by Middlesbrough as a youngster. Sheffield Wednesday snapped him up from South Bank, the well-known North-Eastern

nursery. Had his first chance with the League side in 1932-3 and last season succeeded Blenkinsop when the international was transferred to Liverpool.

Sharp, Wilfred (right half).— Born at Bathgate, West Lothian. Height, 5ft. 10½in. Weight, 11st. 8lb. Had experience with Tunbridge Wells Rangers and Airdrie before going to Sheffield in the summer of last year. Started at Hillsborough as a centre-half, but quickly showed his aptitude for the wing position. Made 24 League appearances and won a Cup medal in his first season of English first-class football.

Millership, Harry (centre half).— Born at Warsop, Notts. Height, 5ft. 10in. Weight, 11st. 12lb. Entered League football with Bradford while still in his 'teens. Helped the Park Avenue club to win the Northern Section Championship in 1928-9 and then moved to the Wednesday where he moved from inside left to centre half during season 1933-4 with immediate success. Played in the Jubilee international against Scotland.

BRENTFORD *v.* SH

BRE

Red and

1—M

2—BATEMAN
Right Back

4—McKENZIE
Right Half

5-
C

7—HOPKINS
Outside Right

8—ROBSON
Inside Right

9—H
Cent

Referee—Mr. E. PINKSTONE

12—RIMMER
Outside Left

13—STARLING
Inside Left

14—PA
Cent

17—BURROWS
Left Half

18—
C

20—CATLIN
Left Back

22-

Blue and V

SHEFFIELD

THE LEAGUE—DIVISION I.

	P.	W.	D.	L.	Goals F.	A.	P.
Huddersfield	8	5	3	0	14	6	13
Manchester C.	7	5	1	1	15	5	11
Middlesbrough	8	5	1	2	28	12	11
Sunderland	8	5	1	2	24	12	11
Derby County	8	5	1	2	14	9	11
Arsenal	8	3	3	2	18	9	9
Liverpool	8	4	1	3	22	13	9
Chelsea	8	4	1	3	14	14	9
Stoke City	8	4	0	4	16	13	8
Sheffield Wed.	8	2	4	2	11	11	8
Blackburn Rovers	7	4	0	3	13	14	8
Wolverhampton	8	3	2	3	12	14	8
Portsmouth	7	3	1	3	10	10	7
Aston Villa	8	3	1	4	14	19	7
Birmingham	8	2	3	3	7	13	7
Leeds United	8	2	2	4	5	11	6
BRENTFORD	7	2	1	4	10	10	5
Everton	8	2	1	5	11	21	5
Bolton Wanderers	7	1	3	3	6	12	5
Preston North End	8	2	1	5	6	16	5
Grimsby Town	7	2	0	5	7	19	4
West Bromwich A.	8	1	1	6	6	20	3

IELD WEDNESDAY

FORD

bes

ESON
per

3—POYSER
Left Back

ES
alf

6—WATSON
Left Half

DAY   10—SCOTT   11—FLETCHER
rd   Inside Left   Outside Left

Linesmen— Messrs. J. E. Gouge (blue flag),
and R. V. Pegg (red flag).

ORPE   15—SURTEES   16—HOOPER
ard   Inside Right   Outside Right

RSHIP   19—SHARP
alf   Right Half

21—NIBLOE
Right Back

WN
er

ical Stripes

EDNESDAY

LONDON COMBINATION

	P.	W.	D.	L.	F.	A.	P
Chelsea	9	6	2	1	25	10	14
Luton Town	9	6	1	2	35	16	13
West Ham	8	5	2	1	24	7	12
Portsmouth	7	5	2	0	22	10	12
Arsenal	8	6	0	2	19	10	12
BRENTFORD	**9**	**6**	**0**	**3**	**16**	**12**	**12**
Coventry City	8	5	0	3	18	9	10
Swansea Town	8	4	2	2	9	10	10
Charlton Athletic	9	4	1	4	19	17	9
Southampton	9	3	3	3	14	14	9
Queen's Park Rgrs.	9	4	1	4	15	16	9
Bournemouth	8	3	2	3	12	17	8
Tottenham	9	3	1	5	30	24	7
Clapton Orient	8	2	3	3	6	17	7
Reading	7	3	0	4	17	23	6
Millwall	7	2	2	3	10	13	6
Southend Utd.	9	3	0	6	14	22	6
Bristol City	9	3	0	6	12	29	6
Crystal Palace	7	2	1	4	11	27	5
Watford	8	2	1	5	18	16	5
Fulham	8	2	0	6	17	17	4
Northampton	7	2	0	5	14	20	4
Leicester City	7	2	0	5	10	17	4
Brighton & Hove A.	7	1	1	5	7	21	3

Burrows, Horace (left half).— Born at Sutton-in-Ashfield, Notts. Height, 5ft. 9½in. Weight, 11st. 3lbs. After gaining experience with local Notts sides he moved to Coventry City and then on to Mansfield Town. Joined the Wednesday in May, 1931. Became a regular first team man in 1933-4. Has several English caps.

Hooper, Mark (outside right).— Born at Darlington. Height, 5ft. 5¾in. Weight, 10st. 3lb. A goalkeeper while at school, he became an inside left with a works side and then an outside right with Darlington. Went to Sheffield from the last-named club in 1926-7 season and has twice helped them to win the League championship as well as being in the Cup-winning side last season.

Surtees, John (inside right).— Born at Willington - on - Tyne. Height, 5ft. 10in. Weight, 12st. 6lb. Not retained by Middlesbrough, Portsmouth, Bournemouth and Northampton within the space of three years, he was about to leave for America last Christmas when he accepted a trial with Wednesday. Gained his first team place at once and was a member of the Cup-winning side.

Palethorpe, John (centre forward) —Born at Leicester. Height, 5ft. 10½in. Weight, 12st. 2lb. Won two Second Division championship medals and a Cup medal in three successive seasons. Stoke secured him from Reading in March, 1933. After helping them into the First Division he lost his place. Moved to Preston, who gained promotion in his first season. Then lost his place once more and was taken by Wednesday with whom he won a Cup medal last season.

Starling, Ronald (inside right or left).—Born at Pelaw, Co. Durham. Height, 5ft. 9½in. Weight, 11st. 8lb. The key-man of the forwards. A great roamer and schemer. Gained county honours while at school. Then played for Washington Colliery and Hull City before going to Newcastle United for a £4,000 fee in May, 1930. Cost Sheffield only £2,500 in June, 1932.

Rimmer, Ellis (outside left).— Born at Birkenhead. Height, 5ft. 11½in. Weight, 11st. 9lb. Needs constant marking. Topped Sheffield Wednesday's goal scoring list last season and netted in every round of the Cup. As a schoolboy he played with Dixie Dean and both started in League football with Tranmere Rovers. Both are now English internationals.

NAMES IN THE GAME.

No. 4.

•

Mr. W. H. WALKER

Secretary-Manager of Sheffield Wednesday, our Cup-holding visitors of to-day, Mr. Walker went straight from a brilliant playing career into his present position. Born in 1898, son of a former Wolves' star, he joined Aston Villa in 1919 and took his chance to play in a cup-tie against Queen's Park Rangers so well that he was, but a few months later, helping the Villa to win the Cup against Huddersfield Town.

Has a splendid international record, having played for England in 13 matches against home countries and nine against overseas teams. Not only a really brilliant inside forward, but a captain of genius.

His tactics on and off the field led to his present appointment in December, 1933. This Aston Villa footballer became manager of one of the most famous clubs in the country. He has justified that confidence to the full. Apart from his keen insight into the game, his aptitude for the difficult job he has taken has become obvious. He also possesses a gift for a quiet kind of showmanship which, in bringing some of the unusual sides of football to the notice of the public, has attracted widespread attention.

NEW CAPITAL

The new capital being raised by the Club takes the form of 6 per cent. Debentures of £50 each, and at the Annual General Meeting held in July last, several shareholders expressed the desire to increase their holdings of shares. The Management have also received many letters from supporters who desire to acquire shares. As the share capital of the Club is fully subscribed, it is not possible to satisfy applicants unless any existing shareholder desires to realise, in which case the shareholder should advise the Secretary *in writing* of the number of shares he desires to sell and the price he is willing to accept. Particulars regarding the new issue of Debentures will be forwarded on request.

BEWARE.

It has come to the Management's knowledge that a person or persons are offering tickets for our game v. Arsenal F.C. on November 2nd, for admission to the ground at 1/3 each. These tickets are a fraud and supporters are requested not to purchase them but to give information to the police as the club are anxious to prosecute the individual or individuals concerned. The usual admission arrangements will be in force on November 2nd, being by payment of 1/- through the turnstiles and 1/6 and 2/- enclosure turnstiles.

GEORGE POYSER
Left Full Back

Born at Stanton Hill in 1910, he had a fine record as a school-boy outside left and played for his home town club before the Wolves took him on at the age of 18. Moved first to Stourbridge, then to Mansfield Town, and finally to Port Vale where Brentford " spotted " him. Since he has been playing with Bateman, he has polished up his game, yet lost none of his speed, fearlessness or dash : with the result that the pair make as fine a couple of backs as there is in the country. His recreations include tennis, bowls and pigeons.

FIXTURES, SEASON 1935-36.

FIRST TEAM

Date. 1935.	Opponents.	Ground.	GOALS F.	A.
Aug. 31	Bolton Wanderers ...	A	2	0
Sept. 5	Blackburn Rovers ...	H	3	1
,, 7	Huddersfield Town ...	H	1	2
,, 14	Middlesbrough ...	A	0	0
,, 18	Derby County ...	A	1	2
,, 21	Aston Villa	H	1	2
,, 28	Wolverhampton Wdrs.	A	2	5
Oct. 5	Sheffield Wednesday ..	A		
,, 12	Portsmouth	A		
,, 19	Stoke City	H		
,, 26	Manchester City ...	A		
Nov. 2	Arsenal	H		
,, 9	Birmingham	A		
,, 16	Sunderland	H		
,, 23	Chelsea	A		
,, 30	Leeds United ...	H		
Dec. 7	Grimsby Town ...	A		
,, 14	Liverpool	H		
,, 21	West Bromwich Albion	A		
,, 25	Preston North End ...	H		
,, 26	Preston North End ...	A		
,, 28	Bolton Wanderers ...	H		
1936.				
Jan. 1	Blackburn Rovers ...	A		
,, 4	Huddersfield Town ...	A		
,, 11	(3)			
,, 18	Middlesbrough ...	H		
,, 25	(4) Aston Villa ...	A		
Feb. 1	Wolverhampton Wdrs.	H		
,, 8	Sheffield Wednesday ...	A		
,, 15	(5) Portsmouth ...	H		
,, 22	Stoke City	A		
,, 29	(6) Manchester City ...	H		
Mar. 7	Arsenal	A		
,, 14	(S.-F.) Birmingham ...	H		
,, 21	Sunderland	A		
,, 28	Chelsea	H		
April 4	Leeds United ...	A		
,, 10	Everton	H		
,, 11	Grimsby Town ...	H		
,, 13	Everton	A		
,, 18	Liverpool	A		
,, 25	(F.) West Brom. Alb.	H		
May 2	Derby County ...	H		

SECOND TEAM

Date. 1935.	Opponents.	Ground.	GOALS F.	A.
Aug. 31	Charlton Athletic ...	H	2	1
Sept. 4	Watford	A	1	3
,, 7	Clapton Orient ...	A	0	0
,, 12	Watford	H	2	1
,, 14	Southend United ...	H	1	0
,, 21	Northampton Town ...	A	1	0
,, 25	Luton Town	A	1	4
,, 28	Crystal Palace ...	H	4	0
Oct. 3	Luton Town	H	4	3
,, 5	Reading	A		
,, 9	Bournemouth & Bos. .	H		
,, 12	Tottenham Hotspur	H		
,, 19	Bristol City	A		
,, 26	Millwall	H		
Nov. 2	West Ham United ...	A		
,, 9	Swansea Town ...	H		
,, 16	Leicester City ...	H		
,, 23	Coventry City ...	H		
,, 30	Arsenal	A		
Dec. 7	Southampton ...	H		
,, 14	Brighton & Hove A.	A		
,, 21	Queen's Park Rgrs. ..	H		
,, 25	Chelsea	A		
,, 26	Chelsea	H		
,, 28	Charlton Athletic ...	A		
1936.				
Jan. 4	Clapton Orient ...	H		
,, 11	Fulham	H		
,, 18	Southend United ...	A		
,, 25	Northampton Town ...	H		
Feb. 1	Crystal Palace ...	A		
,, 8	Reading	H		
,, 15	Tottenham Hotspur ...	A		
,, 22	Bristol City	H		
,, 29	Millwall	A		
Mar. 7	West Ham United ...	H		
,, 14	Swansea Town ...	A		
,, 21	Leicester City ...	H		
,, 25	Bournemouth & Bos. .	A		
,, 28	Coventry City ...	A		
April 4	Arsenal	H		
,, 10	Portsmouth	H		
,, 11	Southampton ...	A		
,, 13	Portsmouth	A		
,, 18	Brighton & Hove A.	H		
,, 25	Queen's Park Rgrs. ..	A		
May 2	Fulham	A		

Half Time Scores.

	F.	A.			F	A
A Arsenal v. Blackburn	......	......	J—Sunderland v. Liverpool		......	......
B—Birmingham v. Chelsea	......	......	K—West Brom. v. Grimsby		......	......
C—Bolton v. Middlesbrough	......	......	L—Charlton v. Bradford C.		......	......
D—Derby County v. Wolves	......	......	M—Fulham v. 'Spurs		......	......
E—Everton v. Aston Villa	......	......	N—West Ham v. Barnsley		......	......
F—Leeds v. Huddersfield	......	......	O—Aldershot v. Millwall		......	......
G—Manchester C. v. Stoke	......	......	P—Bristol R. v. Crystal Palace	......	......	
H—Preston N.E. v. Portsmouth	......	......	R—Newport v. Q.P.R.		......	......

The Next Games.

After to-day, a fortnight elapses before the next First Division game at Griffin Park, when on October 19th, Stoke City are our guests. Despite a home defeat at the hands of the Arsenal on Saturday, they have been enjoying a pretty good season, and the game should be yet another star attraction for our supporters.

Meanwhile, however, there is plenty of interesting football to be seen at Griffin Park.

On Monday we meet the Metropolitan Police in the first round of the London Challenge Cup, and two days later the Bees' Reserves meet Bournemouth Reserves in a London Combination game.

The kick-off for both these matches is timed for 3.30 p.m.

The following Saturday there is another London Combination game, and our visitors on this occasion will be Tottenham Hotspur, who have a line of goal-scoring forwards that will give our defence a very busy afternoon.

The Bees' first side will be at Portsmouth that afternoon, and it is expected that many of our supporters will travel down to see what should prove a very exciting game. The seaside team have proved to be rather inconsistent both this season and last—providing big surprises by unexpected wins and equally unexpected defeats.

We'll leave the matter at that . . .

BRENTFORD FOOTBALL AND SPORTS CLUB, LIMITED.

Registered Office :—GRIFFIN PARK, BRAEMAR ROAD, BRENTFORD.

President and Chairman :
MR. L. P. SIMON.

ALDERMAN W. FLEWITT, J.P.
MR. H. N. BLUNDELL.
MR. H. J. SAUNDERS.

MR. H. W. DODGE.
MR. C. L. SIMON.

Vice-Chairman :
MR. F. A. DAVIS.

MR. F. W. BARTON.
ALDERMAN H. F. DAVIS.
MR. J. R. HUGHES, J.P., C.C.

Hon. Treasurer ;
ALDERMAN W. FLEWITT, J.P.

Club Medical Officer ; DR. A. D. GOWANS.

Secretary-Manager ;
MR. H. C. CURTIS,
" DORINCOURT," BOSTON GARDENS, BRENTFORD.

Telephones :
GROUND : EALING 1744.
PRIVATE HOUSE : EALING 1183.

Telegraphic Address ;
CURTIS, FOOTBALL, BRENTFORD.
Ground ; GRIFFIN PARK, EALING ROAD, BRENTFORD.

No. 5.   Saturday, October 19th, 1935.

Notes from the Hive.

THREE points from the last two games is not bad going. Sorry our boys cannot seem to strike their true form, or at least get results, at home, for the last " at home " engagement saw a point quite unnecessarily sacrificed to Sheffield Wednesday. The loss of an odd point here and there would not give any cause for alarm, but things have been going definitely badly for the Bees in their own hive this season, and it is hoped that the team will have found the winning trail before their own supporters again before the Arsenal bring their big guns from Highbury to Griffin Park in a fortnight's time. To do that Stoke City must be sent empty away to-day. All together lads ! A bit more coolness near goal and the trick will be done.

It does not need the writer to tell the reader that things have changed at Brentford in a very short time. Glance round and see for yourself, then look at the fixture list and see all the famous clubs which have to visit us this season, how the crowds have swelled in spite of the wonderful ground improvements. Yes, things have changed, mostly for the better, but there is one little matter which at the moment seems to have NOT changed for the better. It's to do with the Brentford home record. One has not to trace the years back very far to recall a campaign in which Brentford set up a record by winning every home game they played. How different things have worked out during the present season ! But, of course, in our run in Division I. Brentford have actually done better to date AWAY from home than at Griffin Park.

ANOTHER HOME POINT CONCEDED.

Brentford should have beaten Sheffield Wednesday at Griffin Park a fortnight ago, instead of having to put in all they knew to get an equalising goal to save the game in the later stages. It should never have been. Here is what happened. The visitors commenced in bright style, but their period of ascendency was of short duration—Brentford soon got on top and crowned some storming attacks with a goal, scored by Robson. A goal or two more should have rewarded the work of our boys before the interval. The second half commenced disastrously for the Bees, for the visitors actually got in front by scoring a couple of goals. The equalising goal resulted from a long shot striking Bateman and going into the net. Before the Wednesday actually took the lead their goal experienced some sensational escapes, some due to bad

NOTES FROM THE HIVE—*Continued.*

misses by our own forwards. When the visitors took the lead it was all against the run of the play and the onlookers must have been thinking it was going to turn out another "Huddersfield-cum-Villa" affair. Actually it did not work out quite so bad as that, for Scott did head through an equalising goal before the end.

"POMP" TAKEN OUT OF POMPEY.

Few clubs get any change in the course of a season at Fratton Park, but the Bees are no respectors of reputations and they just went down to the headquarters of the Portsmouth F.C. last week-end, and well and truly beat the men of the Naval town by three goals to one.

There was no fluke about this victory either. Brentford knew the nature of the task on hand and they simply let Pompey have it hot and strong right from the start. Two goals up in ten minutes. My word, that was a great start against a team that had won all their home games to date. The home side managed to reduce the margin before the interval, but a goal by Hopkins restored our two-goals advantage in the second half. Our first goal was also scored by Hopkins, and two minutes later Holliday added a second goal. The whole team played jolly well and compared with Portsmouth, were faster and more methodical; in fact the play of Brentford in this game came as something of a revelation to the habitues of Fratton Park, although I understand that the officials of the Portsmouth club were prepared for a very hard struggle without anticipating anything in the nature of a defeat. But all agreed that the better team had won and after all that is really as it should be—although it oftentimes does not work out like that.

RESERVES AT THE TOP.

At the time of writing our Reserve team figure jointly at the head of the London Combination. That is very gratifying for the team was not showing to great advantage in early season games. Considerable improvement has been seen recently, including a London Challenge Cup Tie win over Metropolitan Police.

This was followed by a 5—2 win over Bournemouth Reserves at Griffin Park, a game in which Brown found the net four times and Muttitt got the other goal to complete a "nap" hand.

On Saturday last Tottenham's second string were beaten by the odd goal in three. Smith (C.) and Dunn were the scorers.

STOKE CITY HERE TO-DAY.

In welcoming Stoke City to Griffin Park to-day, we have visitors of whom we must beware, because they have the second best away record in the First Division. Stoke stand pretty high on the table with a record of equal merit to that of the Arsenal in the matter of points—12 from 10 games. There is nothing particularly wonderful in that some might say, but when we consider that our visitors from the Potteries have actually collected half of their points away from home, that is sufficient for all and sundry to sit up and take notice. That is not all, for the nature of Stoke's successes on foreign pastures, has been rather sensational. Look at these results: 5—3 at Chelsea, 5—0 at Birmingham, and 2—1 at Manchester, against the City. Such performances require no amplification—they speak for themselves! Moral to the story: Bees beware! But our boys never take any opposition easy and what they did to Portsmouth they can . . .

Here's to a thrilling game and that the Bees produce their best form and gain a merited success, is the wish of **"BUSY BEE."**

Jottings from the Board Room.

Special cheap tickets are available to Brentford on the Southern Railway for the Arsenal game by all trains between 11 a.m. and 3 p.m. Details can be obtained from any station. The special train will again be arranged from Reading and excellent return service arrangements have been made for all stations.

Our Reserves play Clapton Orient Reserves on this ground on Monday next, October 21st, 1935 (kick-off 3.15 p.m.), in the second round of the "London Challenge Cup."

Patrons are asked to purchase programmes from sellers wearing the Official Armlet Badge only.

IN CONFIDENCE.

Will the person who purchased six tickets in the Irish Sweep (for the "Cambridgeshire") and has lost them, please see Mr. Curtis. These tickets were picked up in Wing G of Stand, on Saturday, October 5th, when we played Sheffield Wednesday, and it may save a lot of inconvenience when drawing the £30,000.

The Reserves are to-day away to Bristol City Reserves (London Combination).

Charlie Walsh was examined by the Football League Specialist, Dr. J. Collingwood Stewart, at Newcastle-on-Tyne, on Tuesday last, and it is with regret that I have to announce that his report confirms the previous examination reports—that Charlie will not be able to play again. All our sympathy is with this player, but I have no doubt that he will receive just treatment for his future.

Our next home game in the Football League is v. The Arsenal, on Saturday, November 2nd, 1935, kick-off at 2.45 p.m. As previously stated, all the Stand seats have been disposed of. The usual prices of admission will be charged, viz., Ground, 1/-; Enclosure, Brook Road, 1/6; and Enclosure, Braemar Road, 2/-; payment through the turnstiles as usual.

It is hoped that patrons will assist the Club as much as possible by packing together to enable all those who pay for admission to witness the game.

Ernie Muttitt injured his shoulder rather badly on Saturday last when playing against the Spurs Reserves. He was taken to hospital for an X-ray examination, which fortunately showed nothing more serious than a badly bruised shoulder. He is making good progress. Walter Metcalf also hopes to resume training during next week.

Comparative results to date with last season are as follows:—
Football League.

	P.	W.	L.	D.	Goals F.	A.	Pt.
This season ...	9	3	4	2	15	13	8
Last season ...	9	5	1	3	20	12	13

London Combination.

	P.	W.	L.	D.	Goals F.	A.	Pt.
This season ...	12	8	3	1	24	17	17
Last season ...	12	7	3	2	24	15	16

Goal scorers to date are as follows:
Football League: Holliday 6, Fletcher 3, Hopkins 3, Scott 2, Robson 1.—Total, 15.
Jack Holliday has now scored 95 goals for this Club.
London Combination: Brown 7, Dunn 6, Muttitt 4, Sullivan 3, Smith 2, Fenton 1, Gibbons 1.—Total 24.

The Reserves are at home to Millwall Reserves (London Combination) on Saturday next, October 26th, 1935; kick-off at 3 o'clock; while the League team are away to Manchester City.

Our young amateur clerk, Leslie Smith, who with Maurice Batchelor assists Hayes F.C. has been honoured by being selected to play for the London F.A. against Diables Rouges F.C. at Brussels on November 1st. He also played for London F.C. team against Charterhouse on Wednesday last. Congratulations Leslie.
A further honour is that he is to play for the Middlesex F.A. against Norfolk F.A. on Wednesday next, October 23rd, 1935.

A Union door key attached to a large ring has been picked up on the ground. Please apply to the office

Shots from the Spot.

By "Rambler"

No excuses to make this week : the Bees have justified all I have said about them. After holding the Cup-winners to a draw, they beat Portsmouth, where Everton, Aston Villa and the Wednesday have all failed this season.

* * *

In other words the Bees are settling down. Clubs have to have lean patches from time to time, and its as well to get them over early.

* * *

I was glad to see that Bolton Wanderers—who share with Brentford the advantages and disadvantages of the title of League babes—also won away from home, and at Aston Villa at that.

* * *

Brentford's League record is an interesting one, and one that promises well for the rest of the season. They are, in fact, six points behind the leaders, and no fewer than five of their eight points have come from away matches. When the old winning-at-home habit reasserts itself, the gap between the Bees and the leaders should close with some rapidity.

* * *

It was a good day all round for the London clubs last Saturday, for only Fulham lost. However, there were two local Derbies, in both of which points were shared, which takes a little of the gilt off the ginger-bread.

It also does me good to refer briefly to the revival of the Bees' Reserve team, who, after making a rather scrappy start to the season, now share top place—which is where we have grown accustomed to seeing them.

* * *

I see from one of my reference books that Brentford last year had six ever-present players in their team and only called on 17 players for first team duty altogether.

Their nearest rivals to this figure in all four Divisions were Grimsby Town who had four players that never missed a game. In the First and Second Divisions no fewer than 17 clubs did not have a single regular representative.

These figures—they were probably much the same the year before —give a remarkable insight into the reasons for the Club's success.

* * *

Notts County changed their colours, improved their stands and started with a new team manager, Charlie Jones, an ex-Arsenal player. At the end of that season Jones had left and the club was doomed to relegation into the Third Division. Perhaps it is true that to change your colours is to change your luck.

* * *

Do you remember when the Bees adopted their red and white stripes?

OUR VISITORS TO-DAY.

HOW THEY MAY LINE UP.

It is over seventy years since Stoke City Football Club, who were original members of the Football League, visitors to Griffin Park to-day, was founded. During that time it has had a remarkably erratic career.

They have had spells in all three sections of the Football League, both Divisions of the old Southern League, while in 1908 they dropped out of the first-class game altogether. After struggling along in minor leagues they came to the fore again when they were reconstructed at the end of the War.

They have made a good start to this season, under the guidance of Mr. Bob McGrory, and they look like settling down into one of the most formidable sides in the League. Their away record is better than their home results, for although the points gained are the same, they have scored more goals away from home and their average is better.

Lewis, Norman A. (goalkeeper). —Born at Wolverhampton. Height 5ft. 10in. Weight, 12st. 6lb. Wolverhampton Wanderers secured him from a local club after he had made his name in junior circles. Has given excellent service to Stoke whom he joined several years ago.

Spencer, William (right back).— Born at Preston, Lancs. Height, 5ft. 8in. Weight, 11st. Has been at Stoke for ten years. Was secured as a youngster from Hebden Bridge, a Yorkshire junior club. Can play on either flank, and though he played on the left for a long time as partner to McGrory, now the club's manager, he has soon settled down on the right this season.

Scrimshaw, Charles (left back). —Born at Heanor, Notts. Height, 5ft. 10in. Weight, 11st. 6lb. Another product of Hebden Bridge. Has been at Stoke for some time, but despite the fact that he has played half-back and full back, his appearances in the first team have been intermittent. This season he gets his first real chance of becoming a " regular."

Tutin, Arthur (right half).—Born at Coundon, Co. Durham. Height, 5ft. 7in. Weight, 11st. 8lb. Coming to the fore with Crook Town, he was introduced to League football by Aldershot Town. In November, 1933, after less than a season as a Third Division player, he joined Stoke. Was immediately put in the First Division side and has kept his place ever since.

Turner, Arthur (centre half).— Born at Stoke. A six-footer who blocks up the way down the centre without neglecting his forwards. Was formerly employed as an upholsterer and first played for Stoke as an amateur. Has a powerful shot which he uses with deadly effect from a free-kick anywhere near goal.

Soo, Frank (left half or forward). —Born at Liverpool. Height, 5ft. 8in. Weight, 10st. 10lb. English born of Chinese parents. Was signed from Prescot Cables in January, 1933, as a half-back. Became an inside forward and when he made his first team debut in November, 1933, against Middles-

BRENTFORD

BRE

Red a

1—M

2—BATEMAN
Right Back

4—McKENZIE   5—
Right Half   C

7—HOPKINS   8—ROBSON   9—H
Outside Right   Inside Right   Centr

Referee—Mr. B. C. WHITE

12—JOHNSON   13—WESTLAND   14
Outside Left   Inside Left   Cent

17—SOO   18-
Left Half   C

20—SCRIMSHAW
Left Back

22

Red and

STO

THE LEAGUE—DIVISION I.

	P.	W.	D.	L.	F.	A.	P.
Huddersfield T.	10	5	4	1	18	12	14
Middlesbrough	10	6	1	3	33	17	13
Sunderland	10	6	1	3	26	16	13
Derby County	10	6	1	3	17	11	13
Arsenal	10	4	4	2	24	11	12
Stoke City	10	6	0	4	20	15	12
Manchester City ..	9	5	1	3	17	11	11
Sheffield Wed.	10	3	5	2	14	13	11
Birmingham	10	4	3	3	11	15	11
Wolves	10	4	2	4	17	17	10
Chelsea	10	4	2	4	16	17	10
Blackburn Rov.	9	5	0	4	18	20	10
Liverpool	10	4	1	5	23	17	9
Bolton Wanderers .	9	3	3	3	11	14	9
BRENTFORD	**9**	**3**	**2**	**4**	**15**	**13**	**8**
Portsmouth	9	3	2	4	12	14	8
Aston Villa	10	3	2	5	17	23	8
Leeds United	10	2	4	4	8	14	8
Grimsby Town	9	3	0	6	12	23	6
West Bromwich A.	10	2	2	6	11	22	6
Everton	10	2	2	6	13	27	6
Preston N.E.	10	2	2	6	8	19	6

turn to page N

STOKE CITY

'ORD

tripes

SON

er

3—POYSER
Left Back

ES
f

6—J. C. BURNS
Left Half

AY **10—SCOTT** **11—FLETCHER**
d Inside Left Outside Left

Linesmen— Messrs. C. E. Argent (blue flag),
and R. Cooper (red flag)

E **15—STEELE** **16—MATTHEWS**
rd Inside Right Outside Right

NER **19—TUTIN**
lf Right Half

21—SPENCER
Right Back

IS
er

ite Knickers

CITY

LONDON COMBINATION
(Up to and including last Saturday's games)

	P.	W.	D.	L.	F.	A.	P.
Portsmouth	10	7	3	0	32	13	17
BRENTFORD	12	8	1	3	24	17	17
Arsenal	10	8	0	2	23	11	16
Chelsea	12	7	2	3	30	17	16
Swansea Town	11	7	2	2	19	13	16
West Ham United	11	6	3	2	32	12	15
Luton Town	11	7	1	3	39	20	15
Charlton Athletic	13	6	1	6	25	22	13
Queen's Park Rgrs.	12	6	1	5	23	21	13
Coventry City	11	6	0	5	25	14	12
Crystal Palace	11	5	1	5	18	33	11
Millwall	10	4	2	4	14	17	10
Southend United	12	4	2	6	19	26	10
Bournemouth	11	4	2	5	17	29	10
Watford	11	4	1	6	26	22	9
Southampton	12	3	3	6	17	22	9
Tottenham H.	11	3	2	6	32	27	8
Reading	9	4	0	5	21	27	8
Bristol City	12	4	0	8	17	37	8
Clapton Orient	10	2	4	4	8	20	8
Fulham	11	3	1	7	21	20	7
Leicester City	11	3	0	8	19	30	6
Northampton	10	2	1	7	17	26	5
Brighton & Hove A.	10	2	1	7	9	31	5

brough, he was the first Chinaman ever to play in English League football. Has returned to his old position this season.

Matthews, Stanley (outside right) —Born at Stoke. Height, 5ft. 9in. Weight, 10st. 10lb. A product of Stoke St. Peter's, the City's nursery club. Was a schoolboy star and in 1929 played for England. Last season he gained full caps against Wales and Italy. Has started this season in his best form.

Steele, Fred. (inside right).—Was only 17 when he joined Stoke in August, 1933. Within two years he had made several first team appearances and has been playing consistently this season. He was spotted while with Downings, a prominent North Staffordshire club.

Sale, Thomas (centre forward).— Born at Stoke. Like Matthews, he is a product of Stoke St. Peter's. Joined the City in 1929 as a half-back, became inside left, and then in season 1933-4 took over the centre forward berth. Has fine ball control and strong physique. Easily led the club's goal-scorers last season.

Westland, J. (inside left).— Height, 5ft. 8in Weight, 10st. 10lb. A Scot, who came to the club on a month's trial from Aberdeen at the start of this season. Thanks to injuries he soon got his first team chance and has played in the last five matches, scoring once. Prior to joining Aberdeen he played for Inchgarth and Banks o' Dee.

Johnson, Joseph (outside left).— Born at Grimsby. Height, 5ft. 7½in. Weight, 10st. 6lb. Started his football career with Scunthorpe United, the Midland League club. Bristol City secured his signature and then he moved to Stoke in 1932. Played a big part in the club's promotion in his first season. A forceful player with a powerful shot.

NAMES IN THE GAME.
No. 5.

Mr. ROBERT McGRORY

Now manager of Stoke City, our visitors to-day, Mr. McGrory has a marvellous record of consistency for and loyalty to his club. He joined Stoke in April, 1921, from Burnley, having started with Dumbarton as long ago as 1913. For Stoke he made over 500 appearances, but retired from the League side on being appointed second team coach and assistant manager. It was found, though, they needed his personality in the team and he was called back and largely through his influence the team was lifted away from the danger of relegation. In 1934-35 he played in every first team game. Another sport he's good at is golf.

NEW CAPITAL

The new capital being raised by the Club takes the form of 6 per cent. Debentures of £50 each, and at the Annual General Meeting held in July last, several shareholders expressed the desire to increase their holdings of shares. The Management have also received many letters from supporters who desire to acquire shares. As the share capital of the Club is fully subscribed, it is not possible to satisfy applicants unless any existing shareholder desires to realise, in which case the shareholder should advise the Secretary *in writing* of the number of shares he desires to sell and the price he is willing to accept. Particulars regarding the new issue of Debentures will be forwarded on request.

Do You Know ?

394 penalty kicks were awarded last season—and 131 of them were missed !

* * *

A set of second-hand turnstiles was part of the transfer fee the 'Spurs paid Peterborough for the services of James Elliott, half back, just before the war.

Ramage, Derby County's inside left, was the only First Division inside forward to retain his position throughout last season.

* * *

Rotherham United did not have a single penalty awarded against them last season, whilst Bury never had a penalty awarded to them.

IDRIS HOPKINS (Outside Right)

Brentford's only full international—he played for Wales against Ireland and Scotland last season—has played a big part in Club's progress from Third to First Division. Had experience with Sheffield Wednesday before coming South to Dartford and Crystal Palace, where Mr. Curtis spotted him. Has a gift for getting goals that count, and, with a couple at Portsmouth last week, seems to have sprung back to his old form. Didn't miss a game last season. He is a very keen canary-fancier but his real hobby is his work —football.

FIXTURES, SEASON 1935-36.

FIRST TEAM

Date. 1935.	Opponents.	Ground.	GOALS F.	GOALS A.
Aug. 31	Bolton Wanderers ...	A	2	0
Sept. 5	Blackburn Rovers ...	H	3	1
,, 7	Huddersfield Town ...	H	1	2
,, 14	Middlesbrough ...	A	0	2
,, 18	Derby County ...	A	1	2
,, 21	Aston Villa	H	1	1
,, 28	Wolverhampton Wdrs.	A	2	3
Oct. 5	Sheffield Wednesday ..	H	2	2
,, 12	Portsmouth ...	A	3	1
,, 19	Stoke City ...	H		
,, 26	Manchester City ...	A		
Nov. 2	Arsenal	H		
,, 9	Birmingham ...	A		
,, 16	Sunderland ...	H		
,, 23	Chelsea ...	A		
,, 30	Leeds United ...	H		
Dec. 7	Grimsby Town ...	A		
,, 14	Liverpool ...	H		
,, 21	West Bromwich Albion	A		
,, 25	Preston North End ...	A		
,, 26	Preston North End ...	A		
,, 28	Bolton Wanderers ...	H		
1936.				
Jan. 1	Blackburn Rovers ...	A		
,, 4	Huddersfield Town ...	A		
,, 11	(3)			
,, 18	Middlesbrough ...	H		
,, 25	(4) Aston Villa ...	A		
Feb. 1	Wolverhampton Wdrs.	H		
,, 8	Sheffield Wednesday ...	A		
,, 15	(5) Portsmouth ...	H		
,, 22	Stoke City ...	A		
,, 29	(6) Manchester City ...	H		
Mar. 7	Arsenal ...	A		
,, 14	(S.-F.) Birmingham ...	H		
,, 21	Sunderland ...	A		
,, 28	Chelsea ...	H		
April 4	Leeds United ...	A		
,, 10	Everton ...	A		
,, 11	Grimsby Town ...	H		
,, 13	Everton ...	H		
,, 18	Liverpool ...	A		
,, 25	(F.) West Brom. Alb.	H		
May 2	Derby County ...	H		

SECOND TEAM

Date. 1935.	Opponents.	Ground.	GOALS F.	GOALS A.
Aug. 31	Charlton Athletic ...	H	2	1
Sept. 4	Watford ...	A	1	3
,, 7	Clapton Orient ...	A	0	0
,, 12	Watford ...	H	2	1
,, 14	Southend United ...	H	1	0
,, 21	Northampton Town ...	A	1	1
,, 25	Luton Town ...	A	1	4
,, 28	Crystal Palace ...	H	4	0
Oct. 3	Luton Town ...	H	4	3
,, 5	Reading ...	A	1	2
,, 7	Met Police—L.C. Cup	H	2	0
,, 9	Bournemouth & Bos. ..	H	5	2
,, 12	Tottenham Hotspur .....H		2	1
,, 19	Bristol City ...	A		
,, 21	C. Orient—L.C. Cup ...	H		
,, 26	Millwall ...	H		
Nov. 2	West Ham United ...	A		
,, 9	Swansea Town ...	H		
,, 16	Leicester City ...	A		
,, 23	Coventry City ...	H		
,, 30	Arsenal ...	A		
Dec. 7	Southampton ...	H		
,, 14	Brighton & Hove A. ...	A		
,, 21	Queen's Park Rgrs. ..	H		
,, 25	Chelsea ...	A		
,, 26	Chelsea ...	H		
,, 28	Charlton Athletic ...	A		
1936.				
Jan. 4	Clapton Orient ...	H		
,, 11	Fulham ...	H		
,, 18	Southend United ...	A		
,, 25	Northampton Town ...	H		
Feb. 1	Crystal Palace ...	A		
,, 8	Reading ...	H		
,, 15	Tottenham Hotspur ...	A		
,, 22	Bristol City ...	H		
,, 29	Millwall ...	A		
Mar. 7	West Ham United ...	H		
,, 14	Swansea Town ...	A		
,, 21	Leicester City ...	H		
,, 28	Bournemouth & Bos. .	A		
,, 28	Coventry City ...	A		
April 4	Arsenal ...	H		
,, 10	Portsmouth ...	H		
,, 11	Southampton ...	A		
,, 13	Portsmouth ...	A		
,, 18	Brighton & Hove A.	H		
,, 25	Queen's Park Rgrs. ...	H		
May 2	Fulham ...	A		

Half Time Scores.

	F.	A.			F	A
A—Ireland v. England	......	......	J—Preston N.E. v. Man. C.		......	......
B—Aston Villa v. West Brom.	......	......	K—Shef. Wed. v. Birmingham		......	......
C—Bolton Wand. v. Liverpool	......	......	L—W'hampton v. Sunderland		......	......
D—Derby C. v. Blackburn R.	......	......	M—Charlton A. v. Blackpool		......	......
E—Everton v. Chelsea	......	......	N—Fulham v. Norwich City		......	......
F—Huddersfield v. Grimsby T.	......	......	O—Plymouth A. v. West Ham		......	......
G—Middlesbrough v. Leeds U.	......	......	P—Tottenham v. Bradford		......	......
H—Portsmouth v. Arsenal	......	......	R—Notts C. v. Queen's P.R.		......	......

THROUGH THE HOOP——

THE WINNING VEIN

——NOW FOR THE LANDING

The Next Games.

Having beaten the Metropolitan Police in the first round of the London Challenge Cup, Brentford meet Clapton Orient in the second round at Griffin Park, on Monday, the kick-off being at 3.15 p.m. The following Saturday the Reserves are at home to Millwall, the kick-off for that game being at 3 p.m.

On that day, Brentford are away to Manchester City, who will provide very stiff opposition indeed. Their home record is a good one, and the Bees will have to touch the high spots if they are to succeed. The City have never succeeded in winning the First Division championship, but they are the only club to have made two appearances at Wembley in successive seasons, losing to Everton the first time and beating Portsmouth a year later.

Then comes November 2nd—a date long earmarked by Brentford fans—and half London as well—as being one of the biggest occasions of the football season. On that date the Arsenal are our visitors, and it is quite unnecessary to add that all stand seats have been sold long ago.

It is, however, worth pointing out at this early date that the kick-off is timed for 2.45 p.m. There won't be as big a crowd as there was at Chelsea a week ago—but that's only because Griffin Park could not hold it!

BRENTFORD FOOTBALL AND SPORTS CLUB, LIMITED.

Registered Office:—GRIFFIN PARK, BRAEMAR ROAD, BRENTFORD.

President and Chairman:
Mr. L. P. Simon.

Vice-Chairman:
Mr. F. A. Davis.

Alderman W. Flewitt, J.P.
Mr. H. N. Blundell.
Mr. H. J. Saunders.

Mr. H. W. Dodge.
Mr. C. L. Simon.

Mr. F. W. Barton.
Alderman H. F. Davis.
Mr. J. R. Hughes, J.P., C.C.

Hon. Treasurer:
Alderman W. Flewitt, J.P.

Club Medical Officer: Dr. A. D. Gowans.

Secretary-Manager:
Mr. H. C. Curtis,
"Dorincourt," Boston Gardens, Brentford.

Telephones:
Ground: Ealing 1744.
Private House: Ealing 1183.

Telegraphic Address:
Curtis, Football, Brentford.
Ground; Griffin Park, Ealing Road, Brentford.

No. 6.   **Saturday, November 2nd, 1935.**

Notes from the Hive.

THE Bees are slipping back. There can be no blinking at the fact that our favourites are at the moment of writing dangerously near the foot of the League table. It is but cold comfort to know that two or three more famous clubs are beneath us. Yet there is no panic at Griffin Park—just a little anxiety perhaps, which is only natural in such circumstances. That the Bees have proved their worth in the top class no one can honestly deny, but the fact remains that results have not worked out as they should have done. Brentford have earned many more points than they have gained, but that is just the luck of the game. We are not grumbling because experience has taught us that the vagaries of the game are many and varied. Our real trouble lies in the fact that the lean period has been unduly prolonged. A smile or two from Dame Fortune would have made all the difference and in all due respect to our opponents, it is surely not an exaggeration to say that if the luck had run evenly since the start of the campaign, Brentford would have been as near the top of the table as they find themselves to the other end at the moment.

THAT ANNOYING ODD GOAL.

In explanation of the above contention it need only be stated that the Bees have suffered five defeats in eleven games, and every one of those reverses have been by the odd goal. The three games which have been won, two away from home, have all shown a two-goal marginal win for Brentford. Opponents have paid tribute in the highest terms to the play of the Bees, which surely cannot always have been a chivalrous gesture on their part to a beaten opposition. No, the Bees have definitely delivered the goods, but somehow things have not gone just right. Great confidence is still invested in our team to rise to a high position on the League table.

HOME POINT DROPPED.

The conceding of another home point a fortnight ago to Stoke City came as a distinct blow. One had to be present to realise how unlucky the Bees were not to win this game. If Brentford had won by something like six clear goals it would not have exaggerated the extent to which Stoke were overplayed. Even in the first half Brentford were always on top, but nothing to compare with the superiority of our boys after the change of ends. Then it was

NOTES FROM THE HIVE—Continued.

simply a bombardment—no other word will suffice. Goals looked like coming at regular intervals, yet not once was the Stoke goalkeeper asked to pick the ball out of the net. The whole affair was a real tragedy for the Bees.

UNLUCKY AT MANCHESTER.

Yes, unfortunately, much as the writer would have it otherwise, the hard luck story of the Bees has to be again stressed after our visit to Maine Road, Manchester, on Saturday last. The whole affair was rather unsavoury and certainly unsatisfactory. It is not within the province of the writer to comment here on the conduct of the game by the official in charge, so that part of the business must be allowed to pass, but it would be most enlightening to know why the referee awarded a penalty kick to the home side. The Manchester players were certainly amazed at the award and the crowd showed their disapproval in no uncertain manner, and later cheered Mathieson to the echo when he saved the " spot " kick. With eleven fit men on the field Brentford called the tune to some purpose and took the lead through Hopkins. Later Bateman twisted a knee and Scott met with a nasty ankle injury which meant the team had to be reorganised, with Bateman going to outside right. Unfortunately our troubles did not end here for a spot of bother between Brook, the City outside left, and McKenzie, ended in both players being given marching orders. The second half was a scrambling affair in consequence of both teams having depleted forces, with the Bees having only eight fit players on the field.

The City obtained two goals which gave them victory in a game which we prefer to forget for more reasons than one. With considerable pride the fact is recorded that it is the only unpleasant game in which Brentford have been directly concerned this season. May it be the very last.

RESERVES ADVANCING.

Our Reserves have been going great guns of late with two well-cut London Combination wins. At Bristol, against the City, a 3—1 win was recorded, while on Saturday last a four clear goals win resulted from the visit of Millwall Reserves.

TO-DAY'S BIG GAME.

We have the tit-bit of the season to offer our patrons, and presumably many other Metropolitan enthusiasts, this afternoon. Brentford v. Arsenal—the game we have all waited for. Our dreams have come true. A year or two ago the only hope of getting the Arsenal to Griffin Park seemed to lay in being drawn against the Highbury club in the F.A. Cup, but it is better than that for the Bees are now operating in the same sphere and the Arsenal now come of their free will and accord to fulfil a First Division engagement at Griffin Park.

What of the Arsenal? How have they fared in their away games? Five points from six games. Curiously enough Brentford have an identical away record, but this game is a HOME one for Brentford —a doubtful advantage taking a line through this season's results. Arsenal's only win to date on foreign pastures was at Stoke. Drawn games were recorded at Birmingham, Leeds and Stamford Bridge, while defeats were sustained at Grimsby and Portsmouth .

May the game be worthy of the occasion and if the players can forget that it is a London " Derby " game, it surely will be. We extend to Arsenal a most cordial welcome and congratulate them most heartily on their wonderful success during recent years, which has put London on the map of the football world.

" BUSY BEE."

Jottings from the Board Room.

The sending off of our player, Duncan McKenzie, at Manchester, on Saturday, is much regretted; the circumstances which led to this drastic action cannot at this stage be commented on, as the case will be considered by the Football Association.

We anticipate a record crowd to-day, providing the weather is kind to us, and the Management do appeal most sincerely to all patrons to assist in the efforts to pack the ground well, to endeavour to give all present a chance to view the game.

Please close together.
Please do not sit on the terraces and take up unnecessary space.
Please endeavour to carry out the requests of the Stewards.
Please beware of pickpockets.

The Southern Railway are arranging a number of cheap trips to Brentford for our home game against Sunderland in a fortnight's time and patrons are asked to note that a special return train for Feltham, Ashford and Staines will leave at 4.38 p.m. Return trains to stations between Waterloo and Mortlake will leave at frequent intervals.

In connection with the League Match between Birmingham and Brentford, on November 9th, the Great Western Railway is running a half-day excursion to Birmingham as under :—
SATURDAY, NOVEMBER 9th.
Express Restaurant-car Half-Day Excursion to †Bordesley and Birmingham.
Forward—Paddington, dep. 11.5 a.m.; Bordesley, arr. 1.5 p.m.; Birmingham (Snow Hill), arr. 1.10 p.m.
Return—Birmingham (Snow Hill), dep. 6.0, 7.50 p.m.; Paddington, arr. 8.5, 10.5 p.m. Return Fare, 6/6.
†Bordesley Station is about 10 minutes' walk from the Birmingham Football Ground; passengers return from Birmingham (Snow Hill) Station.

Leslie Smith, our young amateur, has been selected to play for the F.A. XI v. Cambridge University at Cambridge, on Thursday, November 7th. Congratulations, Leslie!

Tickets can be purchased for our game v. Sunderland on this ground on November 16th (kick-off 2.30), at 4/- each. Applications by post must be accompanied by remittance and stamped, addressed envelope, otherwise they will not be considered.

Numerous comments were made in the Press about our defeat at Manchester on Saturday last after leading at half-time 1—0, but few recorded the fact that for a good period of the second half our team played as follows :—

Mathieson
†J. C. Burns   Poyser
†Robson   James   †Fletcher
†Bateman †Hopkins   †Scott
(badly injured   (badly injured)
Holliday
†Playing out of position.

We congratulate the team on being good losers.

The Big Fifteen are producing a play, "Who Goes Next?" at the Baths Hall, Brentford, on Thursday, November 21st, at 8 p.m., in aid of the Mayor's Unemployment Christmas Fund. The Mayor and Mayoress will be present and Mrs. Lane-Claypon has invited the Bees to be present.

Both Leslie Smith and Ernie Muttitt played for the London Football Association against Diables Rouges at Brussels yesterday.

Walter Metcalf and Leslie Sullivan are still unfit to play for the Reserves.

The Reserves are away to West Ham Reserves to-day. Unfortunately they have a weakened side owing to injuries.

Comparative records to date with last season are as follows :—

	P.	W.	L.	D.	Goals F.	Goals A.	Pt.
Football League—							
This Season	11	3	5	3	16	15	9
Last Season	11	6	2	3	24	16	15
London Combination—							
This Season	14	10	3	1	31	18	21
Last Season	14	9	3	2	27	15	20

Under no circumstances may boys climb into the playing pitch. They should take advantage of the Special Enclosure for their protection.

The Draw for the Semi-Final of the London Challenge Cup resulted as follows : Brentford v. Fulham, to be played at Griffin Park, on Monday, November 11th. 1935; kick-off at 2.45 p.m.

Shots from the Spot.

By "Rambler"

Very few of those who wrote about the Manchester City game explained that Brentford, after holding the lead, were forced to play eight fit men against ten. With Bateman and Scott on the wings, the suggestion that it was lack of stamina that lost the Bees the game is obviously ridiculous.

* * *

However, we'll skip all that, and talk about pleasanter things . . . the game to-day for example. It is safe to say that the Arsenal's visit to Griffin Park gripped public imagination from the day the date was announced. It would be interesting to know just how many 'phone enquiries for tickets the Club has received. There was certainly an almost continual stream of callers at the office for weeks on end, many of whom appear to have imagined the stands were made of elastic.

* * *

But, as you are reading this, it means that you at any rate have gained admission. If you are standing—remember your fellow fans who perhaps knocked off work a little later than you did, and give them every chance to see the game as well.

* * *

A win to-day would be the first Saturday victory the Bees have notched at Griffin Park this season —and it would be a good occasion to pull off such an event. Sunderland will be along in a fortnight's time— so no one can say the Bees are having a gentle baptism into First League football!

* * *

If the League team are not getting all the points we should like to see, the Reserves at any rate have got over the rather poor period which they went through earlier on in the season, and are now serving up attractive football as well as getting the points. They're now well worth watching . . . and there's some talent for future years which will justify the policy of team-building rather than team-buying.

* * *

And talking of team-buying, it would appear that the fantastic fees asked at the beginning of the season for almost any player in the country—and over the border—are now beginning to drop. Clubs have wisely refused to be stampeded into taking the ridiculous risks that the paying of fancy prices always entails. The result of the more reasoned attitude is that the market has brightened up. Clubs in need of players have been able to get them without ruining themselves financially, and clubs with players whom they can spare can use the fees obtainable for them for their own immediate benefit.

* * *

Our fellow "babes"—Bolton Wanderers—delighted the crowd at Stamford Bridge last Saturday by the dazzling qualities of their play. They were beaten 2—1, but they took away with them the plaudits of a very sporting crowd. Brentford outshone the Wanderers when they met them at Burnden Park in the first game of the season.

* * *

Brentford beat Portsmouth at Fratton Park. Arsenal are defeated. This is just another example of the amazingly difficult job it is to compare football form this season. Let us hope, though, it works out right to-day . . .

OUR VISITORS TO-DAY.
HOW THEY MAY LINE UP.

Arsenal come to Griffin Park to-day, known all over the world as the " luxury " team of the game.

Yet it was not always so. Like practically all clubs they sprang from a humble beginning, and an even more humble one than is usually the case.

Founded in 1866 by two ex-Nottingham Forest players, the original club, Royal Woolwich Arsenal, could not afford the players' kit. They had to play in cast-offs that were sent them by the Forest. It was not until 1926 that they carried off an honour in Division I. Then they were the runners-up. Four times in the last five years they have finished champions and on the other occasion they were runners-up, and in 1930 they won the F.A. Cup.

Wherever the name of the Arsenal is known there also will be known the name of the late Herbert Chapman, the greatest managerial genius the game has ever known. It was his astonishing transfer-deals, and amazing capacity for keeping his club in the " news " that brought the Gunners into the position they hold to-day.

Wilson, Alexander (goalkeeper). —Born at Wishaw, Lanarkshire. Height, 5ft. 11in. Weight, 11st. Joined Arsenal in May, 1933, from Greenock Morton, after he had assisted the Scottish club to gain promotion four years previously. Won London Combination medals in each of the last two seasons and has proved an excellent deputy for Moss

Male, George Charles (right back) —Born at Deptford, London. Height, 6ft. Weight, 12st. 12lb. Used to play centre-half and captained West Ham Schoolboys. Arsenal spotted him while with Clapton, the amateur side. Joined them as a professional in 1930. Had intermittent outings until 1932-3 season, when he moved from half to full back and succeeded Tom Parker on the right. A strong and fearless tackler. English international.

Hapgood, Edris (left back).— Born at Bristol. Height, 5ft. 9in. Weight, 11st. Started with Bristol Rovers as an amateur. They allowed him to move to Kettering, where he quickly attracted attention. Arsenal secured him in October, 1927. He has a Cup-winner's medal, four League Championship medals and a string of international caps. Skippers the Arsenal and England.

Crayston, John (right half).— Born at Grange-over-Sands, Lancs. Height, 6ft. Weight, 13st. Had just over a season with Barrow as a centre forward before moving to Bradford in the summer of 1930. Became a centre half and then a right half. Arsenal secured him soon after the close of season 1933-4.

Roberts, Herbert (centre half).— Born at Oswestry. Height, 6ft. Weight, 13st. Once a constable in the Shrewsbury Police Force. Now football "policeman." Succeeds in "arresting" most centre forwards. Joined Arsenal from Oswestry Town and made his League debut in season 1926-7. An English international.

Copping, Wilfred (left half).— Born at Barnsley, Yorks. Height, 5ft. 7in. Weight, 11st. Discovered by Leeds United while playing with Middlecliffe Rovers, a junior side near Barnsley. Signed in 1930. Quickly came to the fore and gained his first England cap on the Continent in 1933. Has followed it with several others. Arsenal secured him at a big fee in June, 1934.

BRENTFORI

BRE

Red

1—M

2—ASTLEY
Right Back

4—McKENZIE
Right Half

5-
C

7—HOPKINS 8—ROBSON 9—H
Outside Right   Inside Right   Cent

Referee— Mr. T. THOMPSON

12—BASTIN   13—JAMES   14—
Outside Left   Inside Left   Cen

17—COPPING   18—
Left Half

20—HAPGOOD
Left Back

22—

Red, W

AR

THE LEAGUE—DIVISION I.

	P.	W.	D.	L.	Goals F.	A.	P.
Sunderland	12	8	1	3	35	20	17
Derby County	12	7	2	3	18	11	16
Huddersfield Town	12	6	4	2	19	15	16
Arsenal	12	5	4	3	27	14	14
Middlesbrough	12	6	2	4	34	19	14
Stoke City	12	6	2	4	20	15	14
Manchester City	11	6	1	4	19	16	13
Sheffield Wed.	12	4	5	3	18	19	13
Birmingham	12	5	3	4	16	18	13
Liverpool	12	5	2	5	26	17	12
Chelsea	12	5	2	5	19	23	12
Blackburn Rovers	11	5	1	5	19	22	11
Leeds United	12	3	5	4	13	17	11
Wolverhampton W.	12	4	2	6	21	23	10
West Bromwich A.	12	4	2	6	20	23	10
Bolton Wanderers	11	3	4	4	12	16	10
Portsmouth	11	4	2	5	14	19	10
BRENTFORD	11	3	3	5	16	15	9
Everton	12	3	3	6	19	29	9
Preston North End	12	3	2	7	13	21	8
Aston Villa	12	3	2	7	19	34	8
Grimsby Town	11	4	0	7	13	24	8

ARSENAL

ORD

ripes

ESON

r

3—POYSER
Left Back

ES   **6—J. C. BURNS**
Left Half

AY **10—SCOTT**   **11—FLETCHER**
Inside Left   Outside Left

Linesmen—   **Messrs. C. F. Ward (blue flag),**
and R. C. Greenwood (red flag)

15—BOWDEN   **16—HULME**
Inside Right   Outside Right

RTS   **19—CRAYSTON**
Right Half

21—MALE
Right Back

ON

r

and Collars

AL

LONDON COMBINATION

	P.	W.	D.	L.	Goals F.	A.	P.
Swansea Town	15	10	2	3	26	17	22
Portsmouth	13	8	5	0	40	16	21
BRENTFORD	14	10	1	3	31	18	21
Chelsea	15	8	3	4	36	26	19
Crystal Palace	15	9	1	5	27	35	19
Luton Town	15	8	2	5	47	33	18
Arsenal	12	8	1	3	24	15	17
West Ham United .	14	6	4	4	37	22	16
Charlton Athletic ...	15	7	2	6	30	25	16
Queen's Park Rgrs.	15	7	2	6	27	24	16
Coventry City	14	7	0	7	31	18	14
Millwall	13	6	2	5	21	24	14
Watford	13	6	1	6	32	25	13
Southend United ...	14	5	2	7	23	29	12
Tottenham H.	13	4	3	6	37	30	11
Southampton	14	4	3	7	21	26	11
Bournemouth	15	4	3	8	24	40	11
Fulham	14	4	2	8	28	25	10
Reading	11	5	0	6	26	32	10
Clapton Orient	12	3	4	5	11	24	10
Bristol City	16	4	1	11	20	49	9
Leicester City	14	4	0	10	23	35	8
Brighton & Hove A.	13	3	2	8	20	39	8
Northampton	13	2	2	9	19	34	6

x INDEPENDENT—Best Reports and Pictures

Hulme, Joseph (outside right).— Born at Stafford. Height, 5ft. 8in. Weight, 11st. 11lb. Was brought up at York and joined York City at an early age. Moved to Blackburn Rovers in 1923 and to Arsenal two years later. His many honours include a string of international caps against Ireland, Scotland and Wales as well as overseas sides. Made his first appearance this season against Preston last week.

Bowden, Edwin Raymond (inside right).—Born at Looe, Cornwall. Height, 5ft. 9½in. Weight, 10st. 10lb. Came to the fore in 1928-9 with Plymouth Argyle, whom he joined in 1926. Won a Southern Section championship medal in 1930. Toured Canada with F.A. side the following year and went to Arsenal in March, 1933. Won two England caps last season and played against Ireland a week or so back and against the Scottish League this Wednesday.

Drake, Edward Joseph (centre forward).—Born at Southampton. Height, 5ft. 10in. Weight, 11st. 10lb. Became a Southampton player in 1931 after gaining experience with Winchester City (Hampshire League). Became a regular in the "Saints'" League XI. during season 1932-3. After protracted negotiations Arsenal secured his transfer in March, 1934, and last season he set up a club goal-scoring record with 43 goals. Also played twice for England during the campaign.

James, Alexander (inside left).— Born at Mossend, Glasgow. Height 5ft. 6½in. Weight, 11st. Football's wizard. A master juggler with the ball. Exploits the " W " formation brilliantly. Played in same school team as Hughie Gallacher. Later with Bellshill Athletic and Ashfield, two junior clubs. Raith Rovers introduced him to Scottish League football, and Preston North End to the English League game. Cost Arsenal £9,000 in June, 1929. Has many Scottish caps.

Bastin, Clifford Sydney (outside left).—Born at Exeter. Height, 5ft. 8½in. Weight, 11st. 2lb. Has had a meteoric career. Schoolboy international in 1926; played for Exeter City at 15; joined Arsenal at 17; at 19 won a Cup medal; and by the time he reached his majority had won every honour possible for a footballer. Originally an inside-forward and has played for England both on the wing and at inside.

Could you turn out
for a First Division team ?

Not on your life!

45 minutes each way and going hell for leather all the time! What would you feel like when the whistle went? Absolutely sunk—dead to the wide—wouldn't you? That's because your liver's sluggish. Your liver's supposed to pour two pints of digestive bile into your bowels every day. If it doesn't, your food can't digest, so you get all clogged up and easily tired.

The reason why the chaps out on the field are so fit is because hard training wakes up their livers and keeps their digestive bile flowing. You can't train like that, but you can do the next best thing. Wake up your liver with Carter's Little Liver Pills—get a penn'orth on your way home. You'll feel ten times more active and healthy—fighting fit! Be sure you get the genuine CARTER'S (Brand) LITTLE LIVER PILLS. Look for this trade mark on every 1d. twist. Also 1/3 and 3/- sizes.

Tune in to Radio Luxembourg every Sunday Morning at 11 a.m.

The Hanwell Silver Band has arranged for the co-operation in entertaining our patrons to-day of the

News & Chronicle

T.P.RATCLIFF
News & Chronicle
SONG LEADER.

the popular Daily Newspaper, and to help while away the waiting period, in addition to the band performance, we are pleased to announce

COMMUNITY SINGING
Conducted by
T. P. RATCLIFF
Under the auspices of the
" News Chronicle "
Be prepared to let it rip at 2 p.m.

The band will commence their programme at 12.30 under the direction of J. C. Dyson, and a special selection of popular tunes has been prepared, and we hope you will appreciate the entertainment provided. Our Band will broadcast again on November 23rd at 6.30 p.m.

NAMES IN THE GAME.
No. 6.
MR. PETER McWILLIAM

As Mr. George Allison has already been featured in this series, we deal to-day with another famous Arsenal official—Mr. Peter McWilliam, said to be the highest paid " scout " in the game.

Was one of the two greatest left-half-backs of all time, and is still one of the finest judges of a player in England. His greatest form as a footballer he reached when playing for Newcastle United, but his career in that capacity came to an end after receiving a bad injury when playing for Scotland against Wales.

He became manager of Tottenham Hotspur, and produced some of the most brilliant teams that club has ever fielded. His change-over to Middlesbrough caused a football sensation which was equalled during the last close season when, after retiring from Middlesbrough and acting as a scout for the Arsenal, he apparently thought he was free to return to manage the 'Spurs.

J. C. BURNS
Left Half or Inside Forward.

Has probably a unique record for an amateur, in that he helped Brentford to promotion from the Third Division into the Second and thence into the First. Regularly captains England's Amateur XI. He is a schoolmaster and a fine amateur boxer. Came to Brentford in 1931 from Queen's Park Rangers and is one of the most popular men in the side. Essentially an attacking half—inherited from days when regularly an inside—has great gift for cutting through and scoring a snap goal.

FIXTURES, SEASON 1935-36.

FIRST TEAM

Date. 1935.	Opponents.	Ground.	GOALS F.	A.
Aug. 31	Bolton Wanderers ...	A	2	0
Sept. 5	Blackburn Rovers ...	H	3	1
,, 7	Huddersfield Town ...	H	1	2
,, 14	Middlesbrough ...	A	0	0
,, 18	Derby County ...	A	1	2
,, 21	Aston Villa ...	H	1	2
,, 28	Wolverhampton Wdrs.	A	2	3
Oct. 5	Sheffield Wednesday ..	H	2	2
,, 12	Portsmouth ...	A	3	1
,, 19	Stoke City ...	H	0	0
,, 26	Manchester City ...	A	1	2
Nov. 2	Arsenal ...	H		
,, 9	Birmingham ...	A		
,, 16	Sunderland ...	H		
,, 23	Chelsea ...	A		
,, 30	Leeds United ...	H		
Dec. 7	Grimsby Town ...	A		
,, 14	Liverpool ...	H		
,, 21	West Bromwich Albion	A		
,, 25	Preston North End ...	H		
,, 26	Preston North End ...	A		
,, 28	Bolton Wanderers ...	H		
1936.				
Jan. 1	Blackburn Rovers ...	A		
,, 4	Huddersfield Town ...	A		
,, 11	(3)			
,, 18	Middlesbrough ...	H		
,, 25	(4) Aston Villa ...	A		
Feb. 1	Wolverhampton Wdrs.	H		
,, 8	Sheffield Wednesday ...	A		
,, 15	(5) Portsmouth ...	H		
,, 22	Stoke City ...	A		
,, 29	(6) Manchester City ...	H		
Mar. 7	Arsenal ...	A		
,, 14	(S.-F.) Birmingham ...	H		
,, 21	Sunderland ...	A		
,, 28	Chelsea ...	H		
April 4	Leeds United ...	A		
,, 10	Everton ...	H		
,, 11	Grimsby Town ...	H		
,, 13	Everton ...	A		
,, 18	Liverpool ...	A		
,, 25	(F.) West Brom. Alb.	H		
May 2	Derby County ...	H		

SECOND TEAM

Date. 1935.	Opponents.	Ground.	GOALS F.	A.
Aug. 31	Charlton Athletic ...	H	2	1
Sept. 4	Watford ...	A	1	3
,, 7	Clapton Orient ...	A	0	0
,, 12	Watford ...	H	2	1
,, 14	Southend United ...	H	1	0
,, 21	Northampton Town ...	A	1	0
,, 25	Luton Town ...	A	1	4
,, 28	Crystal Palace ...	H	4	0
Oct. 3	Luton Town ...	A	4	3
,, 5	Reading ...	H	1	2
,, 7	Met Police—L.C. Cup	H	2	0
,, 9	Bournemouth & Bos. .	A	5	2
,, 12	Tottenham Hotspur	H	2	1
,, 19	Bristol City ...	A	3	1
,, 21	C. Orient—L.C. Cup	H	3	1
,, 26	Millwall ...	H	4	0
Nov. 2	West Ham United ...	A		
,, 9	Swansea Town ...	A		
,, 16	Leicester City ...	A		
,, 23	Coventry City ...	H		
,, 30	Arsenal ...	A		
Dec. 7	Southampton ...	H		
,, 14	Brighton & Hove A. ...	A		
,, 21	Queen's Park Rgrs. ..	A		
,, 25	Chelsea ...	H		
,, 26	Chelsea ...	H		
,, 28	Charlton Athletic ...	A		
1936.				
Jan. 4	Clapton Orient ...	H		
,, 11	Fulham ...	H		
,, 18	Southend United ...	A		
,, 25	Northampton Town ...	H		
Feb. 1	Crystal Palace ...	A		
,, 8	Reading ...	H		
,, 15	Tottenham Hotspur ...	A		
,, 22	Bristol City ...	H		
,, 29	Millwall ...	H		
Mar. 7	West Ham United ...	H		
,, 14	Swansea Town ...	A		
,, 21	Leicester City ...	H		
,, 28	Bournemouth & Bos. .	A		
,, 28	Coventry City ...	A		
April 4	Arsenal ...	H		
,, 10	Portsmouth ...	H		
,, 11	Southampton ...	A		
,, 13	Portsmouth ...	A		
,, 18	Brighton & Hove A.	H		
,, 25	Queen's Park Rgrs. ..	A		
May 2	Fulham ...	A		

Half Time Scores.

	F.	A.		F	A
A—Aston Villa v. Grimsby	......	......	J—Sheffield W. v. West Brom.	......	......
B—Bolton W. v. Blackburn	......	......	K—Wolves v. Leeds	......	......
C—Derby Cnty. v. Man. City	......	......	L—Charlton v. Norwich	......	......
D—Everton v. Stoke	......	......	M—Fulham v. Sheffield U.	......	......
E—Huddersfield v. Chelsea	......	......	N—Newcastle v. West Ham	......	......
F—Middlesbrough v. Liverpool	......	......	O—'Spurs v. Swansea	......	......
G—Portsmouth v. Sunderland	......	......	P—Clapton Orient v. Q.P.R.	......	......
H—P.N.E. v. Birmingham	......	......	R—Crystal Palace v. Millwall	......	......

The Next Games.

The League team's next three games are all extremely important ones, and all present severe tests for the Bees.

Many of our supporters will, we anticipate, take advantage of the excursion that is being run to Birmingham next Saturday, and will be at St. Andrew's to give our lads a cheer. Those who do not make the journey should see some good football at Griffin Park, where the Reserves meet Swansea Town.

On November 16th, Sunderland, who, at the time of writing, are top of the League, are our visitors, and this game should provide a really thrilling struggle. Five times have Sunderland won the First Division title, though, it is interesting to note, they have never won the Cup and have actually figured in the Final on only one occasion.

This famous side will be given a great welcome when they appear at Griffin Park for the first time.

Then, the Saturday after that, the Bees are engaged in another historic encounter. They visit Stamford Bridge, where their " local Derby " with Chelsea is bound to attract fans from all over London. That Brentford supporters will be there in large numbers goes without saying, and the probabilities are that these teams, both capable of playing football that is a joy to watch, will stage a really worthwhile exhibition of the game. This year the Pensioners are a really efficient football machine.

On the day of that game Brentford Reserves are at home to Coventry City, and the Saturday before are engaged to meet Leicester City away from home.

BRENTFORD FOOTBALL AND SPORTS CLUB, LIMITED.

Registered Office :—GRIFFIN PARK, BRAEMAR ROAD, BRENTFORD.

President and Chairman :
MR. L. P. SIMON.

ALDERMAN W. FLEWITT, J.P.
MR. H. N. BLUNDELL.
MR. H. J. SAUNDERS.

MR. H. W. DODGE.
MR. C. L. SIMON.

Vice-Chairman :
MR. F. A. DAVIS.

MR. F. W. BARTON.
ALDERMAN H. F. DAVIS.
MR. J. R. HUGHES, J.P., C.C.

Hon. Treasurer ;
ALDERMAN W. FLEWITT, J.P.

Club Medical Officer ; DR. A. D. GOWANS.

Secretary-Manager ;
MR. H. C. CURTIS,
" DORINCOURT," BOSTON GARDENS, BRENTFORD.

Telephones ;
GROUND : EALING 1744.
PRIVATE HOUSE : EALING 1183.

Telegraphic Address ;
CURTIS, FOOTBALL, BRENTFORD.
Ground ; GRIFFIN PARK, EALING ROAD, BRENTFORD.

No. 7.   Saturday, November 16th, 1935.

Notes from the Hive.

GREAT show against the Arsenal! I think we are all in agreement about that, so there is no need to ask for a show of hands—carried unanimously!

I told my readers in the last issue that the Bees were more anxious to beat the Arsenal than any other club. That may have been a rather exaggerated statement, but really our boys were extra keen to win against the Highbury club for various reasons. It was the first time the two clubs had met under the auspices of the Football League —every club likes to beat the Arsenal because of the extra spot of limelight such a success gives them, while the fact that the Bees had not done too well in their home games made it more imperative that an overdue win should be recorded at Griffin Park.

BEES RISE TO THE OCCASION.

Well, the Bees realised our best hopes, and exceeded the expectations of many, by beating the Arsenal by the odd goal in three. The success was all the more praiseworthy by virtue of the fact that Bateman and Scott were unable to play owing to injury. It is most heartening to know that Astley and J. C. Burns deputised in great style and both played an important part in the great victory achieved.

Furthermore there was no fluke about the Bees' win, the Arsenal were well and truly beaten on the play, and were good sportsmen enough to admit the fact at the end of the game. Nothing more than one would expect from an organisation with the sporting reputation the Arsenal possess in the football world.

GREAT FIRST HALF DISPLAY.

Brentford won this game mainly owing to the marked superiority shown in the first half during which period a two-goals lead was built up. The first goal was scored by J. C. Burns, who took a centre from Hopkins and shot into the net. What a cheer rent the air when the Bees drew first blood against the mighty Arsenal !

Better was to follow. The cheers when Brentford went further ahead must have been nearly heard at Highbury. The second goal was rightly Hopkins', although some of the critics gave it as Roberts (own goal). Certainly the ball struck Roberts, the Arsenal centre half, before it entered the net, but it seemed highly probable that Hopkins' fast shot would have found the net without any intervention on the part of Roberts.

NOTES FROM THE HIVE—*Continued*.

ARSENAL MORE IN THE PICTURE.

Brentford had positively over-run the Arsenal in the opening half, but the position was rather changed after the interval. The visitors evidently felt that a big effort was needed to pull the game out of the fire and that effort was forthcoming with some intensity. The improvement of the Arsenal was definite and brought all the best out of our defenders, but the Bees' rearguard only conceded one solitary goal and so finished well-merited winners of an always interesting and oftentimes thrilling game.

Team work undoubtedly did the trick. To single out any member of the Brentford team for special praise would be out of place on a day when every player contributed his full quota to the great success gained. Some players were more prominent perhaps, than others, but as none played poorly I feel the case is well met by again emphasising that team work won the day for Brentford.

UNLUCKY AT BIRMINGHAM.

After our success against the Arsenal it was felt that the Bees would at least bring back a point from their game with Birmingham, at St. Andrew's, last week-end. Well, the fact is our boys, without being at their best, deserved half the spoils and but for the fact that the home side were allowed a winning goal, which we contend, and not alone in such an opinion, should never have counted. Mathieson was badly fouled before he had any chance to get the ball. Our attack did not touch the high spots in this game but with the teams on equality at the interval at a goal apiece, we did feel that the Bees looked like running out good winners. The first half was definitely Brentford's although the home team scored first after about 15 minutes' play, but Billy Dunn, who was making his League debut, headed for the Bees quite a good equaliser about ten minutes later. Our boys called the tune in no uncertain manner and should have been leading at the half-way stage. In the second half a hotly disputed point went in the home team's favour to give them a victory. Birmingham infused great vigour into their play in the second half, but the Bees stood up in fine style and certainly earned a point, which was denied them.

RESERVES' REVIEW.

Our Reserves have been doing very well of late and making a bold bid for the London Combination honours. Two points were gained at West Ham, where Brown scored the only goal of the game.

On Saturday last another win was recorded in the home game with Swansea Town by a margin of two clear goals. McAloon and Brown scored.

On Monday last the Bees qualified for the final of the London Challenge Cup once more, by defeating Fulham at Griffin Park. McAloon and Brown scored the two goals to which Fulham failed to reply.

TO-DAY'S GREAT GAME.

Every game is a big attraction at Griffin Park these days. Some are naturally more attractive, and one of the extra tit-bits are offered as the fare this afternoon. First it was Huddersfield, then Aston Villa, followed by Sheffield Wednesday and Arsenal, all Cup winners and League champions at some time or other. To-day we have Sunderland, the present League leaders, believed by many to be the best footballing team in the whole country. Whatever opinion anyone may hold there can be no denying the fact that the Roker Park club are a great side, and we extend to them a very cordial welcome on their first visit to Griffin Park.

" BUSY BEE."

Jottings from the Board Room.

RE PREMIERE FILM SHOW,
London Hippodrome,
Sunday, November 17th, 1935.

As reported by the Press, I have accepted the chairmanship of the above Cinema Performance. The Players and I will act as hosts to welcome our numerous loyal supporters who wish to help the Belgrave Hospital for Children. There will be two Premiere Films and full supporting programme, and well-known artists will provide a surprise item. Every seat is reserved, the prices being 2s., 2s. 6d., 3s. 6d., 6s. and 10s. 6d., and private boxes for a party of four are £2 2s. Box office opens at 4 o'clock.

As a souvenir of this event an autographed photograph of the team will be given with every programme.

Trusting you will come along and support this deserving cause, in which I am taking a keen interest. Doors open 6.30 p.m., commence 7 o'clock sharp.

Mr. L. P. Simon, our popular Chairman, has asked me to announce the annual Brentford Philanthropic Society Dinner will be held at the Star and Garter Hotel, Kew Bridge, on Thursday, December 5th, at 7 p.m. Tickets can be obtained from any member of the Society at 8s. each. Mr. Simon is also Chairman this year of this splendid society, which has done and still continues to do, such great work for the poor and distressed in the district.

Arthur Bateman has resumed training and is now practically fit.

We have a few tickets for numbered and reserved seats for our game v. Chelsea, at Stamford Bridge, on Saturday next. They are at 5s. only.

Our Reserves, by defeating Fulham on Monday last, 2—0 (McAloon and Brown), again qualify to compete in the Final of the London Challenge Cup. The opponents will be the winners of 'Spurs v. Arsenal Semi-final.

The Southern Railway announce special facilities in connection with our match with Chelsea, on Saturday, 23rd November, when special trains will be run direct to Chelsea and back from Windsor at 12.42 p.m., calling at all stations to Feltham inclusive, with connecting services from the Reading line; from Hounslow at 1.11 p.m. and 1.25 p.m., calling at Isleworth, Brentford, etc.; and from Strawberry Hill at 1.30 p.m., calling at Twickenham, Richmond, etc.

Cheap fares at approximately single fare for the return journey will be issued from these and many other stations. For full particulars see Railway Company's announcements.

The Big Fifteen are producing a play, "Who Goes Next?" at the Baths Hall, Brentford, on Thursday, November 21st, at 8 p.m., in aid of the Mayor's Unemployment Christmas Fund. The Mayor and Mayoress will be present and Mrs. Lane-Claypon has invited the Bees to be present.

I have been asked to state that the Boston Park Cricket Club are holding their first Dance on Wednesday, November 27th, at 8 p.m., at the Good Shepherd Hall, South Ealing Road. Tickets may be obtained from Mr. J. Burtenshaw, 18, Jessamine Road, Hanwell, W.7.

The Reserves are to-day away to Leicester City, kick-off at 2.30 p.m.

Comparative records to date with last season are as follows :—

Football League—	P.	W.	L.	D.	F.	A.	Pt.
This Season	13	4	6	3	19	18	11
Last Season	13	7	3	3	25	17	17

London Combination—						Goals	
This Season	16	12	3	1	34	18	25
Last Season	16	10	3	3	32	18	23

Goal-scorers to date :

Football League.—Holliday 6, Hopkins 5, Fletcher 3, Scott 2, Robson 1, J. C. Burns 1, Dunn 1.—Total 19.

London Combination.—Brown 10, Dunn 7, Sullivan 5, Muttitt 5, Gibbons 3, Smith 2, Fenton 1, McAloon 1.—Total 34.

With reference to the incidents that occurred in our game v. Manchester City, on October 26th, the Emergency Committee decided as follows :

" That D. McKenzie, of Brentford Football Club, be suspended for fourteen days from Monday next, November 11th, and that no action be taken against E. Brook, of Manchester City Football Club."

The charges by the Referee were that " Brook fouled McKenzie and the latter turned on Brook and with his hands held Brook by the neck. Brook **then struck a blow at McKenzie.**"

So McKenzie, for holding Brook's neck after being fouled gets 14 days' suspension and in the case of Brook (who, by the way, is an international) no action is taken. Perhaps it is not policy to comment on the above finding.   H.C.C.

FURNISH

AT

WHEATLAND'S

FOR CASH OR
EASY TERMS

43 & 45, THE BROADWAY
WEST EALING

Shots from the Spot.

By "Rambler"

———————◆————————

They say that any team that beats the Arsenal loses the next game. Reference to records will show this to be about as true as most other generalisations, but it certainly worked out in the case of Brentford.

* * *

However, whatever else happens to them during the course of their football lives, it is certain that each of the eleven Brentford men who took part in that great game a fortnight ago will remember it as one of the real highlights of their career.

* * *

There were moments when the Brentford team touched real greatness—notably a movement just before half-time that took the ball from the home area right to the other end of the field in a series of short ground passes without an opponent touching it.

* * *

Defeat at Birmingham followed: that it was by the odd goal it seems hardly necessary to point out! It was not a very great game and if the Bees had got a point no one could have said that it was an unfair result.

* * *

No one wants to harp on bad luck, and so let's turn to the brighter side for a moment: it was a pity that Arthur Bateman was prevented from turning out for the Bees against the Arsenal, but there was not a man on the ground who could have anything but praise for Jack Astley for the splendid way he did what most of us would have said was impossible. His display, far from weakening the defence, drew enthusiastic comment from the Press, and from Brentford and Arsenal fans as well.

* * *

It's a way the men of Griffin Park have. "Rising to the occasion" some people call it. Others just say "club spirit."

* * *

The fine tributes that two Arsenal players—Alex James and Edris Hapgood—paid Brentford in the Press were greatly appreciated at Griffin Park. There was a friendly atmosphere about both which shows that football is still a game despite the efforts of certain people to make us believe otherwise.

* * *

The Reserves are now in the final of the London Challenge Cup, and just below—on goal average—Portsmouth in the London Combination table. The seaside club have yet to be defeated, it is interesting to note, and last Saturday ran up ten goals against Bristol City. Our Reserves' win over the Combination leaders—Swansea—at Griffin Park on Saturday, was a sparkling affair. It all goes to show that Brentford is not suffering from a dearth of reserve talent that our alarmist friends(?) would like us to think!

OUR VISITORS TO-DAY.
HOW THEY MAY LINE UP.

Though they have been champions of the League on five occasions, it is 22 years since Sunderland last gained that distinction, and after finishing last season as runners-up to the Arsenal, they are making a determined effort this season to carry off the honour for the sixth time. They come to Griffin Park as League leaders, and the " Bees " will have their work cut out if they are to stem the run of success.

The club has always been noted for its Scottish stars and the present team is no exception to the rule.

The club began in 1880, and was formed by a band of schoolmasters. Although at one period they possessed " the team of all talents "—generally reckoned to be the finest side of the age—Sunderland have never won the F.A. Cup, and have only reached the Final on one occasion.

Thorpe, James H. (goalkeeper). —Born at Jarrow-on-Tyne. Height 5ft. 9in. Weight 11st. 3lb. Spotted in junior football at Sunderland and joined Jarrow as an amateur at the start of season 1930-1. Became a professional in the September, on reaching the age of 17. Sunderland paid £250 for his transfer the following week, and by the end of October was in the first team. Cool and agile. Used to work in the shipyards.

Morrison, Thomas (right back)— Born at Coyleton, Ayrshire. Height 5ft. 9in. Weight 11st. 6lb. Joining Sunderland last week, this former Liverpool player made his debut for the Roker Park club at right back against Preston last Saturday. Made 132 first team appearances for St. Mirren, with whom he won a Scottish Cup medal. Also has well over 200 English League appearances to his credit. Joined Liverpool in 1927-28.

Hall, Alec (left back).—Born at East Calder, Midlothian. Height 5ft. 10in. Weight 11st. 5lb. Few clubs have had such a good bargain for £500. That was all this grand back cost Sunderland when they took him from Dunfermline Ath-

letic. Has been on the fringe of the first team for several seasons and after making several appearances on both flanks last season, has established himself this campaign. Had early experience with East Calder Swifts.

Thomson, Charles (right half).— Born at Glasgow. Height, 5ft. 8in. Weight 9st. 12lb. Was taken off the doorsteps of the big Scottish clubs. Sunderland signed him as a youngster from Glasgow Pollock. That was in 1930-1 and two seasons later he had established himself in the League side. An engineer by trade, he now "engineers" delightful attacking movements.

Clark, J. M. C. (centre half).— Born at Glasgow. Height 5ft. 10½in. Weight, 11st. 3lb. A youngster who has come into his own this season. Got his first chance with the League side last season, but the consistency of Johnston kept his total of appearances down to four. Coming into the side for the second match this season, he has been an ever-present since. A strong defender.

Hastings, Alec (left half).—Born at Falkirk. Height 5ft. 10½in. Weight 11st. 5lb. Was secured at

BRENTFORD

BRE...
Red

1—M...

2—ASTLEY
Right Back

4—J. C. BURNS   5—
Right Half

7—HOPKINS   8—ROBSON   9—H...
Outside Right   Inside Right   Ce...

Referee—Mr. T. J. BOTHAM

12—CONNOR   13—GALLACHER
Outside Left   Inside Left

17—HASTINGS   18—
Left Half

20—HALL
Left Back

22—

SUND...

THE LEAGUE—DIVISION I.

	P.	W.	D.	L.	F.	A.	P.
Sunderland	14	9	2	3	41	24	20
Derby County	14	8	3	3	22	12	19
Huddersfield T.	14	7	4	3	22	17	18
Arsenal	14	5	5	4	29	17	15
Middlesbrough	14	6	3	5	37	23	15
Liverpool	14	6	3	5	31	21	15
Manchester City	13	7	1	5	20	19	15
Birmingham	14	6	3	5	19	22	15
West Bromwich A.	14	6	2	6	27	25	14
Stoke City	14	6	2	6	22	22	14
Bolton Wanderers	13	5	4	4	17	18	14
Chelsea	14	6	2	6	21	26	14
Leeds United	14	4	5	5	20	22	13
Blackburn Rovers	13	6	1	6	22	26	13
Sheffield Wednesday	14	4	5	5	22	31	13
Wolverhampton W.	14	5	2	7	25	25	12
Grimsby Town	13	6	0	7	21	27	12
BRENTFORD	13	4	3	6	19	18	11
Everton	14	4	3	7	24	31	11
Portsmouth	13	4	3	6	16	23	11
Preston North End	14	4	2	8	18	26	10
Aston Villa	14	3	2	9	23	43	8

SUNDERLAND

ORD
Stripes

ESON
er

3—POYSER
Left Back

ES   6—WATSON
f   Left Half

AY 10—SCOTT 11—FLETCHER
ard   Inside Left   Outside Left

Linesmen— Messrs. P. W. Poulter (blue flag)
and H. H. Rainbow (red flag)

URNEY 15—CARTER 16—DUNS
Forward   Inside Right   Outside Right

RK   19—THOMSON
lf   Right Half

21—MORRISON
Right Back

RPE
er

LAND

LONDON COMBINATION

	P.	W.	D.	L.	F.	A.	P.
					Goals		
Portsmouth	15	10	5	0	53	18	25
BRENTFORD	16	12	1	3	34	18	25
Swansea Town	17	11	2	4	29	21	24
Arsenal	15	11	1	3	43	16	23
Crystal Palace	18	10	3	5	32	38	23
Chelsea	17	9	3	5	41	29	21
Luton Town	17	9	2	6	55	37	20
Queen's Park Rgrs.	17	8	3	6	31	25	19
West Ham United	16	7	4	5	40	23	18
Charlton Athletic	17	8	2	7	34	28	18
Coventry City	16	8	0	8	34	21	16
Millwall	14	7	2	5	22	24	16
Watford	16	6	2	8	37	38	14
Southampton	16	4	5	7	22	27	13
Southend United	16	5	3	8	23	37	13
Tottenham H.	15	4	4	7	41	38	12
Reading	13	6	0	7	30	37	12
Bournemouth	16	4	3	9	24	44	11
Bristol City	18	5	1	12	25	59	11
Clapton Orient	15	3	5	7	13	33	11
Fulham	16	4	2	10	28	29	10
Leicester City	16	5	0	11	27	42	10
Northampton	15	3	3	9	25	55	9
Brighton & Hove A.	15	3	2	10	22	48	8

a substantial fee from Stenousemuir in 1930-1. Since then has built up a fine understanding with his fellow Scots, Gallacher and Connor. The trio form one of the most formidable flanks in the game. Hastings won his first cap against Ireland this week.

Duns, Leonard (outside right).— Born at Newcastle. Height 5ft. 9in. Weight 11st. 6lb. Was spotted by Sunderland soon after leaving school and in October, 1933, when he reached 17 they immediately signed him as a professional. Made his first team debut against Portsmouth a fortnight ago and last week, in his second match, scored twice against Preston.

Carter, Horatio (inside right).— Born at Sunderland. Height 5ft. 8in. Weight 10st. 7½lb. True example of "local boy makes good" theme. As a schoolboy he won caps against Wales and Scotland. After an unsuccessful trial with Leicester City he was placed on the ground staff at Sunderland and signed as a professional in 1932. In season 1932-3 he became a regular with the first team and in the March of that campaign played in an international trial. Has since gained his full cap. An all-round sportsman.

Curney Robert (centre forward).— Born at Silksworth, nr. Sunderland. Height 5ft. 8in. Weight 11st. 3lb. Went to Roker Park on the recommendation of Charlie Buchan, the famous Sunderland, Arsenal and England forward. Has broken both legs during his career, but still plays with the same dash as ever. Gained his first cap v. Scotland last April.

Gallacher, Patrick (inside left).— Born at Bridge of Weir, Renfrew. Height 5ft. 7½in. Weight 11st. 4lb. Another of the club's discoveries from Scottish junior football. Was signed from a church side, Linwood St. Connel's, and had his League chance in 1929-30, when only 19. Plays either inside right or left and is a Scottish international.

Connor, James (outside left).— Born at Renfrew. Height 5ft. 8in. Weight 10st. 5lb. Played with Paisley Carlisle, Glasgow Perthshire and St. Mirren before joining the Wearsiders in May, 1930. Was actually signed twice by Manager Cochrane, who fixed him up while with St. Mirren and later secured him again after he had taken over the Sunderland managership. Very tricky and a consistent goalscorer. Has several caps.

SHARES & SHAREHOLDERS

In spite of our previous notes in this programme, the Management are still receiving enquiries from supporters who are desiring to acquire shares in the Club. We repeat that the shares of the Club are fully issued, and unless existing shareholders desire to realise, there are no shares available.

The 6% Debentures of £50 each are still being issued, but only a small number now remain, and when these have been issued the finances of the Club will have been completely consolidated and settled.

The Club have been the leaseholders of Griffin Park, and supporters will be interested to know that next March the freehold of the ground is being purchased and the Club will then be in the happy position of being the owners of the ground.

Particulars of the 6% Debentures will be forwarded on application to the Secretary.

Shareholders desiring to realise their share-holdings should advise the Secretary, together with a note of the price they are willing to accept.

NAMES IN THE GAME.

No. 7.

Mr. W. P. HARPER

This week, for the first time in this series, we deal with a " knight of the whistle," and one whom many of you will have seen in action at Griffin Park. He has a strong personality which enables him to keep a game going on the lines it should do without officiousness.

Qualified in the " lower circles " and in 1921, his name appeared on the Football League linesmen's list, and he was promoted after a year to the Supplementary List and so to the list proper. He "lined" the F.A. Cup Final in 1931, and the following year was in charge. Other important games in which he has officiated include the Channel Islands Final (Jersey v. Guernsey, 1931) and the semi-final of the Irish Free State Cup, 1931. In private life he is a Civil Servant and has been hon. secretary of the Worcestershire F.A. for many years.

England has called on 65 players to represent their country in sixteen matches. Barker is the only England centre half to play in four successive matches for many years.

Nottingham Forest is the only League club to have four players on its staff who all scored a goal on making their debut. They are Race, Peacock, Burditt and Gardiner.

C. FLETCHER
Outside Left.

Born in East Homerton, Charlie came to Brentford in August, 1933, and has held his place as outside left ever since. He was a left back in West Ham Schools' football, was given a trial by Villa, but signed first professional forms for Crystal Palace, where he stayed for 2½ seasons, before going to Merthyr. He was secured from the Welsh club by Clapton Orient, whom he served for four seasons before Brentford signed him on. Has mastered the art of driving a dead ball to perfection, and can also hit a moving one a good deal harder than most.

FIXTURES, SEASON 1935-36.

FIRST TEAM

Date. 1935.	Opponents.	Ground.	GOALS F.	A.
Aug. 31	Bolton Wanderers ...	A	2	0
Sept. 5	Blackburn Rovers ...	H	3	1
" 7	Huddersfield Town ...	H	1	2
" 14	Middlesbrough ...	A	0	2
" 18	Derby County ...	A	1	2
" 21	Aston Villa ...	H	1	0
" 28	Wolverhampton Wdrs.	A	2	3
Oct. 5	Sheffield Wednesday ..	H	2	2
" 12	Portsmouth ...	A	3	0
" 19	Stoke City ...	H	0	1
" 26	Manchester City ...	A	1	2
Nov. 2	Arsenal ...	H	2	1
" 9	Birmingham ...	A	1	2
" 16	Sunderland ...	H		
" 23	Chelsea ...	A		
" 30	Leeds United ...	H		
Dec. 7	Grimsby Town ...	A		
" 14	Liverpool ...	H		
" 21	West Bromwich Albion	A		
" 25	Preston North End ...	H		
" 26	Preston North End ...	A		
" 28	Bolton Wanderers ...	H		
1936.				
Jan. 1	Blackburn Rovers ...	A		
" 4	Huddersfield Town ...	A		
" 11	(3)			
" 18	Middlesbrough ...	H		
" 25	(4) Aston Villa ...	A		
Feb. 1	Wolverhampton Wdrs.	H		
" 8	Sheffield Wednesday ...	A		
" 15	(5) Portsmouth ...	H		
" 22	Stoke City ...	A		
" 29	(6) Manchester City ...	H		
Mar. 7	Arsenal ...	A		
" 14	(S.-F.) Birmingham ...	A		
" 21	Sunderland ...	A		
" 28	Chelsea ...	H		
April 4	Leeds United ...	A		
" 10	Everton ...	A		
" 11	Grimsby Town ...	H		
" 13	Everton ...	H		
" 18	Liverpool ...	A		
" 25	(F.) West Brom. Alb.	H		
May 2	Derby County ...	H		

SECOND TEAM

Date. 1935.	Opponents.	Ground.	GOALS F.	A.
Aug. 31	Charlton Athletic ...	H	2	1
Sept. 4	Watford ...	A	1	3
" 7	Clapton Orient ...	A	0	0
" 12	Watford ...	H	2	1
" 14	Southend United ...	H	1	0
" 21	Northampton Town ...	A	1	0
" 25	Luton Town ...	A	1	4
" 28	Crystal Palace ...	H	4	0
Oct. 3	Luton Town ...	H	4	3
" 5	Reading ...	A	1	2
" 7	Met. Police—L.C. Cup	H	2	0
" 9	Bournemouth & Bos. .	H	5	2
" 12	Tottenham Hotspur	H	2	1
" 19	Bristol City ...	A	3	1
" 21	C. Orient—L.C. Cup ...	H	3	0
" 26	Millwall ...	H	4	0
Nov. 2	West Ham United ...	A	1	0
" 9	Swansea Town ...	A	2	0
" 11	Fulham (L.C.Cup,S.F.)	H	2	0
" 16	Leicester City ...	A		
" 23	Coventry City ...	H		
" 30	Arsenal ...	A		
Dec. 7	Southampton ...	A		
" 14	Brighton & Hove A. ...	A		
" 21	Queen's Park Rgrs. ..	H		
" 25	Chelsea ...	H		
" 26	Chelsea ...	H		
" 28	Charlton Athletic ...	A		
Jan. 4	Clapton Orient ...	H		
" 11	Fulham ...	A		
" 18	Southend United ...	A		
" 25	Northampton Town ...	H		
Feb. 1	Crystal Palace ...	A		
" 8	Reading ...	H		
" 15	Tottenham Hotspur ...	A		
" 22	Bristol City ...	H		
" 29	Millwall ...	A		
Mar. 7	West Ham United ...	H		
" 14	Swansea Town ...	H		
" 21	Leicester City ...	H		
" 25	Bournemouth & Bos. .	A		
" 28	Coventry City ...	A		
April 4	Arsenal ...	H		
" 10	Portsmouth ...	A		
" 11	Southampton ...	H		
" 13	Portsmouth ...	H		
" 18	Brighton & Hove A. ...	H		
" 25	Queen's Park Rgrs. ..	A		
May 2	Fulham ...	A		

Half Time Scores.

	F.	A.		F	A
A—Aston Villa v. Chelsea	......	......	J—Sheffield W. v. Grimsby	......	......
B—Bolton W. v. Manchester C.	......	......	K—Wolves v. Liverpool	......	......
C—Derby C. v. Birmingham	......	......	L—Charlton v. Sheffield U.	......	......
D—Everton v. Arsenal	......	......	M—Fulham v. Leicester	......	......
E—Huddersfield v. Stoke	......	......	N—Manchester U. v. W. Ham	......	......
F—Middlesbrough v. Blackburn	......	......	O—'Spurs v. Bury	......	......
G—Portsmouth v. Leeds	......	......	P—Crystal Palace v. Watford	......	......
H—P.N.E. v. West Bromwich	......	......	R—Northampton v. Q.P.R.	......	......

FOOTBALL FAN :— "YOU'RE BEGINNING TO WORRY ME WITH YOUR WEEKLY VISITS !"
GHOST OF BRENTFORD :— "ONLY FREE ME FROM THESE SHACKLES, FOR ONLY
THEN CAN I JOIN THE RANKS OF CONTENTED MORTALS !"

The Next Games.

Next Saturday, Brentford are engaged in their second local Derby since attaining First Division status.

Their visit to Stamford Bridge to play against Chelsea—who have cast their dilettante attitude aside and become a real football force—should provide a really great game. Many Brentford supporters will undoubtedly travel across London to see the game, and our team will be pleased to hear them testifying to their presence when they come out from the dressing room.

The following Saturday Leeds United pay us a visit. At the time of writing they are just above Brentford in the table, with two more points than the Bees, who, however have a game in hand. Their goal average is not as good as the men's from Griffin Park, so on form it would appear that the Bees have a good chance of netting a couple of valuable points—and it will be a game worth seeing at any rate.

The Saturday after that (December 7th) Brentford are due to meet old rivals in Grimsby Town, who, it will be remembered, were one of the two teams responsible for Brentford staying two seasons in the Second Division instead of one !

The Reserves—now just behind the leaders of the London Combination on goal average, have an interesting programme. When the Bees are at Chelsea, Coventry City come to Griffin Park, and the following Saturday our juniors go over to Highbury to attempt to show the Arsenal that they also can do what their seniors have done ! A week later Southampton are their guests.

BRENTFORD FOOTBALL AND SPORTS CLUB, LIMITED.

Registered Office :—GRIFFIN PARK, BRAEMAR ROAD, BRENTFORD.

President and Chairman :
MR. L. P. SIMON.

Vice-Chairman :
MR. F. A. DAVIS.

ALDERMAN W. FLEWITT, J.P.
MR. H. N. BLUNDELL.
MR. H. J. SAUNDERS.

MR. H. W. DODGE.
MR. C. L. SIMON.

MR. F. W. BARTON.
ALDERMAN H. F. DAVIS.
MR. J. R. HUGHES, J.P., C.C.

Hon. Treasurer ;
ALDERMAN W. FLEWITT, J.P.
Club Medical Officer ; DR. A. D. GOWANS.

Secretary-Manager ;
MR. H. C. CURTIS,
" DORINCOURT," BOSTON GARDENS, BRENTFORD.

Telephones ;
GROUND : EALING 1744.
PRIVATE HOUSE : EALING 1183.

Telegraphic Address ;
CURTIS, FOOTBALL, BRENTFORD.
Ground ; GRIFFIN PARK, EALING ROAD, BRENTFORD.

No. 8.   Saturday, November 30th, 1935.

Notes from the Hive.

THE Bees are gradually sinking and are now in the danger zone on the League table, but there is a lot of fight left in the patient and before long an improvement is expected. That is not an optimistic view of an ultra enthusiast, but a considered opinion that the lean period has gone on long enough and a turn in fortune's wheel is now due.

After all, Brentford have only had one bad beating, which I am going to deal with later, and every other defeat has been by the narrow margin of an odd goal. Look at the matter how one will, it is obvious that Brentford have not been outclassed so that in spite of the lowly position on the League table, it can still be said that our boys have shown form which proves that they are operating in their rightful class.

Take Sunderland, the present League leaders, who have sustained some fairly heavy reverses, two 3—1 defeats and a four clear goals licking by lowly-placed Grimsby Town. Other highly placed clubs, too, have suffered heavy reverses, so the Brentford results are not really so bad as they might seem. The Bees have not just quite got there, but our team has always proved worthy opposition whatever club they have been playing against, with the exception of the last home game with Sunderland.

AFTER NEW PLAYERS.

It can be definitely stated that, generally speaking, the management has been wholly satisfied with the play of the team,—results are not always a criterion of what really happens. But the position is getting serious and one cannot look blindly on the situation as reflected by the League table.

There is always a danger that a prolonged lean period will have an adverse effect on the players' confidence and when that happens, even the best players begin to show a loss of form. That has not really happened to any great extent as far as the Bees are concerned, but it often happens that the advent of a new player or two when things are going wrong puts the machinery in working order again. With that end in view very big efforts have recently been made to strengthen the team by the acquisition of new players. In almost every instance the club concerned would not part with the player Brentford wanted. Price never entered into the question, for negotiations were not allowed to get to that stage. But team strengthening efforts go on and it is hoped that some news in this connection

NOTES FROM THE HIVE—*Continued*.

will be available in the near future —perhaps in time for the game with Leeds United to-day.

SUPREME SUNDERLAND.

I mentioned in these notes a fortnight ago that many shrewd judges were of the opinion that Sunderland were the best footballing team in the Football League. Well, many of the Bees' supporters probably hold the same views after seeing the Roker Park club at Griffin Park. Sunderland did indeed touch the high spots and probably have not reached such heights in team play this season as they did against the Bees. It was a football treat which everyone would have enjoyed better if it had not come when Brentford needed points so badly. Sunderland won by five goals to one in a game which was packed sardine tight with thrills. Well as Sunderland played, and my word they did do things so swiftly and skillfully, the margin would not have been so wide at the finish if our boys had not faltered in front of goal so much. " Open goal " misses won't get Brentford out of trouble !

An interesting side-light on our game with Sunderland appeared in the " Daily Mail " on Monday last. The question put to Mr. Alexander Brownlee, who has been a director of Cardiff City since the club started, was, " Is the present Sunderland team the equal of the great side of the 'nineties, who were known throughout the football world as the ' team of all talents'?" Mr. Brownlee saw the game between Brentford and Sunderland and his reply was :

" I have never seen a League club play better football. On that form they are the superiors of their great predecessors, whom I used to watch in the vintage years of the Wearside club."

But why pick Brentford out to give such a display !

REVERSE AT STAMFORD BRIDGE.

Another defeat followed at Stamford Bridge on Saturday last when Chelsea won by the odd goal in three, after Brentford had led by a penalty goal, scored by Robson, at the interval. Chelsea got two quick goals in the second half, the second from a penalty, to win a game which fell rather below expectations. It was a cleanly fought contest in spite of the fact that two of the three goals came from penalty kicks. Team changes were made which included the playing of Brown at centre forward. He did reasonably well in the circumstances, but once again little seemed to go right for the Bees.

RESERVES GOING STRONG.

In great contrast to our League side the junior Bees keep picking up points and are level pegging in the matter of points with the present leaders, Portsmouth, of the London Combination.

A win by the odd goal in five was recorded at Leicester, where Dunn (2) and Fenton scored.

On Saturday last Coventry City were beaten at Griffin Park by the convincing margin of four goals to one. Dunn again scored twice, McAloon and Leslie Smith getting the other goals.

TO-DAY'S VISITORS.

We extend a very cordial welcome to Leeds United on their first visit to Griffin Park. Leeds have averaged exactly a point per game which gives them a position half-way on the League table. They have only secured four points from eight away games, having won at Grimsby by the only goal of the game, and effected a division at West Bromwich and Middlesbrough.

" BUSY BEE."

Jottings from the Board Room.

Mr. L. P. Simon, our popular Chairman, has asked me to announce the annual Brentford Philanthropic Society Dinner will be held at the Star and Garter Hotel, Kew Bridge, on Thursday, December 5th, at 7 p.m. Tickets can be obtained from any member of the Society at 8s. 6d. each. Mr. Simon is also Chairman this year of this splendid society, which has done and still continues to do, such great work for the poor and distressed in the district.

To-day we have much pleasure in extending a hearty welcome to Dai Richards, whose transfer was obtained from Wolverhampton Wanderers on Thursday last.

Dai is the proud possessor of eleven International Caps. He is 26 years of age. I am sure all followers join in wishing him a very happy and successful time at Brentford.

At the time of these notes going to Press there is every possibility that we may extend a further welcome to a well-known new forward.

Because the team has not been doing well, the usual wicked rumours have been in circulation. I feel sure that our wise and sporting supporters will ignore these unfair and damaging statements which are the product of evil and malicious imaginations.

The Premiere Film Show held at the London Hippodrome, on Sunday, the 17th November, in aid of the Belgrave Hospital for Children, proved a great success. On behalf of the Hospital Committee I desire to extend sincere thanks to all those kind friends who supported same.

Jimmie Nichols, who dislocated a finger during the game v. Coventry Reserves, on Saturday last, is making fairly good progress. As the accident occurred in the first five minutes of the game, it necessitated George Dumbrell playing goalkeeper and the rest of the game being played with ten players. The Reserves are to be heartily congratulated on recording a win by 4—1 (Dunn 2, McAloon 1 and Leslie Smith 1). Jimmie will be out of the game for about three weeks.

Leslie Smith, our young amateur, was further honoured on Wednesday last by being selected to play for the F.A. Team against the Oxford University F.C. at Oxford.

The Reserves are to-day away to the Arsenal Reserves.

Comparative records to date with last season are as follows :—

	P.	W.	L.	D.	F.	A.	P.
Football League—					Goals		
This Season	15	4	8	3	21	25	11
Last Season	15	9	3	3	34	19	21
London Combination—							
This Season	18	14	3	1	41	21	29
Last Season	18	10	3	5	34	20	25

Goal-scorers to date :

Football League.—Holliday 6, Hopkins 6, Fletcher 3, Scott 2, Robson 2, Dunn 1, J. C. Burns 1.—Total 21.

London Combination.—Dunn 11, Brown 10, Muttitt 5, Sullivan 5, Gibbons 3, Fenton 2, McAloon 2, Smith, C., 2, Smith, L., 1.—Total 41.

Jack Astley was called home to Warrington, on Tuesday owing to serious illness of his father. We trust Mr. Astley (senior) will make a speedy recovery to good health.

Our Reserves will now meet the Arsenal Reserves in the Final of the London Challenge Cup. This will be played in May on a mutual ground. Arsenal Reserves defeated 'Spurs Reserves by 2—1 in the semi-final.

The " News Chronicle " is offering an Art Plate of the Brentford F.C. players and officials, autographed by everyone in the picture. Two vouchers from the " News Chronicle " sports pages and 2d. in stamps secures a copy for you. Send to the address on the voucher.

Next Home Game.
Saturday, December 14th
BRENTFORD v. LIVERPOOL
(Football League)   Kick-off at 2.30 p.m.

Tickets for numbered and reserved seats in Block B, can be obtained at 4s. each. Applications will not be considered unless accompanied by a remittance and stamped addressed envelope.

Arthur Bateman is having a trial run with the Reserves at Highbury to-day after his injury.

Shots from the Spot.

By "Rambler"

The old wives' tale about the club beating the Arsenal losing the next three games has come true so far as Brentford is concerned. Birmingham, Sunderland and Chelsea all collected a couple of points at our expense.

* * *

In two of those games the Bees were defeated by the odd goal of three, and Sunderland in fact are the only club to have scored anything more notable than an odd goal victory over the Bees this season.

* * *

Mr. Cochrane was particularly pleased at Sunderland's win because —as he said afterwards—it showed the Metropolis at last what sort of football his team really can play.

* * *

It is worthy of note that the previous 13 visits Sunderland had paid to London had never brought them a win. Thirty-one goals had been scored against their thirteen. So they really had got something to wipe out!

* * *

The Chelsea programme, introducing the Bees, had a neat heading —" Our Western Brothers—Brentford."

* * *

The consistency of Portsmouth Reserves keeps our juniors just below them in the London Combination table on goal average alone, but there is still a long way to go— and they have yet to meet each other! The success of the junior Bees is really most encouraging in these days when the points are not coming to the first team with the regularity we should all like to see.

* * *

There are not many positions in the field that the versatile George Dumbrell has not occupied at one time or another. On Saturday, after Nichols had been injured, George went into goal and gave a rattling display that had no small effect on the final result of 4—1.

* * *

It is to be hoped that the example of the young autograph hunter who calmly walked about the pitch at Villa Park attempting to get his book signed, will not be generally emulated. The crowd approved of his enterprise, but if they had been the players themselves they might have been tempted to indulge in a little gentle shooting practice! Footballers are in danger of suffering from "writer's cramp" unless the activities of these enthusiasts are curbed a little. If it was all enthusiasm, one might take a kinder view, but when one sees small boys with as many as three or four books each, one begins to suspect that professionalism has entered that sport as well!

OUR VISITORS TO-DAY.
HOW THEY MAY LINE UP.

After a poor start to the season, Leeds United, visitors to Griffin Park to-day, have shown a remarkable revival in recent weeks and have climbed from the bottom of the table to a position in the top half. That they are a powerful attacking force has been shown in the last two home games, when they have netted twelve goals—seven against Sheffield Wednesday and five against Bolton.

The present club only dates back to 1920, but it sprang, of course, from the much older Leeds City which was disbanded at that date by order of the F.A. In their comparatively short career the United have won the Second Division championship once and have twice been runners-up, the last occasion being in 1931-32 when they returned to First Division football.

The club has a reputation for building up their League sides from their own discoveries, rather than by paying high prices for ready-made stars.

McInroy, Albert (goalkeeper).—Born at Preston. Height, 5ft. 10in. Weight, 12st. 8lb. Was missed by Preston North End. Had his early experience with Preston Co-operative Stores and Leyland Rubber Works teams and for two years was on the books at Deepdale. Only got two Reserve team games in that period. Joined Sunderland in 1923, Newcastle six years later, back to Sunderland last year and then to Leeds during the last close season. An English international.

Sproston, Bert (right back).—Born at Elworth, Cheshire. Height 5ft. 9in. Weight 11st. 12lb. Signed from Sandbach Ramblers, the Cheshire club, he got his first run with the seniors within twelve months—at Christmas, 1933, Played in more than half the First Division games last season and this campaign has established himself as a "regular."

Milburn, John (left back).—Born at Ashington, Northumberland. Height 5ft. 10in. Weight 11st. 10lb. A former miner who served his football apprenticeship with Spen Black and White, a well-known North-Eastern nursery. Joined Leeds in 1928 and got his place as a right back, but moved to the other flank to make room for his brother George, who has now lost his place to Sproston.

Edwards, Willis (right half).—Born at Alfreton, Derbyshire. Height 5ft. 7½in. Weight, 11st. 10lb. Was secured by Chesterfield when about to set out for a trial with Blackburn Rovers. Has been at Leeds for ten years, and during that time, built up a reputation as one of the greatest of modern half backs. The possessor of several caps, he has captained England.

McDougall, John (centre half).—Born at Port Glasgow, Renfrewshire. Height 5ft. 10½in. Weight 11st. 12lb. Secured from Sunderland last season to fill the vacancy when English international Hart was injured, this Scotland player has established himself at the former's expense. Joined Sunderland in 1929 from Airdrieonians, with

BRENTFORD *u*

BRE
Red

1—

2—**ASTLEY**
Right Back

4—**McKENZIE**
Right Half

7—**HOPKINS**   8—**ROBSON**   9—
Outside Right   Inside Right   Ce

Referee—MR. J. H. WHITTLE

12—**COCHRANE**   13—**FURNESS**
Outside Left   Inside Left

17—**BROWNE**   18—
Left Half

20—**MILBURN, J.**
Left Back

22—

LEED
Blue and Old

THE LEAGUE—DIVISION I.

	P.	W.	D.	L.	F.	A.	P.
Sunderland	16	11	2	3	48	26	24
Huddersfield T.	16	9	4	3	26	19	22
Derby County	16	8	5	3	24	14	21
Arsenal	16	7	5	4	35	17	19
Manchester C.	15	8	2	5	26	22	18
Middlesbrough	16	7	3	6	44	26	17
Birmingham	16	6	5	5	23	26	17
Chelsea	16	7	3	6	25	29	17
Liverpool	16	6	4	6	32	24	16
Stoke C.	16	7	2	7	25	24	16
Leeds United	16	5	6	5	27	26	16
Bolton Wanderers	15	5	5	5	22	26	15
Sheffield W.	16	5	5	6	25	34	15
West Bromwich A.	16	6	2	8	28	30	14
Wolves	16	6	2	8	28	30	14
Blackburn R.	15	6	2	7	24	33	14
Everton	16	5	3	8	28	33	13
Preston N.E.	16	5	3	8	22	27	13
Portsmouth	15	4	4	7	18	27	12
Grimsby Town	15	6	0	9	21	34	12
BRENTFORD	**15**	**4**	**3**	**8**	**21**	**25**	**11**
Aston Villa	16	3	4	9	27	47	10

(Goals)

LEEDS UNITED

ORD
Stripes
ESON
er

3—POYSER
Left Back

ES   6—RICHARDS
f   Left Half

AY   10—SCOTT   11—FLETCHER
ard Inside Left   Outside Left

Linesmen—Messrs. R. C. Langer (blue flag),
and E. J. Poultin (red flag)

KELLY, J.   15—BROWN 16—DUGGAN
Forward   Inside Right Outside Right

GALL   19—EDWARDS
alf   Right Half

21—SPROSTON
Right Back

ROY
er

UNITED
s), White Knickers

LONDON COMBINATION

	P.	W.	D.	L.	F.	A.	P.
Portsmouth	17	12	5	0	56	18	29
BRENTFORD	**18**	**14**	**1**	**3**	**41**	**21**	**29**
Swansea Town	20	13	2	5	35	28	28
Crystal Palace	20	11	4	5	42	40	26
Arsenal	17	12	1	4	47	19	25
West Ham U.	19	9	4	6	49	27	22
Luton Town	19	10	2	7	59	42	22
Chelsea	19	9	4	6	43	38	22
Charlton Athletic	19	9	2	8	36	31	20
Queen's Park Rgrs.	19	8	3	8	32	34	19
Coventry City	18	9	0	9	38	26	18
Tottenham H.	17	6	4	7	47	40	16
Millwall	16	7	2	7	23	27	16
Southend United	18	6	4	8	28	37	16
Southampton	19	5	5	9	29	32	15
Reading	16	7	1	8	37	43	15
Watford	18	6	3	9	39	48	15
Clapton Orient	18	4	6	8	18	42	14
Northampton	17	5	3	9	36	36	13
Fulham	18	5	2	11	33	35	12
Bournemouth	18	4	3	11	27	51	11
Bristol City	20	5	1	14	27	66	11
Leicester City	18	5	0	13	31	48	10
Brighton & Hove A.	17	3	4	10	24	50	10

whom he won a Scottish Cup medal in 1924. Blocks up the centre of the field.

Browne, Robert (left half).—An Irishman who signed for Leeds last month after helping the Irish League surprise the English League in September. United had to pay £1,500 to Derry City for his signature, but he is proving well worth the money. Established himself in the first team soon after arriving at Elland Road.

Duggan, Harry (outside right).—Born at Dublin. Height 5ft. 7in. Weight 10st. 4lb. A versatile forward who has filled several positions for his club and country. Formerly a monumental mason, he was picked up in 1925 while playing in Dublin junior football with Richmond United. Is a consistent goalscorer.

Brown, George (inside right).—Born at Mickley, Northumberland. Height 5ft. 11in. Weight, 11st. 6lb. When on strike from Mickley Colliery he was given a professional engagement by Huddersfield Town. After scoring nearly 150 goals in over 200 League games for the Yorkshire club, he moved to Aston Villa seven years later (1929). Went to Burnley last season and then on to Leeds soon after the start of this campaign. A great shot and tricky worker of the ball. Has many caps.

Kelly, John (centre forward).—Born at Hetton-le-Hole, Durham. Height 5ft. 8in. Weight 11st. 7½lb. Made his name with Burnley. Newcastle took him in the 1933 close season and then he moved to Leeds last February. Is a tricky fellow with plenty of pace and good ball distribution. Formerly a butcher.

Furness, William (inside left).—Born at New Washington, Co. Durham. Height 5ft. 6in. Weight 10st. 6lb. An English international who has been the schemer-in-chief of the side for several seasons. Was a clerk with Usworth Colliery before joining the Elland Road club.

Cochrane, Thomas (outside left).—Born at Newcastle. Height 5ft. 9in. Weight 11st. 4lb. Another North-Eastern find. Secured from St. Peter's Albion, Newcastle, several years ago, he has long been a stalwart of the club. Is elusive and fast. Used to be a bricklayer.

SHARES & SHAREHOLDERS

In spite of our previous notes in this programme, the Management are still receiving enquiries from supporters who are desiring to acquire shares in the Club. We repeat that the shares of the Club are fully issued, and unless existing shareholders desire to realise, there are no shares available.

The 6% Debentures of £50 each are still being issued, but only a small number now remain, and when these have been issued the finances of the Club will have been completely consolidated and settled.

The Club have been the leaseholders of Griffin Park, and supporters will be interested to know that next March the freehold of the ground is being purchased and the Club will then be in the happy position of being the owners of the ground.

Particulars of the 6% Debentures will be forwarded on application to the Secretary.

Shareholders desiring to realise their share-holdings should advise the Secretary, together with a note of the price they are willing to accept.

NAMES IN THE GAME.

No. 8.

MR. " BILLY " HAMPSON.

Took up the duties of manager of Leeds United in July, 1935, having been one of about 120 applicants for the job. From the revival the club has been staging, looks like making a success of it.

Remembered by Leeds fans for the great games he played for the Leeds City team. Began League career with Bury in 1906, went to Norwich City and then, in January, 1914, went to Newcastle United. Ten years later he played in the Newcastle team which beat Aston Villa in the Cup Final. Left St. James's Park in 1927, played for South Shields and then became manager of Carlisle United, setting that club splendidly on its financial feet. Next came managership of Ashington, and so to Elland Road.

Interested in juvenile football is Mr. Hampson, and has done much coaching under F.A. school scheme.

Official programmes can only be bought from sellers wearing the official armlet.

Ellis Rimmer, Sheffield Wednesday's international winger, scored in each round of the Cup last season.

DUNCAN McKENZIE
Right Half.

Born in Glasgow but has adapted himself to English football without losing his Scots craft. Joined Albion Rovers when only 17 and in 1931-2 played in every game for that club, only in those days he occupied the centre half position. Came to Brentford in 1932-3, and made his place in the side the following season, helping the Bees to the First Division in 1934-5. Has a young brother of whom hopes are entertained.

FIXTURES, SEASON 1935-36.

FIRST TEAM

Date. 1935.	Opponents.	Ground.	GOALS F.	A.
Aug. 31	Bolton Wanderers	A	2	0
Sept. 5	Blackburn Rovers	H	3	1
,, 7	Huddersfield Town	H	1	2
,, 14	Middlesbrough	A	0	0
,, 18	Derby County	A	1	2
,, 21	Aston Villa	H	1	2
,, 28	Wolverhampton Wdrs.	A	2	3
Oct. 5	Sheffield Wednesday ..	H	2	2
,, 12	Portsmouth	A	3	1
,, 19	Stoke City	H	0	0
,, 26	Manchester City	A	1	2
Nov. 2	Arsenal	H	2	1
,, 9	Birmingham	A	1	2
,, 16	Sunderland	H	1	1
,, 23	Chelsea	A	1	2
,, 30	Leeds United	H		
Dec. 7	Grimsby Town	A		
,, 14	Liverpool	H		
,, 21	West Bromwich Albion	A		
,, 25	Preston North End	H		
,, 26	Preston North End	A		
,, 28	Bolton Wanderers	H		
1936.				
Jan. 1	Blackburn Rovers	A		
,, 4	Huddersfield Town	A		
,, 11	(3)	H		
,, 18	Middlesbrough	H		
,, 25	(4) Aston Villa	A		
Feb. 1	Wolverhampton Wdrs.	H		
,, 8	Sheffield Wednesday ...	A		
,, 15	(5) Portsmouth	H		
,, 22	Stoke City	A		
,, 29	(6) Manchester City ...	H		
Mar. 7	Arsenal	A		
,, 14	(S.-F.) Birmingham ...	H		
,, 21	Sunderland	A		
,, 28	Chelsea	H		
April 4	Leeds United	A		
,, 10	Everton	A		
,, 11	Grimsby Town	H		
,, 13	Everton	H		
,, 18	Liverpool	A		
,, 25	(F.) West Brom. Alb.	H		
May 2	Derby County	H		

SECOND TEAM

Date. 1935.	Opponents.	Ground.	GOALS F.	A.
Aug. 31	Charlton Athletic	H	2	1
Sept. 4	Watford	A	1	3
,, 7	Clapton Orient	A	1	0
,, 12	Watford	H	2	1
,, 14	Southend United	H	1	0
,, 21	Northampton Town	A	1	0
,, 25	Luton Town	A	4	0
,, 28	Crystal Palace	H	1	4
Oct. 3	Luton Town	H	4	3
,, 5	Reading	A	3	2
,, 7	Met. Police—L.C. Cup	H	2	0
,, 9	Bournemouth & Bos.	H	5	2
,, 12	Tottenham Hotspur	H	2	1
,, 19	Bristol City	A	3	1
,, 21	C. Orient—L.C. Cup	H	3	1
,, 26	Millwall	H	4	0
Nov. 2	West Ham United	A	1	0
,, 9	Swansea Town	H	2	0
,, 11	Fulham (L.C.Cup,S.F.)	H	2	0
,, 16	Leicester City	A	3	2
,, 23	Coventry City	H	4	1
,, 30	Arsenal	A		
Dec. 7	Southampton	H		
,, 14	Brighton & Hove A.	A		
,, 21	Queen's Park Rgrs. ..	H		
,, 25	Chelsea	A		
,, 26	Chelsea	H		
,, 28	Charlton Athletic	A		
Jan. 4	Clapton Orient	H		
,, 11	Fulham	H		
,, 18	Southend United	H		
,, 25	Northampton Town	H		
Feb. 1	Crystal Palace	H		
,, 8	Reading	H		
,, 15	Tottenham Hotspur	A		
,, 22	Bristol City	H		
,, 29	Millwall	A		
Mar. 7	West Ham United	H		
,, 14	Swansea Town	A		
,, 21	Leicester City	H		
,, 25	Bournemouth & Bos. .	A		
,, 28	Coventry City	A		
April 4	Arsenal	H		
,, 10	Portsmouth	A		
,, 11	Southampton	A		
,, 13	Portsmouth	A		
,, 18	Brighton & Hove A.	H		
,, 25	Queen's Park Rgrs. ..	A		
May 2	Fulham	A		

Half Time Scores.

	F.	A.			F	A
A—Aston Villa v. Stoke	......	......	J—Sheffield W. v. Chelsea		......	......
B—Bolton W. v. Birmingham	......	......	K—Wolves v. Blackburn		......	......
C—Derby C. v. W. Bromwich	......	......	L—Charlton v. Leicester		......	......
D—Everton v. Sunderland			M—Fulham v. West Ham			
E—Huddersfield v. Arsenal	......	......	N—'Spurs v. Blackpool		......	......
F—Middlesbro' v. Man. City	......	......	O—Bristol City v. Crystal P.		......	......
G—Portsmouth v. Liverpool			P—Clapton O. v. Aldershot			
H—P.N.E. v. Grimsby	......	......	R—Margate v. Q.P.R.		......	......

The Villain—" Do you realise, Laddie, that with 20 less against I would have been in the cast of this show?"
Young Griffinian—" In the cast! Why, with 11 more for I should be the HERO and playing IN THE LEAD!"

The Next Games.

Brentford's next First Division game is against Grimsby Town, but for whom the Bees might now have been in their second season in the upper circle, instead of their first! Grimsby are a formidable side, and particularly so on their own ground, and in their big centre forward, Glover, Joe James will find one of his toughest jobs this season!

The Reserves, who are away at Highbury to-day, entertain the Southampton Reserves at Griffin Park next Saturday, and then the following week, Liverpool F.C. come down to Brentford for the first time.

Their away record this season is not impressive, and they have yet to record a win on foreign soil, having drawn three games and lost four.

This points to a good thing for Brentford, but the men from Anfield Road can produce really fine football away as well as at home, so we had better not say too much at the moment.

The week after that Brentford go up to meet West Bromwich Albion, who, although they do not occupy a very exalted position in the League table at the moment, are always a difficult side to beat.

On December 14th, the Reserves are away at Brighton, and on December 21st there is a minor local Derby at Griffin Park, when the visitors are Queen's Park Rangers.

BRENTFORD FOOTBALL AND SPORTS CLUB, LIMITED.

Registered Office :—GRIFFIN PARK, BRAEMAR ROAD, BRENTFORD.

President and Chairman :
MR. L. P. SIMON.

ALDERMAN W. FLEWITT, J.P.
MR. H. N. BLUNDELL.
MR. H. J. SAUNDERS.

MR. H. W. DODGE.
MR. C. L. SIMON.

Vice-Chairman :
MR. F. A. DAVIS.

MR. F. W. BARTON.
ALDERMAN H. F. DAVIS.
MR. J. R. HUGHES, J.P., C.C.

Hon. Treasurer ;
ALDERMAN W. FLEWITT, J.P.
Club Medical Officer ; DR. A. D. GOWANS.

Telephones :
GROUND : EALING 1744.
PRIVATE HOUSE : EALING 1183.

Secretary-Manager ;
MR. H. C. CURTIS,
" DORINCOURT," BOSTON GARDENS, BRENTFORD.

Telegraphic Address ;
CURTIS, FOOTBALL, BRENTFORD.
Ground ; GRIFFIN PARK, EALING ROAD, BRENTFORD.

No. 9.　　　　　　　**Saturday, December 14th., 1935.**

Notes from the Hive.

THAT sinking feeling which I mentioned a fortnight ago still persists as far as the Bees are concerned, but there is a confident feeling that the "patient" is only suffering from an acute, rather than chronic, attack of some mystifying malady.

I mentioned, too, that Brentford were after new players, and two were secured at great cost just in time to be included in the home game against Leeds United. First Dai Richards, the Welsh international half back from Wolverhampton Wanderers was signed, and there immediately followed the transfer of D. McCulloch, centre forward from Hearts, the Scottish League club. A very cordial welcome is extended to these new chums who, it is felt, will prove " stinging " Bees once they settle down in their new surroundings.

Richards has been honoured by his country eleven times and yet is still quite a young man, while McCulloch has played in Scottish representative games and proved himself a fine goal-getter, and also was capped against Wales. May he continue the good work this side of the border. Brentford may be very lowly placed at the moment, but it can be very definitely stated there is no happier family in football than at Griffin Park, where optimism is still strong that the Bees will get out of trouble once the present lean patch is over.

GREAT START AGAINST LEEDS.

Supporters must have felt that the Bees' troubles were at an end after the game with Leeds United had been in progress a few minutes. Brentford got off the mark in such style that a two-goals lead had been built up before thousands of the large crowd had arrived. That was just the tonic our supporters, players and management needed, and which should have ensured a substantial victory, but the "bogy" which has been frustrating the efforts of our boys for some time again made its presence felt. The visitors scored twice before the interval and in the end we had to be content with a division because neither side managed to get a goal in the second half. It was terribly disappointing after such a brilliant start, but it was very heartening to know that the form of the two new players came well up to expectations.

There is nothing so heartening for a new player than to get a quick goal for his new club. Well, McCulloch obliged in this respect in double quick time against Leeds, for

play had only progressed six minutes when he had got the ball in the net to give Brentford a two-goal lead. Just previously our new centre forward had cleverly allowed the ball to go through to Scott to open the score for our side.

Everything in the garden seemed lovely—so nice in fact that everyone must have felt that here was the turn in the tide as far as the fortunes of the Bees were concerned. But it did not work out quite like that for, as I have previously mentioned, the visitors finished on level terms and so took a point away which appeared during the early stages in safe keeping.

WHAT HAPPENED AT GRIMSBY?

One might well ask such a question after the Bees had been beaten by the convincing margin of six goals to one. It was the biggest licking our boys have sustained this season but the story, without any attempt at excuses, can be largely explained away. First of all the troubles of Brentford were added to by the fact that Jack Astley's father died, which left us with only one of the five full backs on the club's books available. Bert Watson, our captain, was therefore called on to fill the breach at full back with Dumbrell, a reserve player, as his partner. But don't think that our defeat was due to our regular full backs not being available, for it wasn't. It was very foggy; in fact up to within forty minutes of the start it seemed certain that no match would take place. Then the fog lifted and left a playing pitch which could be likened to a sheet of ice. The home players used rubber studs and were thus properly shod to suit the conditions, while Brentford had to turn out as usual. This gave Grimsby a tremendous advantage which was soon in evidence, so much so that the play was little more than a farce.

Our players found the greatest of difficulty in keeping their feet on the frozen surface and our defeat in the circumstances caused no great surprise. It was just another scurvy trick on the part of the Goddess of Fate.

RESERVES' REVIEW.

Our Reserves lost a very hard game against Arsenal, at Highbury, by the only goal of the game. Our boys fought desperately hard to save the game, but just failed.

On Saturday last Southampton were beaten by four clear goals at Griffin Park. McAloon (2), Dunn and Brown scored for the Bees.

SEA-SIDE RELAXATION.

Our first team were taken to Brighton on Tuesday, and remained there until this morning. It was felt that the seaside air, brine baths, golf and walking exercise would prove a good tone up for the players and help make them particularly refreshed for the game with Liverpool to-day.

LIVERPOOL HERE TO-DAY.

For the first time we have the pleasure of extending a cordial welcome to Liverpool, who have averaged exactly a point per game to date. It gives us a crumb of comfort to know that Liverpool have collected fifteen of their eighteen points at home, for so far the famous Mersey club has not gained winning brackets on opposing territory this season. There seems no reason why they should break the ice at our expense this afternoon. The best Liverpool have done away from home is three drawn games. They drew 2—2 at Chelsea, 0—0 at Bolton and 2—2 at Middlesbrough. Liverpool have only scored six goals in eight away games and conceded eighteen, which shows an adverse goal average of 3—1, a result which would look very well on paper for the Bees this evening.

" BUSY BEE."

Jottings from the Board Room.

The League team have spent the week at Brighton in an effort to give them a tonic to assist them to regain their confidence. They will return to-day in time for the kick-off.

Our deepest sympathy is extended to Jack Astley at the sad loss he has sustained by the death of his father

Comparative records with last season are as follow :
Football League—
	P.	W.	L.	D.	Goals F.	A.	P.
This Season	17	4	9	4	24	33	12
Last Season	17	11	3	3	41	22	25

London Combination—
	P.	W.	L.	D.	Goals F.	A.	P.
This Season	20	15	4	1	45	22	31
Last Season	20	11	4	5	37	23	27

Goal-scorers to date are :
Football League.—Holliday 6, Hopkins 6, Fletcher 4, Scott 3, Robson 2, Dunn 1, J. C. Burns 1 and McCulloch 1.—Total 24.
London Combination.—Dunn 12, Brown 11, Muttitt 5, Sullivan 5, McAloon 4, Gibbons 3, Fenton 2, Smith (C.) 2, L. Smith 1.—Total 45.

The Reserves are away to Brighton Reserves to-day.

Charlie Walsh, whose injury has permanently finished his playing career, has agreed to accept a sum of money as a settlement. Charlie proposes to start up in business, and I am sure all at Brentford will wish him good luck in his new venture. He has certainly experienced nothing but bad luck as a professional footballer and a portion of good luck is long overdue to him.

We are interested in Monday's F.A. Cup draw (3rd Round)!!! Is it possible to be drawn at home? The date of the games are on January 11th, 1936.

HOME GAMES TO FOLLOW
Saturday, December 21st.
BRENTFORD RES. v.
QUEEN'S PARK RANGERS RES.
(London Combination) Kick-off 2.30 p.m.

Christmas Day, December 25th.
BRENTFORD v.
PRESTON NORTH END
(Football League) Kick-off 11.15 a.m.

Boxing Day, December 26th.
BRENTFORD RES. v.
CHELSEA RES.
(London Combination) Kick-off 2.30 p.m.

Saturday, December 28th.
BRENTFORD v.
BOLTON WANDERERS
(Football League). Kick-off at 2.30 p.m.

Tickets for numbered and reserved seats at 3/6 and 4/- each can be purchased for the game v. Preston North End on Christmas Day, kick-off at 11.15 a.m. Applications by post will not be considered unless accompanied with remittance and stamped addressed envelope.

In connection with the League match between West Bromwich Albion and Brentford on December 21st, the Great Western Railway is running a half-day excursion as follows :
Express Restaurant-Car Trip to Birmingham and the Hawthorns Halt (adjoining West Bromwich Albion F.C. Ground). Forward : Paddington dep. 11.5 a.m.; Birmingham (Snow Hill) arr. 1.10 p.m. Return : Birmingham (Snow Hill) dep. 6.0 or 7.50 p.m.; Paddington arr. 8.5 and 10.5 p.m. Return fare 6/6.
Trains leave Birmingham (Snow Hill) Station for Hawthorns Halt at 1.15, 1.45 and 2.0 p.m. Return trains will leave Hawthorns Halt for Birmingham (Snow Hill) immediately after the match.

Jimmy Nichols, who dislocated a finger against Coventry City Reserves, on November 23rd, has now resumed training and should be fit to play in another week.

As I have said the draw for the third round of the Cup will take place on Monday. The method of drawing the teams has altered vastly since the beginning of the competition. The draw is attended by all 73 members of the Football Association Council. Each team is represented by a red-painted wooden ball with a white number on it. All 64 balls are placed in a cloth bag sufficiently large to enable them to mix and then shaken about by the chairman of the Committee When he is satisfied that he no longer knows what order the balls are in, he extracts them in pairs, and the secretary of the Association announces from the side of the hall which teams are to fight for the honour of playing in the fourth round.

H.C.C.

Shots from the Spot.

By "Rambler"

The Bees, as you have been told elsewhere, have all been at Brighton this week, toning up for to-day, and trying to forget the skating lessons they received on an ice-bound pitch at Grimsby!

* * *

Our fellow " babes " in the First Division wood found Sunderland in very much the same sort of mood as when the leaders visited Griffin Park. I have seen Bolton play this season, and the side that can beat them 7—2 is a very good side indeed.

* * *

Sunderland look like making the championship this year, though there is plenty of time for all sorts of things to happen between now and the final reckoning. If they do, the Bees won't regret that 5—1 defeat at Griffin Park quite so much . . .

* * *

It is divulging no secret to say that Brentford—management and players alike—are very keen to have a decent run in the F.A. Cup this year, and on Monday afternoon we shall know how we have fared in the draw for the third round.

* * *

Last year's 1—0 defeat by Plymouth Argyle may have been a blessing in disguise in that the club was left free to concentrate on promotion, but it is never pleasant to be put out of the Cup at the very first attempt, and it is particularly irritating when the game takes place on one's own ground.

* * *

This year then we all hope for better things. A little luck when the draw takes place and we can hope to break a few club records in our advancement.

* * *

Charlton Athletic, our neighbours and good friends, are making a fine show in their first season in the Second Division. There's plenty of room for another London club in the First Division, and if only the 'Spurs could come up as well, there would be some celebrating.

* * *

The glorious uncertainty of football, about which we hear so much was not a great deal in evidence in First Division circles last Saturday. Every home club won—with a total of thirty-eight goals against nine. (That only includes finished games, of course.)

* * *

We can look with real pleasure at one feature of Brentford football at the moment, and that is the fine form of the Reserves, who now lead the London Combination table. They are getting amongst the goals with a vengeance and got four without a reply from Southampton on Saturday. Pat Clark, the amateur full back, who, like Jackie Burns, is a schoolmaster, gave a very promising display.

OUR VISITORS TO-DAY.
HOW THEY MAY LINE UP.

———◆———

Liverpool and Everton, the two famous Merseyside clubs, used to be one and the same organisation. That club played at Anfield, the present ground of the visitors to Griffin Park to-day, but it was known as the Everton F.C.

The division came about through a dispute over rentals with a local brewer who owned the ground. One section moved to Goodison, while the other stayed on where it was, but it was anomalous for them both to play, as Everton and the F.A. stepped in. Peculiarly enough it was the Anfield club which changed its name, the part that had moved away being allowed to keep the original title.

Liverpool have four times won the League championship, while they share with Everton the distinction of having carried off this honour the season after gaining promotion.

They reached the final of the Cup on one occasion, but were beaten by Burnley.

An interesting feature of the club is the success the South African players have had under its colours.

Riley, Arthur (goalkeeper).— Born at Boksburg, South Africa. Height, 6ft. Weight 12st. 8lb. Took up soccer in order to get to this country. Formerly played Rugby, but developed so rapidly at the Association game that he won a place in the 1924 touring side. Stayed over here as a Liverpool player. Has something like 200 appearances in English League football to his credit.

Cooper, Thomas (right back).— Born at Fenton, Staffs. Height 5ft. 9in. Weight, 12st. Cost a tidy penny when secured from Derby County twelve months ago. Came to the fore with Port Vale, whom he joined in 1924. Derby took him in 1926 and he won many caps while with them, captaining England on several occasions . Stylish and powerful defender.

Blenkinsop, Ernest (left back).— Born at Cudworth, Yorks. Height 5ft. 9½in. Weight 11st. 9lb. Another fine defender who had captained England. Had 1½ seasons with Hull City and 11 years with Sheffield Wednesday before moving from Hillsbrough to Liverpool in March, 1934. Created a post-war record by playing in 15 consecutive internationals for England, and has 25 caps in all. Captain of the club.

Savage, Robert Edward (right half).—Born at Lincoln. Height 5ft. 11½in. Weight 12st. A product of Lincoln City, who established himself in Liverpool's League side last season. Can play in all three half-back positions or at inside forward. Fine constructive player.

Bradshaw, Thomas (" Tiny ") (centre half).—Born at Coatbridge, Lanarkshire. Height 6ft. 1½in. Weight 14st. Started with Bury in 1923, after being spotted playing in a " kick about " on some waste ground. Had seven seasons with them and won a Scottish cap before moving to Liverpool. Not a third back.

BRENTFORD

BREN

Red an

1—M

2—ASTLEY
Right Back

4—McKENZIE
Right Half

5—
Cen

7—HOPKINS
Outside Right

8—ROBSON
Inside Right

9—McC
Cent

Referee—Mr. G. W. JONES

12—HANSON
Outside Left

13—GLASSEY
Inside Left

14—
Centr

17—McDOUGALL
Left Half

18—B
Ce

20—BLENKINSOP
Left Back

22-
G

LIV
Red Jerse

THE LEAGUE—DIVISION I.

	P	W.	D.	L.	F.	A.	P
Sunderland	18	13	2	3	58	28	28
Derby County	18	9	5	4	26	15	23
Huddersfield T.	18	9	5	4	27	23	23
Arsenal	17	7	6	4	35	17	20
Manchester C.	17	9	2	6	31	24	20
Middlesbrough	17	8	3	6	46	26	19
Leeds United	18	6	7	5	30	28	19
Birmingham	18	7	5	6	27	29	19
Liverpool	18	7	4	7	35	27	18
Stoke City	18	8	2	8	29	29	18
Sheffield Wed.	18	6	5	7	31	38	17
Bolton Wand.	17	6	5	6	26	33	17
Chelsea	17	7	3	7	26	33	17
Wolves	18	7	2	9	37	35	16
W. Brom. Albion	18	7	2	9	34	33	16
Blackburn Rov.	17	7	2	8	28	43	16
Preston N.E.	18	6	3	9	24	29	15
Grimsby Town	17	7	0	10	27	36	14
Portsmouth	16	5	4	7	20	28	14
Everton	18	5	3	10	29	42	13
BRENTFORD	**17**	**4**	**4**	**9**	**24**	**33**	**12**
Aston Villa	18	4	4	10	31	52	12

(Goals)

LIVERPOOL

...FORD

Stripes

...IESON
...per

3—POYSER
Left Back

...IES   **6—RICHARDS**
...lf   Left Half

...)CH   **10—HOLLIDAY**   **11—FLETCHER**
...ward   Inside Left   Outside Left

Linesmen—Messrs. A. Wooldridge (red flag),
and A. H. Auberton (blue flag).

...VE   **15—WRIGHT**   **16—NIEUWENHUYS**
...ard   Inside Right   Outside Right

...SHAW   **19—SAVAGE**
...alf   Right Half

21—COOPER
Right Back

...EY
...er

...POOL
...te Knickers

LONDON COMBINATION

	P	W.	D.	L.	F.	A.	P
BRENTFORD	20	15	1	4	45	22	31
Swansea Town	21	14	2	5	37	28	30
Portsmouth	18	12	5	1	56	20	29
Arsenal	19	14	1	4	55	20	29
Crystal Palace	22	12	4	6	47	43	28
Luton Town	21	12	2	7	69	44	26
West Ham United .	21	10	4	7	53	31	24
Chelsea	20	10	4	6	46	40	24
Queen's Park R. ...	21	10	3	8	35	35	23
Charlton Ath.	20	9	2	9	37	33	20
Reading	18	9	1	8	40	43	19
Coventry City	19	9	0	10	39	29	18
Millwall	18	8	2	8	25	29	18
Watford	19	7	3	9	42	50	17
Tottenham H.	18	6	4	8	49	44	16
Southend United ...	19	6	4	9	50	40	16
Northampton	19	6	3	10	42	40	15
Southampton	21	5	5	11	31	39	15
Clapton Orient ...	19	4	6	9	18	43	14
Bournemouth	19	5	3	11	30	52	13
Fulham	19	5	2	12	34	42	12
Bristol City	22	5	1	16	29	74	11
Leicester City	18	5	0	13	31	48	10
Brighton & Hove A.	18	3	4	11	24	57	10

McDougall, James (left half).— Born at Port Glasgow. Height 5ft. 11in. Weight 11st. 6lb. Was an inside left when Liverpool secured him from Partick Thistle seven years ago. Soon moved into the middle line, where he has settled down into a top-class player.

Nieuwenhuys, Berry (outside right).—Born in South Africa. Formerly a mining engineer in his native country. Liverpool heard of him while he was playing football with Boksburg. Joined them early in season 1933-4 and made 34 First Division appearances that season. Fast and centres neatly.

Wright, E. V. (inside right).— Born at Walsall. Height 5ft. 11in. Weight 12st. 6lb. Began career with Bristol City, who transferred him to Rotherham. In 1930 went to Sheffield Wednesday and in 1933 returned to Rotherham, leaving for Anfield the following year. Usually a centre-forward, he is a powerful shot who never wastes time in pretty-pretty stuff.

Howe, Frederick (centre forward) —Born at Stockport. Height 5ft. 9½in. Weight 11st. 7lb. Has jumped to fame this season. Joining Liverpool last season from Hyde United after having had previous experience with Stockport County, he had several first team outings towards the close of the campaign. Has been the regular leader this season and his goal-scoring feats include a hat-trick and a quartet in a match.

Classey, R. J. (inside left).— Another youngster who has gained his initial First Division experience this season. Joined Liverpool from Usworth Colliery in March, 1934. Was injured in his first trial with the club. They gave him another when he was fit again and signed him immediately. Making his first team debut last week, he scored one of the side's goals against Preston North End.

Hanson, Adolf (outside left).— Born at Bootle, nr. Liverpool. Height 5ft. 8in. Weight 10st. 8lb. Was turned down by Everton after trials with " A " team. Got into Liverpool first team during season 1932-3. Has been second fiddle to Carr for the majority of games this season. Fast and elusive, often cuts in and scores.

CHARLIE WALSH.

We would like to take this opportunity of saying good-bye to Charlie Walsh, and to express the hope that he will retain as friendly memories of the Club as we retain of him. As you all know, an injury has put a sudden and tragic stop to his playing career, and his contract is accordingly ended, so that he can make immediate use of the cash settlement, which has now been arranged, to start up in business.

All his footballing life injuries have dogged him and retarded the progress that he would otherwise undoubtedly have made. We know that all our supporters will join with us in this farewell, adding the sincere hope that his future will be a properous and contented one.

ARTHUR BATEMAN.

Arthur Bateman, our popular full back, who injured his knee against Manchester City on October 26th, can rightly claim to be unlucky. He was one of the party who had been to Brighton and it was anticipated that he had fully recovered and would play for certain on Saturday next. Unfortunately in a test he felt much pain in his knee. He was immediately brought to London on Thursday and examined by a London surgeon specialist, and it was discovered that he had injured his cartilege, and an operation was necessary if it was desirous of getting him absolutely fit again.

Arrangements were made for Arthur to be admitted in the Brentford Hospital yesterday (Friday), and this morning the operation was being performed by Mr. A. G. Timbrell Fisher, who, by the way, performs all the necessary operations to the Arsenal players.

Arthur will be discharged from hospital, if all goes well, before Christmas, and within a month should be training again, and fit to play within six weeks. The injury in this case is not serious, and the specialist is absolutely confident that it will in no way affect Arthur's play when he resumes. I am sure all supporters join me in wishing this popular player a speedy recovery. If any supporter desires to write Arthur a cheery note, Arthur Bateman, Brentford Hospital, Brentford, will find him.

FIXTURES, SEASON 1935-36.

FIRST TEAM

Date. 1935.	Opponents.	Ground.	GOALS F.	A.
Aug. 31	Bolton Wanderers	A	2	0
Sept. 5	Blackburn Rovers	H	3	1
,, 7	Huddersfield Town	H	1	2
,, 14	Middlesbrough	A	0	0
,, 18	Derby County	A	1	2
,, 21	Aston Villa	H	1	2
,, 28	Wolverhampton Wdrs.	H	2	3
Oct. 5	Sheffield Wednesday	H	2	2
,, 12	Portsmouth	A	3	1
,, 19	Stoke City	H	0	0
,, 26	Manchester City	A	1	2
Nov. 2	Arsenal	H	2	1
,, 9	Birmingham	A	1	2
,, 16	Sunderland	H	1	5
,, 23	Chelsea	A	1	2
,, 30	Leeds United	H	2	2
Dec. 7	Grimsby Town	A	1	6
,, 14	Liverpool	H		
,, 21	West Bromwich Albion	A		
,, 25	Preston North End	H		
,, 26	Preston North End	A		
,, 28	Bolton Wanderers	H		
1936.				
Jan. 1	Blackburn Rovers	A		
,, 4	Huddersfield Town	A		
,, 11	(3)			
,, 18	Middlesbrough	H		
,, 25	(4) Aston Villa	A		
Feb. 1	Wolverhampton Wdrs.	H		
,, 8	Sheffield Wednesday	A		
,, 15	(5) Portsmouth	H		
,, 22	Stoke City	A		
,, 29	(6) Manchester City	H		
Mar. 7	Arsenal	A		
,, 14	(S.-F.) Birmingham	H		
,, 21	Sunderland	A		
,, 28	Chelsea	H		
April 4	Leeds United	A		
,, 10	Everton	A		
,, 11	Grimsby Town	H		
,, 13	Everton	H		
,, 18	Liverpool	A		
,, 25	(F.) West Brom. Alb.	H		
May 2	Derby County	H		

SECOND TEAM

Date. 1935.	Opponents.	Ground.	GOALS F.	A.
Aug. 31	Charlton Athletic	H	2	1
Sept. 4	Watford	A	1	3
,, 7	Clapton Orient	A	0	0
,, 12	Watford	H	2	1
,, 14	Southend United	H	1	0
,, 21	Northampton Town	A	1	0
,, 25	Luton Town	A	1	4
,, 28	Crystal Palace	H	4	0
Oct. 3	Luton Town	H	4	3
,, 5	Reading	A	1	2
,, 7	Met Police—L.C. Cup	H	2	0
,, 9	Bournemouth & Bos.	H	5	2
,, 12	Tottenham Hotspur	H	2	1
,, 19	Bristol City	A	3	1
,, 21	C. Orient—L.C. Cup	H	3	1
,, 26	Millwall	H	4	0
Nov. 2	West Ham United	A	1	0
,, 9	Swansea Town	H	2	0
,, 11	Fulham (L. Cup.S.F.)	H	2	0
,, 16	Leicester City	A	3	2
,, 23	Coventry City	H	4	1
,, 30	Arsenal	A	0	1
Dec. 7	Southampton	H	4	0
,, 14	Brighton & Hove A.	A		
,, 21	Queen's Park Rgrs.	A		
,, 25	Chelsea	A		
,, 26	Chelsea	H		
,, 28	Charlton Athletic	A		
Jan. 4	Clapton Orient	H		
,, 11	Fulham	A		
,, 18	Southend United	A		
,, 25	Northampton Town	H		
Feb. 1	Crystal Palace	H		
,, 8	Reading	H		
,, 15	Tottenham Hotspur	A		
,, 22	Bristol City	H		
,, 29	Millwall	H		
Mar. 7	West Ham United	H		
,, 14	Swansea Town	A		
,, 21	Leicester City	H		
,, 25	Bournemouth & Bos.	A		
,, 28	Coventry City	A		
April 4	Arsenal	H		
,, 10	Portsmouth	H		
,, 11	Southampton	A		
,, 13	Portsmouth	A		
,, 18	Brighton & Hove A.	H		
,, 25	Queen's Park Rgrs.	A		
May 2	Fulham	A		

Half Time Scores.

	F.	A.		F	A
A—Aston Villa v. Arsenal	......	......	J—Sheffield W. v. Stoke	......	......
B—Bolton W. v. W. Bromwich	......	......	K—Wolves v. Manchester C.	......	......
C—Derby County v. Grimsby	......	......	L—Charlton v. West Ham	......	......
D—Everton v. Leeds	......	......	M—Fulham v. Doncaster	......	......
E—Huddersfield v. Sunderland	......	......	N—'Spurs v. Norwich	......	......
F—Middlesbro' v. Birmingham	......	......	O—Luton v. Bristol City	......	......
G—Portsmouth v. Blackburn	......	......	P—Folkestone v. Clapton O.	......	......
H—P.N.E. v. Chelsea	......	......	R—Margate v. Crystal Palace	......	......

DAI RICHARDS
Left Half

Dai Richards, who joined Brentford a fortnight ago, possesses 11 Welsh caps. He was born in Abercanaid, S. Wales, and went to Wolverhampton from Merthyr Town, helping the Wolves to promotion in 1931-32. He first played in their League team at the age of 17, and is now 26 years of age. His brother, William, plays for Brighton and was with Fulham.

The Next Games.

Next Saturday, the Bees are away to West Bromwich Albion, whilst the Reserves entertain near neighbours and old rivals in Queen's Park Rangers, at Griffin Park.

After that come the Christmas games. On Christmas morning (kick-off at 11.15 a.m.) the Bees have as their visitors Preston North End, who once had the distinction of winning the F.A. Cup without conceding a goal, in the same season that they won the championship without a defeat and dropping only four points.

On Boxing Day, the clubs meet again, this time at Deepdale.

The Reserves have two games with Chelsea, being at home to them on Boxing Day.

There is another big attraction for Brentford fans on Saturday, December 28th, for our visitors on that occasion are Bolton Wanderers who came up with us from the Second Division at the end of last season. Despite a home defeat at our hands in the first game of the season, the Wanderers have settled down nicely in their new sphere, and the Bees will have to go all out to pull off their first First League double. The following Wednesday the Bees have another stiff task as they have to journey up to meet Blackburn Rovers, with Huddersfield also away from home the following Saturday.

BRENTFORD FOOTBALL AND SPORTS CLUB, LIMITED.

Registered Office :—GRIFFIN PARK, BRAEMAR ROAD, BRENTFORD.

President and Chairman :		**Vice-Chairman :**
MR. L. P. SIMON.		MR. F. A. DAVIS.
ALDERMAN W. FLEWITT, J.P.	MR. H. W. DODGE.	MR. F. W. BARTON.
MR. H. N. BLUNDELL.	MR. C. L. SIMON.	ALDERMAN H. F. DAVIS.
MR. H. J. SAUNDERS.		MR. J. R. HUGHES, J.P., C.C.

Hon. Treasurer :
ALDERMAN W. FLEWITT, J.P.

Club Medical Officer : DR. A. D. GOWANS.

Secretary-Manager :
MR. H. C. CURTIS,
" DORINCOURT," BOSTON GARDENS, BRENTFORD.

Telephones :
GROUND : EALING 1744.
PRIVATE HOUSE : EALING 1183.

Telegraphic Address :
CURTIS, FOOTBALL, BRENTFORD.
Ground ; GRIFFIN PARK, EALING ROAD, BRENTFORD.

No. 10.
Christmas Day, 1935.

Notes from the Hive.

BEES STILL ON THE LOW PEDAL.

*T*HINGS don't seem to go right whatever is tried. Two players secured, team changes made, yet the silver lining to the cloud which has been over-hanging the Bees since the early season games refuses to show itself in practical form.

"Brentford are good enough for the company they are in," was the generally expressed opinion after the season started. Astute judges said so in all sincerity, and inside official circles at Griffin Park similar views were held.

This was when Brentford were *not* winning. It showed the confidence of the management in their belief that the team would prove worthy of holding a safe place in the First Division once the team got acclimatised to the new sphere they were operating in.

Well, as you all know, it has not worked out like that. Our plans have not materialised. Yet there is still an optimistic feeling that the Bees will save their place and not suffer relegation.

At the moment Brentford are occupying the last but one rung on the League ladder and the outlook might not seem too bright, but there is a long way to go yet and a lot can happen in the second half of the season. We have a loyal set of players who intend to see the Bees through the lean time now being experienced.

We have too a loyal lot of sup-porters and that is why our en-thusiastic directors have shown such enterprise in not only looking after the comfort of the habitues of Grif-fin Park but gone out and spent big money on the acquisition of new players—your reward for the splen-did support accorded to the club.

ANOTHER HOME DEFEAT.

Two more valuable points were conceded at home from the visit of Liverpool last Saturday week. It was thought that this was a game which might provide the Bees with a much-needed victory, for the An-field club had not gained winning brackets on opposing territory be-fore they came to Griffin Park. The turn of the tide was not seen, how-ever, for Liverpool got a snap goal two minutes after the start, due to Joe James slicing the ball in his effort to clear.

In the second half the visitors added another goal. Then late in the game Robson scored the Bees' solitary point, leaving Liverpool the

NOTES FROM THE HIVE—*Continued.*

winners by the odd goal in three. Territorially, Brentford had far more of the play and had their chances too. Enough to have finished very good winners. The fact that Liverpool lost a player quite early in the game and played with depleted forwards, really handicapped Brentford more than it did the visitors, for it compelled Liverpool, having already gained the lead, to concentrate on defence and naturally our own forwards were crowded out more often than not at close quarters.

It was a poor game with few redeeming features to commend it.

NARROW DEFEAT AT WEST BROMWICH.

Another defeat was sustained on Saturday last, when West Bromwich got the only goal of the game at the Hawthorns.

Here again the luck of the Bees was dead out. To be beaten after having as much of the play as Brentford had in this game was indeed rank bad luck. Brentford adapted themselves better to the conditions which a hard, frozen ground imposed. Our boys should have held a good lead at the interval, for altogether the frame work of the Albion goal was struck four times, but never a goal came to the Bees. Five minutes after the interval Muttitt got the ball into the net but the point was disallowed owing to McCulloch being adjudged offside.

The critics generally gave Brentford credit for their good display, and said our boys were unlucky to lose. It is nice to know that the team played so well but poor consolation when points are wanted so badly. It is not too much to say that the management of the Club were delighted with the football played by the Bees and have no hesitation in fielding an unchanged side for the game against Preston North End to-day.

RESERVES' REVIEW

In striking contrast to the lowly position of the senior side in the League table, our Reserves continue to do well and hold pride of place in the London Combination. Two recent games have resulted in wins being recorded.

Dunn scored at Brighton, while the former Glasgow Celtic player, was again on the mark against Queen's Park Rangers at Griffin Park on Saturday last. The Rangers were beaten by three goals to one, and Dunn did the hat trick for the Bees.

PRESTON HERE TO-DAY.

Preston North End, to whom we extend a most cordial welcome this morning, hold a "half-way" position on the League table as a result of collecting 19 points from 20 games, but their away record is not a very impressive one. Ten "out" games have only yielded three points from a 1—0 win at Leeds on Saturday last and a previous draw at Blackburn. Curiously enough their biggest away defeat was sustained at Villa Park, where Aston Villa won by five goals to one. Can the Bees emulate the feat of their companions in distress?

GOOD BYE, GEORGE.

These notes cannot be concluded without wishing George Robson the best of luck with the Hearts.

As you all know George was recently transferred to the Scottish League club from whom just previously David McCulloch had been secured and we all wish George well after the fine service he has rendered the Bees for five seasons.

GREETINGS TO YOU ALL.

The Festive Season is now with us and the Directors, Management and players wish all supporters of the Club a very happy Christmas and a prosperous time during 1936, —and so does . . .

BUSY BEE.

Jottings from the Board Room.

Arthur Bateman, our popular full back, who is making good progress, following his operation, desires me to thank all the supporters who have written to him. He does appreciate their many kind expressions Arthur will be leaving the hospital any day now.

CUP TIE, JANUARY 11th.

A special excursion is to be run to Leicester in connection with our Cup-tie on January 11th. The train, which will be composed of corridor stock, will leave Kew Bridge Station at 10.15 a.m., calling only at South Acton and Acton Central, and is due to arrive Leicester 12.45 p.m. Fare for the return journey, 5/6. A restaurant car will be run on the train and meals will be served in each direction at the rate of 2/6 per meal. For the convenience of our supporters who wish to take advantage of this trip, it is requested that tickets be purchased in advance in order that adequate arrangements may be made. They can be obtained from the Secretary's Office here or from Messrs. Thos. Cook and Son, Ltd., Berkeley Street, W.1.

The prices of admission for our Cup-tie v. Leicester City will be as follows: Admission to Ground, 1/-; Enclosure, 1/6 and 2/-; Stand Seats (unreserved), 2/6, and Numbered and Reserved Seats at 3/6 and 5/-, which can be obtained from this office. There are only a limited number.

The Reserves are away this morning to Chelsea Reserves (London Combination).

The kick-off on Saturday next, December 28th, v. Bolton Wanderers, is at 2.30 p.m. Numbered and Reserved Seats in Block "B" can be purchased at 4/- each. Applications by post should be sent early owing to the possibility of delay at this time of the year.

Our Reserves play the return London Combination fixture on this ground to-morrow; kick-off at 2.30 p.m., v. Chelsea.

The League Team leave this afternoon at 5 o'clock for the return game at Preston to-morrow.

Comparison records with last season are as follows:—

Football League:—

	P.	W.	L.	D.	F.	A.	P.
This Season ...	19	4	11	4	25	36	12
Last Season ...	19	12	3	4	51	25	28

London Combination:—

	P.	W.	L.	D.	F.	A.	P.
This Season ...	22	17	4	1	49	22	35
Last Season ...	22	12	5	5	38	25	29

Goal scorers to date are:—
Football League: Holliday 6, Hopkins 6, Fletcher 4, Scott 3, Robson 3, Dunn 1, J. C. Burns 1, and McCulloch 1—Total 25.
London Combination: Dunn 16, Brown 11, Muttitt 5, Sullivan 5, McAloon 4, Gibbons 3, Fenton 2, C. Smith 2, L. Smith 1—Total 49.

George Robson had an unfortunate experience during the week-end. He was selected to play for the Hearts Reserves on Saturday at Edinburgh. He travelled on Friday, but owing to fog did not arrive at Edinburgh until well after mid-night, the train being four hours late. He reported at the ground on Saturday, but the game was postponed owing to the ground being unfit. He immediately returned to Brentford to settle up his affairs, and on Monday returned to Edinburgh—over 800 miles' travelling for nothing.

The fact that Jackie Burns, our popular amateur, has signed for the Leyton F.C. does not indicate that he has severed his connection with this Club. He has promised to assist us whenever he may be required.

One of the most outstanding facts so far this season is that of our amateur neighbours. Southall F.C., who by their remarkable success in the F.A. Cup look like making history. In the 3rd Round they are drawn to play Watford F.C. at Southall, and as they defeated Swindon Town in the 1st Round they are fully entitled to anticipate equal success against Watford, especially as the game is again at Southall. We extend hearty congratulations to the Southall F.C. on their great success.

H.C.C.

BOXING DAY
v. **CHELSEA RESERVES**
(London Combination)
Kick-off at 2.30 p.m.

A HAPPY CHRISTMAS.

Shots from the Spot.

By "Rambler"

Brentford have been going through a very bad time we all know, and many of our supporters must have felt downcast in the extreme. I get many letters asking me why this, that and the other is not done, and which also rate me for maintaining my confidence in the boys.

* * *

I hate harping on the "hard luck" story: yet let me quote you two remarks picked at random from Press reports of the West Bromwich Albion game:

"If Brentford can reproduce this form their fortune must change. They are plucky, clever, but unlucky losers."

"Brentford will never again lose a match so undeservedly as they did the one at West Bromwich on Saturday."

So you can see that I am not the only one who writes this sort of thing . . .

* * *

Fate has not been as kind as she might in the F.A. Cup draw either, but we believe the Bees have the makings of a fine Cup-fighting side, and that, given a share of whatever fortune is going, are capable of living to fight again.

* * *

If Charlie Fletcher plays in that game an interesting reunion may take place, as he will meet Dave Jones and Tommy Mills, both Welsh internationals, who were with Charlie at Clapton Orient.

* * *

J. C. Burns, our popular amateur, who is now, together with Pat Clark who occasionally turns out for the Reserves, assisting Leyton when not required by the Bees, scored the winning goal for his club on Saturday. It was the first time Leyton had bagged both points since the third game of the season.

* * *

Southall, our amateur neighbours, whose F.A. Cup feats are commented on elsewhere, showed on Saturday that they do not confine their activities to that particular competition. In the Middlesex Senior Cup they beat Alexandra Park by 9 goals to 2—Willshaw scoring 6!

* * *

With the departure of George Robson from Brentford, the Hearts of Midlothian in particular and Scottish football in general have gained one of the most sportsman-like, gentlemanly players I ever hope to see. We can rest assured that he will add nothing but credit to the name of the club where he has spent the greater part of his football career and to which he has rendered such splendid service. Good luck, George!

* * *

Time now to close down on this chat. There is a thick fog creeping steadily up around my windows as I write, which gives me an uneasy feeling that we may not have Christmas football after all. However a strong wind will do wonders —so here's hoping that you will see a good game and a result that will heighten your appetite for the turkey.

OUR VISITORS TO-DAY.
HOW THEY MAY LINE UP.

——◆——

Preston's accomplishments in recent seasons pale before their brilliant record of the early days of the Football League. In 1888-9 they achieved the remarkable feat of winning the Cup without conceding a goal, and the Cup without losing a match. Again in 1889-90 they won the League, but since then their career has been one of ups and downs in more senses than one. They were first relegated in 1901, and since then have dropped from the First to the Second Divisions three times, in 1912, 1914, and 1925, returning last in 1934. Last season they finished with 42 points, going to the sixth round of the Cup.

The Club was originally formed for cricket, but they became members of the Football League in 1888.

Holdcroft, George Harry (goalkeeper).—Born at Stoke-on-Trent. Height, 5ft. 11½in. Weight, 11st. 11lb. An agile custodian who is among the best in the country to-day. At 17 was a professional with Port Vale. Moved to Darlington two years later and then to Everton in 1931. Was allowed to move to Deepdale three years ago and has been an ever-present since.

Gallimore, Frank (right-back). Born at Northwich, Cheshire. Height 5ft. 8in. Weight, 11st. Secured as a junior from Witton Albion (Cheshire League). Developed with the Colts and graded the first team in 1932. Lost his place to Hough following injury in 1933-4, but turned the tables last season when the latter was injured. Not spectacular but a determined defender who is difficult to pass.

Lowe, Harry (left back).—Born at Skelmersdale, Lancs. Height 5ft. 9in. Weight, 11st 6lb. Southport gave him his introduction to League football after a spell with Skelmersdale United. Went to Everton, where his chances were limited. At Christmas three years

ago he was transferred to Deepdale together with Holdcroft. Has been a consistent performer ever since.

Shankly, William (right half).— Born at Glenbuck, Lanarkshire. Height 5ft. 8½in. Weight 11st. Came out with Glenbuck Cherrypickers, that picturesquely named Scottish Junior club that has been the starting point of several first class players. Came South to join Carlisle United. Preston took him two and a half years ago. Ever-present last season.

Tremelling, William (centre half) --Born at Birmingham. Height 5ft. 9in. Weight, 11st 7lb. Captain of the side. Previously with Shirebrook Albion, Retford Town and Blackpool. Was six and a half years with the latter club before joining North End in December five years ago. Made his name as an inside forward, but three years ago made his place secure as the club's pivot. Brother of Dan Tremelling, former England goalkeeper.

Milne, James (left half)—Born at Dundee. Height, 5ft. 10in. Weight 12st. After experience with Dundee Violet, he joined Dundee United. Was an ever present in his

See the "MIDDLESEX COUNTY TIMES" ever

BRENTFORD *v.* P

BRE

Red a

1—M

2—ASTLEY
Right Back

4—McKENZIE
Right Half

5-
Ce

7—HOPKINS
Outside Right

8—SCOTT
Inside Right

9—McC
Centr

Referee— Mr. W. B. BRISTOW (Stafford).

14—
C

12—O'DONNELL, H.
Outside Left

13—O'DONNEL
Inside Left

17—MILNE
Left Half

18—1
C

20—LOWE
Left Back

22—H

PRESTON

White Shir

THE LEAGUE—DIVISION I.

	P.	W.	D.	L.	F.	A.	P.
Sunderland	20	14	2	4	61	30	30
Derby C.	20	10	5	5	29	18	25
Huddersfield T.	19	10	5	4	28	23	25
Arsenal	19	9	6	4	44	18	24
Birmingham	20	9	5	6	33	31	23
Liverpool	20	9	4	7	38	28	22
Stoke City	20	9	3	8	31	30	21
Middlesbrough	20	8	4	8	47	31	20
Manchester City	18	9	2	7	34	28	20
Leeds United	20	6	8	6	30	29	20
Wolves	20	8	3	9	43	40	19
Preston N.E.	20	8	3	9	27	29	19
Bolton W.	18	7	5	6	29	34	19
W.B. Albion	20	8	2	10	36	36	18
Portsmouth	18	7	4	7	25	30	18
Chelsea	19	7	4	8	28	37	18
Blackburn R.	19	8	2	9	34	47	18
Sheffield W.	20	6	5	9	31	40	17
Grimsby T.	19	7	0	12	28	40	14
Everton	20	5	4	11	31	46	14
BRENTFORD	19	4	4	11	25	36	12
Aston Villa	20	4	4	12	33	64	12

"RAMBLER" writes exclusively for the County of M

STON NORTH END

FORD

Stripes

IESON
per

3—POYSER
Left Back

IES
lf

6—RICHARDS
Left Half

OCH   10—HOLLIDAY   11—MUTTITT
ard   Inside Left   Outside Left

Linesmen— Messrs. W. E. Wood (blue flag)
and W. G. Cranstone (red flag)

WELL
orward

15—BERESFORD   16—DOUGAL
Inside Right   Outside Right

ELLING   19—SHANKLY
alf   Right Half

21—GALLIMORE
Right Back

CROFT
per

ORTH END

Blue Knickers

LONDON COMBINATION.

	P.	W.	D.	L.	F.	A.	P.
BRENTFORD	22	17	1	4	49	23	35
Swansea Town	23	15	3	5	42	29	33
Portsmouth	20	13	6	1	59	22	32
Arsenal	21	15	1	5	57	21	31
Crystal Palace	24	12	5	7	49	46	29
Chelsea	22	11	5	6	48	41	27
West Ham Utd.	23	11	4	8	53	34	26
Luton Town	23	12	2	9	69	46	26
Queen Park R.	23	11	3	9	37	38	25
Charlton Athletic	22	10	3	9	42	36	23
Millwall	20	9	3	8	29	30	21
Reading	20	9	2	9	40	47	20
Coventry City	21	9	1	11	43	36	19
Watford	21	8	3	10	46	56	19
Tottenham H'spur	20	7	4	9	54	47	18
Southampton	23	6	6	11	34	41	18
Northampton	21	7	3	11	44	43	17
Southend Utd.	21	6	5	10	32	45	17
Leicester City	21	7	1	13	34	48	15
Fulham	21	6	2	13	37	45	14
Bournemouth	22	5	4	13	32	57	14
Clapton Orient	20	4	6	10	20	46	14
Bristol City	23	6	1	16	33	75	13
Brighton & H.A.	20	3	4	13	25	58	10

first season of Scottish League football (1931-2). Secured by Preston soon after the start of the following season, he went straight into their League side. Was kept out in the second part of last season by Batey. A shrewd, constructive player.

Dougal, James (outside right).— Born at Denny, Scotland. Height 5ft. 8in. Weight 11st 6lb. Was an outside right when he joined Preston in the early part of 1934, from Falkirk. Lost his place last season and moved to the inside berth. Has also played at outside left. Brother of Peter Dougal (Arsenal).

Beresford, Joseph (inside right). —Born at Chesterfield. Height, 5ft. 5in. Weight 10st 13lb. Was at Mansfield with the Town before joining Aston Villa in May, 1927. Had much First Division experience with the Birmingham club before going to Preston soon after the start of this term. A former miner, and his early clubs were Bentley Colliery, Askern Road Working Men's Club (Doncaster) and Mexborough.

Maxwell, James (centre forward). —Born at Kilmarnock. Height 5ft. 8½in. Weight 10st. 7lb. Former Scottish schoolboy international. After leaving Kilmarnock Loanhead School he went to the Kilmarnock club in 1930, and was soon in the news. In 1933-4 he got Scottish League cap. Preston paid high for his signature in 1934 close season. Missed only one League game last season and scored 23 goals, but injury has troubled him this campaign. Small but tricky.

O'Donnell, Frank (inside left).— Born at Buckhaven, Fifeshire. Was signed, together with his brother Hugh, from Glasgow Celtic during the summer. A former miner, he was with Wellesley Juniors before going to Celtic. Understudied McGrory, the international leader, at first, but got a regular first team place in season 1933-4, and was the club's top scorer. Is now recognised as partner to his brother, but has played centre-forward since going to North End.

O'Donnell, Hugh (outside left). —Also born at Buckhaven. Height 5ft. 7in. Weight, 10st 11lb. Came out with the same club as his brother. Gained his first team place at Celtic in 1932-3 and secured a Scottish Cup medal that season. Has a fine understanding with Frank and they work many moves to upset the best defences.

HANWELL BAND'S SUCCESS.

As a result of winning the recent East Ham Band Contest our Hanwell Silver Band has been engaged for a further Broadcast to be given on January 19th next, and also for a stage performance at a West End theatre. This latter is to be given at the Prince of Wales Theatre, Coventry Street, on Sunday, December 29th, in connection with the popular Non-Stop Variety shows which are having such a successful run at this theatre. The Hanwell Band will welcome Brentford patrons on this occasion, which is the first time a London brass band has appeared on a West End theatre stage.

Mr. Arthur East and Master Bravington, of Hanwell Band, have recently won the Senior and Junior Championships of the London Association for solo playing.

SHARES & SHAREHOLDERS

In spite of our previous notes in this programme, the Management are still receiving enquiries from supporters who are desiring to acquire shares in the Club. We repeat that the shares of the Club are fully issued, and unless existing shareholders desire to realise, there are no shares available.

The 6% Debentures of £50 each are still being issued, but only a small number now remain, and when these have been issued the finances of the Club will have been completely consolidated and settled

The Club have been the leaseholders of Griffin Park, and supporters will be interested to know that next March the freehold of the ground is being purchased and the Club will then be in the happy position of being the owners of the ground.

Particulars of the 6% Debentures will be forwarded on application to the Secretary.

Shareholders desiring to realise their share-holdings should advise the Secretary, together with a note of the price they are willing to accept.

DAVID McCULLOCH
Centre Forward.

Born in Hamilton, this energetic young Scot has a fine goal-scoring record behind him. He came to Brentford from Hearts of Midlothian only a week or so back, and has already shown his value. Last season he scored 38 goals in 35 League games. That was his first season for Hearts, and before that he saw service with Shotts and Third Lanark. When he has fully settled down, he should become of great value to the side.

FIXTURES, SEASON 1935-36.

FIRST TEAM

Date. 1935.	Opponents.	Ground.	Goals F.	Goals A.
Aug. 31	Bolton Wanderers ...	A	2	0
Sept. 5	Blackburn Rovers ...	H	3	1
,, 7	Huddersfield Town ...	H	1	2
,, 14	Middlesbrough ...	A	0	0
,, 18	Derby County ...	A	1	2
,, 21	Aston Villa	H	1	2
,, 28	Wolverhampton Wdrs.	A	2	3
Oct. 5	Sheffield Wednesday ..	H	2	2
,, 12	Portsmouth ...	A	3	1
,, 19	Stoke City ...	H	0	0
,, 26	Manchester City ...	A	1	2
Nov. 2	Arsenal	H	2	1
,, 9	Birmingham ...	A	1	2
,, 16	Sunderland ...	H	1	5
,, 23	Chelsea ...	A	1	2
,, 30	Leeds United ...	H	2	2
Dec. 7	Grimsby Town ...	A	1	6
,, 14	Liverpool	H	1	2
,, 21	West Bromwich Albion	A	0	1
,, 25	Preston North End ...	H		
,, 26	Preston North End ...	A		
,, 28	Bolton Wanderers ...	H		
1936.				
Jan. 1	Blackburn Rovers ...	A		
,, 4	Huddersfield Town ...	A		
,, 11	(3)			
,, 18	Middlesbrough ...	H		
,, 25	(4) Aston Villa ...	A		
Feb. 1	Wolverhampton Wdrs.	A		
,, 8	Sheffield Wednesday ...	A		
,, 15	(5) Portsmouth ...	H		
,, 22	Stoke City	A		
,, 29	(6) Manchester City ...	H		
Mar. 7	Arsenal	A		
,, 14	(S.-F.) Birmingham ...	H		
,, 21	Sunderland	H		
,, 28	Chelsea	H		
April 4	Leeds United ...	A		
,, 10	Everton	A		
,, 11	Grimsby Town ...	H		
,, 13	Everton	H		
,, 18	Liverpool	A		
,, 25	(F.) West Brom. Alb.	H		
May 2	Derby County ...	H		

SECOND TEAM

Date. 1935.	Opponents.	Ground.	Goals F.	Goals A.
Aug. 31	Charlton Athletic ...	H	2	1
Sept. 4	Watford	A	1	3
,, 7	Clapton Orient ...	A	0	0
,, 12	Watford	H	2	1
,, 14	Southend United ...	H	1	0
,, 21	Northampton Town ...	A	1	0
,, 25	Luton Town ...	A	1	4
,, 28	Crystal Palace ...	H	4	0
Oct. 3	Luton Town ...	H	4	3
,, 5	Reading	A	1	2
,, 7	Met. Police—L.C. Cup	H	2	0
,, 9	Bournemouth & Bos. .	H	5	2
,, 12	Tottenham Hotspur	H	2	1
,, 19	Bristol City	A	3	1
,, 21	C. Orient—L.C. Cup ...	A	3	1
,, 26	Millwall	H	4	0
Nov. 2	West Ham United ...	A	1	0
,, 9	Swansea Town ...	H	2	0
,, 11	Fulham (L. Cup,S.F.)	H	2	0
,, 16	Leicester City ...	A	3	2
,, 23	Coventry City ...	H	4	1
,, 30	Arsenal	A	0	1
Dec. 7	Southampton ...	H	4	0
,, 14	Brighton & Hove A.	A	1	0
,, 21	Queen's Park Rgrs. ..	A	3	1
,, 25	Chelsea	A		
,, 26	Chelsea	H		
,, 28	Charlton Athletic ...	A		
Jan. 4	Clapton Orient ...	H		
,, 11	Fulham	H		
,, 18	Southend United ...	A		
,, 25	Northampton Town ...	H		
Feb. 1	Crystal Palace ...	A		
,, 8	Reading	H		
,, 15	Tottenham Hotspur ...	A		
,, 22	Bristol City	H		
,, 29	Millwall	A		
Mar. 7	West Ham United ...	H		
,, 14	Swansea Town ...	A		
,, 21	Leicester City ...	H		
,, 25	Bournemouth & Bos. .	H		
,, 28	Coventry City ...	A		
April 4	Arsenal	H		
,, 10	Portsmouth ...	H		
,, 11	Southampton ...	A		
,, 13	Portsmouth ...	A		
,, 18	Brighton & Hove A.	H		
,, 25	Queen's Park Rgrs. ..	A		
May 2	Fulham	A		

TO OUR SUPPORTERS.

On behalf of the Directors, Players and Management, I desire to wish all our Supporters and Friends a very Happy Christmas and a Prosperous New Year. May 1936 bring you, one and all, the best of good luck, but more important, may you all enjoy the best of GOOD HEALTH.

HARRY C. CURTIS.

A MODERN " MUNCHAUSEN "?

THE QUICKSANDS OF MISFORTUNE

According to the fairy tale, Baron Munchausen was so strong that when stuck in a bog he seized himself by the hair and lifted himself clear to safety. (This seems to be the Bees' only course to avoid a sticky end.)

The Next Games.

To-night the Bees are travelling up to Preston, where they meet to-day's visitors in the return game on Boxing Day. Not many supporters, one supposes, will be travelling up there with them, and so it is all to the good that there is a very attractive Reserve game here on Boxing afternoon.

Chelsea always put a strong side into the field; the game should be a very interesting one as the Bees Reserves are serving up some splendidly effective football.

On Saturday, our fellow League "babes," Bolton Wanderers, pay us a visit and they'll get a very hearty welcome from the crowd indeed.

Brentford beat them 2—0 at Burnden Park in the first game of the season, but since then the Wanderers have settled down nicely in First Division football and they occupy quite a creditable position. Their visit to Griffin Park last season provided one of the most thrilling games of the year—and we can look forward to another just like that.

On New Year's Day, the first team are away to Blackburn Rovers, on the following Saturday away to Huddersfield Town and then away again for the third game in succession—this time to Leicester City in the Third Round of the F.A. Cup.

A tough programme, most people will agree.

On January 4th the Reserves are at home to Clapton Orient and this is followed by another local Derby the very next Saturday, when Fulham provide the opposition at Griffin Park.

BRENTFORD FOOTBALL AND SPORTS CLUB, LIMITED.

Registered Office :—GRIFFIN PARK, BRAEMAR ROAD, BRENTFORD.

President and Chairman :
Mr. L. P. Simon.

Mr. H. W. Dodge.
Mr. C. L. Simon.

Alderman W. Flewitt, J.P.
Mr. H. N. Blundell.
Mr. H. J. Saunders.

Vice-Chairman :
Mr. F. A. Davis.

Mr. F. W. Barton.
Alderman H. F. Davis.
Mr. J. R. Hughes, J.P., C.C.

Hon. Treasurer :
Alderman W. Flewitt, J.P.
Club Medical Officer ; Dr. A. D. Gowans.

Telephones ;
Ground : Ealing 1744.
Private House : Ealing 1183.

Secretary-Manager :
Mr. H. C. Curtis,
"Dorincourt," Boston Gardens, Brentford.

Telegraphic Address :
Curtis, Football, Brentford.
Ground ; Griffin Park, Ealing Road, Brentford.

No. 11.   Saturday, December 28th, 1935.

Notes from the Hive.

AFTER the very lean time the Bees have experienced for some little while, causing a drop into the lower places of the League table, it came as an excellent Christmas box to the supporters of the Club to find their favourites getting all four points from Preston North End. No more appropriate present could have been made to our supporters, and having now, we all hope, turned the corner, perhaps it is not too much to expect the Bees to carry on the good work in the New Year and so climb to a position free from the anxiety which has been with us all for some time now.

BEES "NAP" HAND AGAINST PRESTON

Brentford came back to their best form with a vengeance against Preston North End, at Griffin Park on Christmas morning, winning in great style by five goals to two. Goals by Holliday and Muttitt gave the Bees a two goal lead which was reduced to a single goal advantage at the interval. Five minutes after the change of ends, McCulloch scored our third goal, and our centre forward obtained a fourth after Preston had scored their second. While the score was 3—2 anything might have happened for it was only five minutes from the close when McCulloch got his second goal. Before the end, however, Scott put the issue beyond all doubt by scoring the fifth goal.

The whole Brentford team played really well and it was a delight to watch the smooth running teamwork which brought back happy memories of other days when Brentford used to carry everything before them at Griffin Park. The fact that the team had at last broken the spell had an obvious effect on the players, who showed marked confidence in all they did. Such spirit, skill and co-operation will bring a quick rise away from the foot of the League table if the Bees can only keep it up.

BAD TRANSPORT FACILITIES.

Unfortunately the attendance was not up to expectations. True there were counter-attractions at Craven Cottage and Shepherds Bush, but even so it is felt that the bad transport facilities mainly accounted for the "gate" at Griffin Park on Christmas morning being so much below anticipation. 'Bus services had been cut to a skeleton which seemed bad business on the part of the London Transport Board. Surely it is the business of this public company to cater for the needs

of the public, whether it be Christmas or any other day. It would not have required much organisation to have put a better service on the roads to enable people in the surrounding districts to get to the game and home again and Still Enable The Servants Of The Company To Have Had Their Christmas Dinner At Home With Their Families.

Football provides a big source of revenue to the respective transport services in London and they should be more considerate to the needs of the clubs at holiday times.

A "DOUBLE" AGAINST PRESTON.

"Single" wins this season have been so few and far between that to get a "double" win against any club seemed almost a prize too great to expect. Well, our boys did the trick in good style by following up their Christmas Day win against Preston by winning the return game at Deepdale by four goals to two.

The Bees again played great football and really won the game by the brilliance they showed in the first half. By the time the interval arrived, Brentford had built up a 3—1 lead and all the three goals had been scored by Idris Hopkins. It must surely be a rare feat for a wingman to perform the "hat-trick" in any one half of a First Division game. Twenty minutes from the end David McCulloch increased our lead to 4—1 and later the home side scored, to leave the Bees very good winners by four goals to two.

The whole team played well on a very heavy ground. In view of the fact that Joe Wilson, our reserve centre half, was brought into the side at right back, it is perhaps fitting to record that he played a splendid game and the writer will perhaps be pardoned for making this individual mention in this particular instance.

RESERVES' REVIEW.

Our Reserves again did well on Christmas morning in equally sharing four goals with Chelsea at Stamford Bridge, after being two goals down at one period and, furthermore were without the services of Metcalf for the last twenty minutes. He pulled a thigh muscle and is likely to be out of the game for several weeks. Dunn and McAloon scored our goals . . .

The return game with Chelsea at Griffin Park, on Boxing Day was one of the best Reserve games seen at Brentford for quite a while. The Bees won by the odd goal in three. Chelsea took the lead after twenty minutes' play, but Dunn equalised before half-time. The visitors' goal was almost bombarded during the second half, but it was not until midway through that McAloon scored what proved to be the winning goal.

BOLTON HERE TO-DAY.

The visit of Bolton Wanderers to Griffin Park to-day is particularly interesting because this Lancashire club was promoted with Brentford last season and the two clubs met in the opening game of the present campaign, when the Bees won at Burnden Park by two clear goals. Having tasted over the Christmas holiday period what it is like to gain a double win, can our boys emulate that feat at the expense of Bolton?

Bolton have secured seven points from ten away games, having won 2—1 at Villa Park and 2—1 at Stoke, while drawn games have been played at Sheffield (2—2), Huddersfield (0—0), Wolverhampton (3—3).

HERE'S THE ANNUAL WISH OF A HAPPY AND PROSPEROUS NEW YEAR TO ALL SUPPORTERS OF THE BEES.

" BUSY BEE."

Jottings from the Board Room.

A gent's scarf was found in Block "E" of Stand on Christmas morning. This can be had on application at the office.

Congratulations to those responsible for the running services of our local trams, who on Christmas Day did all in their power to assist the public to get to Griffin Park to see our game v. Preston North End; but those responsible for the 'bus service gave one the impression that the 'buses do not run for the public convenience. I have received many complaints and must say I agree with them all. It is difficult to understand such a decision to cut completely certain services on such an occasion.

Some time ago a young enthusiast sent to the Club a painted drawing of the players for same to be autographed. Unfortunately we have mislaid this young man's address. If this note catches his eye, will he write to the Club and the autographed drawing will be returned to him immediately.

Walter Metcalf pulled a thigh muscle in the Reserve game v. Chelsea Reserves at Chelsea on Christmas Day and was compelled to leave the field 20 minutes from time. The injury will keep him from playing for three or four weeks.

CUP TIE, JANUARY 11th.

A special excursion is to be run to Leicester in connection with our Cup-tie on January 11th. The train, which will be composed of corridor stock, will leave Kew Bridge Station at 10.15 a.m., calling only at South Acton and Acton Central, and is due to arrive Leicester 12.45 p.m. Fare for the return journey, 5/6. A restaurant car will be run on the train and meals will be served in each direction at the rate of 2/6 per meal. For the convenience of our supporters who wish to take advantage of this trip, it is requested that tickets be purchased in advance in order that adequate arrangements may be made. They can be obtained from the Secretary's Office here or from Messrs. Thos. Cook and Son, Ltd., Berkeley Street, W.1.

The prices of admission for our Cup-tie v. Leicester City will be as follows: Admission to Ground, 1/-; Enclosure, 1/6 and 2/-; Stand Seats (unreserved), 2/6, and Numbered and Reserved Seats at 3/6 and 5/-, which can be obtained from this office. There are only a limited number.

The Reserves are away to-day to Charlton Reserves, who on Christmas Day defeated Portsmouth Reserves by 4 goals to 1.

Arthur Bateman will be leaving the Brentford Hospital this week-end. His progress is very satisfactory.

The League Team are away to Blackburn Rovers on New Year's Day, January 1st, 1936.

Comparative results with last season are as follows:—

Football League—	P.	W.	L.	D.	Goals F.	A.	P.
This season... ...	21	6	11	4	34	40	16
Last Season... ...	21	13	3	5	53	26	31
London Combination—							
This Season... ...	24	18	4	2	53	26	38
Last Season... ...	24	12	6	6	40	28	30

Goal scorers to date are:—

Football League: Hopkins 9, Holliday 7, McCulloch 4, Fletcher 4, Scott 4, Robson 3, Dunn 1, J. C. Burns 1, Muttitt 1—Total 34.

London Combination: Dunn, 18, Brown 11, McAloon 6, Muttitt 5, Sullivan 5, Gibbons 3, Fenton 2, Smith (C.) 2, L. Smith 1—Total 53.

The Management on behalf of the Directors and Players desire to extend a special welcome to our visitors of to-day—Bolton Wanderers. It will be remembered that last season both teams gained promotion to Division I., and strangely enough were drawn to play each other in the opening game of this season. The Directors of our visitors took the opportunity of inviting our Players and Directors to dinner with their Players and Officials after the game to commemorate the occasion, and gave us a real good time, and without doubt proved that the Bolton Wanderers have a Board of Directors of splendid sportsmen, and we do with all sincerity offer them a very hearty welcome. We cannot wish them success to-day, but after we do hope they get all the success they so richly deserve.

1936.

On behalf of the Directors, Players and Management I wish all our supporters a very happy and prosperous New Year. May you all have the best of good luck during 1936, but chiefly may you all enjoy the BEST OF GOOD HEALTH.

H.C.C.

Shots from the Spot.

By "Rambler"

Well, if you have not had a happy Christmas, you can't blame the Brentford Football Club for it.

* * *

My pessimism about the fog proved unjustified, and a bright sun shone on the faces of our contented spectators as they left the ground on Christmas morning, on their way to the turkeys that they could face with a new zest.

* * *

The Bees' first double in First Division football has been completed in sensational style at the expense of Preston North End who, it will be remembered, gained promotion from the Second Division in the Bees' first season there.

* * *

We still have a long and arduous path ahead of us. Directors, Management and players all appreciate that, but also they all feel that the holiday games must have silenced the more bitter and impetuous critics who have been putting their vitriolic pens to paper during the last few weeks with more than usual freedom.

* * *

No one who saw the two games against Preston could fail to be impressed by the new spirit of confidence that characterised the Bees' play, and that, we feel, is chiefly what has been lacking in the past few weeks.

* * *

The next few weeks are going to be tough ones for the Bees. Three away games in succession and the last one a cup-tie! Not easy going by a long chalk.

* * *

The West Bromwich game is past history now, but one comment is worth repeating. After Jim McMullan had sat watching both sides trying hard to keep upright on a ground like a skating rink, he said : " Few spectators have any idea what it means to be out there on such a day. You feel utterly helpless."

* * *

That's a point for the fan to remember when the ground is frozen. It may be easy enough for him to stand up and shout—it's not so easy for a player to stand up and play.

* * *

The sorting-out of the clubs at this stage of the season is always interesting. There are remarkably few points separating the clubs in the middle of the table from those at the foot. A slip or a sprint— however slight—might make a big difference to the position of a club.

* * *

Did you know, by the way, that it is illegal, according to a law passed ages ago and which has not yet been repealed, to play football on Christmas Day? Skating and billiards, too, are crimes on that particular day and arrests can be made of those participating in them. We need not take this too seriously, of course, but a repeal of the laws in question would be, surely, merely a matter of common sense..

OUR VISITORS TO-DAY.
HOW THEY MAY LINE UP.

———————◆———————

A disagreement with a vicar really started Bolton Wanderers on their career as a first-class club. Originally they were a Sunday school organisation, but following the disagreement this was disbanded and the club as it is now known came into being.

In 1888 they were one of the original clubs that formed the League. They have since been relegated five times, but on three occasions they have won back to the top section at the first attempt and their last spell in the Second Division, from which they returned together with the Bees this year, lasted only two seasons.

The result of the corresponding game last season was Brentford 1, Bolton Wanderers 0.

Holliday got the Bees' point on that occasion. Earlier this season the Bees beat Bolton at Burnden Park by two clear goals.

Since the war, the Wanderers have appeared at Wembley three times and won the Cup on each occasion.

Jones, Robert (goalkeeper).— Born at Liverpool. Height 6ft. 0½in. Weight, 11st. About the unluckiest 'keeper in the game. Started his first-class career with Southport. While playing with them had to turn out in a match with two broken fingers in splints. Moved to Bolton, October, 1929. Soon afterwards received a kick on the back which paralysed his legs for six weeks. Recovered to be put out again by appendicitis. Last season damaged his shoulder. Has so far this season escaped mishap.

Finney, Alexander (full back). —Born at St. Helen's, Lancs. Height 5ft. 8¾in. Weight 11st. 11lb. Captain of the side. Starting with St. Helen's and New Brighton, he joined Bolton in 1922. Played in the Cup-winning side of 1923-29. Is the only survivor of the club's first Wembley Cup-winning team. Formerly a barber's lather boy and then a miner. Very stylish.

Connor, John (full back).—Born at Mossley. Height 5ft. 9in. Weight 11st. Was playing for home town team in the Cheshire League, at the beginning of 1934-35 season. Had experience with Bolton Reserve eleven, and deputised for Finney in two F.A. Cup-ties with marked success.

Goslin, Harry (right half).—Born at Willington, Co. Durham. Height 5ft. 11¼in. Weight 11st. Was brought up at Nottingham and came into prominence with Boots' factory side, after having previous experience with the local Boys' Brigade side. Joined Bolton in April, 1930. Is a versatile fellow and has appeared at full back and inside forward as well as all three half-back positions.

Atkinson, J. E. (centre half).— Born at New Washington, Co. Durham. Height 6ft. 0½in. Weight 11st. 5½lb. Was spotted while with Washington Colliery. In order to speed him up was allowed to stay with that club, playing as a forward, after Bolton had signed him. Had his first team chance in 1932-3 after Tom Griffiths had gone to Middlesbrough. Feeds his forwards well and is strong in defence, though not a third-back.

Taylor, George (left half).—Born at Ashton-under-Lyne, Lancs. Height 5ft. 6¾in. Weight 10st. 5lb. Captained England's schoolboys against Scotland in 1924, and was

BRENTFORD *v.*

BRE
Red

1—

2—WILSON
Right Back

4—McKENZIE   5
Right Half   C

7—HOPKINS   8—SCOTT   9—Mc
Outside Right   Inside Right   Cen

Referee— Mr. J. MILLWARD (Derby)

1

12—COOK   13—WESTWOO
Outside Left   Inside Left

17—TAYLOR (G.)   18—
Left Half   C

20—CONNOR
Left Back

22

BOLTON
White

THE LEAGUE—DIVISION I.

	P.	W.	D.	L.	F.	A.	P.
					Goals		
Sunderland	21	15	2	4	63	31	32
Huddersfield T.	21	11	5	5	33	28	27
Arsenal	21	10	6	5	46	20	26
Derby County	22	10	6	6	30	22	26
Stoke City	22	11	3	8	34	30	25
Liverpool	22	10	4	8	40	30	24
Birmingham	22	9	6	7	34	33	24
Wolves	22	9	4	9	49	43	22
Manchester C.	20	9	3	8	35	30	21
Portsmouth	20	8	5	7	29	31	21
Chelsea	21	8	5	8	30	38	21
Middlesbrough	21	8	4	9	49	36	20
West Brom. A.	21	9	2	10	41	38	20
Leeds U.	21	6	8	7	31	31	20
Bolton W.	20	7	6	7	32	40	20
Preston N.E.	22	8	3	11	31	38	19
Blackburn R.	21	8	2	11	34	50	18
Sheffield Wed.	21	6	5	10	34	44	17
Grimsby T.	21	8	1	12	30	41	17
BRENTFORD	21	6	4	11	34	40	16
Everton	21	6	4	11	35	49	16
Aston Villa	22	5	4	13	38	69	14

ON WANDERERS

RD
ripes
SON

3—POYSER
Left Back

6—RICHARDS
Left Half

H 10—HOLLIDAY   11—MUTTITT
Inside Left   Outside Left

Linesmen—   Messrs. G. V. Searle (blue flag),
and S. E. Bragg (red flag)

OM
ward

5—EASTHAM 16—TAYLOR (G. T.)
Inside Right   Outside Right

19—GOSLIN
Right Half

21—FINNEY
Right Back

S

DERERS
nickers

LONDON COMBINATION.

	P.	W.	D.	L.	F.	A.	P.
BRENTFORD ...	24	18	2	4	53	25	38
Portsmouth	22	14	6	2	63	27	34
Swansea	24	15	3	6	43	32	33
Arsenal	23	16	1	6	60	24	33
Crystal Palace	26	13	5	8	57	52	31
Q.P.R.	25	13	3	9	48	39	29
Chelsea	24	11	6	7	51	45	28
West Ham	25	12	4	9	56	37	28
Luton Town	25	12	3	10	71	58	27
Charlton	24	11	3	10	47	40	25
Millwall	22	11	3	8	34	30	25
Reading	22	10	2	10	49	54	22
Coventry	22	10	1	11	46	37	21
Southend	23	7	5	11	39	54	19
Northampton	22	8	3	11	47	45	19
Watford	23	8	3	12	47	57	19
Southampton	25	6	6	13	34	46	18
'Spurs	21	7	4	10	56	50	18
Fulham	23	7	3	13	49	47	17
Leicester	23	8	1	14	40	56	17
Clapton Orient	22	5	7	10	25	50	17
Bournemouth	24	5	5	14	36	62	15
Bristol City	25	6	2	17	35	81	14
Brighton & H.A. ...	22	4	5	13	31	60	13

taken up by Bolton soon afterwards. Was carefully "nursed" and signed professional as soon as he was of age. Formerly an inside or outside left. Is a hard worker with plenty of tricks.

Taylor, George T. (outside right). —Born at Walsall. Height 5ft. 6¾in. Weight 10st. 12lb. Also a schoolboy international. Gained two caps in 1921. Played with Talbot Stead, Walsall Wood, Bloxwich Strollers and Stourbridge (Birmingham League). Started his first class career with Notts County in 1925, and after playing in close on 300 senior games for them he joined Bolton two years ago. Has been a "regular" ever since.

Eastham, George (inside right). —Born at Blackpool. Height 5ft. 7¾in. Weight, 9st. 9lb. A delightful player whose one failing is that he is inclined to overdo the dainty stuff. Arsenal were rumoured to have offered many thousands for him last season. Was spotted by Bolton while with Cambridge Juniors, a Fylde club, in 1932. Formerly in a baker's shop.

Milsom, John (centre forward).— Born at Bristol. Height 5ft. 11¼in. Weight 10st. 10lb. Had an unsuccessful trial with Exeter City when a junior. Then had a season as a professional with Bristol Rovers. Did not get a League game and went on to Kettering Tn. Rochdale took him back to the League game in 1928, and the following year Bolton secured his transfer. A dashing player who needs constant watching.

Westwood, Raymond (inside left). Born at Brierley Hill, nr. Birmingham. Height 5ft. 6½in. Weight 10st. 3lb. Played for his school team at 9, was captain at 11, in Stourbridge Reserves at 14, with Brierley Hill Alliance (Birmingham League) at 15, and a Bolton Wanderers' amateur at 16. Got his first England cap in September last year and has added several to it since.

Cook, William L. (outside left).— Born at Dundee. Height 5ft. 3¾in. Weight, 9st. 6¼lb. Little but good. Knows all the "tricks of the trade" and is a most elusive fellow. Experience with Dundee North End and Forfar Athletic preceded his coming into prominence with Dundee. Joined Bolton seven years ago. Plays on either wing and has been capped for Scotland as an outside right.

HANWELL BAND'S SUCCESS.

As a result of winning the recent East Ham Band Contest our Hanwell Silver Band has been engaged for a further Broadcast to be given on January 19th next, and also for a stage performance at a West End theatre. This latter is to be given at the Prince of Wales Theatre, Coventry Street, on Sunday, December 29th, in connection with the popular Non-Stop Variety shows which are having such a successful run at this theatre. The Hanwell Band will welcome Brentford patrons on this occasion, which is the first time a London brass band has appeared on a West End theatre stage.

Mr. Arthur East and Master Bravington, of Hanwell Band, have recently won the Senior and Junior Championships of the London Association for solo playing.

SHARES & SHAREHOLDERS

In spite of our previous notes in this programme, the Management are still receiving enquiries from supporters who are desiring to acquire shares in the Club. We repeat that the shares of the Club are fully issued, and unless existing shareholders desire to realise, there are no shares available.

The 6% Debentures of £50 each are still being issued, but only a small number now remain, and when these have been issued the finances of the Club will have been completely consolidated and settled

The Club have been the leaseholders of Griffin Park, and supporters will be interested to know that next March the freehold of the ground is being purchased and the Club will then be in the happy position of being the owners of the ground.

Particulars of the 6% Debentures will be forwarded on application to the Secretary.

Shareholders desiring to realise their share-holdings should advise the Secretary, together with a note of the price they are willing to accept.

BILLIE SCOTT
Inside Left or Right.

Born at Willington Quay, Northumberland, Billie is a member of what has become known as " the Middlesbrough contingent." When with that club he made 24 appearances in First Division games. Came to Brentford in 1932-33 season. He got five goals against Barnsley last season. A 90-minute man who never knows when he or his side is beaten. Roams—but with a method and a purpose.

FIXTURES, SEASON 1935-36.

FIRST TEAM

Date. 1935.	Opponents.	Ground.	GOALS F.	A.
Aug. 31	Bolton Wanderers	A	2	0
Sept. 5	Blackburn Rovers	H	3	1
,, 7	Huddersfield Town	H	1	2
,, 14	Middlesbrough	A	0	0
,, 18	Derby County	A	1	2
,, 21	Aston Villa	H	1	2
,, 28	Wolverhampton Wdrs.	A	2	3
Oct. 5	Sheffield Wednesday	H	2	2
,, 12	Portsmouth	A	3	1
,, 19	Stoke City	H	0	0
,, 26	Manchester City	A	2	1
Nov. 2	Arsenal	H	1	2
,, 9	Birmingham	A	1	2
,, 16	Sunderland	H	1	5
,, 23	Chelsea	A	1	2
,, 30	Leeds United	H	2	2
Dec. 7	Grimsby Town	A	1	6
,, 14	Liverpool	H	1	2
,, 21	West Bromwich Albion	A	0	1
,, 25	Preston North End	H	5	2
,, 26	Preston North End	A	4	2
,, 28	Bolton Wanderers	H		
1936.				
Jan. 1	Blackburn Rovers	A		
,, 4	Huddersfield Town	A		
,, 11	(3)			
,, 18	Middlesbrough	H		
,, 25	(4) Aston Villa	A		
Feb. 1	Wolverhampton Wdrs.	H		
,, 8	Sheffield Wednesday	A		
,, 15	(5) Portsmouth	H		
,, 22	Stoke City	A		
,, 29	(6) Manchester City	H		
Mar. 7	Arsenal	A		
,, 14	(S.-F.) Birmingham	H		
,, 21	Sunderland	A		
,, 28	Chelsea	H		
April 4	Leeds United	A		
,, 10	Everton	A		
,, 11	Grimsby Town	H		
,, 13	Everton	H		
,, 18	Liverpool	A		
,, 25	(F.) West Brom. Alb.	H		
May 2	Derby County	H		

SECOND TEAM

Date. 1935.	Opponents.	Ground.	GOALS F.	A.
Aug. 31	Charlton Athletic	H	2	1
Sept. 4	Watford	A	1	3
,, 7	Clapton Orient	A	0	0
,, 12	Watford	H	2	1
,, 14	Southend United	H	1	0
,, 21	Northampton Town	A	1	0
,, 25	Luton Town	A	1	4
,, 28	Crystal Palace	H	4	0
Oct. 3	Luton Town	H	4	3
,, 5	Reading	A	1	2
,, 7	Met. Police—L.C. Cup	H	2	0
,, 9	Bournemouth & Bos. .	H	5	2
,, 12	Tottenham Hotspur	H	2	1
,, 19	Bristol City	A	3	1
,, 21	C. Orient—L.C. Cup .	H	3	1
,, 26	Millwall	A	4	0
Nov. 2	West Ham United	A	1	0
,, 9	Swansea Town	A	2	0
,, 11	Fulham (L.C.Cup, S.F.)	H	2	0
,, 16	Leicester City	A	3	2
,, 23	Coventry City	A	4	1
,, 30	Arsenal	A	0	1
Dec. 7	Southampton	H	4	0
,, 14	Brighton & Hove A.	A	1	0
,, 21	Queen's Park Rgrs. .	A	3	1
,, 25	Chelsea	A	2	2
,, 26	Chelsea	H	2	1
,, 28	Charlton Athletic	H		
Jan. 4	Clapton Orient	H		
,, 11	Fulham	A		
,, 18	Southend United	H		
,, 25	Northampton Town	H		
Feb. 1	Crystal Palace	H		
,, 8	Reading	H		
,, 15	Tottenham Hotspur	A		
,, 22	Bristol City	H		
,, 29	Millwall	H		
Mar. 7	West Ham United	H		
,, 14	Swansea Town	H		
,, 21	Leicester City	H		
,, 25	Bournemouth & Bos. .	A		
,, 28	Coventry City	A		
April 4	Arsenal	H		
,, 10	Portsmouth	H		
,, 11	Southampton	A		
,, 13	Portsmouth	A		
,, 18	Brighton & Hove A.	A		
,, 25	Queen's Park Rgrs. .	A		
May 2	Fulham	A		

Half Time Scores.

	F.	A.			F	A
A—Birmingham v. Wolves	......	......	J—Sunderland v. Arsenal		......	......
B—Derby County v. Everton	......	......	K—W. Bromwich v. Man. C.		......	......
C—Grimsby v. Blackburn	......	......	L—Burnley v. Charlton		......	......
D—Leeds v. Stoke	......	......	M—Fulham v. Hull City		......	......
E—Liverpool v. Chelsea	......	......	N—'Spurs v. Bradford C.		......	......
F—Portsmouth v. Middlesboro'	......	......	O—West Ham v. Norwich		......	......
G—P.N.E. v. Huddersfield	......	......	P—Cardiff v. Crystal Palace		......	......
H—Shef. Wed. v. Aston Villa	......	......	R—Millwall v. Q.P.R.		......	......

WHAT NEXT?

" Steady, oh Master of Destiny, this is already approaching the giddy limit!"

The Next Games.

After to-day's game, the Bees' first team are away for three successive matches.

On New Year's Day they travel up to Blackburn to meet the Rovers who are not very far ahead of the Bees.

On the following Saturday the Bees travel again, their venue this time being the Leeds Road ground where Huddersfield Town are the hosts. The Town were rather lucky 2—1 winners down here in September, and the Bees will be out for revenge.

Then comes the Cup—and whilst Fate might have been kinder than to have drawn us against Leicester City away from home, we have at least the consolation of knowing that the journey is an easy one. Consequently we hope that many of our supporters will be at the City's ground to give the boys a cheer.

To-day the Reserves are away at Charlton, carrying on a series of local "derbies" with which they are now engaged.

On January 4th they are at home to Clapton Orient and the following week they entertain Fulham.

The next First Division game on the ground is against Middlesbrough—and that will be worth seeing. When the teams met earlier in the season there was a fierce but goalless draw. The return is fixed for January 18th.

BRENTFORD FOOTBALL AND SPORTS CLUB, LIMITED.

Registered Office :—GRIFFIN PARK, BRAEMAR ROAD, BRENTFORD.

President and Chairman :
MR. L. P. SIMON.

ALDERMAN W. FLEWITT, J.P.
MR. H. N. BLUNDELL.
MR. H. J. SAUNDERS.

MR. H. W. DODGE.
MR. C. L. SIMON.

Vice-Chairman:
MR. F. A. DAVIS.

MR. F. W. BARTON.
ALDERMAN H. F. DAVIS.
MR. J. R. HUGHES, J.P., C.C.

Hon. Treasurer:
ALDERMAN W. FLEWITT, J.P.
Club Medical Officer; DR. A. D. GOWANS.

Telephones:
GROUND : EALING 1744.
PRIVATE HOUSE : EALING 1183.

Secretary-Manager;
MR. H. C. CURTIS,
" DORINCOURT," BOSTON GARDENS, BRENTFORD.

Telegraphic Address:
CURTIS, FOOTBALL, BRENTFORD.
Ground; GRIFFIN PARK, EALING ROAD, BRENTFORD.

No. 12.   Saturday, January 18th, 1936.

Notes from the Hive.

A MIXED GRILL.

Recent happenings as far as the Bees are concerned resemble very much a " mixed grill," for the last three League games have resulted in one victory, one defeat and one drawn game. The " sweets " to follow were not so palatable—defeat in the F.A. Cup never is !

FINE WIN OVER BOLTON.

The visit of Bolton Wanderers to Griffin Park on the last Saturday of the old year was made all the more attractive by the fact that we had the honour and pleasure of being promoted along with the Wanderers, at the close of last season. Bolton had been in the Top Class before, but it was our first venture into the land of our dreams. Curiously enough the opening game of the present season saw Brentford and Bolton in opposition at Burnden Park. That day Brentford commenced their career in a new sphere in great style by winning two goals to nil.

The return game gave our boys the chance of concluding the Old Year in similar style, to which they had started it by again beating the Wanderers, and thus recording their second " double " since becoming members of the First Division—Preston North End providing the Bees with their first " double " of the season during the Christmas holiday games.

Well, the Bees accomplished the trick in great style against Bolton, winning by a margin of four clear goals, which left no doubt as to the merit of our boys' success.

Brentford were a " new " team compared with the form they had been showing for some time, and undoubtedly gained much confidence—just the thing needed—from the success attained in the holiday games.

David McCulloch was in a pretty deadly form from a penetrative viewpoint. The other forwards did a lot of good foraging and then Dave obliged by finishing off the good play by getting three goals. McKenzie got the other goal to complete a convincing success.

BEATEN AT BLACKBURN.

Brentford finished the Old Year in great style, but did not start 1936 too well, for on New Year's Day our boys were beaten at Blackburn by the only goal of the game. As the narrowness of the defeat might imply it was a very close and hard game. Candidly, on the play, Brentford earned a division of points and seemed certain to save the game more than once during the latter stages.

NOTES FROM THE HIVE—Continued.

DIVISION AT HUDDERSFIELD

A very valuable point was collected at Huddersfield which came in part consolation for an early season defeat inflicted by the Yorkshire club on the Bees at Griffin Park.

Huddersfield are a stiff proposition on their own ground and their strength before their own supporters can in some measure be gauged by the fact that prior to our visit only three goals had been conceded in ten home games by this famous Yorkshire club. Brentford had the honour of being the first club to score two goals at Huddersfield this season.

BEES NOT FOR WEMBLEY.

Brentford will not figure in this season's Cup Final at Wembley. A little affair at Leicester on Saturday last cut short the aspirations of our team, for the Bees took the count at the first hurdle.

Mid-way through the first half the home side got a very good goal and that proved to be the only tangible success which came to either side and so enabled Leicester City to pass on and the Bees to pass out. A large contingent of Brentford supporters went up to Leicester to cheer their favourites on and there must have been almost universal agreement that Brentford were good value for a replay after the second half display. In the second half our boys enjoyed much more of the play, but the much-looked-for goal to save the game would not come.

It may seem poor consolation, but the fact that we are out of the Cup will at least leave our attention undivided and perhaps give our boys a better chance of retaining our First Division status.

RESERVES' REVIEW.

A rather unexpected reverse was sustained against Charlton Athletic at the Valley, where the home side won by three goals to one. The Bees played well in this game and were unlucky in striking the framework of the goal on more than one occasion. McAloon scored our goal. Next followed a big win, five goals to one, against Clapton Orient at Griffin Park. Dunn (3), Gibbons and McAloon were responsible for our " nap " hand in this game.

On Saturday last Fulham Reserves were well beaten by four clear goals at Griffin Park. Sullivan (2), McAloon and Gibbons were the scorers.

MIDDLESBROUGH HERE TO-DAY.

We shall all be specially pleased to welcome Middlesbrough to Griffin Park to-day, because it was from the Ayresome Park Club we secured the transfers of five players —Watson, Scott, Holliday, Mathieson and Muttitt—who in no small way have helped along the advancement of the Bees from the Third to First Division of the Football League.

No doubt those former Middlesbrough players who are figuring in our team to-day will be particularly keen to shine against their old club and in view of the fact that our visitors have not a very imposing away record this season, we are hopeful that the Bees will collect the full spoils at stake. Brentford played a goalless draw at Ayresome Park early in the season and with ground advantage and an improved team something better will be expected to-day.

To date Middlesbrough have only gained five points from eleven away games. Their two away successes were rather amazing performances before the season was a fortnight old. They won 5—0 at Preston and in the following game chalked up a 7—2 win at Villa Park. The other point was secured at Bolton, where six goals were equally divided.

" BUSY BEE."

Jottings from the Board Room.

Arthur Bateman has now left the hospital, having made splendid progress. He resumed light training during the past week, and should be fit to play again within a month.

Comparative records with last season are as follows :
Football League—

	P.	W.	L.	D.	F.	A.	P.
This Season	24	7	12	5	40	43	19
Last Season	24	14	4	6	58	29	34

London Combination—

	P.	W.	L.	D.	F.	A.	P.
This Season	27	20	5	2	63	30	42
Last Season	27	14	7	6	46	31	34

Goal scorers to date are :—
Football League : Hopkins 9, McCulloch 8, Holliday 7, Fletcher 5, Scott 4, Robson 3, Dunn 1, J. C. Burns 1, Muttitt 1, McKenzie 1.—Total 40.
London Combination : Dunn 21, Brown 11, McAloon 9, Sullivan 7, Muttitt 5, Gibbons 5, Fenton 2, Smith (C.) 2, L. Smith 1.—Total 63.

The Reserves are to-day away to Southend Reserves (London Combination).

Some time ago a young enthusiast sent to the Club a painted drawing of the players for same to be autographed. Unfortunately we have mislaid this young man's address. If this note catches his eye, will he write to the Club and the autographed drawing will be returned to him immediately .

On Sunday, February 16th, 1936, a Grand Concert will be held at the Chiswick Empire in aid of the funds of the Brentford Philanthropic Society. Numbered and reserved seats are 5/-, 3/6 and 2/6 (including tax). Un-reserved seats 1/- (including tax). Tickets can be purchased at this Club's Office or at the Chiswick Empire, or from Mr. L. R.

Winter, of 84, Albany Road, Brentford, and also from any member of the Society.

The following artistes will form the all-star programme : Naughton and Gold, Jose Fearson and Robert Naylor, Murray and Mooney (of Command Performance fame), Mamie Soutar, Mario De Pietro, Freddy Bamberger, Esther Coleman, Tom Lynch, Charles Forwood and Danny Walters and His Band. Book your seats early to prevent disappointment.

Telegrams of good wishes for success were received at Leicester on Saturday last from old favourites in Patsy Hendren, George Robson, Harry Rae and Billy Lane.

To-day we offer a very sincere welcome to Bobby Reid, whose transfer was obtained on Thursday night from the Hamilton Academical F.C., and we wish him a very happy and successful time at Brentford. Bob is only 23 years of age and has been honoured by the Scottish League by his selection on the last three occasions to assist them in the international inter-league games.

Heartiest congratulations to our two players, Dai Hopkins and Dai Richards who have both again been honoured by their selection to play for Wales in the International game v. England at Wolverhampton, on Wednesday, February 5th. We also wish them the best of good luck personally, although cannot wish them such success against England.

A half-day excursion in connection with our game against Aston Villa, on January 25th, is being run from Paddington. Tickets at 6/6 are available on the 11.5 a.m. train, returning at 6 p.m. or 7.50 p.m., and can be purchased at Paddington on the day.

Shots from the Spot.

By "Rambler"

It seems a long time since I last had the pleasure of writing this page for you. There have, in fact, been three away games in succession. The Cup, as far as Brentford is concerned, is no longer of any importance, and we can settle down to the important task of getting away and keeping away from the danger zone at the foot of the table.

* * *

There are also certain defeats, revenge for which would be sweet indeed, and with our players keeping up the form they displayed over Christmas, we can feel confident that some useful points will be coming our way.

* * *

To-day Middlesbrough are our guests. The goalless draw at Ayresome Park earlier in the season was one of the most hectic struggles we have yet had to face —and that's saying something! The circumstances of the game brought something extra out of each team—and it may well do so to-day.

* * *

Naturally, our early exit from the Cup—the third 1—0 third round defeat in three years—is disappointing, but at least the huge crowd of spectators who made the journey up saw an exciting and typical Cup-tie, with 90 minutes' keen and vigorous play on each side.

* * *

There was a rather amusing incident on the return journey. The train was not, to put it mildly, exactly an express over the last few miles. It did in fact, stop for what seemed ages, time after time. In the coach in which I was sitting there was a deal of good-humoured comment during what seemed a particularly long wait. The train seemed to have given up all idea of moving—and eventually the appearance of a guard explained this occurrence. We had been in Kew Station for over five minutes without realising it and the rest of the train was deserted!

* * *

The Reserves look like making a fine effort to hold on to their lead of the London Combination. There are youngsters in that forward line that I can see developing in time into big names in the football world and who are already well worth watching. The loyal fans who turn up to these games week after week evidently think so too.

* * *

An interesting personality in the Fulham Reserves side last Saturday was young M. Edelstone, son of J. Edelstone, the club's well-known assistant manager-coach. Evidently his father's knowledge of the game has been handed on to his son, for he gave a promising display.

* * *

It is an interesting point that Aston Villa—whom we meet at Villa Park next week—have, in their anxiety to get away from the relegation places, spent money equal to about £1,000 per game for the whole season.

OUR VISITORS TO-DAY.
HOW THEY MAY LINE UP.

Middlesbrough's career since they were founded in 1892 has been a rather variable one with many trials. This season they promised very well at the start, but have failed to keep up their early good form.

All their distinctions of note have been won in Second Division circles. They were champions in 1927 and 1929 and runners-up in 1902.

They created a record for the period when they paid Sunderland £1,000 for Alf Common.

Last term they narrowly avoided relegation, finishing only one point above Leicester City. They play clever, attractive football, however, and should prove attractive visitors.

Gibson, Frederick (goalkeeper). —Born at Summercoats, Yorkshire. Height 6ft. 1in. Weight 13st. 7lb. Had experience with Dinnington Colliery and Denaby United before entering League football with Hull City. After helping the latter club reach the Cup semi-final in 1930, he moved to Middlesbrough in 1932. After being deposed by Hillier for part of last season he has re-established himself.

Brown, William (right back)— Born at West Stanley, Co. Durham. Height 5ft. 10in. Weight 11st. 4lb. Went full back in team reshuffles due to injuries and when the club were hard pressed for a right back this season, he stepped into the breach. Joined 'Boro from West Stanley (North-Eastern League) in 1929 as a junior. Has been a regular with the senior side in the last few seasons, when he played on both flanks of the middle line.

Stuart, Robert William (left back) —Born at Middlesbrough. Height 5ft. 9in. Weight 11st. 4lb. Played for English schoolboys against Wales and Scotland in 1928. Was "nursed" by South Bank, the Northern League club, and joined Middlesbrough in 1931. At the age of 19, in season 1932-3, he became

a regular First Division player. Leg injury kept him out of the Cup match last week.

Parkin, Raymond (right half).— Born Crook, Co. Durham. Height 5ft. 11in. Weight 12st. Recently secured from the Arsenal, for whom he played at Griffin Park earlier in the season. Played for the famous London side at the age of 17, and has six London Combination medals. Is good at golf and tennis.

Baxter, Robert Denholme (centre half).—Born at Edinburgh. Height 5ft. 10in. Weight 11st. "Versatility" should be his middle name. Was signed as an outside left. Became an inside forward, but injuries caused him to be swopped from one position to another. Revealed equal aptitude for full back, half back or forward berths. Settled down at centre half at the beginning of this season, deposing Tom Griffiths, now of Villa.

Forrest, William (left half).— Born at Glasgow. Height 5ft. 9in. Weight 11st. 6lb. Developed in Scottish junior football with Tranent. Then had experience in Division II. of the Scottish League. Joined Middlesbrough in 1929. Like Martin, is a fine supporter of his forwards. Used to work in the pit.

BRENTFORD *v.*

BREN

Red an

1—M

2—WILSON
Right Back

4—McKENZIE   5—
Right Half   Cen

7—HOPKINS   8—SCOTT   9—McC
Outside Right Inside Right   Centre

Referee—   Mr. G. HEWITT

14
C

12—CUNLIFFE   13—FENTON
Outside Left   Inside Left

17—FORREST   18—
Left Half   Ce

20—STUART
Left Back

22—
G

MIDDLE
Red Shirts, Whi

THE LEAGUE—DIVISION I.

	P.	W.	D.	L.	Goals F.	A.	P
Sunderland	24	17	2	5	70	38	36
Derby County	24	11	7	6	35	25	29
Huddersfield T.	23	11	6	6	35	34	28
Arsenal	23	10	7	6	51	26	27
Stoke City	24	12	3	9	38	36	27
Birmingham	24	9	8	7	35	34	26
Liverpool	24	10	5	9	42	33	25
Wolverhampton	24	10	5	9	51	44	25
Middlesbrough	24	10	4	10	54	38	24
Leeds United	23	8	8	7	38	32	24
Portsmouth	23	9	5	9	32	39	23
Chelsea	23	9	5	9	33	42	23
West Bromwich A.	24	10	2	12	49	45	22
Grimsby Town	24	10	2	12	36	42	22
Bolton Wanderers	23	8	6	9	36	46	22
Manchester City	23	9	3	11	36	39	21
Preston North End	24	9	3	12	35	40	21
Blackburn Rovers	24	9	3	12	36	54	21
BRENTFORD	**24**	**7**	**5**	**12**	**40**	**43**	**19**
Sheffield Wed.	23	7	5	11	40	48	19
Everton	23	6	6	11	38	52	18
Aston Villa	25	7	4	14	47	77	18

...IDDLESBROUGH

...FORD
Stripes

...ESON
...per

3—POYSER
Left Back

...ES   6—RICHARDS
...lf   Left Half

...OCH 10—HOLLIDAY   11—REID
...rd   Inside Left   Outside Left

Linesmen—   Messrs. C. F. Ward (blue flag),
             and R. V. Pegg (red flag).

...MSELL
...orward

15—YORSTON   16—BIRKETT
   Inside Right   Outside Right

...TER   19—PARKIN
...alf   Right Half

         21—BROWN
          Right Back

...SON
...per

...ROUGH
, White Knickers

LONDON COMBINATION

	P.	W.	D.	L.	F.	A.	P
BRENTFORD ...	27	20	2	5	63	30	42
Portsmouth	25	16	7	2	69	30	39
Arsenal	26	18	2	6	67	25	38
Swansea Town	28	16	5	7	49	38	37
Queen's Park Rgrs.	28	15	3	10	57	43	33
Crystal Palace	29	13	6	10	63	61	32
Charlton Ath.	27	14	3	10	55	43	31
Chelsea	27	12	7	8	57	49	31
West Ham Utd. ...	28	13	4	11	63	47	30
Luton Town	27	13	3	11	73	62	29
Reading	25	12	3	10	58	57	27
Millwall	25	11	4	10	35	36	26
Coventry City	25	11	2	12	50	41	24
Tottenham H.	24	8	6	10	64	57	22
Northampton	25	8	5	12	47	47	21
Southend United ...	25	7	6	12	43	61	20
Bristol City	28	9	2	17	43	86	20
Fulham	26	8	3	15	55	55	19
Southampton	27	6	7	14	37	52	19
Leicester City	25	9	1	15	44	60	19
Watford	26	8	3	15	51	77	19
Clapton Orient ...	25	6	7	12	28	60	19
Bournemouth	27	6	6	15	40	66	18
Brighton & Hove A.	25	5	5	15	37	66	15

3

famous grounds entirely re-constructed by

The Arsenal Arena, entirely reconstructed in six weeks.

The White City Arena, entirely reconstructed in six weeks.

The West Ham Stadium Dog Track.

Birkett, Ralph (outside right).—Born at Torquay. Height 5ft. 9in. Weight 11st. 9lb. Was at school at Ashford, Middlesex, where many Brentford fans live. Returned to his native Devonshire where he was employed as a clerk and played for Dartmouth United. Joined Torquay United as soon as he was old enough to turn professional. Moved to Arsenal in 1933, and on to Middlesbrough last season. Has never looked back since going to Ayresome and is now an England player. Very fast.

Yorston, Benjamin (inside right) —Born at Aberdeen. Height 5ft. 4in. Weight 9st. 12lb. Has succeeded despite his lack of inches. Is elusive and sturdy with a powerful shot. Played with Nugiemoss and Montrose before going to Aberdeen, with whom he entered the first-class game in 1927. Sunderland paid well for his transfer in 1932, but he did not settle down and moved to Ayresome in March, 1934. Can also play centre forward.

Camsell, George (centre forward) —Born at Framwellgate Moor, Co. Durham. Height 5ft. 9in. Weight 11st. Went to Middlesbrough from Durham City in October, 1925, and soon became the goalkeepers' terror. In season 1926-7 he set up a League record with 59 goals in 37 matches. This has since been beaten by one goal by "Dixie" Dean, but still stands as a Division II. record. Camsell first played for England in season 1928-9 and after a spell of obscurity he is still an England player this term.

Fenton, M. (inside left).—This young player was one of the discoveries of Mr. Peter McWilliam when he was manager at Ayresome. He had his first runs with the League side in 1934 and last season played in exactly half the First Division matches. Can play in various half back positions or at wing half.

Cunliffe, Arthur (outside left).—Born at Blackrod, Lancs. Height 5ft. 7½in. Weight 11st. The club's latest capture. Was signed at midnight on Friday after Christmas; played against Portsmouth following day. Scored his first goal for the club last Saturday. Joined Blackburn Rovers in 1928 as an outside right, but became famous on the other flank, winning international honours. Went to Villa Park with Dix at the end of season 1932-3. Middlesbrough secured him from the Birmingham club.

Do You Know ?

Only three contemporary forwards can claim the remarkable record of having gone through three consecutive seasons without missing a Football League match. They are George Mee (now with Accrington) who actually went better than that with four ever-present seasons for Blackpool; Mark Hooper of Sheffield Wednesday; and Eric Brook of Manchester City.

* * *

George Mee can also claim another unusual distinction. In 42 games for Blackpool in 1922-23 he only got one goal!

* * *

In 1930-31 Aston Villa scored 128 goals. This year they have had 77 scored against them.

* * *

Last season Middlesbrough called on 20 players for their League games and had only one ever-present. The 'Spurs called on no fewer than 36, and no one appeared in every game. Brentford only called on 15, a figure far below any other club, and 6 were ever-present.

SHARES & SHAREHOLDERS

In spite of our previous notes in this programme, the Management are still receiving enquiries from supporters who are desiring to acquire shares in the Club. We repeat that the shares of the Club are fully issued, and unless existing shareholders desire to realise, there are no shares available.

The 6% Debentures of £50 each are still being issued, but only a small number now remain, and when these have been issued the finances of the Club will have been completely consolidated and settled

The Club have been the leaseholders of Griffin Park, and supporters will be interested to know that next March the freehold of the ground is being purchased and the Club will then be in the happy position of being the owners of the ground.

Particulars of the 6% Debentures will be forwarded on application to the Secretary.

Shareholders desiring to realise their share-holdings should advise the Secretary, together with a note of the price they are willing to accept.

ERNEST MUTTITT

Another one of the ex-Middlesbrough men who has rendered valuable service to the Brentford Club and one who has recently come back into the limelight. At the age of 17 scored winning goal for Middlesbrough v. Arsenal at Highbury. He is a utility forward of boundless and untiring energy. Keen eye for an opening.

FIXTURES, SEASON 1935-36.

FIRST TEAM

Date. 1935.	Opponents.	Ground.	Goals F.	A.
Aug. 31	Bolton Wanderers	A	2	0
Sept. 5	Blackburn Rovers	H	3	2
" 7	Huddersfield Town	H	1	2
" 14	Middlesbrough	A	0	0
" 18	Derby County	A	1	2
" 21	Aston Villa	H	1	2
" 28	Wolverhampton Wdrs.	A	2	3
Oct. 5	Sheffield Wednesday	H	2	2
" 12	Portsmouth	A	3	1
" 19	Stoke City	H	0	0
" 26	Manchester City	A	1	2
Nov. 2	Arsenal	H	2	1
" 9	Birmingham	A	1	2
" 16	Sunderland	H	1	5
" 23	Chelsea	A	1	2
" 30	Leeds United	H	2	6
Dec. 7	Grimsby Town	A	1	2
" 14	Liverpool	H	1	1
" 21	West Bromwich Albion	A	0	2
" 25	Preston North End	H	5	2
" 26	Preston North End	A	4	0
" 28	Bolton Wanderers	H	4	
1936.				
Jan. 1	Blackburn Rovers	A		1
" 4	Huddersfield Town	A	2	2
" 11	(3) Leicester City	A	0	1
" 18	Middlesbrough	H		
" 25	(4) Aston Villa	A		
Feb. 1	Wolverhampton Wdrs.	H		
" 8	Sheffield Wednesday	A		
" 15	(5) Portsmouth	H		
" 22	Stoke City	A		
" 29	(6) Manchester City	H		
Mar. 7	Arsenal	A		
" 14	(S.-F.) Birmingham	H		
" 21	Sunderland	A		
" 28	Chelsea	H		
April 4	Leeds United	A		
" 10	Everton	A		
" 11	Grimsby Town	H		
" 13	Everton	H		
" 18	Liverpool	A		
" 25	(F.) West Brom. Alb.	A		
May 2	Derby County	H		

SECOND TEAM

Date. 1935.	Opponents.	Ground.	Goals F.	A.
Aug. 31	Charlton Athletic	H	2	1
Sept. 4	Watford	A	1	3
" 7	Clapton Orient	A	0	0
" 12	Watford	H	2	1
" 14	Southend United	H	1	0
" 21	Northampton Town	A	1	0
" 25	Luton Town	A	1	4
" 28	Crystal Palace	H	4	0
Oct. 2	Luton Town	H	4	3
" 5	Reading	A	1	2
" 7	Met Police—L.C. Cup	H	2	0
" 9	Bournemouth & Bos.	A	5	2
" 12	Tottenham Hotspur	H	2	1
" 19	Bristol City	A	3	1
" 21	C. Orient—L.C. Cup	H	3	1
" 26	Millwall	H	4	0
Nov. 2	West Ham United	A	4	0
" 9	Swansea Town	H	2	0
" 11	Fulham (L.C.Cup,S.F.)	H	2	6
" 16	Leicester City	A	3	2
" 23	Coventry City	H	4	1
" 30	Arsenal	A	0	1
Dec. 7	Southampton	H	4	0
" 14	Brighton & Hove A.	A	1	0
" 21	Queen's Park Rgrs.	H	3	1
" 25	Chelsea	A	2	2
" 26	Chelsea	H	2	1
" 28	Charlton Athletic	H	1	3
Jan. 4	Clapton Orient	H	5	0
" 11	Fulham	H	4	0
" 18	Southend United	A		
" 25	Northampton Town	H		
Feb. 1	Crystal Palace	A		
" 8	Reading	H		
" 15	Tottenham Hotspur	A		
" 22	Bristol City	H		
" 29	Millwall	A		
Mar. 7	West Ham United	H		
" 14	Swansea Town	A		
" 21	Leicester City	H		
" 25	Bournemouth & Bos.	A		
" 28	Coventry City	A		
April 4	Arsenal	H		
" 10	Portsmouth	H		
" 11	Southampton	A		
" 13	Portsmouth	A		
" 18	Brighton & Hove A.	H		
" 25	Queen's Park Rgrs.	A		
May 2	Fulham	A		

Half Time Scores.

	F.	A.		F	A
A—Birmingham v. Man. City	......	......	J—Sunderland v. Stoke	......	......
B—Derby C. v. Huddersfield	......	......	K—W. Bromwich v. Blackburn	......	......
C—Everton v. Bolton W.	......	......	L—Charlton v. Hull City	......	......
D—Grimsby v. Liverpool	......	......	M—Fulham v. Plymouth	......	......
E—Leeds v. Chelsea	......	......	N—'Spurs v. Sheffield U.	......	......
F—Portsmouth v. Wolves	......	......	O—West Ham v. Blackpool	......	......
G—Preston N.E. v. Aston Villa	......	......	P—Aldershot v. Q.P.R.	......	......
H—Sheffield W. v. Arsenal	......	......	R—Bournemouth v. Crystal P.	......	......

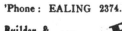

Sinbad the Sailor and the "Old Man of the Sea" (new version).

The Next Games.

The next home First Division game falls on February 1st, when our opponents are Wolverhampton Wanderers, who beat us earlier in the season on their own ground by the odd goal of five.

Before that game, however, the Bees go to Villa Park, where two teams, both involved in the struggle against relegation, should provide a thrilling encounter. The Villa have spent vast sums of money to reinforce their playing strength, and been showing signs that they are getting at least some return for their money.

Brentford fans would much appreciate, however, seeing the Villa pegged back for, while they have no wish to add to the discomfiture of any club, they can remember a very lucky couple of points for the Villa achieved at the expense of Brentford at Griffin Park earlier in the season.

Many of our supporters are planning to make the trip to Villa Park.

The Reserves, who are away to-day at Southend, are at home next week to Northampton Town, and that game is followed on February 1st by a visit to Crystal Palace.

On February 8th the Bees visit the Cup-holders, with whom a draw was staged at Griffin Park early in October.

BRENTFORD FOOTBALL AND SPORTS CLUB, LIMITED.

Registered Office :—GRIFFIN PARK, BRAEMAR ROAD, BRENTFORD.

President and Chairman :
Mr. L. P. Simon.

Vice-Chairman :
Mr. F. A. Davis.

Alderman W. Flewitt, J.P.   Mr. H. W. Dodge.   Mr. F. W. Barton.
Mr. H. N. Blundell.   Mr. C. L. Simon.   Alderman H. F. Davis.
Mr. H. J. Saunders.   Mr. J. R. Hughes, J.P., C.C.

Hon. Treasurer :
Alderman W. Flewitt, J.P.

Secretary-Manager :
Mr. H. C. Curtis,

Club Medical Officer ; Dr. A. D. Gowans.   " Dorincourt," Boston Gardens, Brentford.

Telephones :
Ground : Ealing 1744.
Private House : Ealing 1183.

Telegraphic Address ;
Curtis, Football, Brentford.
Ground ; Griffin Park, Ealing Road, Brentford.

No. 13.   Saturday, February 1st, 1936.

Notes from the Hive.

THINGS have changed definitely for the better since we last met, for two welcome points were collected in the home game with Middlesbrough, the only goal of the game deciding the issue, and then on Saturday last four goals were equally divided with Aston Villa, at Villa Park, where the Bees played sparkling football in a vital relegation struggle between two lowly placed teams. It was a " relegation " game with a vengeance, and although our boys only managed half the spoils, they called the tune for lengthy periods and were congratulated on their clever football at the end of the game by the Villa officials.

WELCOME HOME VICTORY.

Two welcome and valuable points were collected by the Bees from the visit of Middlesbrough to Griffin Park a fortnight ago, when our boys claimed the only goal of the game.

The game was notable for the fact that both teams included a new player, Reid, from Hamilton Academicals, making his debut for the Bees at outside left, and Parkin from the Arsenal figuring for the first time in the Middlesbrough team. Curiously enough, these two players were directly opposed to each other.

It was not a good day to pass judgment on new players, but our new chum, Bobbie Reid, did well enough to tell us all that he is going to prove a great acquisition when he settles down in his new surroundings. He comes to Brentford with a fine reputation which we all hope and believe he will live up to.

The only goal came fairly late in the game, being scored by Scott, after some good combined work in which at least four Brentford players had a direct interest.

This victory took Brentford away from the last two places on the League table and there is every confidence that the Bees' team, as at present constituted, will gradually rise to a place of safety and so relieve the anxiety many have felt at the decline of their favourites.

POINT FROM VILLA PARK.

When teams either at the top or bottom meet the points become double in value, so that our meeting with Aston Villa, at Villa Park, on Saturday last was a very vital one for both clubs. A win for either club meant success at the vital expense of the losers, but as the game ended in a draw the result really reflected greater credit on the Bees insomuch that it was a point gained away from home, while with the

NOTES FROM THE HIVE—Continued.

Villa it meant the conceding of a point at home—a rather serious matter for a club on the bottom rung of the League ladder.

Brentford played great football and in the matter of football skill there could be no two opinions which team was the better. The reason why Brentford did not collect the full spoils was mainly the brilliance of Biddlestone in the Villa goal. He repeatedly saved his side.

The more one looks back on the game the more mystifying does it become. Take the case of the Brentford forwards, whose brilliance was the salient feature of the game, with David McCulloch a real " star " as leader of our attack. Yet with all their skill and persistent attacking sufficient goals could not be got to win the game. And McCulloch actually failed with a penalty kick. And furthermore the Villa led by the odd goal in three until a few minutes from the end. It seems almost unbelievable that such things should have been, considering the superiority of Brentford from a territorial viewpoint.

VILLA LEAD TWICE.

Mid-way through the first half the Villa took the lead, but before half-time the Bees had an excellent chance of levelling the scores from a penalty kick. McCulloch took the " spot " kick, but Biddlestone effected a brilliant save and thus our boys were a goal down at the breather. After the change of ends Reid, our new Scottish chum, scored from short range to level the scores. Later, however, the Villa succeeded in getting in front again. The minutes sped on and on, with Biddlestone doing his stuff in the Villa goal in great style. It seemed that his brilliance was going to foil the Bees, but it did not work out quite so bad as that, for with only four minutes to go, Scott, who got

the valuable goal against Middlesbrough the previous week, scored again, to enable the game to be drawn.. Well played everybody!

RESERVES' REVIEW.

Our Reserves now hold a lead of six points at the head of the London Combination over their nearest rivals, Arsenal and Portsmouth, although both these clubs have two games in hand at the time of writing.

At Southend a fortnight ago our Reserves won by four goals to two. Dunn (2), McAloon and Brown scored for the Bees.

On Saturday last, at Griffin Park, Northampton were beaten by five goals to one. Dunn again scored twice, Fletcher also got two and McAloon completed the " nap " hand. Keep it up Junior Bees.

TO-DAY'S VISITORS.

There is every promise of a particularly stern struggle at Griffin Park to-day for we have as visitors Wolverhampton Wanderers, who will be keen to repeat their success of last September, when on their own ground the Wolves beat our boys by the odd goal in five. On the other hand the Bees will be just as anxious to avenge that defeat and so move a step nearer safety. So far this season our visitors have not done too well away from home, for only one victory, a 3—0 win at Bolton on Christmas Day, has been recorded in thirteen " out " games, three of which have resulted in draws, viz., at Sheffield (0—0), at Chelsea (2—2), and Birmingham (0—0). Since Brentford played at Wolverhampton early in the season one of their players, Dai Richards, has been transferred to Brentford, and we hope to see him at the top of his form against his old clubmates this afternoon.

BUSY BEE.

Jottings from the Board Room.

BRENTFORD PHILANTHROPIC SOCIETY

On Sunday, February 16th, 1936, a **Grand All-Star Concert** will be held at the Chiswick Empire in aid of the funds of the Brentford Philanthropic Society. Numbered and reserved seats are 5/-, 3/6 and 2/6 (including tax). Un-reserved seats 1/- (including tax). Tickets can be purchased at this Club's Office or at the Chiswick Empire, or from Mr. L. R. Winter, of 34, Albany Road, Brentford, and also from any member of the Society. The following artistes will form the all-star programme : **Naughton and Gold, Jose Fearon and Robert Naylor, Murray and Mooney** (of Command Performance fame), **Mamie Soutar, Mario de Pietro, Freddy Bamberger, Esther Coleman, Tom Lynch, Charles Forwood and Danny Walters and his Band.** Book your seats early to prevent disappointment. Tickets can be booked by application at the Secretary's Office TO-DAY.

Comparative records with last season are as follows :

	P.	W.	D.	L.	F.	A.	P.
Football League—							
This Season	26	8	6	12	43	45	22
Last Season	26	15	6	5	60	32	36
London Combination—							
This Season	29	22	2	5	72	33	46
Last Season	29	15	6	8	49	35	36

Goal Scorers to date are :

Football League.—Hopkins 9, McCulloch 8, Holliday 7, Scott 6, Fletcher 5, Robson 3, J. C. Burns 1, Dunn 1, Muttitt 1, McKenzie 1, Reid 1.—Total 43.

London Combination.—Dunn 25, Brown 12, McAloon 11, Sullivan 7, Muttitt 5, Gibbons 5, Fenton 2, C. Smith 2, Fletcher 2, L. Smith 1.—Total 73.

The Reserves are to-day away to Crystal Palace Reserves (London Combination), kick-off at 3.15 p.m.

Both I. Hopkins and D. Richards are playing for Wales against England, at Wolverhampton, in the International game on Wednesday next. We wish them both personal success, but we cannot wish their country the same fortune.

Both Arthur Bateman, who it will be remembered, was operated on for the removal of a cartiledge, and Walter Metcalf who pulled a thigh muscle, are now in full training. Arthur should be fit to play within two weeks, while Walter has now fully recovered and is fit to play.

Jimmy Nichols, our goalkeeper, who fractured a finger in the Reserve game on November 23rd, 1935, is now in full training. He is not yet able to play as he has not quite regained the full action of the injured finger.

Jackie Burns, our popular amateur, who has given such splendid service to this club, is now assisting the Leyton F.C. pretty regularly.

The F.A. Cup Draw, 5th Round, to be played on Saturday, February 15th, resulted as follows :

Barnsley v. Stoke City.
Sheffield United v. Leeds United
Grimsby Town v. Manchester City
Newcastle United v. Arsenal
Bradford City or Blackburn Rovers v. Derby County .
Bradford or West Bromwich Albion v. Tottenham Hotspur
Middlesbrough v. Leicester City
Chelsea v. Fulham

A special return train will leave Brentford to-day at 5.9 p.m. for Feltham, Ashford and Staines.

The following team will represent England v. Wales on Wednesday next at Wolverhampton :—

Hibbs (Birmingham) ; Male, Hapgood (Arsenal) ; Crayston (Arsenal), Barker (Derby), Bray (Manchester City) ; Crooks (Derby), Bowden, Drake, Bastin (Arsenal), Brook (Manchester City).

Reserves : Keen (Derby), Barclay (Sheffield United).

For six players to be selected from the Arsenal F.C. is a great compliment to the Club, who are to be heartily congratulated on such a record.

The League Team are away to Sheffield Wednesday F.C. on Saturday next, February 8th, 1936.

Leslie Smith, our young Amateur, has again been honoured by being selected to play for the Middlesex F.A. against Suffolk F.A. on Wednesday, February 12th, 1936 ; also for the Athenian League against the Royal Air Force on Saturday, February 15th, 1936. We wish him the best of good luck

GRAND EVENING CONCERT,
SUNDAY, FEBRUARY 16th, 1936,
At CHISWICK EMPIRE

BOOK YOUR SEATS TO-DAY.

Shots from the Spot.

By "Rambler"

———◆———

Football last week was played under strange and tragic circumstances. Naturally there were the very moving ceremonies on the grounds all over the country, but even more impressive than those was the almost complete absence of rattles and club favours which usually form so gay and noisy a part of football crowds. This was just another illustration of the natural good taste of the Britisher, who can be relied upon to do the right thing without having to be told to.

* * *

I think that events are proving that my confidence in the team—even in their darkest moments—has not been misplaced. As I see many of the away games as well as those at Griffin Park, I have been able to form a fairly accurate opinion of the general level of First Division football and how the Bees have fitted in during their first season.

* * *

My own honest opinion is that if they were as near to the top as they now are to the bottom, fate would have been giving them a fairer deal than she actually has—and that no one could say even then that she had been over-generous.

* * *

If you don't believe me, reckon up the number of points that the Bees have dropped through sheer ill-luck, and then see what their position in the table would be.

* * *

Everywhere I travel in the North too, I come into contact with local Pressmen and club officials who have the highest opinion of the Bees' skill.

* * *

After last Saturday's game one prominent figure in Midland sport said to be, "The Bees gave the neatest display we've seen at the Villa Park this season."

Yet they only got a point!

* * *

There is something about our boys which seems to inspire the opposing goalkeepers to amazing heights of brilliance. Cast your mind back to the number of clubs who can only thank their very last line of defence for escaping severe defeat. We never seem to catch one on an "off day," and Biddlestone, of the Villa, is the latest to join the ranks of those who have, almost single-handed, kept the Bees at bay.

* * *

In view of the danger in which the Villa find themselves of relegation, a number of correspondents have written asking whether the club has had to face that before. What actually happened was that at the end of the 1889-90 season there was only a fractional part of a goal difference between the goal averages of Bolton Wanderers and Villa (who occupied the eighth and ninth position in the final table), and as a certain Bolton result was in dispute, the standing order of the Football League was suspended and both Villa and Bolton were allowed to remain in membership. At the end of the following season, when Villa occupied the ninth position, they had to seek re-election and got it. That season the League was extended from 12 to 14 clubs, but this extension had been decided upon before Villa were in danger.

* * *

Our friends and neighbours, Charlton Athletic, appear to stand an excellent chance of beating our record and moving from Third to First Division with only the lapse of one season. If they do, they'll get a great welcome at Griffin Park.

OUR VISITORS TO-DAY.
HOW THEY MAY LINE UP.

Wolverhampton Wanderers, founded in 1879, were members of the English League on its foundation in 1888. In 1906 they dropped into Division II., and did not win back to the top section until 1932. Since then they have had rather a struggle, but this season looks like being by far their most successful since their return.

They have never carried off the First Division Championship, but have figured in five Finals, winning two—against Everton in 1893 and Newcastle U. in 1908. So proud were the people of Wolverhampton of that first success that a special row of villas—Wanderers Avenue—was built and each given the name of one of the victorious side.

Curnow, C. (goalkeeper). — Height 6ft. 2in. Weight 12st. 6lb. Has had a meteoric rise. Last September he was playing with Whitby United in the Northern League. By Christmas he had graded the first team. Had only nine games with the club's reserves before making his first team debut at Chelsea. Is the tallest and heaviest man in the side.

Taylor, John (right back).—Born Barnsley. Height 5ft. 8½in. Weight 11st. Joined the Wolves in season 1933-34 from Worsboro Bridge F.C., a Barnsley club, and has come on well. Has a strong kick with a good idea of where to place the ball. Plays tennis well.

Shaw, Cyril (left back).—Born at Mansfield. Height 5ft. 10in. Weight 12st. 2lb. Was only 17 when recruited from Rufford Colliery. Signed forms outside a cinema, where the Wanderers' official had located him. Since making his first team place secure three years ago he has missed only one game. Has been described as " the best uncapped back in England " and that's no idle flattery.

Galley, Thomas (right half).— Born at Hednesford, Staffs. Height 5ft. 11in. Weight 10st. 12lb. Joined the club as soon as he was old enough to sign professional and has now been with them two years. Was actually signed in April, 1934 from Cannock Town. Played several games for the first team as an inside forward at the end of last season and the start of this, but definitely secured his place last October when he was given a chance at half-back.

Morris, William (centre half).— Born at Handsworth, Birmingham. Height 5ft. 10in. Weight 11st. 7lb. Was an outside-right when signed by the club in May, 1933. Tried in various positions before settling down as pivot last campaign. Has been an ever-present in the position this season. Blocks up the middle, but makes surprise dribbles down the field at times. Was previously with Halesowen Town (Birmingham Combination) and had trials with West Bromwich Albion.

Gardiner, Joseph (left half).— Born at Bear Park, Co. Durham. Height 5ft. 9in. Weight 11st. Yet another converted forward. Was secured from Bear Park Juniors and played in practically every forward position before settling down in the middle line last season. Gained first team place this season after being reserve to Richards, now with us (Brentford). Delightful constructive player.

BRENTFORD *v.* W

BRENT

Red an

1—M

2—WILSON
Right Back

4—McKENZIE
Right Half

5—
Cer

7—HOPKINS   8—SCOTT   9—McC
Outside Right   Inside Right   Centre

Referee— Mr. G. STEPHENSON (Liverpool)

14
C

12—WRIGGLESWORTH   13—CLAYT
Outside Left   Inside Left

17—GARDINER   18—
Left Half   Ce

20—SHAW
Left Back

22—
G

WOLVERHAMPT
Old Gold S

THE LEAGUE—DIVISION I.

	P.	W.	D.	L.	F.	A.	P.
Sunderland	25	18	2	5	71	38	38
Derby County	26	13	7	6	40	25	33
Huddersfield T.	26	13	6	7	39	38	32
Arsenal	24	10	7	7	53	29	27
Stoke City	25	12	3	10	38	37	27
Liverpool	25	10	6	9	42	33	26
Leeds United	24	9	8	7	40	32	26
Birmingham	25	9	8	8	35	35	26
Wolverhampton	25	10	5	10	51	45	25
Bolton Wand.	25	9	7	9	43	49	25
Portsmouth	24	10	5	9	33	39	25
Middlesbrough	26	10	4	12	54	42	24
West Bromwich A.	25	11	2	12	57	46	24
Preston N.E.	25	10	3	12	38	40	23
Manchester C.	25	10	3	12	38	41	23
Grimsby T.	26	10	3	13	36	46	23
Chelsea	24	9	5	10	33	44	23
BRENTFORD	**26**	**8**	**6**	**12**	**43**	**45**	**22**
Sheffield Wed.	24	8	5	11	43	50	21
Blackburn R.	25	9	3	13	37	62	21
Everton	25	6	7	12	42	57	19
Aston Villa	27	7	5	15	49	82	19

VERHAMPTON W.

ORD
Stripes
ESON
er

3—POYSER
Left Back

ES   6—RICHARDS
f   Left Half

CH 10—HOLLIDAY   11—REID
rd   Inside Left   Outside Left

Linesmen— Messrs. D. W. Paget (blue flag)
and C. H. D. Hurdle (red flag)

ALLEY
orward

15—THOMPSON   16—JONES
Inside Right   Outside Right

RIS   19—GALLEY
alf   Right Half

21—TAYLOR
Right Back

OW
er

WANDERERS
e Knickers

LONDON COMBINATION

	P.	W.	D.	L.	F.	A.	P.
BRENTFORD ...	29	22	2	5	72	33	46
Arsenal	27	19	2	6	74	26	40
Portsmouth	27	16	8	3	74	36	40
Swansea	29	16	6	7	50	39	38
Charlton Ath.	29	16	3	10	60	43	35
Chelsea	29	13	8	8	60	50	34
Crystal Palace	30	14	6	10	69	64	34
Queen's Park Rgrs.	28	15	3	10	57	43	33
West Ham U.	30	14	4	12	70	51	32
Luton Town	29	13	4	12	78	69	30
Reading	28	13	3	12	63	65	29
Coventry City	27	13	2	12	58	46	28
Millwall	27	12	4	11	38	40	28
Tottenham H.	27	9	7	11	69	67	25
Northampton	28	9	6	13	50	53	24
Southend U.	27	7	7	13	47	67	21
Watford	28	9	3	16	56	85	21
Clapton Orient	28	7	7	14	34	66	21
Fulham	27	8	4	15	56	56	20
Bournemouth	29	7	6	16	47	73	20
Bristol City	30	9	2	19	44	90	20
Southampton	28	6	7	15	38	54	19
Leicester City	26	9	1	16	44	64	19
Brighton & Hove A.	27	6	5	16	45	72	17

The Arsenal Arena, entirely reconstructed in six weeks.

The White City Arena, entirely reconstructed in six weeks.

The West Ham Stadium Dog Track.

3 famous grounds entirely re-constructed by

Jones, Brynmor (inside left or outside right).—Born at Merthyr Tydfil. Height 5ft. 6in. Weight 10st. This tricky young Welsh international joined Wolverhampton from Aberaman (Welsh League) in November, 1933, after being on trial for some weeks. Before the end of that month he secured his first team place and has retained it ever since. Has played inside right and left, whilst last Saturday in the " friendly " with Southampton, he played outside right.

Thompson, Harry (inside right).—Born at Mansfield, Notts. Height 5ft. 9½in. Weight 10st. 8lb. Came to the fore as a junior with Mansfield Town. Was only a youngster when the Wanderers took him up in June, 1933. Has had his initial chances with the senior side this season. Tricky and fast with a powerful shot.

Smalley, Thomas. — Born at Kinsley, Yorks. Height 5ft. 7½in. Weight 11st. 7lb. Secured from South Kirkby Colliery in 1931. Made several first team appearances in the League side at inside right or centre forward before being tried at right half in October,

1933. Played regularly in that berth until last October, when he moved back to centre forward. Leads his line intelligently but has been rather out of luck from a marksmanship point of view.

Clayton, James (inside left).—Born at Sunderland. Height 5ft. 11in. Weight 12st. Joined the club from Shotton Colliery, Sunderland, in October, 1932. His activities were practically confined to the club's junior sides, though he did make one or two appearances with the League side. Then in March last year he left the club to join the Sunderland Police Force. By October, however, he had returned to Molineux.

Wrigglesworth, William (outside left).—Born at South Elmsall, Yorkshire. Height 5ft. 4in. Weight 9st. 7lb. Joined Wolves from Chesterfield in December, 1934. Quickly made his mark in the First Division game, playing 16 times for the League eleven and scoring seven goals. Is the club's top scorer to date this term. Plays on either flank though preferring the left. Early experience with Frickley Colliery.

Do You Know ?

Stoke hold the record for gaining the lowest number of points in First Division football. In the season 1889-90 they only collected 10. In the Second Division in 1904-5, though, Doncaster Rovers only collected eight.

* * *

Within seven weeks at the end of last season three Everton footballers—Cook, Coulter and Stein—broke a leg.

NAMES IN THE GAME

MAJOR FRANK BUCKLEY.

Major Buckley, the secretary-manager of the Wolverhampton Wanderers, is one of the best known managers in the game, with a reputation for unearthing young talent and making the best of it. In his playing days he was an international centre-half, playing for the Villa, Birmingham and Derby County. It was while he was with the last-named club that he was capped against Ireland. Before taking over his present post he was manager of Norwich City and also of Blackpool.

SHARES & SHAREHOLDERS

In spite of our previous notes in this programme, the Management are still receiving enquiries from supporters who are desiring to acquire shares in the Club. We repeat that the shares of the Club are fully issued, and unless existing shareholders desire to realise, there are no shares available.

The 6% Debentures of £50 each are still being issued, but only a small number now remain, and when these have been issued the finances of the Club will have been completely consolidated and settled

The Club have been the lease-holders of Griffin Park, and supporters will be interested to know that next March the freehold of the ground is being purchased and the Club will then be in the happy position of being the owners of the ground.

Particulars of the 6% Debentures will be forwarded on application to the Secretary.

Shareholders desiring to realise their share-holdings should advise the Secretary, together with a note of the price they are willing to accept.

ROBERT REID
Outside Left.

One of our new chums who has settled down very nicely. Scored his first goal for the Bees against Villa last week. Born in Hamilton—Dave McCulloch's home town—he learnt his football with the Academicals. Has League honours and the reputation of being the fastest winger in Scottish football.

FIXTURES, SEASON 1935-36.

FIRST TEAM

Date. 1935.	Opponents.	Ground.	GOALS F.	A.
Aug. 31	Bolton Wanderers	A	2	0
Sept. 5	Blackburn Rovers	H	3	1
,, 7	Huddersfield Town	H	1	2
,, 14	Middlesbrough	A	0	0
,, 18	Derby County	A	1	2
,, 21	Aston Villa	H	1	2
,, 28	Wolverhampton Wdrs.	A	2	3
Oct. 5	Sheffield Wednesday	H	2	2
,, 12	Portsmouth	A	3	1
,, 19	Stoke City	H	0	0
,, 26	Manchester City	A	1	2
Nov. 2	Arsenal	H	2	1
,, 9	Birmingham	A	1	2
,, 16	Sunderland	H	1	5
,, 23	Chelsea	H	1	2
,, 30	Leeds United	H	2	2
Dec. 7	Grimsby Town	A	1	6
,, 14	Liverpool	H	1	2
,, 21	West Bromwich Albion	A	0	1
,, 25	Preston North End	H	5	2
,, 26	Preston North End	A	4	2
,, 28	Bolton Wanderers	H	4	0
1936.				
Jan. 1	Blackburn Rovers	A	0	1
,, 4	Huddersfield Town	A	2	2
,, 11	(3) Leicester City	A	0	1
,, 18	Middlesbrough	H	1	0
,, 25	(4) Aston Villa	A	2	2
Feb. 1	Wolverhampton Wdrs.	H		
,, 8	Sheffield Wednesday	A		
,, 15	(5) Portsmouth	H		
,, 22	Stoke City	A		
,, 29	(6) Manchester City	H		
Mar. 7	Arsenal	A		
,, 14	(S.-F.) Birmingham	H		
,, 21	Sunderland	A		
,, 28	Chelsea	H		
April 4	Leeds United	A		
,, 10	Everton	H		
,, 11	Grimsby Town	H		
,, 13	Everton	A		
,, 18	Liverpool	A		
,, 25	(F.) West Brom. Alb.	H		
May 2	Derby County	H		

SECOND TEAM

Date. 1935.	Opponents.	Ground.	GOALS F.	A.
Aug. 31	Charlton Athletic	H	2	1
Sept. 4	Watford	A	1	3
,, 7	Clapton Orient	A	0	0
,, 12	Watford	H	2	1
,, 14	Southend United	H	1	0
,, 21	Northampton Town	A	1	0
,, 25	Luton Town	A	1	4
,, 28	Crystal Palace	H	4	0
Oct. 3	Luton Town	H	4	3
,, 5	Reading	A	1	2
,, 7	Met Police—I.C.Cup	H	2	0
,, 9	Bournemouth & Bos.	A	5	2
,, 12	Tottenham Hotspur	H	2	1
,, 19	Bristol City	A	3	1
,, 21	C. Orient—L.C.Cup	A	3	1
,, 26	Millwall	H	4	0
Nov. 2	West Ham United	A	1	0
,, 9	Swansea Town	H	2	0
,, 11	Fulham (L.C.Cup.S.F.)	H	2	6
,, 16	Leicester City	A	3	2
,, 23	Coventry City	H	2	1
,, 30	Arsenal	A	0	1
Dec. 7	Southampton	H	4	0
,, 14	Brighton & Hove A.	A	1	0
,, 21	Queen's Park Rgrs.	H	3	1
,, 25	Chelsea	A	2	2
,, 26	Chelsea	H	2	1
,, 28	Charlton Athletic	A	1	3
Jan. 4	Clapton Orient	H	5	1
,, 11	Fulham	H	4	0
,, 18	Southend United	A	4	2
,, 25	Northampton Town	H	5	1
Feb. 1	Crystal Palace	A		
,, 8	Reading	A		
,, 15	Tottenham Hotspur	A		
,, 22	Bristol City	A		
,, 29	Millwall	A		
Mar. 7	West Ham United	H		
,, 14	Swansea Town	A		
,, 21	Leicester City	H		
,, 25	Bournemouth & Bos.	A		
,, 28	Coventry City	A		
April 4	Arsenal	H		
,, 10	Portsmouth	H		
,, 11	Southampton	A		
,, 13	Portsmouth	A		
,, 18	Brighton & Hove A.	H		
,, 25	Queen's Park Rgrs.	A		
May 2	Fulham	A		

Half Time Scores.

	F.	A.			F	A
A—Arsenal v. Stoke C.	......	......	J—Sunderland v. Chelsea		......	......
B—Birmingham v. Blackburn	......	......	K—W. Brom. A. v. Liverpool		......	......
C—Bolton W. v. Huddersfield	......	......	L—Charlton A. v. Plymouth A.		......	......
D—Derby C. v. Aston Villa	......	......	M—Fulham v. Newcastle		......	......
E—Everton v. Middlesboro	......	......	N—Port Vale v. 'Spurs		......	......
F—Leeds U. v. Grimsby T.	......	......	O—West Ham U. v. Bury		......	......
G—Portsmouth v. Man. City	......	......	P—Coventry C. v. Q.P.R.		......	......
H—Preston N.E. v. Shef. W.	......	......	R—Luton T. v. Reading		......	......

So much of this sort of luck has been our lot recently that we understand some of our supporters are organising a petition to claim the following addition to the Rules, i.e., " **THAT ALL GOALPOSTS SHALL BE NEUTRAL.**"

The Next Games.

Next Saturday the Bees face a tough proposition when they visit Sheffield Wednesday, the holders of the English Cup. on the Hillsborough ground. The Wednesday, who shared four goals with us rather luckily earlier in the season, have yet to produce the real form of which they are capable, but they are always a dangerous side.

The following Saturday the Bees have a chance of completing another double, as Portsmouth are the visitors to Griffin Park.

When Brentford went to Fratton Park earlier in the season they staged one of the best performances of their First Division career, winning by three goals to one.

This game should provide real football entertainment for our supporters if anything like the same quality play is served up.

After that (on February 22nd) the Bees are away to Stoke City.

Next Saturday the Reserves are at home to Reading and the following Saturday cross London to White Hart Lane, where they meet the challenge of the junior 'Spurs, whom they beat 2–-1 at Griffin Park in October.

BRENTFORD FOOTBALL AND SPORTS CLUB, LIMITED.

Registered Office :—GRIFFIN PARK, BRAEMAR ROAD, BRENTFORD.

President and Chairman :
Mr. L. P. Simon.

Vice-Chairman :
Mr. F. A. Davis.

Alderman W. Flewitt, J.P.
Mr. H. N. Blundell.
Mr. H. J. Saunders.

Mr. H. W. Dodge.
Mr. C. L. Simon.

Mr. F. W. Barton.
Alderman H. F. Davis.
Mr. J. R. Hughes, J.P., C.C.

Hon. Treasurer :
Alderman W. Flewitt, J.P.
Club Medical Officer ; Dr. A. D. Gowans.

Secretary-Manager ;
Mr. H. C. Curtis,
" Dorincourt," Boston Gardens, Brentford.

Telephones ;
Ground : Ealing 1744.
Private House : Ealing 1183.

Telegraphic Address ;
Curtis, Football, Brentford.
Ground ; Griffin Park, Ealing Road, Brentford.

No. 15   Saturday, February 29th, 1936.

Notes from the Hive.

Our last home game against Portsmouth could not be played owing to fog, so that the issue of the Official Programme published for that game did not get into circulation. Consequently, for the benefit of our supporters who keep these programmes as a record of the Bees doings, it seems appropriate that some reference should be made to the games played which will enable the records to be a complete one for reference back if needed.

This takes us back to the home game against Wolverhampton, which was won by five clear goals, followed by two drawn games away from home—at Hillsbrough and Stoke.

Thus four valuable points have been obtained and lifted the Bees away from the last two dreaded places, but not yet free from the danger zone.

BEES' NAP HAND AGAINST WOLVES.

The Bees stung the Wolves very badly when the Wanderers visited Griffin Park four weeks ago, and did not cry enough until the Wolves goalkeeper had picked the ball out of the net five times, and as the visitors could not reply with a solitary goal, the victory of our boys was most substantial; in fact the most decisive recorded this season. Brentford laid the foundation of their success by scoring twice before the interval –Reid and McCulloch getting the goals.

Better still was to follow, for the Bees did not make the mistake of adopting the policy of " what we have we hold." Not a bit of it, they went all out to consolidate their advantage and such aggressive efforts were rewarded with three more goals. McCulloch, Scott and Holliday were the net-finders in this half.

Incidentally it is interesting to note that this was the first time the Wolves had conceded as many as five goals in a game, and the Bees more than avenged an odd goal in five defeat sustained at Wolverhampton earlier in the season.

DIVISION AT SHEFFIELD.

Brentford supporters must have experienced two mild, and distinct, shocks over the Bees' visit to Sheffield to oppose the Wednesday. Firstly the half-time score showing Brentford leading by three clear goals must have caused smiles on broad lines among the Brentford " fans," while secondly a pang of disappointment must have been felt when the final score came through indicating that the game had ended in a 3—3 draw.

On the face of things it certainly seems that having held such a substantial lead at the interval the Bees should have made no mistake about finishing in front. Normally that would have no doubt been the case, but circumstances alter cases, and this was truly an abnormal case, governed solely by the atmospheric conditions.

The ground was like a sheet of ice with a gale blowing from end to end. Winning the toss meant a big advantage. Brentford had the conditions in their favour in the first half and scored three times. After ends were changed it was naturally a very different story. The Wednesday were heartened by a quick goal and were not long in getting a second, a state of affairs which made the issue an open one. Cheered on by their supporters, the home side eventually managed to score a third goal and so divide the spoils. We give Sheffield Wednesday all the credit they deserve for the splendid way they hit back after being so much behind. Holliday, McCulloch and Hopkins scored for Brentford in the first half.

ANOTHER AWAY POINT.

Another valuable point was collected away from home on Saturday last, when four goals were equally divided with Stoke City, which put us all square with the " Potters " for this season, as they played a goalless draw at Griffin Park last October.

Although Stoke twice led in this game, the critics were in general agreement that they were fortunate to finish on level terms. Both from a football and territorial viewpoint Brentford held a distinct advantage over the City, but things simply did not go just right near goal.

Stoke took the lead at the end of half an hour's play, but before the interval the Bees had levelled the scores through McCulloch. Almost immediately after the restart the home side again took the lead, but once again there was a quick equaliser—Scott doing the needful this time. The Bees fought hard to get the winning goal their play deserved, but the luck of our boys was dead out. Just one outstanding incident is worth recording to show how the Goddess of Fortune smiled on the home side. Ten minutes from the end McCulloch gave Hopkins a perfect pass which left our wingman with only the goalkeeper to beat from ten yards range. Hopkins fired in a great shot which struck the inside of a post and actually came right back into the Stoke goalkeeper's hands—a most amazing happening.

RESERVES' REVIEW.

Our Reserves have been on the soft pedal of late and two successive reverses cost them the leadership of the London Combination for the moment at any rate.

A 3—1 defeat against Crystal Palace, at Selhurst Park, was a bit unexpected, but did not come as such a shock as Reading's 1—0 win at Griffin Park a week later. That was the first defeat sustained by our second string at home this season, in fact not even a point had been conceded in previous games of the present campaign. To add to our troubles in this game, Fletcher failed with a penalty kick in the first half, long before the visitors claimed the only goal mid-way through the second half.

On Saturday last a much better showing was made against Bristol City Reserves, who were beaten at Griffin Park by three clear goals, Brown 2, McAloon 1, scored by the Bees.

This win put us at the top of the London Combination again, being level on points with Portsmouth Reserves, for the previous week Pompey's second team was beaten at home by Fulham Reserves.

BUSY BEE.

Jottings from the Board Room.

The Players and Officials of this Club have received an invitation to see the performance of " Twenty to One " at the Coliseum Theatre, on Friday, March 6th, 1936, at the first performance (6.15 p.m.). The cast includes Lupino Lane, Clifford Mollison, Joyce Barbour, Arthur Rigby, Jnr., and Betty Norton. The management of the Coliseum has also agreed to permit a limited number of supporters of this Club to attend the same performance at a reduced admission, viz., 3/6 for the Fauteuils. Any desiring to take advantage of this offer should write to Mr. Curtis stating his requirements. Mr. Curtis will obtain tickets for any supporter.

Supporters are asked to note that no further applications can be considered for Cup Final Tickets. When this Club's allocation is known, those supporters who have applied previously will be considered, and to those few who are allocated any tickets a notification will be sent. (Cup Final Day is April 25th, the day on which we play West Bromwich Albion at home.)

Comparative records with last season are as follows :—
Football League—

	P.	W.	D.	L.	F.	A.	P.
This Season	29	9	8	12	53	50	26
Last Season	29	17	6	6	65	37	40

London Combination—

	P.	W.	D.	L.	F.	A.	P.
This Season	32	23	2	7	76	37	48
Last Season	32	17	6	9	55	38	40

Goal scorers to date are :—
Football League.—McCulloch 12, Hopkins 10, Holliday 9, Scott 8, Fletcher 5, Robson 3, Reid 2, J. C. Burns 1, Dunn 1, Muttitt 1, McKenzie 1.—Total 53.

London Combination.—Dunn 25, Brown 14, McAloon 12, Sullivan 7, Muttitt 6, Gibbons 5, Fenton 2, Smith (C.) 2, Fletcher 2, L. Smith 1.—Total 76.

With reference to the Football League game v. Portsmouth, postponed on Saturday, February 15th, 1936, we are trying to arrange to play it on Wednesday, April 22nd, 1936, with an evening kick-off, but the Portsmouth Club have not yet agreed to this date.

The Reserves are away to-day to Millwall Reserves (London Combination), and on Saturday next, March 7th, 1936, West Ham Reserves will be the visitors to this ground.

Seats numbered and reserved in Block " B," at 4/- each, can be booked for our game (Football League) on this ground on Saturday, March 14th, 1936. Applications by post will not be considered unless accompanied by remittance and a stamped addressed envelope.

Presuming our game v. Arsenal F.C. is played at Highbury on Saturday next, March 7th, 1936, as per the original fixture list the only bookable seats are at 5/- each. Applications should be sent direct to the Arsenal Club.

Football League games will be definitely played on THIS ground on the following dates :— February 29th, March 14th, March 28th, April 11th, April 13th (Easter Monday), April 25th and May 2nd, and the Portsmouth game date is to be definitely arranged. The following teams have to be met at home : Manchester City, Birmingham, Chelsea, Grimsby, Everton, West Bromwich, Derby County and Portsmouth.

We are pleased to announce that Archie Scott proved a very worthy deputy for Joe James at Stoke, on Saturday last. He played splendidly.

To the supporters who have not yet witnessed an Ice Hockey game, I recommend them for excitement. Below I append fixtures at the Wembley Empire Pool and at the Empress Stadium, Ltd., Earl's Court.

Wembley Empire Pool.

Saturday, February 29th.—International Cup—Wembley Lions v. Stade Francais. London-Paris Tournament.

Thursday, March 5th.—U.S.A. Olympic team v. Wembley Lions.

Saturday, March 7th.—Wembley Canadians v. Richmond Hawks. London Cup.

Monday, March 9th.—British Olympic Team v. U.S.A. Olympic Team.

Thursday, March 12th.—Wembley Lions v. Earl's Court Rangers. London Cup.

Empress Stadium, Limited.

Monday, March 2nd—Kensington Corinthians v. Canadians.

Friday, March 6th.—Earl's Court Rangers v. Brighton Tigers.

Monday, March 9th.—Kensington Corinthians v. Wembley Lions.

Friday, March 13th.—Earl's Court Rangers v. Richmond Hawks.

Monday, March 16th.—Kensington Corinthians v. Streatham.

Shots from the Spot.

To Our Supporters

During the past week I have received numerous letters complaining of the proposed new scheme, which has resulted in our fixtures being altered and our opponents not being known until the day before the game. In many instances the contents of the letters were sensible and reasonable, and I confess I am in agreement with much that was said. The contents of other letters were unreasonable and not worth commenting on. Nearly all the writers appear to be of the opinion that the Football Association are responsible for the alteration, and I desire to rectify this wrong impression. The F.A. and the Football League Management Committee are two distinct bodies. Even in this respect, it is only fair to point out that the League clubs at a meeting in Manchester, by a majority gave the Management Committee power to put the scheme into operation, so the responsibility must be with the clubs.

In the first place the Rules of the F.A. are quite clear, that any player or official who takes part in any betting on football results will be suspended. So under these circumstances it would not be advisable for me to express my personal views on the merits of football pools. What the members of the public do is quite another matter, and I fully appreciate their desire to please themselves.

I would like to assure our supporters that my Board are not in favour of the proposed new scheme and this Club will be represented at a meeting in Leeds on Monday, with a view to supporting the immediate return to the original fixture list.

HARRY C. CURTIS,
Secretary-Manager.

TO-DAY'S GAME.

We welcome to Griffin Park this afternoon, Birmingham. It will be remembered that when the Bees opposed them away earlier in the season Brentford lost by the narrow margin of two goals to one. We are all hopeful that with ground advantage the Bees will reverse this result.

A good game should be seen as the visitors play the kind of football that spectators enjoy watching. Their position in the League —sixth—goes to prove that they are a good team. The Bees, however, should proved a little too good for them.

* * *

RESERVES.

It is interesting to note that the Reserves have regained their place as leaders of the London Combination. It is very difficult for a team leading its own particular division to hold that position, for every opposing team fights with a cup-final tenacity in the hope of having the honour of lowering their colours.

* * *

THE LEAGUE TABLE.

The League Table is very interesting reading just now. The Bees are sixteenth with 26 points and 53 goals for and 50 against. West Bromwich Albion are ninth with 28 points and 68 goals for and 53 against.

* * *

PROPOSED RE-UNION DINNER.

Footballers' Battalion, 17th Middlesex Regiment propose to hold a re-union dinner on April 25th, 1936 (Cup Final night) in London. Will all members interested please communicate with Mr. Angus Seed, manager, Aldershot Football Club, Aldershot, Hants., or ex-Sergeant C. Dale, 18, Delorme Street, Hammersmith, London, W.6, when full particulars will be supplied.

OUR VISITORS TO-DAY.
HOW THEY MAY LINE UP.

Though their history dates back to 1875, Birmingham have always been somewhat overshadowed by the greater fame of their neighbours, Aston Villa. With things going badly for Villa this season, however, the "Blues" have proved themselves the most consistent of the three Birmingham First Division clubs—Villa, Birmingham and Albion. They have fallen away somewhat since the turn of the year, but will not be easy to overcome.

Their League distinctions have all been won in the Second Division, of which they have carried off the championship on two occasions, being runners-up on a similar number of occasions.

Hibbs, Harry (goalkeeper) — Born at Wilnecote, near Tamworth, Warwick. Height 5ft. 9½in. Weight 11st. 6lb. Has been called the "prince of present day goal keepers" and not without reason. Is agile and fearless, while his anticipation is remarkable. Brought out by Wilnecote Holy Trinity and Tamworth Castle. Joined Birmingham in the 1924 summer. Has over 20 caps for England.

Barkas, Edward (right back).— Born at Wardley Colliery, Northumberland. Height 5ft. 7¾in. Weight 12st. 6lb. Had experience with Bedlington, South Shields and Hebburn Colliery before joining Huddersfield in 1921-2. Played in 119 League matches for them and helped them win two championships, 1925 and 1926. Transferred to Birmingham in 1929 and became their captain. Is a keen cyclist. Robust but fair.

Steel, William (left back).—Born at Blantyre, Lanark. Height 5ft. 8in. Weight 11st. 8lb. A cool and thoughtful defender who clears judiciously. While with St. Johnstone he did not miss a Scottish League match for three seasons and attracted the attention of several English clubs. Joined Liverpool in September, 1931, after a month's trial, and soon established himself. Moved to Birmingham in March, 1935, after losing his place to Tom Cooper.

Stoker, Lewis (right half).— Born at Wheatley Hill, County Durham. Height 5ft. 8¾in. Weight 10st. 7lb. Previously with Brandon Juniors, Esh Winning Juniors, Bearpark (Durham Central League) and West Stanley (North Eastern League). Came to Birmingham in 1930 and soon gained his first team place. Is an English international. Used to be an electrician.

Morrall, George (centre half).— Born at Smethwick, near Birmingham. Height 6ft. 0½in. Weight 12st. 12½lb. Was spotted locally playing in works football for Allen Everitt's F.C. Had a trial with West Bromwich Albion before joining Birmingham in 1927. Defends well and feeds his forwards with long, swinging passes.

Sykes, Jack (wing half).—Born at Wombwell, Yorks. Height 5ft. 8½in. Weight 11st. 2lb. Was centre half when he joined the club in May, 1932, but soon settled down in the flank positions, making his First Division debut against Huddersfield Town in the final match of 1933-4 season. Getting his chance at left half earlier this year, he has shown consistent form. Previously with Wombwell (Midland League).

Jennings, Dennis Bernard (outside right)—Born at Kidderminster. Height 5ft. 6in. Weight 10st. 3lb. Was overlooked while playing with Kidderminster Harriers in the Birmingham League and cost his pre-

BRENTFORD

BRE

Red a

1—M

2—WILSON
Right Back

4—McKENZIE
Right Half

5—
C

7—HOPKINS
Outside Right

8—SCOTT
Inside Right

9—McC
Centre

Referee— MR. A. J. BROWN (Bristol)

C

12—MORRIS
Outside Left

13—HARRIS
Inside Left

17—SYKES
Left Half

18—
Ce

20—STEEL
Left Back

22-

BIRM

Royal Blue Shirts W

THE LEAGUE—DIVISION I.

	P.	W.	D.	L.	F.	A.	P.
Sunderland	30	21	4	5	84	44	46
Derby	30	14	9	7	44	29	37
Huddersfield	30	15	7	8	47	43	37
Stoke	30	14	5	11	45	42	33
Arsenal	27	12	7	8	57	32	31
Birmingham	29	11	9	9	42	40	31
Portsmouth	28	12	6	10	39	44	30
Bolton W.	29	10	9	10	49	55	29
W.B. Albion	28	13	2	13	68	53	28
Leeds	28	10	8	10	45	39	28
Grimsby	30	12	4	14	44	53	28
Liverpool	29	10	7	12	44	45	27
Preston	29	11	5	13	43	44	27
Man. City	29	12	3	14	43	46	27
Middlesbro'	30	11	5	14	58	51	27
BRENTFORD	29	9	8	12	53	50	26
Chelsea	27	9	8	10	38	49	26
Wolves	29	10	6	13	53	57	26
Everton	30	8	10	12	57	66	26
Sheffield W.	29	9	7	13	51	60	25
Blackburn R.	30	9	5	16	40	70	23
Aston V.	30	8	6	16	56	88	22

BIRMINGHAM

...ORD

...stripes

...ESON
...er

3—POYSER
Left Back

...ES   **6—RICHARDS**
...lf   Left Half

...CH **10—HOLLIDAY**   **11—REID**
...d   Inside Left   Outside Left

Linesmen— Messrs. G. Johnson (blue flag)
and F. E. Mitchell (red flag)

...ONES
...rward

15—DEVINE   **16—JENNINGS**
Inside Right   Outside Right

...ALL   **19—STOKER**
...f   Right Half

21—BARKAS
Right Back

...3S
...er

...HAM

...rs, White Knickers

LONDON COMBINATION

	P.	W.	L.	D.	F.	A.	P.
BRENTFORD	32	23	7	2	76	37	48
Portsmouth	32	20	4	8	84	42	48
Arsenal	31	21	7	3	80	31	45
Reading	34	19	12	3	79	67	41
Swansea Town	33	17	10	6	57	48	40
Charlton A.	34	17	13	4	73	56	38
Crystal Palace	33	16	11	6	75	72	38
West Ham U.	34	16	13	5	81	56	37
Chelsea	33	14	11	8	67	59	36
Queen's P.R.	31	16	12	3	64	49	35
Millwall	32	15	12	5	51	51	35
Coventry City	32	15	13	4	66	55	34
Luton Town	33	14	15	4	89	82	32
Tottenham H.	30	11	11	8	77	69	30
Clapton O.	34	10	15	9	47	77	29
Northampton	33	10	15	8	59	64	28
Fulham	32	10	16	6	60	60	26
Southend U.	32	9	15	8	53	78	26
Leicester C.	31	12	18	1	56	77	25
Watford	32	10	19	3	60	92	23
Bournemouth	33	8	19	6	56	86	22
Southampton	32	7	18	7	40	58	21
Bristol City	34	9	22	3	49	102	21
Brighton & H.	31	7	18	6	59	78	20

The Arsenal Arena, entirely reconstructed in six weeks.

The White City Arena, entirely reconstructed in six weeks.

The West Ham Stadium Dog Track.

3

famous grounds entirely re-constructed by

B. *Sunley* and Co. Ltd.

Sunley's Island . Great West Road . Brentford . Middlesex

Telephone : Ealing 1412/3

Makers of the famous "De Luxe" Non-attention hard tennis courts.   Sports grounds.   Gardens.   Bowling greens.   Racing tracks.   Consult Sunley about your garden.   Estimates and plans prepared without cost or obligation.

sent club a substantial fee when secured from Grimsby this January. Had spell with West Bromwich Albion, but really came to fore with Huddersfield Town, who introduced him to the League game. Joined Grimsby at the start of season 1932-3. Can also play inside-forward.

Devine, Joseph (inside right).— Born at Motherwell. Height 5ft. 8in. Weight 11st. 4lb. An experienced player who has a fine steadying effect on the young Birmingham forward line. Began his career with Cledale Juniors and Bathgate, crossing the border in 1925. His first English club was Burnley. Then followed spells with Newcastle and Sunderland before reaching Queen's Park Rangers in the 1933 close season. Moved on to Birmingham at substantial fee in January, 1935. Is an adaptable player who has filled many positions.

Jones, Charles Wilson (centre forward). — Born at Wrexham. Height 5ft. 9in. Weight 10st. 2lb. Was secured from Wrexham's reserve team last season and was an immediate success in First Division football. Gained his Welsh international cap—against Ireland—before the end of the season. Is a dashing leader with a shot in either foot.

Harris, Frederick (inside left).— Born at Birmingham. Height 5ft. 9in. Weight 10st. 1½lb. A schoolboy international who joined Birmingham in May, 1933, as a junior. Made rapid progress and came into the first team at the start of last season. Scored in his first Division I. game. Is hard-working and clever. Gets many goals with his head. Used to play with Osborn's Athletic in the Birmingham Suburban League.

Morris, Seymour (outside left).— Born at Pontypridd, South Wales. Height 5ft. 8in. Weight 11st. Gained his early football experience in the Rhondda Valley, where he went to school and later worked as a pit lad. Joined Huddersfield Town as an inside forward or wing half from Aberaman in 1932. Settled down on the wing after moving to Birmingham in March, 1935. Has been a regular goal-scorer with the Reserves and has recently been showing up well with the League side as a deputy for Guest.

Do You Know ?

That Glasgow Rangers won every match in the Scottish League Competition in the season 1898-99. No other club has accomplished this performance.

* * *

That Billie Meredith has a record of 51 international caps and played in a semi-final of the English Cup at the age of 50.

* * *

That in all the years he never had a transfer fee paid for him.

* * *

That Bob Benson, now deceased, was known before the Great War as the " Penalty King." Was with Sheffield United for four seasons and only failed with one spot kick. A colleague placed the ball for him, Benson ran from his position at full back and never stopped until he had shot. And what a shot !

* * *

That Referees never make mistakes ! In a game recently played, a " rough-house " was developing. The Ref. called a player to one side. Said he : " Now then, cut out the rough stuff. I know you So-and-so, and your record. You can't do that there 'ere." Unfortunately— *for the Ref.*—So-and-so wasn't playing !

SHARES & SHAREHOLDERS

In spite of our previous notes in this programme, the Management are still receiving enquiries from supporters who are desiring to acquire shares in the Club. We repeat that the shares of the Club are fully issued, and unless existing shareholders desire to realise, there are no shares available.

The 6% Debentures of £50 each are still being issued, but only a small number now remain, and when these have been issued the finances of the Club will have been completely consolidated and settled

The Club have been the leaseholders of Griffin Park, and supporters will be interested to know that next March the freehold of the ground is being purchased and the Club will then be in the happy position of being the owners of the ground.

Particulars of the 6% Debentures will be forwarded on application to the Secretary.

Shareholders desiring to realise their share-holdings should advise the Secretary, together with a note of the price they are willing to accept.

JAMES A. MATHIESON

Goalkeeper.

Was born at Methil, Fifeshire, and transferred to Middlesbrough from Raith Rovers, 1926. At Ayresome he secured Second Division Medals in 1927 and 1929. Came to Griffin Park in 1934. The Club's best goalkeeper in recent years. Height is 6ft. 1½in.

FIXTURES, SEASON 1935-36.

FIRST TEAM

Date. 1935.	Opponents.	Ground.	GOALS F.	A.
Aug. 31	Bolton Wanderers	A	2	0
Sept. 5	Blackburn Rovers	H	3	1
„ 7	Huddersfield Town	H	1	2
„ 14	Middlesbrough	A	0	0
„ 18	Derby County	A	1	2
„ 21	Aston Villa	H	1	2
„ 28	Wolverhampton Wdrs.	A	2	5
Oct. 5	Sheffield Wednesday	H	2	2
„ 12	Portsmouth	A	3	1
„ 19	Stoke City	H	0	0
„ 26	Manchester City	A	1	2
Nov. 2	Arsenal	H	2	1
„ 9	Birmingham	A	1	1
„ 16	Sunderland	H	1	5
„ 23	Chelsea	A	1	2
„ 30	Leeds United	H	2	2
Dec. 7	Grimsby Town	A	1	6
„ 14	Liverpool	H	1	2
„ 21	West Bromwich Albion	A	0	1
„ 25	Preston North End	H	5	2
„ 26	Preston North End	A	4	2
„ 28	Bolton Wanderers	H	4	0
1936.				
Jan. 1	Blackburn Rovers	A	0	1
„ 4	Huddersfield Town	A	2	2
„ 11	(3) Leicester City	A	0	1
„ 18	Middlesbrough	H	1	0
„ 25	(4) Aston Villa	A	2	2
Feb. 1	Wolverhampton Wdrs.	H	5	0
„ 8	Sheffield Wednesday	A	3	3
„ 15	(5) Portsmouth	H		
„ 22	Stoke City	A	2	2
„ 29	(6) Birmingham	H		
Mar. 7	Arsenal	A		
„ 14	(S.-F.) Manchester City			
„ 21	Sunderland	A		
„ 28	Chelsea	H		
April 4	Leeds United	A		
„ 10	Everton	A		
„ 11	Grimsby Town	H		
„ 13	Everton	H		
„ 18	Liverpool	A		
„ 25	(F.) West Brom. Alb.	H		
May 2	Derby County	H		

SECOND TEAM

Date. 1935.	Opponents.	Ground.	GOALS F.	A.
Aug. 31	Charlton Athletic	H	2	1
Sept 4	Watford	A	1	3
„ 7	Clapton Orient	A	0	0
„ 12	Watford	H	2	1
„ 14	Southend United	H	1	0
„ 21	Northampton Town	A	1	0
„ 25	Luton Town	A	1	4
„ 28	Crystal Palace	H	4	0
Oct. 2	Luton Town	H	4	3
„ 5	Reading	A	1	2
„ 7	Met. Police—I.C. Cup	H	2	0
„ 9	Bournemouth & Bos.	H	5	2
„ 12	Tottenham Hotspur	H	2	1
„ 19	Bristol City	A	3	1
„ 21	C. Orient—L.C. Cup	A	3	1
„ 26	Millwall	H	4	0
Nov. 2	West Ham United	A	1	0
„ 9	Swansea Town	H	2	0
„ 11	Fulham (L.C.Cup,S.F.)	H	2	0
„ 16	Leicester City	A	3	2
„ 23	Coventry City	H	4	1
„ 30	Arsenal	A	0	1
Dec. 7	Southampton	H	4	0
„ 14	Brighton & Hove A.	A	1	0
„ 21	Queen's Park Rgrs.	H	3	1
„ 25	Chelsea	A	2	2
„ 26	Chelsea	H	2	1
„ 28	Charlton Athletic	A	1	3
Jan. 4	Clapton Orient	H	5	1
„ 11	Fulham	H	4	0
„ 18	Southend United	A	4	2
„ 25	Northampton Town	H	5	1
Feb. 1	Crystal Palace	A	1	3
„ 8	Reading	H	0	1
„ 15	Tottenham Hotspur	A		
„ 22	Bristol City	H	3	0
„ 29	Millwall	A		
Mar. 7	West Ham United	H		
„ 14	Swansea Town	A		
„ 21	Leicester City	H		
„ 25	Bournemouth & Bos.	A		
„ 28	Coventry City	A		
April 4	Arsenal	H		
„ 10	Portsmouth	H		
„ 11	Southampton	A		
„ 13	Portsmouth	A		
„ 18	Brighton & Hove A.	H		
„ 25	Queen's Park Rgrs.	A		
May 2	Fulham	A		

Half Time Scores.

	F.	A.			F	A
A—Arsenal v. Barnsley	......	......	J—Portsmouth v. West Brom.		......	......
B—Fulham v. Derby C.	......	......	K—Sheffield W. v. Leeds		......	......
C—Grimsby v. Middlesbro'	......	......	L—P.N.E. v. Sunderland		......	......
D—Sheffield U. v. 'Spurs	......	......	M—Burnley v. W. Ham		......	......
E—Aston Villa v. Liverpool	......	......	N—Charlton v. Swansea		......	......
F—Bolton W. v. Stoke City	......	......	O—Bournemouth v. Q.P.R.		......	......
G—Everton v. Man. City	......	......	P—Bristol R. v. Millwall		......	......
H—Huddersfield v. Blackburn	......	......	R—Crystal Palace v. Coventry		......	......

"GET YOUR FAT HEAD OUT O' THE LIGHT, POTTIE. I'M AS INTERESTED IN THIS PROBLEM AS YOU ARE!"

The Next Games.

Next Saturday Brentford Reserves will entertain West Ham United Reserves. When the teams met earlier in the season at West Ham, the Bees won by the only goal scored. West Ham are eighth in the London Combination, but even so Brentford should complete a " double."

* * *

The Saturday following the Reserves will travel across country to Swansea. They have an opportunity there to complete yet another " double " for at Griffin Park earlier in the season the Bees won by two clear goals.

* * *

On March 21st, the Reserves will be at home to Leicester City Reserves, who they defeated by three goals to two at Leicester.

The attention of supporters is drawn to the fact that the prices of seats bookable for the Bees' visit to Highbury is 5s. each, and applications should be made direct with the Arsenal Club. This is, of course, providing that the original fixture is carried out and the Bees oppose the Highbury men next Saturday.

" BUSY BEE " CONTINUES.

I cannot let this opportunity pass without wishing both Jack Astley and Charlie Fletcher the best of luck with their new clubs. As you all probably know the first-named was recently transferred to Coventry City, and Fletcher left us for Burnley after the London Combination game with Bristol City on Saturday last. Both have rendered good service to the Bees.

BRENTFORD FOOTBALL AND SPORTS CLUB, LIMITED.

Registered Office:—GRIFFIN PARK, BRAEMAR ROAD, BRENTFORD.

President and Chairman:
MR. L. P. SIMON.

ALDERMAN W. FLEWITT, J.P.   MR. H. W. DODGE.
MR. H. N. BLUNDELL.   MR. C. L. SIMON.
MR. H. J. SAUNDERS.

Hon. Treasurer:
ALDERMAN W. FLEWITT, J.P.
Club Medical Officer: DR. A. D. GOWANS.

Telephones:
GROUND: EALING 1744.
PRIVATE HOUSE: EALING 1183.

Vice-Chairman:
MR. F. A. DAVIS.

MR. F. W. BARTON.
ALDERMAN H. F. DAVIS.
MR. J. R. HUGHES, J.P., C.C.

Secretary-Manager:
MR. H. C. CURTIS,
"DORINCOURT," BOSTON GARDENS, BRENTFORD.

Telegraphic Address:
CURTIS, FOOTBALL, BRENTFORD.
Ground: GRIFFIN PARK, EALING ROAD, BRENTFORD.

No. 16   Saturday, March 14th, 1936.

Notes from the Hive.

"BITTERS"—AND SWEETS.

The strange thing about our team is that we appear to be playing better football on foreign grounds. Naturally every game has to be taken on its individual merits for there are often circumstances which can almost wholly account for an unexpected result, but there can be no two opinions that Brentford are playing remarkably well away from home and what is more, getting results.

Two games have been played since the last issue of the Official Programme, and both might be termed unexpected results, for few could have anticipated the defeat of the Bees against Birmingham, at Griffin Park, to be followed by a well-earned success at Leeds on Saturday last.

Now take a glance at the First Division table! Has anyone seen such a state of affairs before! The equality of the whole lot outside say the first three clubs is amazing. It might be said, without much stretch of imagination, that all the clubs, apart from those occupying the three leading places, are directly concerned with the relegation bogey. This unusual position makes the position less fraught with anxiety for the clubs concerned, because the risk is shared by so many, and in a brief period the position can be so completely changed. It is all very helpful from an interest sustaining viewpoint.

FATE BEATS THE BEES.

Fate beat Brentford in the home game with Birmingham a fortnight ago. This is not the name of a player new to League football, but a goddess who sometimes makes her presence felt either in favour or against a club. We experienced the frowns, instead of the smiles, of Dame Fortune in our game with Birmingham. The first blow came at the end of twelve minutes' play when Poyser sustained a groin injury and had to leave the field for good. The Bees played up in great style with depleted numbers, and enjoyed much the better of the play, so much so, that actually a good win should have been recorded instead of a 1—0 defeat. Unfortunately the control of the game left something to be desired, as some of the critics pointed out in their reviews of the game, but that apart Brentford should have still finished well on the right side, if our boys had received their deserts. Nothing would go right, however, for try as they would, and no team could have put more endeavour into their

play than did the Bees, nothing of a tangible nature rewarded our superhuman efforts.

The framework of the Birmingham goal was struck several times and other efforts missed by inches —then there was that almost impassable barrier, Harry Hibbs, to contend with. To England's goalkeeper we offer our heartiest congratulations. He kept a magnificent goal throughout; in fact it was Harry Hibbs and Fanny Fate who beat Brentford, although Birmingham, as a team, got the credit, the points and the bonus money.

VICTORY AT LEEDS.

The Bees soon showed Leeds at Leeds, on Saturday last, that the home defeat of the previous week had had no adverse effect on either their play or confidence. Our boys started on the top notes and scored in the first minute of the game. McCulloch gave Reid a chance right from the kick-off and our left wingman made no mistake, the ball being in the net before many had realised that the game had started.

Ten minutes before the interval the home side equalised, and ten minutes before the close good play by Wilson provided Hopkins with a chance and the last named took a shot from twenty yards range, the ball entering the net off the far post.

After having the better of the opening half, the superiority of the Bees was even more pronounced after ends were changed.

Three or four goals might easily have come our way in the closing half, for early on a penalty should have been awarded, then McCulloch had a goal disallowed which looked a perfectly good one, and in the last minute our centre forward again got the ball in the net, but was adjudged offside. It is pleasing to record that in this game Bateman resumed after his operation for cartilage trouble and played a fine game.

RESERVES' REVIEW.

Brentford Reserves have regained the leadership of the London Combination by collecting three points from their last two games.

Against Millwall, at New Cross, a hard game resulted in a goalless draw. On Saturday last West Ham Reserves were beaten at Griffin Park by four clear goals. Mc-Aloon, who has been doing extremely well for some time, performed the "hat trick," and Sullivan, from a penalty, got the other goal.

LANCASHIRE VISITORS HERE TO-DAY.

We have the pleasure of according a warm welcome to Manchester City this afternoon. It will be remembered that when the teams met at Maine Road last October the game was a none too pleasant one, and incidents led up to the ordering off of Duncan McKenzie and Brook, the City outside left. We sincerely trust that there will be no repetition of such incidents in to-day's game, which it is hoped will be fought out on the best sporting lines and so provide an enjoyable entertainment for all concerned.

Although Manchester City have only two more points than Brentford, our visitors are many places higher on the League Table, which just proves the point already stressed that there is precious little to choose between the big majority of teams in the First Division at the moment.

The City have collected ten points from 15 away games by virtue of four wins and two drawn games. They have won 2—0 at Liverpool, 3—2 at Highbury, 1—0 at Birmingham and 2—1 at Portsmouth, while draws have been effected at Bolton (3—3) and Everton (2—2)

"BUSY BEE."

Jottings from the Board Room.

At the meeting of the Football League Clubs held at Manchester, on Monday last, March 9th, the following resolution was unanimously passed :

"This meeting of clubs and members of the Football League, Limited, hereby decide to revert as from to-day to the fixtures approved at the annual fixtures meeting of the League in June, 1935, for the 1935-36 season, save for the changes made necessary by the alteration of fixtures on Saturday, February 29th and Saturday, March 7th."

Thus by this we now play Manchester City to-day and on Saturday, April 4th, we play the Arsenal F.C. at Highbury. The fixture list in to-day's programme is now in order.

The following games postponed on February 15th, owing to fog, have been re-arranged as follows :

v. Portsmouth (Football League), at Brentford, on Wednesday, March 25th.

v. 'Spurs Reserves (London Combination), at Tottenham, on Wednesday, April 1st.

Comparative records with last season are as follows :

Football League—

	P.	W.	D.	L.	F.	A.	P.
This Season	31	10	8	13	55	52	28
Last Season	31	18	7	6	16	37	43

London Combination—

	P.	W.	D.	L.	F.	A.	P.
This Season	34	24	3	7	80	37	51
Last Season	34	18	7	9	57	39	43

Goal scorers to date are :—

Football League.—McCulloch 12, Hopkins 11, Holliday 9, Scott 8, Fletcher 5, Robson 3, Reid 3, J. C. Burns 1, Dunn 1, Muttitt 1, McKenzie 1.—Total 55.

London Combination.—Dunn 25, McAloon 15, Brown 14, Sullivan 8, Muttitt 6, Gibbons 5, Fenton 2, Smith (C.) 2, Fletcher 2, L. Smith 1.—Total 80.

Heartiest congratulations to our Band —the Hanwell Silver Band—on their great performance in being awarded Second Prize in the big Leicester Contest, held on Saturday last, March 7th. Over 80 bands competed. A great achievement.

We had rather an anxious time during our visit to Leeds on Saturday last. Our train was due to arrive at 1.46 p.m., but owing to some trouble with the engine, we did not arrive until about 2.45 p.m. By a hurried charabanc trip to the ground —during which the players began dressing for the game—we were able to take the field in good time, and celebrated our haste by Bobby Reid scoring our first goal within one minute of the start of the game.

It is with regret that Portsmouth F.C. are unable to accept our proposed date— April 22nd (Wednesday)—for our postponed game, as we would have been able to kick off at 6 or 6.15 p.m. The game will therefore be played on this ground on Wednesday, March 25th, kick-off at 3.30 p.m.

Supporters are asked to note that no further applications can be considered for F.A. Cup Final tickets. The few this Club are to receive have already been allocated, and those who are to receive them have been notified. The same remark applies to International Tickets for the England v. Scotland game at Wembley on Saturday, April 4th.

The Reserves are to-day away to Swansea Town Reserves, and on Saturday next, March 21st, will be at home to Leicester City Reserves, kick-off at 3.30.

Tickets for seats, numbered and reserved at 3/6 and 4/- can be obtained for our game v. Chelsea, on Saturday, March 28th. Applications by post must be accompanied with remittance and stamped addressed envelope, otherwise they will not be considered.

The following fixtures have been arranged at the Empire Pool and Sports Arena, Wembley :

Saturday, March 14th. — Wembley Canadians v. Brighton Tigers. National League.

Monday, March 16th.—Final Play-off (Semi-final Round) London-Paris Tournament—Wembley Lions v. Stade Francais; also Miss Cecilia Colledge, runner-up in the Olympic Championships of 1936, will perform the full Olympic schedule of figures and free skating.

Thursday, March 19th.—Wembley Lions v. Kensington Corinthians. London Cup.

Saturday, March 21st.—A.A.A. Indoor Athletic Championships.

Thursday, March 26th. — Wembley Lions v. Richmond Hawks. London Cup.

Saturday, March 28th. — Wembley Canadians v. Earl's Court Rangers. London Cup.

Wednesday, March 25th.
BRENTFORD v. PORTSMOUTH
(Football League) Kick-off at 3.30 p.m.

Shots from the Spot.

Alex James, Arsenal's inimitable inside left, writing in the " Evening News " during the week, and discussing Scotland's team for their match against England at Wembley, on April 4th, says Davey McCulloch is first favourite for the centre-forward position.

* * *

Alex is inclined to fancy Bobby Reid's chances for the outside-left position, too, and Jackson, the Chelsea reserve 'keeper, is probably marked down for the place between the sticks. That's three London Scots as possibles already !

* * *

London clubs are clustered together at the top of the Second Division table, and with three points separating Charlton Athletic, West Ham and Tottenham Hotspur, it would take a brave man to prophesy which one or two or none at all will move into the upper circle. If any should be successful they would be heartily welcomed to the higher sphere.

* * *

Many supporters will remember Mapson, the young Reading goalkeeper, for it was his brilliant display that was largely responsible for our Reserves' defeat when Reading visited Griffin Park in February. During the week he was transferred to Sunderland.

There is a great chance for an all-London Cup Final this year. Should it come off it will make history, for it will be the first time that two Metropolitan clubs have opposed each other in the Final at Wembley.

Arsenal, who are the favourites, are opposed to Grimsby Town in the semi-final, while the other London club, Fulham, is meeting Sheffield United.

* * *

Dean (Everton), Watson (Southampton), Johnson (Mansfield) and Camsell (Middlesbrough) are men who are still in first class football who have scored over 300 goals in Football League games.

* * *

George Poyser, our left back, was injured in the game with Birmingham, and had to be carried off the field, having pulled a thigh muscle. George has made a splendid recovery and is now in full training.

* * *

Hopkins and Richards were again " capped " and played for Wales against Ireland, on Wednesday. Wales lost by the odd goal in five and are out of the running for the international championship, which now rests between England and Scotland at Wembley, on April 4th. England must win to finish at the top, but a draw would suffice Scotland.

OUR VISITORS TO-DAY.
HOW THEY MAY LINE UP.

———◆———

Founded nearly sixty years ago, Manchester City, our visitors to-day, have twice been runners-up for the League Championship, and have finished at the head of matters in Division II. on four occasions. They have reached the Cup Final four times also, winning the trophy twice.

In 1933 and 1934 they reached the last round in successive years, taking the Cup at the second attempt.

Swift, Frank V. (goalkeeper).—Born at Blackpool. Height 6ft. 2in. Weight 13st. 6lb. Had rapid rise to fame. Went to Maine Road from Blackpool junior club in 1933 and by December of that year was in first team. In following April he was a member of the Cup-winning side. Collapsed under the strain at the end of the final against Portsmouth. Did not miss a single game last season and has gained inter-League honours this campaign.

Dale, William (right back).—Born at Manchester. Height 5ft. 8½in. Weight 10st. 10lb. Joined Manchester United as an amateur in 1925 from Sandbach Ramblers (Cheshire League). Became professional soon afterwards and midway through season 1931-32 moved over to the City. Played in the Cup Finals of 1933 and 1934. Can play on either flank.

Barkas, Samuel (left back).—Born at Tyne Dock, South Shields. Height 5ft. 8¾in. Weight 12st. 4lb. Tried his hand at mining and farming before taking up football as a profession. Joined Bradford City from Middle Dock, a Tyneside junior club, in 1928. Helped them to gain the Northern section championship in his first season, and received a benefit at the unusually young age of 23. In April, 1934, the City paid a substantial fee for his transfer. Has been their first choice ever since and has assisted the English League. Robust but fair.

Percival, John (wing half)—Born at Low Pettington, Co. Durham. Height, 5ft. 7½in. Weight 11st. 3lb. Has had the misfortune to understudy players of the calibre of Busby, Bray and McLuckie since joining City from the North-East in the early part of season 1932-3. Injury to Busby permitted him a fairly long run this year, while he played outside right at Preston.

Marshall, Robert (centre half).—This player was born at Hucknall, Nottingham. Height 5ft. 10¾in. Weight 12st. 4lb. Is the club's utility man. Can adapt himself to an attacking or defensive position as is required, though first and foremost an inside right. Was secured by Sunderland from Hucknall Olympic in 1920, and moved to Maine Road seven seasons later. Won Second Division championship medal in first season with City (1927-8) and was also in the Cup-winning side two years ago.

Bray, John (left half).—Born at Oswaldtwistle, Lancs. Height 5ft. 8½lb. Weight 10st. 6lb. First choice for England this season. Went to Maine Road from Manchester Central in 1929. It was two years before he got his first team place and then his appearances were intermittent. Plays cricket for Accrington in the Lancashire League. First played for England against Wales last year.

Toseland, Ernest (outside right). Born at Northampton. Height 5ft. 5½in. Weight 10st. A product of

BRENTFORD v. M

BREN

Red an

1—M

2—WILSON
Right Back

4—McKENZIE
Right Half

5—
C

7—HOPKINS   8—SCOTT   9—McC
Outside Right   Inside Right   Centr

Referee—
MR. E. C. MILLS (Warminster, Wilts.)

1
C

12—BROOK   13—DOHERT
Outside Left   Inside Left

17—BRAY   18—
Left Half   Ce

20—BARKAS
Left Back

22—
G

MANCHE
Sky Blue Sh

THE LEAGUE—DIVISION I.

	P.	W.	D.	L.	F.	A.	P.
Sunderland	32	21	5	6	89	50	47
Derby County	32	15	9	8	47	33	39
Huddersfield T.	32	15	9	8	49	45	39
Stoke City	32	15	5	12	49	46	35
Arsenal	30	13	8	9	62	34	34
Birmingham	31	12	10	9	43	40	34
Manchester C.	32	14	4	14	52	48	32
Portsmouth	30	13	6	11	42	47	32
Preston N.E.	31	12	6	13	46	46	30
Bolton W.	31	10	10	11	50	57	30
West Brom. A.	31	12	3	15	71	61	29
Middlesbrough	32	12	5	15	62	58	29
Liverpool	31	11	7	13	46	48	29
Sheffield Wed.	31	11	7	13	56	61	29
Grimsby Town	32	12	5	15	44	54	29
BRENTFORD	31	10	8	13	55	52	28
Leeds United	30	10	8	12	46	44	28
Wolves	31	11	6	14	54	58	28
Everton	32	8	12	12	62	71	28
Chelsea	29	9	9	12	42	57	27
Aston Villa	32	10	6	16	62	90	26
Blackburn R.	32	10	6	16	42	71	26

NCHESTER CITY

FORD

Stripes

ESON
per

3—BATEMAN
Left Back

ES   6—RICHARDS
alf   Left Half

CH   10—HOLLIDAY   11—REID
ard   Inside Left   Outside Left

Linesmen—   Messrs. W. E. Howard (blue flag)
and C. F. B. Harding (red flag)

LSON
orward

15—HERD   16—TOSELAND
Inside Right   Outside Right

HALL   19—PERCIVAL
alf   Right Half

21—DALE
Right Back

FT
er

ER CITY

te Knickers

LONDON COMBINATION

	P.	W.	D.	L.	Goals F.	A.	P.
BRENTFORD	34	24	3	7	80	37	51
Portsmouth	34	21	8	5	93	45	50
Arsenal	34	23	3	8	85	34	49
Reading	36	19	5	12	79	67	43
Swansea Town	35	18	6	11	64	52	42
Crystal Palace	35	18	6	11	87	75	42
Chelsea	36	16	8	12	74	66	40
West Ham U.	36	17	5	14	87	61	39
Queen's Park Rgrs.	34	17	5	12	68	51	39
Charlton Ath.	37	17	4	16	76	66	38
Coventry City	35	16	5	14	69	62	37
Millwall	35	15	6	14	53	56	36
Luton Town	35	15	4	16	93	89	34
Tottenham H.	32	12	8	12	82	73	32
Northampton T.	35	11	9	15	64	64	31
Leicester City	35	14	3	18	63	81	31
Fulham	34	11	7	16	64	62	29
Clapton Orient	35	9	11	15	46	78	29
Southend U.	34	9	8	17	55	82	26
Watford	34	11	3	20	65	100	25
Bournemouth	35	9	6	20	55	88	24
Brighton & Hove A.	34	8	7	19	54	90	23
Southampton	34	7	8	19	42	63	22
Bristol City	36	9	4	23	50	104	22

x INDEPENDENT—Best Reports and Pictures

Higham Ferrers Town, Northants. Entered League Football with Coventry City, but moved to Manchester before completing a season with that club. Is very fast and carries a powerful shot. Was a member of the Cup-winning side in 1934 and also the defeated finalist team in the previous year.

Herd, Alexander (inside forward).—Born at Bowhill, Lanarkshire. Height 5ft. 7in. Weight 10st. 7lb. After a short spell with Hearts of Beith, a Scottish junior side, he entered the first class game with Hamilton Academicals. Joined the latter club at the age of 16. Was secured by Manchester City in February, 1933, and two months later led their attack at Wembley. Gained a Cup-winner's medal in 1934. Fills any of the inside forward berths and has also played on the wing.

Tilson, Samuel Frederick (inside forward). — Born at Barnsley. Height 5ft. 9in. Weight 11st. 9½lb. Came to the front with Barnsley, from whom he joined City along with Eric Brook in 1928. Has been dogged by injury throughout his career. Missed schoolboy international honours, while for a similar reason he has since been deprived of an England cap and a place in the 1933 Cup Final team. Scored four goals in his first match after being moved from inside left to centre forward and has led England's attack.

Doherty, Peter Dermont (inside forward).—Born at Coleraine, Ireland. Height 5ft. 10in. Weight 11st. 1lb. This fine utility forward was signed from Blackpool on 19th February at a fee stated to be a record for both clubs. Was brought out by Glentoran and had twice been reserve for his country when signed by Blackpool at the age of 20 in November, 1933. Has now caps against England, Scotland and Wales. Is red-headed.

Brook, Eric (outside left).—Born at Mexborough, Yorks. Height 5ft. 6¾in. Weight 11st. 9lb. After playing for Mexborough and District Schools had experience with Oxford Road Y.M.C.A., Swinton Prims., Mexborough Athletic (Midland League) and Wath Athletic. Barnsley took him from the latter club and he moved to Maine Road with Tilson in 1928. Has numerous England caps.

How to get Rich Quick

At a meeting at which representatives of this Club attended, the following particulars in connection with one of the leading Pool firms were given :

It was alleged that—

1. The attendances in all 44 League games one Saturday was **550,000** odd.

2. This represented gate proceeds of approximately **£48,125.**

3. On this same day ONE Pool company received the amazing income of nearly **£700,000,** which, it will be noted, is 14½ times the amount of income from gate proceeds received in all Football League games played on the one day.

4. Pool companies take either 5, 7½ or 10 per cent. of the total income, so taking the percentage as 7½, it gives the pool company the huge sum of nearly **£50,000** as their share for ONE week.

It must be admitted that the Pool companies' weekly expenses are considerable, yet to think that any business can receive such huge sums weekly without any business risks seems like a fairy tale. Some people are making fortunes at a quick rate.

Well ! Well ! ! Well ! ! !

SHARES & SHAREHOLDERS

In spite of our previous notes in this programme, the Management are still receiving enquiries from supporters who are desiring to acquire shares in the Club. We repeat that the shares of the Club are fully issued, and unless existing shareholders desire to realise, there are no shares available.

The 6% Debentures of £50 each are still being issued, but only a small number now remain, and when these have been issued the finances of the Club will have been completely consolidated and settled

The Club have been the leaseholders of Griffin Park, and supporters will be interested to know that next March the freehold of the ground is being purchased and the Club will then be in the happy position of being the owners of the ground.

Particulars of the 6% Debentures will be forwarded on application to the Secretary.

Shareholders desiring to realise their share-holdings should advise the Secretary, together with a note of the price they are willing to accept.

JOSEPH JAMES
Centre Half.

Born at Battersea, 1911. First big club— Brentford. A Curtis discovery who was taken on as an assistant on the ground after a trial at age of 17. Turned professional 1929. Seized his chance in 1933-34 season when he stepped into Jimmy Bain's shoes. Essentially a defensive pivot, but constructive play is steadily improving.

FIXTURES, SEASON 1935-36.

FIRST TEAM

Date. 1935.	Opponents.	Ground.	GOALS F.	A.
Aug. 31	Bolton Wanderers	A	2	0
Sept. 5	Blackburn Rovers	H	3	2
,, 7	Huddersfield Town	H	1	2
,, 14	Middlesbrough	A	0	0
,, 18	Derby County	A	1	2
,, 21	Aston Villa	H	1	2
,, 28	Wolverhampton Wdrs.	A	2	3
Oct. 5	Sheffield Wednesday	H	2	2
,, 12	Portsmouth	A	3	1
,, 19	Stoke City	H	0	0
,, 26	Manchester City	A	1	2
Nov. 2	Arsenal	H	2	1
,, 9	Birmingham	A	1	2
,, 16	Sunderland	H	1	5
,, 23	Chelsea	A	1	2
,, 30	Leeds United	H	2	0
Dec. 7	Grimsby Town	A	1	6
,, 14	Liverpool	H	1	2
,, 21	West Bromwich Albion	A	0	1
,, 25	Preston North End	H	5	2
,, 26	Preston North End	A	4	2
,, 28	Bolton Wanderers	H	4	0
1936.				
Jan. 1	Blackburn Rovers	A	0	1
,, 4	Huddersfield Town	A	2	2
,, 11	(3) Leicester City	A	0	1
,, 18	Middlesbrough	H	1	0
,, 25	(4) Aston Villa	A	2	2
Feb. 1	Wolverhampton Wdrs.	H	5	0
,, 8	Sheffield Wednesday	A	3	3
,, 15	(5)			
,, 22	Stoke City	A	2	2
,, 29	(6) Birmingham	H	0	1
Mar. 7	Leeds United	A	2	1
,, 14	Manchester City	H		
,, 21	(S.-F.) Sunderland	A		
,, 25	Portsmouth	H		
,, 28	Chelsea	H		
April 4	Arsenal	A		
,, 10	Everton	A		
,, 11	Grimsby Town	H		
,, 13	Everton	H		
,, 18	Liverpool	A		
,, 25	(F.) West Brom. Alb.	H		
May 2	Derby County	H		

SECOND TEAM

Date. 1935.	Opponents.	Ground.	GOALS F.	A.
Aug. 31	Charlton Athletic	H	2	1
Sept. 4	Watford	A	1	3
,, 7	Clapton Orient	A	0	0
,, 12	Watford	H	2	1
,, 14	Southend United	H	1	0
,, 21	Northampton Town	A	1	0
,, 25	Luton Town	A	1	4
,, 28	Crystal Palace	H	4	0
Oct. 3	Luton Town	H	4	3
,, 5	Reading	A	1	2
,, 7	Met Police—L.C.Cup	H	2	0
,, 9	Bournemouth & Bos.	H	5	2
,, 12	Tottenham Hotspur	H	2	1
,, 19	Bristol City	A	3	1
,, 21	C. Orient—L.C.Cup	H	3	1
,, 26	Millwall	A	4	0
Nov. 2	West Ham United	A	1	0
,, 9	Swansea Town	H	2	0
,, 11	Fulham (L.C.Cup.S.F.)	H	2	0
,, 16	Leicester City	A	3	2
,, 23	Coventry City	H	4	1
,, 30	Arsenal	A	0	1
Dec. 7	Southampton	H	4	0
,, 14	Brighton & Hove A.	A	1	0
,, 21	Queen's Park Rgrs.	A	3	1
,, 25	Chelsea	A	2	2
,, 26	Chelsea	H	2	1
,, 28	Charlton Athletic	A	1	5
Jan. 4	Clapton Orient	H	5	1
,, 11	Fulham	H	4	0
,, 18	Southend United	A	4	2
,, 25	Northampton Town	H	5	1
Feb. 1	Crystal Palace	A	1	3
,, 8	Reading	H	0	1
,, 15				
,, 22	Bristol City	H	3	0
,, 29	Millwall	A	0	0
Mar. 7	West Ham United	H	4	0
,, 14	Swansea Town	A		
,, 21	Leicester City	H		
,, 25	Bournemouth & Bos.	A		
,, 28	Coventry City	A		
	Arsenal	H		
April 1	Tottenham Hotspur	A		
,, 10	Portsmouth	H		
,, 11	Southampton	A		
,, 13	Portsmouth	A		
,, 18	Brighton & Hove A.	H		
,, 25	Queen's Park Rgrs.	A		
May 2	Fulham	A		

Half Time Scores.

	F.	A.			F	A
A—Aston Villa v. Leeds U.	......	......	J—Sheffield W. v. Sunderland		......	......
B—Bolton W. v. Chelsea	......	......	K—Wolves v. West Brom. A.		......	......
C—Derby C. v. Stoke C.	......	......	L—Burnley v. Sheffield U.		......	......
D—Everton v. Blackburn R.	......	......	M—Charlton v. Southampton		......	......
E—Huddersfield v. Liverpool	......	......	N—Fulham v. Bradford		......	......
F—Middlesbrough v. Grimsby	......	......	O—Manchester U. v. Swansea		......	......
G—Portsmouth v. Birmingham	......	......	P—Tottenham v. West Ham		......	......
H—Preston N.E. v. Arsenal	......	......	R—Bristol R. v. Q.P.R.		......	......

MODERN TIMES (Modern Version!) (Based on an episode in Char'ie Chaplin's film)

" For heaven's sake come out! You'll get killed as well as ruin the whole machinery."

" Well, I heard a little squeak that sounded like ' Pools,' so I chucked this spanner in to stop it!"

The Next Games.

Next Saturday the Bees are away to Sunderland. This is a very stiff hurdle, for they are the leaders of the First Division, being well clear of their nearest rivals on points, and seem almost certain to carry off the championship. It will be remembered that when they visited Griffin Park they gave a grand display of football, and beat the Bees by five goals to one. They are not, however, invincible on their own ground, having lost to Aston Villa, whilst last Saturday they only drew with Everton. The Bees will do their utmost to wipe out that heavy defeat, but they will have to go all out to pull off a draw.

On Wednesday, March 25th, Brentford will be at home to Portsmouth. This game should have been played on February 15th, but was postponed owing to fog.

The following Saturday, Chelsea will visit Griffin Park. This should be a big attraction, for besides being a local Derby, Chelsea are fighting to avoid relegation. When Brentford went to Stamford Bridge they lost a close game by two goals to one.

On April 4th, Brentford will be engaged in another local Derby, this time having to visit Highbury for their re-arranged fixture with the Arsenal.

Next Saturday the Reserves will be at home to Leicester City Reserves, and then have three away fixtures. On March 25th they visit Bournemouth and Boscombe; on March 28th, Coventry City, and on April 1st, Tottenham Hotspur.

BRENTFORD FOOTBALL AND SPORTS CLUB, LIMITED.

Registered Office:—GRIFFIN PARK, BRAEMAR ROAD, BRENTFORD.

President and Chairman:
MR. L. P. SIMON.

Vice-Chairman:
MR. F. A. DAVIS.

ALDERMAN W. FLEWITT, J.P.
MR. H. N. BLUNDELL.
MR. H. J. SAUNDERS.

MR. H. W. DODGE.
MR. C. L. SIMON.

MR. F. W. BARTON.
ALDERMAN H. F. DAVIS.
MR. J. R. HUGHES, J.P., C.C.

Hon. Treasurer:
ALDERMAN W. FLEWITT, J.P.
Club Medical Officer: DR. A. D. GOWANS.

Secretary-Manager:
MR. H. C. CURTIS,
" DORINCOURT," BOSTON GARDENS, BRENTFORD.

Telephones:
GROUND: EALING 1744.
PRIVATE HOUSE: EALING 1183.

Telegraphic Address:
CURTIS, FOOTBALL, BRENTFORD.
Ground: GRIFFIN PARK, EALING ROAD, BRENTFORD.

No. 17.   Wednesday, March 25th, 1936.

Notes from the Hive.

BEES MOVING UPWARDS.

If things continue to go on as they have been doing it is conceivable that Brentford will finish with a better away record than at Griffin Park. At the moment the Bees have actually collected fifteen points in eighteen away games, while at home as many as fourteen have been conceded. If those home points had not been lost . . . but why lay too much stress on these home failures? Surely it is better to mete out due praise to our boys for such splendid performances away from home, which, after all, shows the fine fighting spirit which permeates the whole team on foreign territory.

Consistency may not have been the Bees' motto this season, but after all it is the aggregate which counts.

The loss of a home point to Manchester City was very unfortunate for all concerned, but the fact that the City could not score was something to be proud about. The previous game they had found the net six times and after drawing a blank against the Bees, went on to notch no fewer than seven goals against Bolton Wanderers.

Then there was that affair at Sunderland last week-end. You have probably heard what happened —but read on to get the stories in their right rotation.

Then to-day the two teams bang in the centre of the League table, right next to each other, are in opposition at Griffin Park. A win for the Bees and we just steal into the top half—never, we hope, to descend any lower again this season.

ANOTHER HOME POINT CONCEDED.

Another valuable home point, the fourteenth this season, was conceded on the occasion of Manchester City's visit last Saturday week. Fortunately very few clubs in the First Division have done better than Brentford away from home this season, otherwise the lapses of the Bees at Griffin Park would have proved much more serious than they have done—and things are quite bad enough now.

The game under review proved a goalless affair and as a spectacle not as thrilling as some anticipated. Yet there were some very bright moments when things seemed likely to happen. Quite early in the game Reid made a very good scoring effort that only missed by inches, and just after the same player, with a very good chance, finished poorly.

SWIFT—AND SURE.

In the second half the Bees exerted great pressure and were very unlucky not to score on more than one occasion. The fact that

no tangible reward came the way of our boys from the many attacks they made was largely due to the brilliance of Swift, in the City goal. Some really fine scoring attempts were made, in which most of our forwards had a direct hand, or should it be foot, but everything came alike to the City 'keeper. He simply refused to be beaten. It certainly did seem that Brentford would get their just deserts when McCulloch essayed a brilliant solo run, but once again Swift came to the rescue of the visitors with an equally brilliant save. Great credit must go to the City defenders, particularly Swift, for the skill and resolution they showed in the circumstances, but when all is said and done, it was very evident that this was not one of the Bees' lucky days; in fact a very unlucky one.

BEES' STARTLING WIN.

No doubt our supporters remember a little affair at Griffin Park last November, when Sunderland came along and stung our boys to the extent of five goals to one. That is easily the worst defeat sustained by the Bees at home this season. Ever since that big victory the famous Roker Park club have made such headway that they seem practically certain to win the championship.

Well, the return game took place at Roker Park on Saturday last, and not unnaturally the prophets marked down Sunderland as home winners. That fact did not worry our boys one little bit; in fact it probably added an incentive to prove the prophets all wrong and at the same time go all out for revenge. Whatever the reason, the Bees won a great victory over the prospective champions by the convincing margin of three goals to one. That was the best bit of news received at Griffin Park for a long time—a real startler for the whole football world. That great win brought two very valuable points, but what is more pleasing was the fine form displayed by our team, and with ordinary good fortune that decisive defeat sustained at home would have been completely wiped out. Brentford were much steadier and more resourceful in defence, while our attack was a much more potent force than the Sunderland quintette.

AN INTERVAL LEAD.

Fifteen minutes after the start Brentford took the lead through Holliday, who was distinctly unfortunate not to score at least three times before the breather.

The Bees continued to call the tune after the change of ends, but goals did not come, and when the home side equalised ten minutes from the end there were visions of a point being undeservedly lost. Happily that did not turn out to be the case, for McCulloch soon restored the Bees' advantage and just to make certain of success, McCulloch scored again before the end to give the Bees a well merited victory.

RESERVES' REVIEW.

Our Reserves came a cropper at Swansea last Saturday week, when the Welsh side scored no fewer than five times to which our boys were unable to reply.

On Saturday last, at Griffin Park, two valuable points were collected against Leicester City, which kept the Bees in striking distance of the present leaders of the London Combination — Portsmouth Reserves. Brentford only won by the narrow margin of a goal to nil, and many late-comers were deprived of seeing that rather remarkable goal scored. The visitors won the toss and Dunn kicked off, passed the ball to McAloon, back to Dunn, out to Fenton, centre to Dunn and the ball was in the net without a Leicester City player touching the ball.

BUSY BEE.

Jottings from the Board Room.

It is with deepest regret that we announce the death of Mr. John McKenna, President of the Football League and also a member of the Emergency Committee of the Football Association.

Mr. McKenna was taken suddenly ill and was removed to the Walton Hospital, Liverpool, on Friday last, where he died. He was 81 years of age.

By his death Football has lost a great personality. We extend our deepest sympathy to the members of Mr. McKenna's family.

Comparative records with last season are as follows:
Football League—

	P.	W.	D.	L.	F.	A.	P.
This Season	33	11	9	13	58	53	31
Last Season	33	20	7	6	71	40	47

London Combination—

	P.	W.	D.	L.	F.	A.	P.
This Season	36	25	3	8	81	42	53
Last Season	36	19	7	10	64	40	45

Goal scorers to date are:—
Football League.—McCulloch 14, Hopkins 11, Holliday 10, Scott 8, Fletcher 5, Robson 3, Reid 3, J. C. Burns 1, Dunn 1, Muttitt 1, McKenzie 1.—Total, 58.
London Combination.—Dunn 26, McAloon 15, Brown 14, Sullivan 8, Muttitt 6, Gibbons 5, Fenton 2, Smith (C.) 2, Fletcher 2, Smith (L.) 1.—Total 81.

Regarding our game v. the Arsenal on Saturday, April 4th, at Highbury, we are informed that the only bookable seats are at 5/- each. Applications should be sent direct to the Arsenal Club enclosing remittance and stamped addressed envelope.

The Reserves are to-day away to Bournemouth F.C. (London Combination).

In connection with our game v. Chelsea on this ground on Saturday next, March 28th, the kick-off is at 3.30 p.m. There are still a few tickets for numbered and reserved seats at 3/6 left. All the 4/- tickets have been disposed of. Applications by post must be accompanied with remittance and stamped addressed envelope. Seats in the Wing Stands will be UNRESERVED for Saturday next.

George Poyser, who was injured in the game v. Birmingham on February 29th, is still unfit. It was his intention to have a trial run out with the Reserves on Saturday last, but while training on Friday he again strained his groin (slightly).

The Reserves are away to Coventry City Reserves on Saturday next, and on April 1st (Wednesday) they play 'Spurs Reserves at Tottenham.

Heartiest congratulations to the Arsenal F.C. on their great achievement in reaching the Final. We wish them the best of good luck, and trust that they will be this year's Cup Holders.

Supporters still continue to write in for F.A. Cup Final tickets. I repeat that this club's small allocation has already been disposed of.

Two keys and a gent's pair of leather gloves were found in the ground on Saturday, March 14th. Please apply at the office.

Supporters are asked to " BEWARE OF PICKPOCKETS," as on March 14th, when we played Manchester City, two supporters had the misfortune to have their wallets stolen.

Including to-day's game v. Portsmouth we have six home and three away games to complete our programme. The three away games are: April 4th v. Arsenal; April 10th (Good Friday) v. Everton; and April 18th v. Liverpool.

The home games for the Easter programme will be as follows:
Good Friday, April 10th, v Portsmouth (London Combination), kick-off at 3.30 p.m.
Saturday, April 11th, v. Grimsby Town (Football League), kick-off at 3.30 p.m.
Easter Monday, April 13th, v. Everton (Football League), kick-off at 3.30 p.m.

The following events will take place at the Empire Pool and Sports Arena, Wembley:
Saturday, April 18th.—Rugby League Challenge Cup Final—Leeds v. Warrington.
Tuesday, May 5th.—At the Empire Pool, " Golden Gloves " Amateur Boxing Tournament—England v. America.
Thursday, May 7th.—At the Empire Stadium. Opening of the Speedway season. National League match—Wembley v. Wimbledon.
The British Ice Hockey Association fixtures at the Empire Pool are as follows:
Thursday, March 26th, Lions v. Hawks (London Cup); Saturday, March 28th, Canadians v. Rangers (London Cup); Thursday, April 2nd, Lions v. Streatham (London Cup); Saturday, April 4th, Canadians v. Corinthians (Final, Channel Cup).

Shots from the Spot.

We have the pleasure of extending a very cordial welcome to Portsmouth this afternoon. It will be remembered that this game was originally arranged to take place on February 15th, but the referee decided that the visibility was too bad for the game to take place.

* * *

The Bees won at Portsmouth last October by a 3—1 margin, so we are hopeful that our boys, with ground advantage, coupled with the added confidence which their great win at Sunderland should give them, that a " double " will be recorded to-day.

* * *

Away from home, Portsmouth have won three and drawn three out of sixteen games this season. They won 2—1 at Grimsby, 1—0 at Sheffield, and 3—2 at Highbury—but let us hope it will be a case of " you can't do that there 'ere !"

* * *

Portsmouth qualified for promotion to the First Division of the League in 1926-27 after a thrilling race with Manchester City, by the two-hundredth part of a goal— 1.7755 against 1.77049. On the last day of the season Pompey defeated Preston North End 5—1 at Fratton Park, and Manchester City conquered Bradford City 8—0 at Maine Road.

* * *

Rochford, Pompey's clever back, will not be seen to-day. The F.A. refused to release him from his international trial obligations. We sympathise with our visitors and hope that Rochford's detention may lead in due course to a cap.

It appears fairly certain now that another London First Division club will be seen at Griffin Park next season; possibly two. West Ham lead the Second Division with a one-point lead over Charlton and Sheffield United. The 'Spurs, despite their Bradford contingent, seem to have dropped out of the race for good.

* * *

By the way, have you noticed something rather unusual about this season with regard to the colours of the shirts of the leading clubs? Arsenal and Sheffield United, the Cup finalists, both wear red and white shirts; the United stripes and Arsenal red with white sleeves. Sunderland, easy champions, also wear red and white— stripes again. The Bees wear red and white, of course. This should help them gain added confidence for their terrific battle of the next few weeks !

* * *

So Arsenal and Sheffield United are to meet at Wembley. It will not only be a North v. South, but a First Division versus Second Division clash. Congratulations to our London neighbours and our Sheffield friends upon their success. It should be a splendid game. Arsenal bring to Wembley all their tradition and science, but in Sheffield United they will meet a truly gallant club whose run of 22 matches without a defeat spells " trouble," with a capital T for the Gunners.

* * *

The Cup records of the clubs are interesting. Sheffield United have won the Cup four times in five previous appearances in the final, twice since the beginning of the war, in 1914-15 and 1924-25; Arsenal once in three attempts, in 1930.

OUR VISITORS TO-DAY.

HOW THEY MAY LINE UP.

An interesting feature of the visit of Portsmouth to Griffin Park to-day is that until we gained promotion last year, " Pompey " were the only club to have won through from the Southern Section to Division I.

They were champions of the Third Division (South) in 1923, and four years later were runners-up in Division II.

Though they have never carried off the coveted trophy, twice in recent years—1929 and 1934—they have reached the Cup Final.

Gilfillan, John (goalkeeper).—Born at Townhill, Scotland. Height 5ft. 11½in. Weight 12st. Was formerly in the pit. Left that employment to enter professional soccer with Heart of Midlothian. Had to understudy Harkness, the famous international, and was loaned to East Fife. While with that club took the eye of Portsmouth, whom he joined in 1928. Also plays golf.

Morgan, Lewis (right back).—Born at Woodend, Fifeshire. Height 5ft. 8½in. Weight 11st. 7lb. Schoolboy international as inside left. Formerly with Bowhill Juns. (Fife), and then with Dundee. Played for Scottish League v. Irish League, 1933-34. Recreation : Walking.

Smith, William (left back).—Born at Whitburn, Co. Durham. Height 5ft. 8½in. Weight 12st. One of the famous family, brothers being English internationals—Jack (ex-Portsmouth and now with Bournemouth) and Septimus (Leicester City). Had experience in the Tottenham nursery at Northfleet and with South Shields before going to Fratton Park in 1929. Has played in every forward and half back position as well as full back.

Nichol, James (right half).—Born at Glasgow. Height 5ft. 11½in. Weight 11st. 7lb. Formerly with Gillingham. F.A. Cup medals : 1929, Portsmouth v. Bolton Wanderers ; 1934, Portsmouth v. Manchester City. Recreation : Golf.

Salmond, Robert (centre half).—Born at Kilmarnock, Scotland. Height 6ft. Weight 12st. Started with Abercainey Thistle, a Perthshire junior club. Then followed a spell with Dundee Vale End before arriving at Portsmouth in 1930. Was understudy to Jimmy Allen until the international joined Aston Villa in 1934. Has since been first choice for the berth. Is strong and untiring, favouring the third-back game. Son of a farmer.

Symon, James Scot (left half).—Born at Errol, Perthshire. Height 5ft. 11in. Weight 12st. Was secured from Dundee at the beginning of this season. Has spent five seasons with the Scottish League clubs, of which he was captain. A worthy successor to David Thackeray, for some years captain of the club. Plays cricket for Perthshire, being an opening batsman and a good fast bowler.

BRENTFORD u...

BRE...
Red a...

1—M...

2—WILSON
Right Back

4—McKENZIE   5—
Right Half   C...

7—HOPKINS   8—SCOTT   9—McC
Outside Right   Inside Right   Centr...

Referee— Mr. C. P. WEST (Brighton)

14...
C...

12—PARKER   13—BAGLEY
Outside Left   Inside Left

17—SYMON   18—
Left Half   Ce...

20—SMITH
Left Back

22—...
C...

PORT...
Royal Blue

THE LEAGUE—DIVISION I.

	P.	W.	D.	L.	F.	A.	P.
Sunderland	34	21	6	7	90	53	48
Derby County	34	16	9	9	50	36	41
Huddersfield	34	16	9	9	50	46	41
Stoke City	34	17	5	12	51	46	39
Birmingham	33	13	10	10	48	43	36
Manchester City	34	15	5	14	59	46	35
Arsenal	31	13	8	10	62	35	34
Preston N.E.	33	14	6	13	51	48	34
Middlesbrough	34	13	6	15	69	61	32
Wolverhampton	33	13	6	14	58	58	32
Portsmouth	32	13	6	13	42	51	32
BRENTFORD	**33**	**11**	**9**	**13**	**58**	**53**	**31**
Leeds United	33	11	9	13	51	49	31
Liverpool	34	12	7	15	48	52	31
Chelsea	32	11	9	12	46	59	31
Everton	33	9	12	12	66	71	30
Sheffield Wed.	32	11	8	13	56	61	30
Bolton Wand.	33	10	10	13	52	67	30
West Brom. A.	33	13	3	17	73	67	29
Grimsby Town	33	12	5	16	45	59	29
Aston Villa	34	10	7	17	65	94	27
Blackburn Rov.	34	10	7	17	44	77	27

PORTSMOUTH

ORD
Stripes
ESON
er

3—BATEMAN
Left Back

ES
alf

6—RICHARDS
Left Half

CH 10—HOLLIDAY
Inside Left

11—REID
Outside Left
rd

Linesmen— Messrs. K. D. Eames (blue flag)
and A. L. R. Bellion (red flag)

DDLE
orward

15—GROVES
Inside Right

16—WORRALL
Outside Right

OND
alf

19—NICHOL
Right Half

21—MORGAN
Right Back

LAN
er

OUTH
hite Knickers

LONDON COMBINATION

	P.	W.	L.	D.	Goals F.	A.	P.
Portsmouth	37	23	6	8	104	51	54
BRENTFORD	36	25	8	3	81	42	53
Arsenal	35	24	8	3	91	37	51
Swansea Town	38	19	12	8	70	55	46
Reading	38	20	13	5	83	72	45
Crystal Palace	38	19	12	7	90	80	45
Chelsea	37	17	12	8	80	67	42
Charlton Ath.	39	18	16	5	80	68	41
Queen's Park Rgrs.	38	17	16	6	68	57	40
West Ham U.	38	17	16	5	90	66	39
Coventry City	38	16	15	7	71	69	39
Luton Town	37	17	16	4	99	89	38
Northampton	38	14	15	9	72	66	37
Millwall	37	15	16	6	56	64	36
Clapton Orient	37	12	16	11	58	89	35
Fulham	37	13	17	7	68	65	33
Tottenham H.	35	13	13	9	83	78	33
Bournemouth	38	12	20	6	64	93	30
Leicester City	37	13	21	3	61	86	29
Southend United	37	10	18	9	61	85	29
Watford	37	12	22	3	69	107	27
Southampton	37	9	20	8	48	68	26
Brighton & Hove A.	37	9	21	7	59	99	25
Bristol City	39	9	25	5	54	116	23

The Arsenal Arena, entirely reconstructed in six weeks.

The White City Arena, entirely reconstructed in six weeks.

The West Ham Stadium Dog Track.

3

famous grounds entirely reconstructed by

B. Sunley and Co. Ltd.

Sunley's Island . Great West Road . Brentford . Middlesex

Telephone : Ealing 1412/3

Makers of the famous "De Luxe" Non-attention hard tennis courts. Sports grounds. Gardens. Bowling greens. Racing tracks. Consult Sunley about your garden. Estimates and plans prepared without cost or obligation.

Worrall, Frederick (outside right). — Born at Warrington, Lancs. Height 5ft. 6½in. Weight 11st. 2lb. Developed with Witton Albion (Cheshire League). Moved to Bolton Wanderers, but on a technical objection his registration was not sanctioned by the F.A. Oldham Athletic then snapped him up. Made quite a name for himself before joining Portsmouth in season 1931-32. Has played for England and the Football League. Needs continual watching for he is an adept at snapping up half chances.

Groves, Arthur (inside right).— Born at Langwith, Notts. Height 5ft. 10½in. Weight 10st. 12lb. Joined the club some weeks ago from Derby County and seems likely to establish himself. Was an inside right when secured by Blackburn Rovers from Halifax Town With the Lancs club, however, he played most of his 65 League games at inside left. Derby got him for a fee of less than £1,000 and he played 64 times with their League side. An astute schemer who knows how to shoot.

Weddle, John (centre forward).— Born at Sunderland. Height 5ft. 9in. Weight 12st. Joined Pompey from Fatfield Albion, a North-Eastern junior club. Played inside left before taking over the first-team leadership several years ago. Is a whole-hearted bustling type of player.

Bagley, William (inside left).— Born at Newport, Monmouthshire. Height 5ft. 7in. Weight 10st. 7lb. A product of Lovell's Athletic, the Newport club that has given several players to League football. Made a name for himself with Newport County and then moved to Portsmouth in the 1933 close season. Played regularly in the League side towards the close of last season, and has passed his half century of First Division appearances.

Parker, Clifford (outside left).— Born at Denaby, Yorks. Height 5ft. 6in. Weight 10st. Was once turned down by Mexborough Athletic (Midland League). Soon afterwards was in League football with Doncaster Rovers. Joined Portsmouth at substantial fee in December, 1933, and made six First Division appearances in that season. That total rose to 15 last term, while he now seems to have established himself. Early experience with Denaby United.

FOOTBALL VETERANS PASS.

A week-end of splendid sport was marred by the death of two well-known and popular figures in football circles—Mr. John McKenna and Mr. Arthur Chadwick.

* * *

Eighty-one years of age and President of the Football League, Mr. McKenna was sometimes referred to as the " John Blunt " of football, and was a convert from the Rugby code. He has been a member of the F.A. Council since 1905, and in 1928 was elected vice-president; his presidency of the Football League dates from 1910. Connected with Liverpool Football Club for nearly 30 years.

* * *

Five weeks ago he travelled to Inverness as a member of the International Selection Committee of the Football Association to watch the Scotland v. England amateur game, and was taken ill on the return journey.

* * *

While watching the Exeter City—Clapton Orient game at Exeter on Saturday, Mr. Arthur Chadwick felt ill and left his seat. He died soon afterwards. Mr. Chadwick, formerly known as a Southampton F.C. centre half and England international, was the first manager of Exeter City F.C. upon their acquiring professional status.

SHARES & SHAREHOLDERS

In spite of our previous notes in this programme, the Management are still receiving enquiries from supporters who are desiring to acquire shares in the Club. We repeat that the shares of the Club are fully issued, and unless existing shareholders desire to realise, there are no shares available.

The 6% Debentures of £50 each are still being issued, but only a small number now remain, and when these have been issued the finances of the Club will have been completely consolidated and settled

The Club have been the leaseholders of Griffin Park, and supporters will be interested to know that next March the freehold of the ground is being purchased and the Club will then be in the happy position of being the owners of the ground.

Particulars of the 6% Debentures will be forwarded on application to the Secretary.

Shareholders desiring to realise their share-holdings should advise the Secretary, together with a note of the price they are willing to accept.

JOSEPH WILSON
Right Back.

Was born in Scotland. First big club was Newcastle United, with whom he remained for two and a half years. He was then transferred to Southend United and his displays at centre half soon attracted many clubs. He remained with that club for five years. During the last close season he was secured by Brentford as a centre-half. Made his first appearance with the first team during Christmas games at right back—the position he has held ever since. He is 5ft. 11½in. in height and weighs 12st. 6lbs.

FIXTURES, SEASON 1935-36.

FIRST TEAM

Date. 1935.	Opponents.	Ground.	GOALS F.	A.
Aug. 31	Bolton Wanderers ...	A	2	0
Sept. 5	Blackburn Rovers ...	H	3	1
,, 7	Huddersfield Town	H	1	2
,, 14	Middlesbrough ...	A	0	0
,, 18	Derby County ...	A	1	2
,, 21	Aston Villa ...	H	1	2
,, 28	Wolverhampton Wdrs.	A	2	3
Oct. 5	Sheffield Wednesday ..	H	2	2
,, 12	Portsmouth ...	A	3	1
,, 19	Stoke City ...	H	0	0
,, 26	Manchester City ...	A	1	2
Nov. 2	Arsenal ...	H	2	1
,, 9	Birmingham ...	A	1	2
,, 16	Sunderland ...	H	1	5
,, 23	Chelsea ...	A	1	2
,, 30	Leeds United ...	H	2	2
Dec. 7	Grimsby Town ...	A	1	6
,, 14	Liverpool ...	H	1	2
,, 21	West Bromwich Albion	A	0	1
,, 25	Preston North End ...	H	5	2
,, 26	Preston North End ...	A	4	2
,, 28	Bolton Wanderers ...	H	4	0
1936.				
Jan. 1	Blackburn Rovers ...	A	0	1
,, 4	Huddersfield Town ...	A	2	2
,, 11	(3) Leicester Ci y ...	A	0	1
,, 18	Middlesbrough ...	H	1	0
,, 25	(4) Aston Villa ...	A	2	2
Feb. 1	Wolverhampton Wdrs.	H	5	0
,, 8	Sheffield Wednesday ...	A	3	3
,, 15	(5)			
,, 22	Stoke City ...	A	2	2
,, 29	(6) Birmingham ...	H	0	1
Mar. 7	Leeds United ...	A	2	1
,, 14	Manchester City ...	A	0	0
,, 21	(S.-F.) Sunderland ...	A	3	1
,, 25	Portsmouth ...	H		
,, 28	Chelsea ...	H		
April 4	Arsenal ...	A		
,, 10	Everton ...	A		
,, 11	Grimsby Town ...	H		
,, 13	Everton ...	H		
,, 18	Liverpool ...	A		
,, 25	(F.) West Brom. Alb.	H		
May 2	Derby County ...	H		

SECOND TEAM

Date. 1935.	Opponents.	Ground.	GOALS F.	A.
Aug. 31	Charlton Athletic ...	H	2	1
Sept. 4	Watford ...	A	1	3
,, 7	Clapton Orient ...	A	0	0
,, 12	Watford ...	H	2	1
,, 14	Southend United ...	H	1	0
,, 21	Northampton Town ...	A	1	1
,, 25	Luton Town ...	A	1	4
,, 28	Crystal Palace ...	H	4	0
Oct. 3	Luton Town ...	H	4	3
,, 5	Reading ...	A	1	2
,, 7	Met. Police—I .C.Cup	H	2	0
,, 9	Bournemouth & Bos. .	H	5	2
,, 12	Tottenham Hotspur	H	2	1
,, 19	Bristol City ...	A	3	1
,, 21	C. Orient—L.C.Cup ...	H	3	1
,, 26	Millwall ...	H	4	0
Nov. 2	West Ham United ...	A	1	0
,, 9	Swansea Town ...	H	2	0
,, 11	Fulham (L.C.Cup.S.F.)	H	2	0
,, 16	Leicester City ...	A	3	2
,, 23	Coventry City ...	A	4	1
,, 30	Arsenal ...	A	0	1
Dec. 7	Southampton ...	H	4	0
,, 14	Brighton & Hove A.	A	1	0
,, 21	Queen's Park Rgrs. ..	A	3	1
,, 25	Chelsea ...	A	2	2
,, 26	Chelsea ...	A	2	1
,, 28	Charlton Athletic ...	A	1	3
Jan. 4	Clapton Orient ...	H	5	1
,, 11	Fulham ...	H	4	0
,, 18	Southend United ...	A	4	2
,, 25	Northampton Town ...	A	5	1
Feb. 1	Crystal Palace ...	H	1	0
,, 8	Reading ...	H	0	1
,, 15				
,, 22	Bristol City ...	A	3	0
,, 29	Millwall ...	A	0	0
Mar. 7	West Ham United ...	H	4	0
,, 14	Swansea Town ...	A	0	5
,, 21	Leicester City ...	H	1	0
,, 25	Bournemouth & Bos. .	A		
,, 28	Coventry City ...	A		
April 1	Tottenham Hotspur ...	A		
,, 4	Arsenal ...	H		
,, 10	Portsmouth ...	A		
,, 11	Southampton ...	A		
,, 13	Portsmouth ...	A		
,, 18	Brighton & Hove A.	H		
,, 25	Queen's Park Rgrs. ..	A		
May 2	Fulham ...	A		

Notes from the Hive.—Contd.

The Bees' wonderful victory at Sunderland, on Saturday has created confidence in their ability to keep up in the First Division. There has been a very real danger, these last few weeks, of relegation, because there is a terrific scramble going on in the bottom half of the League table, where only five points cover fourteen teams. Every point is valuable in such a situation. If the Bees can beat Sunderland 3—1 at Roker Park, they should have no difficulty in steering clear of the bottom of the table.

DO YOU KNOW?

Scottish selectors, along with Mr. George Graham, secretary of the Scottish Football Association, were at Sunderland on Saturday. They were there no doubt to have under review McCulloch and Reid. The Scottish team to oppose England at Wembley will be known on Monday.

* * *

Ronald Rooke, the young Crystal Palace centre forward, has scored in his last three games in the London Combination, twelve goals. Six of these were obtained against Brighton.

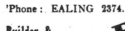
RETURNED WITH THANKS!

The Next Games.

On Saturday Brentford entertain Chelsea, their West London neighbours. This should be a grand game. In November of last year, at Stamford Bridge, the Pensioners sent the Bees away empty-handed by the odd goal in three. That defeat was sustained during the slump that followed Brentford's victory over Arsenal. For seven games in succession the Bees did not win, and one point alone they added to their total, until on Christmas Day they beat Preston North End at Griffin Park by five goals to two, and on Boxing Day at Preston by four goals to two.

Chelsea are three places below Brentford in the league table on goal average alone, as the Bees have the same number of points—31. Brentford have won the same number of games—11, drawn the same number—9, and have lost one game more than Chelsea, who have played one game less. So the records are almost identical. With ground advantage in their favour and with the memory of the Sunderland win to inspire the players, Brentford should just about get home.

The following Saturday Brentford are engaged in another local Derby as they have to visit Highbury. This should be one of the classics of the season. When the Highbury men visited Griffin Park they were beaten by two goals to one, so they will try their utmost to gain revenge. The Bees, however, will be as equally keen to complete a " double," at the same time maintaining their fine away record.

On April 10th, Brentford have another away game, this time with Everton. The clubs have not been opposed to each other yet this season, for the Goodison Park men come to Griffin Park on April 13th.

Dividing these games will be a home game with Grimsby Town on Easter Saturday (April 11th).

The Bees' Reserves are away next Saturday to Coventry City, and the week following they are at home to Arsenal Reserves. This is rather unusual, for it is the same day as the first team are at Highbury.

BRENTFORD FOOTBALL AND SPORTS CLUB, LIMITED.

Registered Office :—GRIFFIN PARK, BRAEMAR ROAD, BRENTFORD.

President and Chairman :
MR. L. P. SIMON.

Vice-Chairman :
MR. F. A. DAVIS.

ALDERMAN W. FLEWITT, J.P.   MR. H. W. DODGE.   MR. F. W. BARTON.
MR. H. N. BLUNDELL.   MR. C. L. SIMON.   ALDERMAN H. F. DAVIS.
MR. H. J. SAUNDERS.   MR. J. R. HUGHES, J.P., C.C.

Hon. Treasurer :
ALDERMAN W. FLEWITT, J.P.

Secretary-Manager :
MR. H. C. CURTIS,

Club Medical Officer : DR. A. D. GOWANS.   " DORINCOURT," BOSTON GARDENS, BRENTFORD.

Telephones :
GROUND : EALING 1744.
PRIVATE HOUSE : EALING 1183.

Telegraphic Address :
CURTIS, FOOTBALL, BRENTFORD.
Ground : GRIFFIN PARK, EALING ROAD, BRENTFORD

NO. 18.   **Saturday, March 28th, 1936.**

Notes from the Hive.

INTO THE TOP HALF.

A convincing success over Portsmouth at Griffin Park, on Wednesday last enabled the Bees to move up into the top half of the table, and we all hope our boys will continue to retain a place above the half-way line and so relieve all anxiety as to relegation, which for some time Brentford were concerned with.

AN EARLY SET-BACK.

There was a very early thrill in the game with Portsmouth, but not of the appetising kind as far as the Bees were concerned—for Pompey took the lead straight from the kick-off. It was a very good movement in which the cleverness and speed of Parker, the Portsmouth outside left was a salient feature. He " made " and " got " the goal which put the Bees behind so early in the game.

That early goal gave Pompey much confidence, but gradually the Bees got over their early set-back and then put on much pressure.

Both Holliday and McCulloch experienced very bad luck in efforts made from short range. Then Reid missed with a good chance—striking a post when a goal appeared certain to accrue. Later Gilfillan saved in thrilling style a header from McCulloch.

The large crowd must have wondered whether the Bees were going to score at all—but the happy event came just before the interval, when McCulloch and Salmond went up for the ball at the same time, and it cannoned into the net to make an interval score of 1—1.

Brentford were a much better side after the interval. The whole team played with more method and confidence. The lead was soon gained when McCulloch headed a great goal from Hopkins' centre.

Scott was extremely unlucky to see a really great shot strike the underside of the crossbar and come out for McCulloch to head over the bar.

NOTES FROM THE HIVE—*Continued.*

Mid-way through the second half Brentford went further ahead. McCulloch was again the scorer—a fine first-time shot from Hopkins' centre leaving Gilfillan helpless to save.

It was practically a case of all-Brentford after this, but nothing further was added to the score.

CHELSEA HERE TO-DAY.

To-day we stage our local Derby game at Griffin Park, when Chelsea provide the opposition. From the positions of the two clubs on the League table, everything portends to a close struggle, and if the players can forget that it is a local " Derby " game—and the on-lookers, too, play their part in this important matter, it should be a fine spectacle from a footballing viewpoint.

When the clubs met at Stamford Bridge last November, Chelsea won by the odd goal in three, but with ground advantage, allied to great improvement shown by the Bees since the teams last met, we feel that our boys should prove equal to reversing that verdict.

At the same time, games between neighbouring club are more or less levelled up in the matter of territory in view of the fact that the visitors always have a large contingent of supporters present to urge them on. We took many thousands to Stamford Bridge and no doubt Chelsea " fans " will be present in strong force to-day.

What have Chelsea done away from home this season? Eleven points from sixteen games! Not too bad this.

Here are a list of games in which the Stamford Bridge club at least avoided defeat on opposing territory. They won 3—1 at Grimsby, 2—1 at West Bromwich, 3—2 at Bolton and 3—2 at Liverpool, while drawn games were played with Aston Villa (2—2), Manchester City (0—0) and Sunderland (3—3). We shall expect to see a " full house " at Griffin Park to-day.

AT HIGHBURY NEXT WEEK.

A week to-day the Bees will be opposing the F.A. Cup finalists at Highbury. This is a game many thousands of our supporters have been looking forward to with intense interest. No doubt they feel that it will be nice to see their favourites in action at Highbury, with a chance of recording a " double " win over the famous London team. Recent results should give the Bees all the confidence needed to achieve this feat, and here's luck to our boys.

BUSY BEE.

Jottings from the Board Room.

The funeral of the late Mr. John McKenna, the popular president of the Football League, took place at Liverpool on Thursday last.

Regarding our game v. the Arsenal on Saturday, April 4th, at Highbury, we are informed that the only bookable seats are at 5/- each. Applications should be sent direct to the Arsenal Club enclosing remittance and stamped addressed envelope.

The Reserves drew with Bournemouth and Boscombe Reserves, at Bournemouth, on Wednesday last, 1—1. Dunn scored our goal.

Comparative records with last season are as follows :
Football League—

	P.	W.	D.	L.	Goals F	A.	P.
This Season .	34	12	9	13	61	54	33
Last Season .	34	21	7	6	74	40	49

London Combination—

	P.	W.	D.	L.	Goals F	A.	P.
This Season .	37	25	4	8	82	43	54
Last Season .	37	20	7	10	65	40	47

Goal scorers to date are :—
Football League.—McCulloch 17, Hopkins 11, Holliday 10, Scott 8, Fletcher 5, Robson 3, Reid 3, J. C. Burns 1, Dunn 1, Muttitt 1, McKenzie 1.—Total 61.

London Combination.—Dunn 27, McAloon 15, Brown 14, Sullivan 8, Muttitt 6, Gibbons 5, Fenton 2, Smith (C.) 2, Fletcher 2, Smith (L.) 1.—Total 82.

The Reserves are to-day away to Coventry City Reserves, kick-off at 3 p.m.

Supporters still continue to write in for F.A. Cup Final tickets. I repeat that this club's small allocation has already been disposed of.

Supporters are asked to "BEWARE OF PICKPOCKETS," as on March 14th, when we played Manchester City, two supporters had the misfortune to have their wallets stolen.

The following articles have been found on the ground and can be claimed on, application at the Secretary's Office :—Keys, book, one odd lady's glove, gent's leather gloves, pair of gaiters.

The home games for the Easter programme will be as follows :
Good Friday, April 10th, v Portsmouth (London Combination), kick-off at 3.30 p.m.
Saturday, April 11th, v. Grimsby Town (Football League), kick-off at 3.30 p.m.
Easter Monday, April 13th, v. Everton (Football League), kick-off at 3.30 p.m.

The selection of the Scottish team to play England in the International game at Wembley, on April 4th, will be selected on Monday. We trust our popular centre forward, Dave McCulloch, will be honoured. This club has agreed to release him if selected.

We have much pleasure in stating that on Wednesday last, March 25th, the purchase of this ground was completed. The Club are now in the happy position of being the owners of Griffin Park.

Seats, numbered and reserved, can now be booked for our game v. Grimsby, on April 11th, at 4/- each, and v. Everton on Easter Monday at 3/6 and 4/-. Applications by post will not be considered unless accompanied with remittance and stamped addressed envelope.

The following events will take place at the Empire Pool and Sports Arena, Wembley :

Tuesday, May 5th.—At the Empire Pool, " Golden Gloves " Amateur Boxing Tournament—England v. America.

Thursday, May 7th.—At the Empire Stadium. Opening of the Speedway season. National League match—Wembley v. Wimbledon.

The British Ice Hockey Association fixtures at the Empire Pool are as follows : Saturday, March 28th, 1936, Canadians v. Rangers (London Cup); Thursday, April 2nd, Lions v. Streatham (London Cup); Saturday, April 4th, Canadians v. Corinthians (Final, Channel Cup).

FURNISH

AT

WHEATLAND'S

FOR CASH OR
EASY TERMS

43 & 45, THE BROADWAY
WEST EALING

Shots from the Spot.

Walking from the ground on Wednesday evening it was obvious how delighted Brentford fans were with their team's display. Loyal support is one of the greatest assets a club can have. If a team can feel that they have a broad-minded following who understand that no eleven can always be on the top of their form, it gives them confidence. If the supporters show the same tolerant and understanding spirit when things are not going so well, they will prove a great asset.

* * *

The Reserves are putting up a fine fight to bring back the London Combination Shield to Griffin Park. They are level on points with the present leaders, Portsmouth, and only forced back into second place on goal average. There is every prospect of a very exciting finish for the Arsenal, now third with 51 points, have two games in hand.

* * *

They and the Bees will meet at Griffin Park next Saturday and this needle game is likely to decide which will continue to be the challengers to Pompey for supremacy.

* * *

When they visited Highbury earlier in the season the Bees lost a very close game by the only goal scored. Altogether the Bees have nine more matches to play before the end of the season.

* * *

Will the three brothers Male all figure in cup finals? That is a question which will have its answer after to-day's F.A. Amateur Cup Semi-Final between Ilford and Maidenhead United. C. G. Male, the Arsenal player, has already qualified for the F.A. Cup Final, and Charles Male is in the New Scotland Yard Team that has reached the final of the Civil Service League Shield. If Ilford, who include L. V. Male, defeat Maidenhead United, a family hat-trick will be completed.

* * *

A sports writer in a London newspaper, on Thursday, writing on when " hands " cannot be ignored, mentioned an incident that happened in the Bees' game with Portsmouth, when the ball actually lodged between a player's hanging arm and his body during a hot attack on the Pompey goal.

* * *

Quite obviously, the writer states, the player had no idea the ball was coming his way at all, yet the incident interfered with play to such an extent that the referee had no hesitation at all in blowing up for a free kick. Things like this are bound to happen in many matches. He could only reiterate that it was in the referee's power to " decide all disputed points."

OUR VISITORS TO-DAY.
HOW THEY MAY LINE UP.

———◆———

Though they have probably had as many internationals on their books as any other club, Chelsea have not a particularly distinguished record.

They reached the Final of the English Cup on one occasion—in 1913 —and were then beaten 3—0 by Sheffield United.

The Pensioners were founded in 1905.

Woodley, Victor Robert (goalkeeper). Born at Chippenham, Wiltshire. Height 5ft. 11½in. Weight 12st. 2lb. The fact that he keeps Jackson in reserve shows the true worth of this young 'keeper. Helped Windsor and Eton to win the Spartan League Championship and played for Berks and Bucks. Had trials with Aldershot before joining Chelsea in 1931. Was soon in the League side. Since Jackson joined the club in 1933, the two have more or less shared the position.

O'Hare, J. (right back).—Born at Armadale, Scotland. Height 5ft. 8in. Weight 11st 4lb. Has been with the Stamford Bridge club for some years, but up to this season his appearances were not very frequent. Got his chance in the third match of this campaign, and has played in some twenty games since. A fearless tackler who kicks with power.

Barber, George (left back).— Born at West Ham. Height 6ft. 1in. Weight 12st. 4lb. Played with Fairbairn House Lads' club and Redhill (Athenian League) before turning professional with Luton Town. Did not satisfy and in 1930, after less than a season, was given a free transfer. Chelsea snapped him up and he made rapid improvement.

Allum, J. (right half).—Born at Reading. Height 5ft. 8in. Weight 10st. One of the several Chelsea players who have been developed in amateur circles. Won amateur honours with Maidenhead United in the Spartan League. Went to Stamford Bridge in the summer of 1932 and played in 13 first team matches in his first season. Plays a cool and thoughtful game.

Craig, Alan (centre half).—Born at Paisley. Height 5ft. 10in. Weight 11st. 7lb. Joined Chelsea in 1932 from Motherwell shortly after assisting Scotland against England. In his first full season played principally at wing half, but in season 1933-4 ousted O'Dowd from the pivotal berth. Was ever-present last season. A resolute defender.

Hutcheson, John (left half).— Born at Falkirk. Height 5ft. 9½in. Weight 11st. 6lb. A product of Falkirk local football. Had his first outings in the Scottish League with Falkirk in season 1927-28. Joined Chelsea in March, 1934, and, though unable to establish himself has played a number of First Division games. Used to be a miner.

BRENTFORD

BREN

Red an

1—M

2—WILSON
Right Back

4—McKENZIE
Right Half

5—
C

7—HOPKINS
Outside Right

8—SCOTT
Inside Right

9—McC
Centr

Referee— Mr. L. E. GIBBS (Reading)

1
C

12—BARRACLOUGH
Outside Left

13—BURGESS
Inside Left

17—HUTCHESON
Left Half

18—
Ce

20—BARBER
Left Back

22—V
G

CH

Royal Blue White C

THE LEAGUE—DIVISION I.

	P.	W.	D.	L.	Goals F.	A.	P.
Sunderland	34	21	6	7	90	53	48
Derby County	34	16	9	9	50	36	41
Huddersfield	34	16	9	9	50	46	41
Stoke City	34	17	5	12	51	46	39
Birmingham	33	13	10	10	48	43	36
Arsenal	32	13	0	10	63	36	35
Manchester City	34	15	5	14	59	48	35
Preston N.E.	33	14	6	13	51	48	34
BRENTFORD	**34**	**12**	**9**	**13**	**61**	**54**	**33**
Middlesbrough	34	13	6	15	69	61	32
Wolverhampton	33	13	6	14	58	58	32
Portsmouth	33	13	6	14	43	64	32
Leeds United	33	11	9	13	51	49	31
Liverpool	34	12	7	15	48	52	31
Everton	34	9	13	12	67	72	31
Grimsby Town	34	13	5	16	49	59	31
Chelsea	32	11	9	12	46	59	31
Sheffield Wed.	33	11	8	14	56	65	30
Bolton Wand.	33	10	10	13	52	67	30
West Brom. A.	33	13	3	17	73	67	29
Aston Villa	34	10	7	17	65	94	27
Blackburn Rov.	34	10	7	17	44	77	27

v. CHELSEA

FORD

Stripes

IESON
per

3—BATEMAN
Left Back

IES
alf

6—RICHARDS
Left Half

OCH 10—HOLLIDAY   11—REID
ard   Inside Left   Outside Left

Linesmen—   Messrs. A. V. Boorer (blue flag)
and F. J. Chambers (red flag)

ILLS
orward

15—ARGUE   16—SPENCE
Inside Right   Outside Right

19—ALLUM
AIG   Right Half
alf

21—O'HARE
Right Back

DLEY
per

SEA
rts, White Knickers

LONDON COMBINATION

	P.	W.	L.	D.	Goals F.	A.	P.
Portsmouth	37	23	6	8	104	51	54
BRENTFORD	37	25	8	4	81	43	54
Arsenal	35	24	8	3	91	37	51
Swansea Town	38	19	12	8	70	55	46
Reading	38	20	13	5	83	72	45
Crystal Palace	38	19	12	7	90	80	45
Chelsea	37	17	12	8	80	67	42
Charlton Ath.	40	18	17	5	81	70	41
Queen's Park Rgrs.	38	17	16	6	68	57	40
West Ham U.	38	17	16	5	90	66	39
Coventry City	38	16	15	7	71	69	39
Luton Town	37	17	16	4	99	89	38
Northampton	38	14	15	9	72	66	37
Millwall	37	15	16	6	56	64	36
Clapton Orient	37	12	16	11	58	89	35
Fulham	37	13	17	7	68	65	33
Tottenham H.	35	13	13	9	83	78	33
Bournemouth	39	12	20	7	65	94	31
Leicester City	37	13	21	3	61	86	29
Southend United ...	38	10	19	9	62	87	29
Watford	38	13	22	3	71	108	29
Southampton	38	10	20	8	50	69	28
Brighton & Hove A.	37	9	21	7	59	99	25
Bristol City	39	9	25	5	54	116	23

The Arsenal Arena, entirely reconstructed in six weeks.

The White City Arena, entirely reconstructed in six weeks.

The West Ham Stadium Dog Track.

3

famous grounds entirely reconstructed by

B. Sunley and Co. Ltd.

Sunley's Island . Great West Road . Brentford . Middlesex

Telephone : Ealing 1412/3

Makers of the famous "De Luxe" Non-attention hard tennis courts. Sports grounds. Gardens. Bowling greens. Racing tracks. Consult Sunley about your garden. Estimates and plans prepared without cost or obligation.

Spence, Richard (outside right). —Born at Platts Common, nr. Barnsley. Height 5ft. 5in. Weight 9st. 4lb. Was playing for Thorne Colliery, Yorkshire, when taken by Barnsley. Had only one full season with the latter club (1933-4) and his 21 goals in 41 appearances that term played a big part in their promotion to Division II. Joined Chelsea in 1934 and was their top scorer last season with 19 goals in 34 First Division matches.

Argue, James (inside right).— Born at Glasgow. Height 5ft. 10½in. Weight 11st. 4lb. Came out with St. Roch's, a junior side at Glasgow. Was brought South by Birmingham in season 1931-2. Had very little scope with that club and moved on to Chelsea in 1933, when Mr. Leslie Knighton left Birmingham to become manager of Chelsea. Made numerous appearances in the League side last season.

Mills, George (centre forward).— Born at Deptford, London. Height 6ft. Weight 12st. Began his first-class career in Athenian League football with Bromley. Scored over 100 goals in this class of game. First joined Chelsea as an amateur in 1929, turning professional later. Keeps his employment in an office, however. Toured the Continent with the F.A. in 1933, but did not play in the internationals.

Burgess, Harry (inside left).— Born at Alderley Edge, Cheshire. Height 5ft. 8in. Weight 11st. 10lb. Had First League experience with Stockport County. Was secured by Sheffield Wednesday after Wolverhampton Wanderers had made unsuccessful overtures for his signature. Won four English caps before moving to Chelsea twelve months ago. Can play in either inside forward positions.

Barraclough, Wm. (outside left). —Born at Hull. Height 5ft. 6in. Weight 10st. 12lb. Was with Bridlington Town (Yorkshire League) and Hull City as an amateur before joining the paid ranks with Wolverhampton Wanderers in 1928. Took a benefit in April, 1934, and six months later moved to Chelsea. A former clerk. Still practises shorthand.

NAMES IN THE GAME.

Mr. A. L. Knighton.

Mr. Albert Leslie Knighton, the secretary-manager of Chelsea, is one of the best known officials in the popular game of soccer at the present time.

He has had a long career and has been in charge of some of the leading first-class teams. He is very popular, just as much so in the dressing room as in the directors' box.

Mr. Knighton commenced his official career as team manager of Castleford Town.

From there, however, he joined Huddersfield Town as assistant secretary-manager, and afterwards served in a similar capacity with Manchester City. He then came to London as secretary-manager of the Arsenal

From Highbury, Mr. Knighton joined the ranks of Bournemouth in a similar position, and then went to Birmingham. Under his direction Birmingham reached the F.A. Cup Final in 1931, when they were beaten at Wembley by the odd goal in three by West Bromwich Albion.

Later Mr. Knighton came back to London to guide the affairs of Chelsea.

Mr. Knighton was born at Church Gresley, Burton-on-Trent.

SHARES & SHAREHOLDERS

In spite of our previous notes in this programme, the Management are still receiving enquiries from supporters who are desiring to acquire shares in the Club. We repeat that the shares of the Club are fully issued, and unless existing shareholders desire to realise, there are no shares available.

The 6% Debentures of £50 each are still being issued, but only a small number now remain, and when these have been issued the finances of the Club will have been completely consolidated and settled.

The Club have been the leaseholders of Griffin Park, and supporters will be interested to know that the freehold of the ground was purchased on the 25th March, and the Club are in the happy position of being the owners of the ground.

Particulars of the 6% Debentures will be forwarded on application to the Secretary.

Shareholders desiring to realise their share-holdings should advise the Secretary, together with a note of the price they are willing to accept.

ROBERT KANE
Trainer

Was born at Glasgow. He joined the Navy and played football all over the world. He then joined Gillingham and also played for Portsmouth as an inside forward. Bob, as he is popularly called, has been with Brentford ten seasons. During that time he has seen Brentford come from the Third Division (Southern Section) through Division II into Division I. He has been in no small way responsible for the success of the team..

FIXTURES, SEASON 1935-36.

FIRST TEAM

Date. 1935.	Opponents.	Ground.	GOALS F.	A.
Aug. 31	Bolton Wanderers ...	A	2	0
Sept. 5	Blackburn Rovers ...	H	3	1
" 7	Huddersfield Town ...	H	1	2
" 14	Middlesbrough ...	A	0	0
" 18	Derby County ...	A	1	2
" 21	Aston Villa ...	A	1	2
" 28	Wolverhampton Wdrs.	A	2	3
Oct. 5	Sheffield Wednesday ..	H	2	2
" 12	Portsmouth ...	A	3	1
" 19	Stoke City ...	H	0	0
" 26	Manchester City ...	A	1	2
Nov. 2	Arsenal ...	H	2	1
" 9	Birmingham ...	A	1	2
" 16	Sunderland ...	H	1	5
" 23	Chelsea ...	A	1	2
" 30	Leeds United ...	H	2	2
Dec. 7	Grimsby Town ...	A	1	6
" 14	Liverpool ...	H	1	2
" 21	West Bromwich Albion	A	0	1
" 25	Preston North End ...	H	5	2
" 26	Preston North End ...	A	4	2
" 28	Bolton Wanderers ...	H	4	0
1936.				
Jan. 1	Blackburn Rovers ...	A	0	1
" 4	Huddersfield Town ...	A	2	2
" 11	(3) Leicester City ...	A	0	1
" 18	Middlesbrough ...	H	1	0
" 25	(4) Aston Villa ...	A	2	2
Feb. 1	Wolverhampton Wdrs.	H	5	0
" 8	Sheffield Wednesday ...	A	3	3
" 15	(5) ...			
" 22	Stoke City ...	A	2	2
" 29	(6) Birmingham ...	H	0	1
Mar. 7	Leeds United ...	A	2	1
" 14	Manchester City ...	H	0	
" 21	(S.-F.) Sunderland ...	A	3	1
" 25	Portsmouth ...	H	3	
" 28	Chelsea ...	H		
April 4	Arsenal ...	A		
" 10	Everton ...	A		
" 11	Grimsby Town ...	H		
" 13	Everton ...	H		
" 18	Liverpool ...	A		
" 25	(F.) West Brom. Alb.	H		
May 2	Derby County ...	H		

SECOND TEAM

Date. 1935.	Opponents.	Ground.	GOALS F.	A.
Aug. 31	Charlton Athletic ...	H	2	1
Sept. 4	Watford ...	A	1	3
" 7	Clapton Orient ...	A	0	0
" 12	Watford ...	H	2	1
" 14	Southend United ...	H	1	0
" 21	Northampton Town ...	A	1	0
" 25	Luton Town ...	A	1	4
" 28	Crystal Palace ...	H	4	0
Oct. 3	Luton Town ...	H	4	3
" 5	Reading ...	A	1	2
" 7	Met. Police—L.C. Cup	H	2	0
" 9	Bournemouth & Bos. .	H	5	1
" 12	Tottenham Hotspur	H	2	1
" 19	Bristol City ...	A	3	1
" 21	C. Orient—L.C. Cup ...	H	3	1
" 26	Millwall ...	H	4	0
Nov. 2	West Ham United ...	A	1	0
" 9	Swansea Town ...	H	2	0
" 11	Fulham (L.C.Cup,S.F.)	H	2	0
" 16	Leicester City ...	A	3	2
" 23	Coventry City ...	H	4	1
" 30	Arsenal ...	A	0	1
Dec. 7	Southampton ...	A	1	0
" 14	Brighton & Hove A. ...	A	1	0
" 21	Queen's Park Rgrs. ..	H	3	1
" 25	Chelsea ...	A	2	2
" 26	Chelsea ...	H	2	1
" 28	Charlton Athletic ...	A	1	3
Jan. 4	Clapton Orient ...	H	5	1
" 11	Fulham ...	A	4	0
" 18	Southend United ...	A	4	2
" 25	Northampton Town ...	H	5	1
Feb. 1	Crystal Palace ...	A	1	0
" 8	Reading ...	H	0	1
" 15				
" 22	Bristol City ...	H	3	0
" 29	Millwall ...	A	0	0
Mar. 7	West Ham United ...	H	4	0
" 14	Swansea Town ...	A	0	5
" 21	Leicester City ...	A	1	0
" 25	Bournemouth & Bos. .	A	1	1
" 28	Coventry City ...	A		
April 1	Tottenham Hotspur ...	A		
" 4	Arsenal ...	H		
" ..	Portsmouth ...	H		
" 11	Southampton ...	A		
" 18	Portsmouth ...	A		
" 18	Brighton & Hove A.	H		
" 25	Queen's Park Rgrs. ..	A		
May 2	Fulham ...	A		

Half Time Scores.

	F.	A.			F	A
A—Aston Villa v. Birmingham	......	......	J—Shef. W. v. Manchester C.		......	......
B—Bolton W. v. Leeds U.	......	......	K—Wolves v. Arsenal		......	......
C—Derby County v. Liverpool	......	......	L—Charlton A. v. Bury		......	......
D—Everton v. Grimsby T.	......	......	M—Fulham v. Blackpool		......	......
E—Huddersfield v. W. Brom.	......	......	N—Hull City v. West Ham		......	......
F—Middlesbro' v. Sunderland	......	......	O—Tottenham H. v. Soton		......	......
G—Portsmouth v. Stoke C.	......	......	P—Bristol R. v. Coventry C.		......	......
H—P.N.E. v. Blackburn R.	......	......	R—Crystal Pal. v. Q.P.R.		......	......

WITH THE BEST INTENTIONS

Pensioner—" Is Mr. Brentford at home to-day?"
" B "—" Sure he is, old timer. Come inside and I'll see if I can entertain you
as well as I did your friend " The Gunner!" ...

The Next Games.

Next Saturday Brentford visit the Arsenal. This local "Derby" should be one of the classics of the season. The Bees have a fine opportunity of completing a "double," for when the Arsenal came to Griffin Park they went away beaten by the odd goal in three. Both teams are likely to be weakened as the International game between England and Scotland takes place on the same day. There is every likelihood of one or more of the Scottish players in the Bees' team being selected, while Arsenal usually contribute in forming the team to represent England.

Then come the Easter holiday games. On Good Friday (April 10th) Brentford have to journey to Goodison Park to meet Everton. The clubs have not been opposed to each other yet this season.

On the day following, Brentford will be at home to Grimsby Town, Cup semi-finalists this season, and they will have a fine chance of revenging that six goals to one defeat they sustained when they were away to the Fishermen.

On Easter Monday Brentford will have the return game with Everton.

The Bees will then have only three more games before the end of the season—Liverpool (away) and West Bromwich Albion and Derby County at home.

Brentford Reserves have another mid-week fixture for next Wednesday, when they oppose Tottenham Hotspur Reserves at White Hart Lane.

On Saturday next they will receive as their visitors to Griffin Park Arsenal Reserves.

BRENTFORD FOOTBALL AND SPORTS CLUB, LIMITED.

Registered Office :—GRIFFIN PARK, BRAEMAR ROAD, BRENTFORD.

President and Chairman :
MR. L. P. SIMON.

ALDERMAN W. FLEWITT, J.P.
MR. H. N. BLUNDELL.
MR. H. J. SAUNDERS.

MR. H. W. DODGE.
MR. C. L. SIMON.

Vice-Chairman :
MR. F. A. DAVIS.

MR. F. W. BARTON.
ALDERMAN H. F. DAVIS.
MR. J. R. HUGHES, J.P., C.C.

Hon. Treasurer ;
ALDERMAN W. FLEWITT, J.P.

Club Medical Officer ; DR. A. D. GOWANS.

Secretary-Manager ;
MR. H. C. CURTIS,
" DORINCOURT," BOSTON GARDENS, BRENTFORD.

Telephones :
GROUND : EALING 1744.
PRIVATE HOUSE : EALING 1183.

Telegraphic Address ;
CURTIS, FOOTBALL, BRENTFORD.
Ground ; GRIFFIN PARK, EALING ROAD, BRENTFORD.

No. 19.   **Saturday, April 11th, 1936.**

Notes from the Hive.

Three points from two London " Derby " games is very good going—and it might easily have been four. Chelsea were beaten at Griffin Park by the odd goal in three, and two goals were equally divided with the Arsenal at Highbury last week-end. If things continue in such a strain it would seem that the Bees are going to finish in a high position on the League table in their first year in the First Division. That is an achievement in any case, but when we come to consider that Brentford were languishing very near the foot of the table, on the last rung at one time, earlier in the season, the change in fortune has been as welcome as it has been meritorious.

REVENGE AGAINST CHELSEA

Last November Chelsea beat Brentford at Stamford Bridge by the odd goal in three. Naturally our boys, and our supporters too, were very anxious to square the account with the Pensioners by winning the return game at Griffin Park last Saturday week. That is exactly what happened—even to the score—the Bees winning this time by the same margin they had been beaten by at the Bridge.

Actually there should have been a wider margin in our favour at the close, for the Bees were far and away the better side from start to finish. Yet, in spite of such great territorial advantage, the Bees could not get goals in numbers to more adequately represent the run of the play.

Brentford were much faster and better together in attack, more solid at half back, showed better positional play and resource at full back than the visitors, which made our boys a most persistent attacking force by comparison, and the fact that only two goals came our way was due to a combination of circumstances, including some good work by Woodley, the Chelsea goalkeeper, some indifferent finishing at times by our own forwards, allied to some rank bad luck on other occasions. Still, the fact that the Bees played so well and finished winners is all that really matters. Brentford had done far less pressing and won more convincingly on other days. That is the uncertainty of the game.

Brentford took the lead nearly mid-way through the opening half, when some smart play between Scott and Hopkins ended in the first

named giving McCulloch possession and the ball was in the net true and quick. The Bees went further ahead fifteen minutes after the change of ends. This goal was scored by Hopkins from an opening provided by McCulloch. Before the end the visitors managed to get a goal, but they never really looked like saving a game in which the final score certainly flattered them.

DIVISION AT HIGHBURY.

Unfortunately there were some disappointing features about our game at Highbury on Saturday last. Firstly the conditions which a strong cold wind entailed rather spoiled the play as a spectacle, secondly the Arsenal had a number of star players absent on international duty, which also meant the withdrawal of David McCulloch from our team, then the attendance was a big disappointment—a " gate " around 30,000 being one of the smallest the Arsenal have had this season for a Saturday game.

Against this it must be said that there was one good feature—the result. A division of a goal apiece was a most equitable one to all concerned. For either team to have lost in the circumstances would have been an injustice in spite of the fact that Brentford led until the latter stages of the game.

Brentford got in front in the first half when Holliday obtained a goal of the opportunist order.

The Arsenal levelled the scores near the end and thus the spoils were divided.

RESERVES' REVIEW

The struggle for the championship of the London Combination persists with three clubs, Portsmouth, Brentford and Arsenal, all standing a chance of gaining the honour.

Our boys collected two very valuable points at Coventry, where they won 3—1. Dunn, Brown and Sullivan were the scorers.

On Saturday last the vital game with Arsenal Reserves, at Griffin Park, resulted in a goalless draw. The conditions were all against good football, and the game in consequence was lacking in sparkle and fell below anticipations in every respect.

EASTER HOLIDAY GAMES

There are now only six games remaining for Brentford to play, four of which are at Griffin Park. At the moment we are mainly concerned with the Easter Holiday fixtures, which comprise home and away games with Everton and a home game with Grimsby Town.

To-day's game is with Grimsby, and we extend a most cordial welcome to Grimsby Town, and congratulate them on qualifying for the semi-final of the F.A. Cup. At the moment of writing, before the games played yesterday (Good Friday) Grimsby Town, although only three points less than the Bees were in the danger zone of relegation, so we can expect a very keen fight.

On Monday next the return game with Everton, another club not too well off for points, takes place at Griffin Park, so it seems that before the holiday games are over our boys will have taken part in three strenuous games and will probably be thankful for a few days' rest, which they will enjoy before the game at Liverpool next week-end. Here's to a very productive Easter Egg for the Bees.

" BUSY BEE."

Jottings from the Board Room.

The Final of the London Challenge Cup —Arsenal Reserves v. Brentford Reserves —will be played on Monday, May 4th, 1936, and it is anticipated that it will be played at Stamford Bridge.

The kick-off in our game v. Everton, on this ground on Easter Monday is at 3.30 p.m. There are still some tickets for numbered and reserved seats at 3/6 and 4/- each.

The Reserves are to-day away to Southampton Reserves, and owing to a schoolboys' game following ours, the kick off is at 2.30 p.m.

Comparative records with last season is as follows :
Football League—

	P.	W.	D.	L.	Goals F.	A.	P.
This Season	36	13	10	13	64	56	36
Last Season	36	22	8	6	75	40	52
London Combination—							
This Season	40	26	5	9	86	46	57
Last Season	40	21	7	12	69	46	49

Goal scorers to date :
Football League.—McCulloch 18, Hopkins 12, Holliday 11, Scott (W.) 8, Fletcher 5, Robson 3, Reid 3, J. C. Burns 1, Dunn 1, Muttitt 1, McKenzie 1. —Total 64.
London Combination.—Dunn 28, McAloon 15, Brown 15, Sullivan 10, Muttitt 6, Gibbons 5, Fenton 2, Smith (C.) 2, Fletcher 2, Smith (L.) 1.—Total 86.

George Poyser is now in training and ready to play when required, although a further rest is advisable to assure absolute fitness. George strained a groin muscle against Birmingham on Saturday, February 29th.

There are still a number of articles unclaimed which have been found on the ground after various games. These include keys, gloves, gaiters, lady's purse containing silver and copper coins and an umbrella found in Block " C " of stand. Please apply at secretary's office.

Patrons are warned to BEWARE OF PICKPOCKETS. At recent games one or two supporters have complained of losses.

The B.B.C. Football Club will play our Reserves on this ground on Thursday, April 23rd, kick-off at 6.15 p.m. in the Brentford Philanthropic Cup competition. Admission 6d., entrance in Braemar Road only. Tickets can be purchased from any member of the Philanthropic Society. Tommy Handley, of B.B.C. fame, will kick off. An old favourite of this club plays for the B.B.C. Club in Billy Hodge. If you cannot come and witness the game, please purchase a ticket (6d.) and thus assist to help the poor and distressed of the district.

Little has been seen this season of our goalkeeper Jimmy Nichols. Unfortunately he met with a rather bad injury against Coventry City Reserves on November 23rd, 1935, when he fractured a finger. Complications set in and proved more serious than at first anticipated. Even now, after such a long lapse, he is unable to get proper use of the injured finger. Bad luck for Jimmy and the Club.

The 6 per cent. Debentures issue has now been fully taken up and therefore no further applications can be considered.

The Southern Railway announce cheap trips from Reading, Ascot, Chertsey, Egham, Feltham and other stations to Brentford, for the match Brentford v. Everton on Easter Monday. Return trains leave Brentford at 5.10 and 5.41 p.m.

NEXT HOME GAME

Easter Monday, April 13th.

BRENTFORD v. EVERTON

(Football League)   Kick-off at 3.30 p.m.

Tickets at 3/6 and 4/- for numbered and reserved seats can be purchased to-day.

Shots from the Spot.

Grimsby, our visitors to-day, were originally an amateur club. They joined Football Alliance in 1889 and moved to Abbey Park. They have a very strong defence and it earned them many points last season when they finished fifth in the table.

* * *

This year they had a successful run in the Cup, reaching the semi-final, when they were beaten by the Arsenal by the only goal of the game.

* * *

The Reserves have a very difficult task in trying to regain the London Combination Championship. Only a point divides the top three teams, who are well in the lead of the rest of the teams.

* * *

With only four more games to be played, it seems that there is going to be a very exciting race. Of the Bees' remaining games three are away, and they have only one at home.

* * *

That is a very stiff programme, and more so as two of the games are local " Derbys." One is with Queen's Park Rangers and the other, the last game of the season, with Fulham.

* * *

Chesterfield had eleven penalties awarded against then last season— more than any other club.

McCulloch was chosen to lead his country's attack against England at Wembley, on Saturday. Scotland, by forcing a draw, have won the international championship.

* * *

The 'Spurs' sudden revival has completely changed the promotion chances at the head of the Second Division table. Four points cover the top six clubs and the Easter scramble is upon them. West Ham, touch wood, seem fairly safe, but Charlton's heavy defeat at Leicester, on Saturday, has shaken them a bit.

* * *

What a battle it will be these next few weeks ! Manchester United and Sheffield United are also to be accounted for.

* * *

Oldham Athletic are the only Football League team since the war to start each of two consecutive seasons with the identical team. That occurred in 1929-30 and 1930-31.

* * *

History, if it can be termed as such, was made on Saturday. Walker, of Hearts, had the distinction of being the first player to use the penalty spot at Wembley. Never before in Cup Final or international game has it been required.

OUR VISITORS TO-DAY.

HOW THEY MAY LINE UP.

One of the oldest clubs in the games, Grimsby Town—our visitors to-day—have never, however, been regarded as one of the " fashionable " clubs. Despite lack of support and financial troubles (their successful Cup career this season only results in a net gain of a few hundred pounds to their exchequer) they have produced many well-known players and have their share of distinctions.

They gained their First League honour in 1901 when they won the Second Division championship; a feat they repeated in season 1933-4. They have once finished runners-up in that section and in 1925-6 won the Northern Section Championship.

Tweedy, George Jacob (goalkeeper).—Born at Willington, Co. Durham. Height 6ft. Weight 12st. 4lb. This fine custodian was picked up as a youngster, his only previous experience being with the junior club of his native town. Developed rapidly and got his first chance in League football in season 1932-3. Became the regular man last term when he was ever present. Has remarkable agility, but is very sure.

Kelly, James Edward (right back).—Born at Seaham Harbour, Co. Durham. Height 5ft. 9in. Weight 11st. 6lb. Played for Durham City in his early days. Then moved to Barrow. Was secured as a right-back by Grimsby in March, 1933. Has played on both flanks this season.

Hodgson, James Venner (left back).—Born at Seaham Harbour. Height 6ft. 1½in. Weight 12st. 12lb. Was a centre half when secured from Seaham Colliery Welfare. Proved a capable deputy for Betmead until this season, when he showed his adaptability by taking over the left back berth, in which position he has given some grand displays.

Hall, Frederick (right half).—Born at Cleethorpes, Lincs. Height 5ft. 8in. Weight 11st. 2lb. Made his name with Cleethorpes Town. Was snapped up by Grimsby in 1930 and has been the regular right half for several seasons, being an ever present for something like three campaigns. A full 90-minute player, hard working in attack and defence.

Betmead, Harry (centre half).—Born at Grimsby. Height 6ft. 1in. Weight 11st 6lb. This local is the son of a former Grimsby Town trainer. Was only a youngster when he joined the club's playing staff in 1931. Got his League chance in 1932-3 season and made the most of it. Plays a game of similar style to Barker, not confining himself to defensive duties.

Buck, Edward (left half).—Born at Dipton, Co. Durham. Height 5ft. 11in. Weight 12st. After ex-

BRENTFORD *v.*

BREN

Red an

1—MA

2—WILSON
Right Back

4—McKENZIE
Right Half

5—
Cen

7—HOPKINS
Outside Right

8—SCOTT
Inside Right

9—McC
Centr

Referee—Mr. A. TAYLOR (Wigan)

12—LEWIS
Outside Left

13—CRAVEN
Inside Left

14—G
Centre

17—BUCK
Left Half

18—B
Ce

20—HODGSON
Left Back

22—T
G

GRIMS
Shirts, Black and W

THE LEAGUE—DIVISION I.
Up to April 4th inclusive.

	P.	W.	D.	L.	F.	A.	P.
Sunderland	36	22	6	8	95	59	50
Derby County	36	16	10	10	52	39	42
Stoke City	36	18	5	13	53	49	41
Huddersfield	36	16	9	11	52	50	41
Arsenal	35	13	12	10	67	40	38
Manchester City	36	16	5	15	60	49	37
Preston N.E.	35	15	7	13	53	48	37
Birmingham	35	13	11	11	49	45	37
BRENTFORD	36	13	10	13	64	56	36
Middlesbrough	36	14	7	15	77	63	35
Bolton Wanderers	36	12	11	13	59	68	35
Portsmouth	35	14	6	15	45	59	34
Leeds United	35	12	9	14	53	52	33
Everton	36	10	13	13	72	74	33
Wolverhampton	35	13	7	15	60	62	33
Liverpool	36	12	9	15	52	56	33
Sheffield Wednesday	35	12	9	14	59	67	33
Grimsby Town	36	14	5	17	53	64	33
Chelsea	34	12	9	13	48	61	33
West Bromwich A.	36	14	4	18	78	74	32
Aston Villa	37	12	7	18	71	99	31
Blackburn	36	10	7	19	44	82	27

GRIMSBY TOWN

FORD
e Stripes

IESON
eper

3—BATEMAN
Left Back

IES   6—RICHARDS
alf   Left Half

LOCH 10—HOLLIDAY 11—REID
ward   Inside Left   Outside Left

Linesmen—Messrs. F. S. E. Riggs (blue flag)
and M. E. Love (red flag)

ER 15—BESTALL 16—BALDRY
ard   Inside Right   Outside Right

MEAD   19—HALL
Half   Right Half

21—KELLY
Right Back

EDY
eper

TOWN

ipes ; Knickers Black

LONDON COMBINATION

Up to April 4th inclusive.

	P.	W.	L.	D.	F.	A.	P.
BRENTFORD ...	40	26	9	5	86	46	57
Arsenal	39	26	9	4	99	42	56
Portsmouth	39	24	7	8	111	54	56
Swansea Town ...	42	19	14	9	70	62	47
Reading	40	21	14	5	86	75	47
Crystal Palace	39	19	13	7	90	85	45
Chelsea	39	17	13	9	84	72	43
Queen's Park Rgrs.	41	18	16	7	71	61	43
West Ham U.	40	18	16	6	93	67	42
Charlton Ath.	41	18	17	6	82	70	42
Luton Town	39	19	16	4	105	92	42
Northampton T. ...	41	15	16	10	81	74	40
Millwall	40	17	17	6	60	67	40
Tottenham H.	38	15	14	9	93	78	39
Coventry City	40	16	17	7	72	74	39
Fulham	39	14	17	8	73	68	36
Bournemouth	42	13	20	9	66	93	35
Clapton Orient	40	11	16	13	55	88	35
Leicester City	40	14	21	5	68	91	33
Southend Utd.	40	11	20	9	65	90	31
Watford	41	14	24	3	78	116	31
Southampton	39	10	21	8	53	73	28
Brighton & Hove A.	39	9	22	8	60	104	26
Bristol City	40	10	25	5	57	116	25

The Arsenal Arena, entirely reconstructed in six weeks.

The White City Arena, entirely reconstructed in six weeks.

The West Ham Stadium Dog Track.

3 famous grounds entirely re-constructed by

perience with West Stanley, he joined Leeds United. Did not make much of an impression with them. Has steadily improved since joining Grimsby in December, 1929, and completes a fine half back line.

Baldry, George (outside right).— Born at Cleethorpes. Height 5ft. 7in. Weight 10st. 6lb. Has had a swift rise this season. Signing as a part-time pro. at the start of the campaign, he graded to the first team before Christmas and has kept his place. Is a deadly shot and frequently cuts in. Still works in the fish business all day and plays in a dance band at night.

Bestall, John Gilbert (inside right) —Born at Beighton, Sheffield. Height 5ft. 2½in. Weight 9st. 7lb. The smallest player in regular First Division football. Also one of the cleverest. Started his football career with Beighton Miners' Welfare. Then moved to Rotherham County (now Rotherham United). Was secured by Grimsby 10 years ago. Captains the club. Has played for England and the Football League.

Glover, Ernest Matthew (centre forward). — Born at Swansea. Height 6ft. Weight 13st. 9lb. A Welsh schoolboy international who had a trial with Swansea Town. Joined Grimsby in December, 1928. and got his chance three years later when Coleman moved to Arsenal. Keeps up the club's tradition for centre forwards. Has several Welsh caps. Used to be a railway porter.

Craven, Charles (inside left)— Born at Boston, Lincs. Height 5ft. 9in. Weight 10st. 10lb. Previously with Boston Town, where he played with Eric Houghton, Aston Villa's international. Used to be a clerk in a printing works. Was a schoolboy international trialist and has been reserve for England in " full " internationals.

Lewis, A. C. (outside left).—Born at Trealaw, Wales. Height 5ft. 5½in. Weight 10st. 3lb. This Welsh amateur international outside right went to Grimsby in June, 1933. Made five appearances in his first season and six last term. He has shown that outside left is his better position. Grimsby was his first club as a professional.

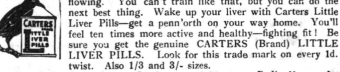

NAMES IN THE GAME.

MR. WILLIAM HOOTON

Mr. William Hooton, the secretary of Grimsby Town Football Club, is one of the best-known men in Grimsby football.

He was born in Grimsby and he has had a varied experience not only as a club and competition official, but as a referee, and his expert knowledge of the game is never doubted.

For several years he was a director of the Town, until his appointment as assistant secretary. In March, 1932, he was appointed to his present position.

Mr. FRANK WOMACK

Mr. Frank Womack is the name of the Grimsby Town manager, and is probably one of the best known in the annals of English football. He had a very long association with Birmingham Football Club and for twenty years he was in the service of the club as a player.

His great displays at full back are still talked of when footballers and football fans chat over old times and old games.

He was twice chosen to play for the English League against the Scottish League. In 1931-32 he was appointed Manager of Torquay United. His stay with that club, however, was short, for in May, 1932, he came to Grimsby Town.

A SHORT REVIEW

It is now a seasonable time to have a short review of the events that have taken place since our first season in Division I commenced, and it can be looked upon as one of "ups and downs."

We opened the season in good style, winning the first two games. After that the tides of fortune seemed to turn on us with a vengeance, and for several weeks we lost matches at home and away by the narrowest of margins.

At intervals we managed to obtain points but throughout it will be generally agreed that it was rarely through being out-played that the Bees lost. We did everything but score. The result was that we were fighting at the bottom of the table to steer clear of relegation.

With the coming of the New Year there commenced a brighter outlook and the team, with some fine football, commenced to obtain results that their performances warranted.

Now it is only a few more weeks before our first experience of the First Division comes to a close. The position in the League is bright and with a few more points from the Easter games, the outlook will be still more cheerful.

There is one thing remaining and that is that the supporters have backed up the club in an admirable way throughout the season.

JACK CARTMELL
Assistant Trainer

Born at Blackpool in 1900. He was with the Gillingham Football Club at the same time as Mr. Harry Curtis, the Bees' secretary-manager. He played for the team at outside left and was one of those wingers with a touch of "class." When Mr. Curtis came to Brentford "Jack," as he is popularly known, soon afterwards joined him at Griffin Park as assistant trainer, a position he has since held.

FIXTURES, SEASON 1935-36.

FIRST TEAM

Date. 1935.	Opponents.	Ground.	Goals F.	Goals A.
Aug. 31	Bolton Wanderers ...	A	2	0
Sept. 5	Blackburn Rovers ...	H	3	1
,, 7	Huddersfield Town ...	H	1	2
,, 14	Middlesbrough ...	A	0	0
,, 18	Derby County ...	A	1	2
,, 21	Aston Villa	H	1	2
,, 28	Wolverhampton Wdrs.	A	2	3
Oct. 5	Sheffield Wednesday ..	H	2	2
,, 12	Portsmouth ...	A	3	1
,, 19	Stoke City	A	0	0
,, 26	Manchester City ...	A	1	2
Nov. 2	Arsenal	H	2	1
,, 9	Birmingham	A	1	2
,, 16	Sunderland ...	H	1	5
,, 23	Chelsea	A	1	2
,, 30	Leeds United ...	H	2	2
Dec. 7	Grimsby Town ...	A	1	6
,, 14	Liverpool	H	1	1
,, 21	West Bromwich Albion	A	0	1
,, 25	Preston North End ...	H	5	2
,, 26	Preston North End ...	A	4	2
,, 28	Bolton Wanderers ...	H	4	0
1936.				
Jan. 1	Blackburn Rovers ...	A	0	1
,, 4	Huddersfield Town ...	A	2	2
,, 11	(3) Leicester City ...	A	0	1
,, 18	Middlesbrough ...	H	1	0
,, 25	(4) Aston Villa ...	A	2	2
Feb. 1	Wolverhampton Wdrs.	H	5	1
,, 8	Sheffield Wednesday ...	A	3	3
,, 15	(5)			
,, 22	Stoke City	A	2	2
,, 29	(6) Birmingham ...	H	0	1
Mar. 7	Leeds United ...	A	2	1
,, 14	Manchester City ...	H	0	0
,, 21	(S.-F.) Sunderland ...	A	3	1
,, 25	Portsmouth ...	H	3	1
,, 28	Chelsea	H	2	1
April 4	Arsenal	A	1	1
,, 10	Everton	A		
,, 11	Grimsby Town ...	H		
,, 13	Everton	H		
,, 18	Liverpool	A		
,, 25	(F.) West Brom. Alb.	H		
May 2	Derby County ...	H		

SECOND TEAM

Date. 1935.	Opponents.	Ground.	Goals F.	Goals A.
Aug. 31	Charlton Athletic ...	H	2	1
Sept. 4	Watford	A	1	3
,, 7	Clapton Orient ...	A	0	1
,, 12	Watford	H	2	1
,, 14	Southend United ...	H	1	0
,, 21	Northampton Town ...	A	1	0
,, 25	Luton Town	A	1	4
,, 28	Crystal Palace ...	H	4	0
Oct. 2	Luton Town	H	4	3
,, 5	Reading	A	1	2
,, 7	Met. Police—L.C. Cup	H	2	0
,, 9	Bournemouth & Bos. .	H	5	2
,, 12	Tottenham Hotspur	H	2	1
,, 19	Bristol City	A	3	1
,, 21	C. Orient—L.C. Cup ...	A	3	1
,, 26	Millwall	H	1	0
Nov 2	West Ham United ...	A	1	0
,, 9	Swansea Town ...	H	2	0
,, 11	Fulham (L.C.Cup,S.F.)	H	2	0
,, 16	Leicester City ...	A	3	2
,, 23	Coventry City ...	H	4	1
,, 30	Arsenal	A	0	1
Dec 7	Southampton ...	H	4	0
,, 14	Brighton & Hove A.	A	1	0
,, 21	Queen's Park Rgrs. ..	H	3	1
,, 25	Chelsea	A	2	2
,, 26	Chelsea	H	2	1
,, 28	Charlton Athletic ...	A	1	3
Jan. 4	Clapton Orient ...	H	5	1
,, 11	Fulham	H	4	0
,, 18	Southend United ...	A	4	2
,, 25	Northampton Town ...	H	5	1
Feb. 1	Crystal Palace ...	A	1	
,, 8	Reading	H	0	1
,, 22	Bristol City	H	3	0
,, 29	Millwall	A	0	4
Mar	West Ham United ...	H	4	0
,, 14	Swansea Town ...	A	0	5
,, 21	Leicester City ...	H	1	0
,, 25	Bournemouth & Bos. .	A	1	1
,, 28	Coventry City ...	A	3	1
April 1	Tottenham Hotspur ...	A	1	2
,, 4	Arsenal	H	0	0
,, 10	Portsmouth ...	H		
,, 11	Southampton ...	A		
,, 13	Portsmouth ...	A		
,, 18	Brighton & Hove A.	H		
,, 25	Queen's Park Rgrs. ..	A		
May 2	Fulham	A		

Half Time Scores.

	F.	A.			F	A
A—Aston Villa v. Man. City	......	......	J—Sheffield Wed. v. Blackburn	......	......	
B—Bolton W. v. Sunderland	......	......	K—Wolves v. Stoke		......	......
C—Derby County v. Leeds	......	......	L—Bradford C. v. West Ham	......	......	
D—Everton v. West Bromwich	......	......	M—Charlton v. Notts Forest	......	......	
E—Huddersfield v. Birm'ham	......	......	N—Fulham v. Southampton	......	......	
F—Middlesbrough v. Arsenal	......	......	O—'Spurs v. Leicester	......	......	
G—Portsmouth v. Chelsea	......	......	P—Cardiff v. Q.P.R.	......	......	
H—P.N.E. v. Liverpool	......	......	R—Reading v. Brighton	......	......	

GETTING ON THE MAP

Professor—" Now, can any boy tell me what very well-known place is missing from this map?"
Chorus of Boys (anywhere within 30 miles of London)—"Yes sir, Brentford!"

The Next Games.

We are now midway through the Easter holiday games, and when the Bees entertain Everton at Griffin Park on Monday the programme will be concluded.

The Goodison Park men have not had a very happy season, but are now finding their feet, although it is getting late in the season. They have that great centre forward, Dixie Dean, and when he is at his best he is a match-winning player. Their away record is very poor, however, as they have only won one away match all the season. Everton are not out of the relegation zone yet and will put up a fine fight for points.

The following Saturday Brentford conclude their away fixture list with a visit to Liverpool.

When Liverpool came to Griffin Park they won by the odd goal in three. The Bees will go all out to obtain revenge and also to collect points to assist them in reaching a higher place in the League than the other London clubs.

On Cup Final day the visitors to Griffin Park will be West Bromwich Albion, who were another team to defeat the Bees earlier in the season. With ground advantage, however, Brentford should not let them repeat this performance.

To conclude the season, the Bees have another home game, this time the visitors being Derby County.

A better game to end the season could not have been arranged —except with Sunderland—for the men from Derby have a bright chance of being the runners-up for the League championship.

BRENTFORD FOOTBALL AND SPORTS CLUB, LIMITED.

Registered Office :—GRIFFIN PARK, BRAEMAR ROAD, BRENTFORD.

President and Chairman :
Mr. L. P. Simon.

Alderman W. Flewitt, J.P.
Mr. H. N. Blundell.
Mr. H. J. Saunders.

Mr. H. W. Dodge.
Mr. C. L. Simon.

Vice-Chairman :
Mr. F. A. Davis.

Mr. F. W. Barton.
Alderman H. F. Davis.
Mr. J. R. Hughes, J.P., C.C.

Hon. Treasurer :
Alderman W. Flewitt, J.P.
Club Medical Officer ; Dr. A. D. Gowans.

Telephones ;
Ground : Ealing 1744.
Private House : Ealing 1183.

Secretary-Manager ;
Mr. H. C. Curtis,
" Dorincourt," Boston Gardens, Brentford.

Telegraphic Address ;
Curtis, Football, Brentford.
Ground ; Griffin Park, Ealing Road, Brentford.

No. 20. **Easter Monday, April 13th, 1936.**

Notes from the Hive.

The printers of this programme want a holiday at Easter, like most other people, consequently no comment can be made regarding our games against Everton, at Goodison Park on Good Friday and Grimsby Town, at Griffin Park, on Saturday last.

We naturally hope that the Bees did well and assuming such to be the case, express the hope that the good work will be carried on against Everton in the return game to-day.

* * *

With no games to review, as these notes have to be written before any of the Easter holiday games were played, the opportunity is taken to have a look back on the season's work.

For a club playing in the First Division for the first time it will be generally agreed that Brentford have justified their promotion to the top class of English football.

. Not unnaturally, it took our boys some time to get acclimatised, but even in the early stages of the campaign when things were not going too well, especially at home, it was generally admitted that Brentford were displaying form better than the actual results might suggest.

But if points are being dropped with any degree of regularity there is always the possibility that the players' confidence will be affected and the play of the team suffer accordingly.

That kind of thing was happening as far as the Bees were concerned and in an effort to bring back the old confidence into the side new players were secured. Things got to such a pitch that it was imperative that something should be done. Having earned the right to a place in the First Division, the directors were anxious to retain their place, particularly in view of the fact that the club was being so well supported. Everything in the garden looked lovely except for the fact that defeats were being sustained, oftentimes against the run of the play, and generally by the narrowest of margins—the odd goal.

* * *

The directors felt that the supporters of the club deserved all the enterprise that could be shown, so they went boldly into the transfer market and secured the transfer of three high-priced players. First came Dai Richards, the Welsh international half back from Wolverhampton Wanderers. Then David McCulloch, the Scottish international centre forward from the

Hearts followed, and later Bobby Reid, outside left from Hamilton Academicals, packed his bag to journey south to join Brentford.

Naturally the transfer of three such well-known players cost big money, offset to some extent by the transfers of George Robson to Hearts and Charlie Fletcher to Burnley, but the wisdom of such team strengthening soon became apparent and the critics were in perfect agreement that Brentford had bought right. When a team buys right, expenditure, however great, does not really matter, because it is sure to come back through the turnstiles and after all the assets of a club must be improved if the playing strength is represented by players for whom a club could get big fees if they were of a mind to part with them.

* * *

It is highly probable that some of the early season reverses were due to our team knowing they were playing in the First Division for the first time. A sort of inferiority complex—just like a fellow starting a new job. He knows he can do the work, but is looking for snags all the time before he settles down.

It was like that with Brentford. Started off with two wins—the first one at Bolton, too! "Bees are good enough," the critics said. Not a win in the next six games—"Are the Bees good enough?" was the next chant we heard. But it must be remembered that in those games were four odd-goal defeats, and a couple of drawn games. The poor sequence was broken by a fine 3—1 win at Portsmouth. In the game which followed against Stoke City at Griffin Park, the Bees pressed for something like eighty minutes out of ninety and yet had to be content with a goalless draw. Later an odd goal in three win over the Arsenal raised the hopes of our supporters, rather prematurely, for

three successive defeats followed—one a terrible hiding at home against Sunderland.

* * *

Christmas saw the turn in the tide. Plenty of goals and full points from three games and although, like all other clubs, Brentford have tasted the bitters of defeat since the upward swing in the fortunes of our club has been maintained. Included in the achievements during the second half of the season was a great 3—1 win at Sunderland, a draw at Highbury and five clear goals win over the Wolves at Griffin Park. Without assuming an attitude of counting one's chickens before the shells are broken, it seems a reasonable supposition that the Bees will finish in a fairly respectable position in the League table in their first venture in the Highest Circle.

PLAYERS HONOURED

It is with considerable pride that we record the fact that three of our players have been honoured by their country this season. Richards and Hopkins have again been chosen for Wales, while McCulloch recently led the Scottish attack against England at Wembley. In addition there was Duncan McKenzie, who was chosen as reserve for Scotland. May it be a case of coming events casting their shadows before in the case of our popular right half back.

FREEHOLD OF GROUND BOUGHT

Another big step forward made by the club is the purchase of the freehold of Griffin Park. That important stroke of business was accomplished recently and the way is now made clear for the club to undertake any further alterations and improvements they wish.

How the fortunes have changed for the Bees during say, the last ten years?

BUSY BEE.

Jottings from the Board Room.

The kick-off for all remaining games to be played on this ground this season (Football League and London Combination) will be at 3.30 p.m., with the exception of our game v. Derby County (Football League) on Saturday, May 2nd, when the match will be commenced at 3.15 p.m.

The Final of the London Challenge Cup —Arsenal Reserves v. Brentford Reserves —will be played on Monday, May 4th, 1936, and it is anticipated that it will be played at Stamford Bridge.

The Reserves are to-day away to Portsmouth Reserves, kick-off at 3.15 p.m. Their two holiday games will no doubt have decided the chances of winning the London Combination Championship.

Comparative records with last season is as follows :

Football League—

	P.	W.	D.	L.	Goals F.	Goals A.	P.
This Season	36	13	10	13	64	56	36
Last Season	36	22	8	6	75	40	52

London Combination—

	P.	W.	D.	L.	Goals F.	Goals A.	P.
This Season	40	26	5	9	86	46	57
Last Season	40	21	7	12	69	46	49

The B.B.C. Football Club will play our Reserves on this ground on Thursday, April 23rd, kick-off at 6.15 p.m. in the Brentford Philanthropic Cup competition. Admission 6d., entrance in Braemar Road only. Tickets can be purchased from any member of the Philanthropic Society. Tommy Handley, of B.B.C. fame, will kick off. An old favourite of this club plays for the B.B.C. Club in Billy Hodge. If you cannot come and witness the game, please purchase a ticket (6d.) and thus assist to help the poor and distressed of the district.

The 6 per cent. Debenture issue has now been fully taken up and therefore no further applications can be considered.

The League team complete this season's away fixtures on Saturday next, April 18th when they pay a visit to Liverpool, while the Reserves complete their London Combination home fixtures on the same day when they meet Brighton and Hove Reserves, kick-off at 3.30 p.m.

Jackie Burns and Pat Clark, our two popular amateurs, are both assisting Leyton F.C. these days.

Brighton and Hove F.C. have agreed to compete against us on Thursday, April 30th, kick-off at 6.15 p.m., for the Brentford Hospital Cup. Please book this date.

The Championship of the Billiards and Table Tennis Tournaments between the players this season has resulted as follows :

Table Tennis.—D. McKenzie defeated G. McAloon in the Final.

Billiards.—R. Kane defeated C. Smith in the Final.

NEXT HOME LEAGUE MATCH
Saturday, April 25th.
BRENTFORD v. WEST BROM. A.

(Football League) Kick-off at 3.30 p.m.

Tickets at 4/- for numbered and reserved seats can be purchased to-day.

Patrons are warned to BEWARE OF PICKPOCKETS. At recent games one or two supporters have complained of losses.

Shots from the Spot.

Returning from Highbury on Saturday afternoon, delight was expressed by the Bees' supporters who had seen the match with Arsenal, at Brentford's performance. There were many arguments as to the merits of the displays of the players but everyone was unanimous in the opinion that Mathieson was outstanding in goal.

* * *

Several supporters, whose first visit is was to Highbury, were a trifle disappointed in the ground. From the boosting it had received they expected to find a larger ground, one similar to that of Stamford Bridge. The double-decker stand, although it was not used to a great extent on Saturday, was greatly admired.

* * *

At this time of the year it is unusual for players to have as much ball practice as they do in the earlier stages of the season. But that is not because the players are in any way getting " fed up " with the sight of the ball. As a matter of fact, if any proof were really needed that professionals enjoy football it was forthcoming at Griffin Park the other day.

* * *

Usually the players train on the field, but owing to the wet state of the ground they used the small open space in front of the manager's office. There the players had two old balls out and were indulging in a little game on their own.

* * *

Alec James, Arsenal's famous Scottish forward, who watched the Arsenal-Brentford clash at Highbury, on Saturday, pays a striking tribute to the players on both sides in his weekly article in a London evening newspaper. Says Alec : "I must admit I enjoyed my watching brief, for it is not often that you see a " Derby " game so cleanly played, despite the keenness.

* * *

" It was very pleasant too to see my old friend and colleague in the Raith Rovers' team, Jim Mathieson, have a real day out, even against my present club. Although Jim has been in the game so long, he does not seem to have lost any of his form in goal—or his Fife accent.

* * *

" The last time I saw Jack Holliday play for Brentford I remarked how well he, as a centre forward, had fitted into an inside position. He did even better on Saturday and more than one of our team said how well he had played. No one, I think, expected him to turn out to be such a great inside artist.

* * *

" In addition to his foraging, Holliday showed by the practically unstoppable shot with which he scored Brentford's goal that he is still a great opportunist with a wonderful eye for an opening." Thanks very much Alec for a very nice little note. We appreciate it and accept it in the spirit in which it was written.

* * *

Arsenal Reserves' point obtained at Griffin Park on Saturday, with the nil-nil result of their clash with our boys, must be just about the first point they have ever taken away from our second string at Griffin Park.

OUR VISITORS TO-DAY.

HOW THEY MAY LINE UP.

———◆———

Founded in 1878 and reformed fourteen years later, Everton, our visitors to-day, have had their full share of ups and downs. These last six years, however, have been easily the most remarkable and hectic in that long career.

Relegated in 1930 they topped the Second Division the following year and followed that by gaining the Division I championship in 1932 and the F.A. Cup the year after that—a run that is without parallel in the history of the game.

This year they have not been without their relegation troubles, but have staged a revival recently that has considerably diminished those fears.

Sagar, Edward (goalkeeper).—Born at Moorends, Yorkshire. Height 5ft. 10in. Weight 10st. 8lb. Next to Hibbs is considered England's best. Played against Scotland this month, but that was not his first experience of representative football. Has played for the Football League as well as England. Started with a colliery side. Was offered trial with Hull City before joining Everton in March, 1929.

Cook, William (right back).—Born at Coleraine, Ireland. Height 5ft. 7½in. Weight 11st. 10lb. Has only played in Ireland in internationals. Moved to Scotland as a boy and after developing with Port Glasgow Juniors, joined Celtic. Won a Scottish Cup medal in his first season with that club (1930-1). Joined Everton December, 1932, and won an English Cup medal in his first season with them. Has captained Ireland.

Jones, John E. (left back).—Born at Bromborough, Cheshire. Height 5ft. 9½in. Weight 10st. 10lb. A tribute to the club's nursing system. Signed first as an amateur. Turned professional in 1933 and in 1933-4 had his first League outings.

Mercer, Joseph (right half).—Born at Ellesmere Port, Cheshire. Height 5ft. 9½in. Weight 10st. 8lb. Another youngster who has developed with the junior sides at Goodison. Had trials with Blackburn as a youngster, but was not kept. After playing second fiddle to Britton and Thomson for some time has come into his own this season. Played first on the left flank and is now keeping international Britton in the Reserves.

White, Thomas (centre half).—Born at Manchester. Height 5ft. 9½in. Weight 13st. Utility man of the club. Was a pivot with Stockport Schoolboys. Played as an amateur for Southport's League side while still a boy. Joined Everton in February, 1927. Had to be content with understudy's role for some time. Established himself at centre half in 1932 and played for England in that position the following year. Has often played as a forward and in emergency at full back.

Thomson, John (left half).—Born at Thornton, Fifeshire. Height 6ft. Weight 12st. 13lb. Played for Thornton Rangers (junior) and Dundee before joining Everton in March, 1930. Has since played in well over 200 first team games. Lost his form at the beginning of this season, but is now back in form.

BRENTFORD

BRE...

Red a...

1—MA...

2—WILSON
Right Back

4—McKENZIE
Right Half

5—
Ce...

7—HOPKINS   8—SCOTT   9—McC...
Outside Right   Inside Right   Centr...

Referee— Mr. A. W. BARTON (Derbyshire)

14—
Cen...

12—GILLICK   13—STEVENSON
Outside Left   Inside Left

17—THOMSON
Left Half

18—
Ce...

20—JONES
Left Back

22—
C...

EVE...
Shirts, Royal Blue ;

THE LEAGUE--DIVISION I.
Up to April 4th inclusive.

	P.	W.	D.	L.	F.	A.	P.
Sunderland	36	22	6	8	95	59	50
Derby County	36	16	10	10	52	39	42
Stoke City	36	18	5	13	53	49	41
Huddersfield	36	16	9	11	52	50	41
Arsenal	35	13	12	10	67	40	38
Manchester City	36	16	5	15	60	49	37
Preston N.E.	35	15	7	13	53	48	37
Birmingham	35	13	11	11	49	45	37
BRENTFORD	**36**	**13**	**10**	**13**	**64**	**56**	**36**
Middlesbrough	36	14	7	15	77	63	35
Bolton Wanderers	36	12	11	13	59	68	35
Portsmouth	35	14	6	15	45	59	34
Leeds United	35	12	9	14	53	52	33
Everton	36	10	13	13	72	74	33
Wolverhampton	35	13	7	15	60	62	33
Liverpool	36	12	9	15	52	56	33
Sheffield Wednesday	35	12	9	14	59	67	33
Grimsby Town	36	14	5	17	53	64	33
Chelsea	34	12	9	13	48	61	33
West Bromwich A.	36	14	4	18	78	74	32
Aston Villa	37	12	7	18	71	99	31
Blackburn	36	10	7	19	44	82	27

⟩. EVERTON

ORD
Stripes

ESON
er

3—BATEMAN
Left Back

ES   6—RICHARDS
Left Half

OCH 10—HOLLIDAY 11—REID
Inside Left   Outside Left

Linesmen— Messrs. W. F. Tucker (blue flag)
and F. E. Hawkes (red flag)

AN
ard

15—CUNLIFFE   16—GELDARD
Inside Right   Outside Right

TE   19—MERCER
lf   Right Half

21—COOK
Right Back

AR
er

ON

White (Blue Seams)

LONDON COMBINATION

Up to April 4th inclusive.

	P.	W.	L.	D.	F.	A.	P.
BRENTFORD ...	40	26	9	5	86	46	57
Arsenal	40	26	10	4	99	43	56
Portsmouth	39	24	7	8	111	54	56
Reading	40	21	14	5	86	75	47
Swansea Town ...	42	19	14	9	70	62	47
Chelsea	40	18	13	9	85	72	45
Crystal Palace	39	19	13	7	90	85	45
Queen's Park Rgrs.	41	18	16	7	71	61	43
West Ham U.	40	18	16	6	93	67	42
Luton Town	39	19	16	4	105	92	42
Charlton Ath.	41	18	17	6	82	70	42
Northampton T. ...	41	15	16	10	81	74	40
Millwall	40	17	17	6	60	67	40
Tottenham H.	38	15	14	9	93	78	39
Coventry City	40	16	17	7	72	74	39
Fulham	39	14	17	8	73	68	36
Bournemouth	42	13	20	9	66	93	35
Clapton Orient	40	11	16	13	55	88	35
Leicester City	40	14	21	5	68	91	33
Southend Utd.	40	11	20	9	65	90	31
Watford	41	14	24	3	78	116	31
Southampton	39	10	21	8	53	73	28
Brighton & Hove A.	39	9	22	8	60	104	26
Bristol City	40	10	25	5	57	116	25

Goals (heading over F. and A. columns)

The Arsenal Arena, entirely reconstructed in six weeks.

The White City Arena, entirely reconstructed in six weeks.

The West Ham Stadium Dog Track.

3

famous

grounds

entirely re-

constructed

by

B. Sunley and Co. Ltd.

Sunley's Island . Great West Road . Brentford . Middlesex

Telephone : Ealing 1412/3

Makers of the famous "De Luxe" Non-attention hard tennis courts. Sports grounds. Gardens. Bowling greens. Racing tracks. Consult Sunley about your garden. Estimates and plans prepared without cost or obligation.

Geldard, Albert (outside right)—Born at Manningham, Bradford. Height 5ft. 7in. Weight 10st. 10lb. Was training with professionals at the age of 12 and made his English League debut with Bradford (Park Avenue) when only 15. Joined Everton at 19, in November, 1932. That season he helped them to gain the Cup and also toured the Continent with the F.A. Hobby—conjuring.

Cunliffe, James Nathaniel (inside right).—Born at Blackrod, Lancs. Height 5ft. 10in. Weight 10st. 7lb. Was discovered as a junior with Adlington, a Lancashire minor club. Went to Goodison in May, 1930, and made his first team debut three years later. Can fill any of the three inside forward positions and has been an international reserve.

Dean, William Ralph (centre forward).—Born at Birkenhead. Height 5ft. 10½in. Weight 12st. 12lb. Well known wherever the game is played. Came from that famous centre forward "nursery," Tranmere Rovers, which also brought out Pongo Waring and Bell (now with Everton too), who holds the League goal scoring record for one match. Dean holds the record for a season,. Set it up in season 1927-8 when he scored 60 goals (82 in all matches). Dislikes the nickname " Dixie." Much prefers " Bill." English international of course.

Stevenson, Alex (inside left).—Born at Dublin. Height 5ft. 5in. Weight 10st. 7lb. Was discovered in Irish junior football by Arthur Dixon, coach and trainer of Glasgow Rangers. That was five years ago. Soon got his Irish cap. Joined Everton in February, 1934. Though a schemer, does not neglect scoring opportunities.

Gillick, Terrance (outside left).—Born at Airdrie. Height 5ft. 7in. Weight 10st. 10lb. Cost £8,000—a record for the club—when secured from Glasgow Rangers last December. Has had a rapid rise. Joined Rangers from Petershill two years ago at the age of 17. Made two first team appearances that season and last term in 17 Scottish League matches he scored an average of a goal per match, also gained a Cup-winner's medal.

NAMES IN THE GAME.

" BILL " McCRACKEN

" Big Bill " McCracken, until recently manager of Millwall, will always be known by his hard-won title—the " Offside King."

He went to Newcastle United from Belfast Distillery in 1903, and in his time was the most barracked player there was. He completely confounded opposing forward lines, so bluffing them into offside positions and holding up the game by his amazingly clever exploitation of the laws, that in time the laws had to be altered !

McCrackned has often been credited with inventing the offside game, but that is to be doubted. Notts County had a back called Morley who was the first " villain," but McCracken improved upon Morley's plans.

Bill played many times for Ireland, of course, and was in the Newcastle team when they made a habit of getting to the Cup Final. They did it five times in seven seasons, though, strangely enough they won the Cup only once—against Barnsley in 1910.

Because McCracken was such an expert at the offside game, many folk lost sight of his brilliance as a full back. He was a master tactician. His speed of recovery was excellent and he could kick with both feet. His tackling was careful and deliberate.

When Newcastle United played away from home, " hostile " crowds could never upset Mc-Cracken—and they tried hard enough. The truth of course was that McCracken had, and for that matter still has, a brilliant football brain.

After finishing his playing career McCracken managed Hull City and then Gateshead. The effect of his stay at Hull is still to be seen—they are the modern Newcastle United so far as offside tactics are concerned. When Brentford were in the Second Division and Hull visited Griffin Park, they demonstrated how the offside game should be played.

DO YOU KNOW ?

The King, as did his late father, has become a Patron of the Football Association. It will indeed be a popular position should he decide to grace the Final Tie proceedings with his presence at Wembley.

* * *

The name of Alec James has been coupled with the Preston North End managership.

SAMUEL BRIDDON
Right Half.

Hailing from Derbyshire, he is known among his team mates as Sam. His football career is very short. He played for Mansfield Town for a season as an amateur, but his performances soon attracted attention and he came to Brentford, signing on as a professional. He has not made any appearances with the first team although he has played on several occasions with the Reserves. He is 6ft. in height and 11 stone 10 pounds in weight.

FIXTURES, SEASON 1935-36.

FIRST TEAM

Date. 1935.	Opponents.	Ground.	Goals F.	A.
Aug. 31	Bolton Wanderers	A	2	0
Sept. 5	Blackburn Rovers	H	3	1
,, 7	Huddersfield Town	H	1	2
,, 14	Middlesbrough	A	0	0
,, 18	Derby County	A	1	2
,, 21	Aston Villa	H	1	2
,, 28	Wolverhampton Wdrs.	A	2	3
Oct. 5	Sheffield Wednesday	H	2	2
,, 12	Portsmouth	A	3	1
,, 19	Stoke City	H	0	0
,, 26	Manchester City	A	1	2
Nov. 2	Arsenal	H	2	1
,, 9	Birmingham	A	1	2
,, 16	Sunderland	A	1	5
,, 23	Chelsea	A	1	2
,, 30	Leeds United	H	2	2
Dec. 7	Grimsby Town	A	1	6
,, 14	Liverpool	H	1	2
,, 21	West Bromwich Albion	A	0	1
,, 25	Preston North End	H	5	2
,, 26	Preston North End	A	4	2
,, 28	Bolton Wanderers	H	4	0
1936.				
Jan. 1	Blackburn Rovers	A	0	1
,, 4	Huddersfield Town	A	2	2
,, 11	(3) Leicester City	A	0	1
,, 18	Middlesbrough	H	1	0
,, 25	(4) Aston Villa	A	2	2
Feb. 1	Wolverhampton Wdrs.	H	5	0
,, 8	Sheffield Wednesday	A	3	3
,, 15	(5)			
,, 22	Stoke City	A	2	2
,, 29	(6) Birmingham	H	0	1
Mar. 7	Leeds United	A	2	1
,, 14	Manchester City	H	0	0
,, 21	(S.-F.) Sunderland	A	3	1
,, 25	Portsmouth	H	3	1
,, 28	Chelsea	H	2	1
April 4	Arsenal	A	1	1
,, 10	Everton	A		
,, 11	Grimsby Town	H		
,, 13	Everton	H		
,, 18	Liverpool	A		
,, 25	(F.) West Brom. Alb.	H		
May 2	Derby County	H		

SECOND TEAM

Date. 1935.	Opponents.	Ground.	Goals F.	A.
Aug. 31	Charlton Athletic	H	2	1
Sept. 4	Watford	A	1	3
,, 7	Clapton Orient	A	0	0
,, 12	Watford	H	2	1
,, 14	Southend United	H	1	0
,, 21	Northampton Town	A	1	0
,, 25	Luton Town	A	1	4
,, 28	Crystal Palace	H	4	0
Oct. 3	Luton Town	H	4	3
,, 5	Reading	A	1	0
,, 7	Met. Police—L.C.Cup	H	2	0
,, 9	Bournemouth & Bos.	A	5	2
,, 12	Tottenham Hotspur	H	2	1
,, 19	Bristol City	A	3	1
,, 21	C. Orient—L.C. Cup	H	3	1
,, 26	Millwall	A	4	0
Nov. 2	West Ham United	A	1	0
,, 9	Swansea Town	H	2	0
,, 11	Fulham (L.C.Cup,S.F.)	H	2	0
,, 16	Leicester City	A	3	2
,, 23	Coventry City	A	4	1
,, 30	Arsenal	A	1	0
Dec. 7	Southampton	H	4	0
,, 14	Brighton & Hove A.	H	3	1
,, 21	Queen's Park Rgrs.	H	2	2
,, 25	Chelsea	H	2	1
,, 26	Chelsea	H	1	5
	Charlton Athletic	A	5	3
Jan. 4	Clapton Orient	H	4	1
,, 11	Fulham	A	4	0
,, 18	Southend United	A	5	2
,, 25	Northampton Town	A	1	
Feb. 1	Crystal Palace	H		
,, 8	Reading	H	0	1
,, 22	Bristol City	H	3	0
,, 29	Millwall	A	0	0
Mar	West Ham United	H	4	0
,, 14	Swansea Town	A	0	5
,, 21	Leicester City	H	1	0
,, 25	Bournemouth & Bos.	A	1	1
,, 28	Coventry City	A	3	2
April 1	Tottenham Hotspur	A	1	0
,, 4	Arsenal	H	0	
,, 10	Portsmouth	H		
,, 11	Southampton	A		
,, 19	Portsmouth	A		
,, 18	Brighton & Hove A.	H		
,, 25	Queen's Park Rgrs.	A		
May 2	Fulham	A		

Half Time Scores.

	F.	A.			F	A
A—Birmingham v. Sunderland	......	......	J—Charlton A. v. 'Spurs		......	......
B—Derby County v. Chelsea	......	......	K—Fulham v. Port Vale		......	......
C—Leeds U. v. Man. City	......	......	L—Leicester C. v. West Ham		......	......
D—Liverpool v. Blackburn R.	......	......	M—Man. United v. Burnley		......	......
E—Middlesbro v. Shef. Wed.	......	......	N—Bristol City v. Q.P.R.		......	......
F—Stoke C. v. Grimsby T.	......	......	O—Luton Town v. Bristol R.		......	......
G—West Brom. v. Arsenal	......	......	P—Reading v. Crystal Pal.		......	......
H—Wolves v. Aston Villa	......	......	R—Swindon v. Coventry		......	......

THE FINEST KICK WE HAVE SEEN AT BRENTFORD FOR MANY A DAY

THE RELEGATION BOGEY

The Next Games.

After to-day's game the end of the season will soon be with us, there being only three more games before the curtain is rung down. Of these, two are at home.

The away game is with Liverpool, who the Bees visit next Saturday. It will be remembered that when they came to Griffin Park they won a very close game by two goals to one. They will try hard to complete a double while the Bees will try hard to reverse the defeat.

On the following Saturday Brentford entertain West Bromwich Albion, when a keen game should be witnessed

Then comes the last game of the season. Derby County provide the opposition at Griffin Park, and a better fixture to the ringing down of the curtain could not have been arranged, except with Sunderland, as Derby have bright prospects of being the runners-up for the League championship.

The Reserves are not so fortunate with their fixtures for out of their three games, two are away and one at home.

Next Saturday they will have as their opponents at Griffin Park, Brighton and Hove Albion.

Then they are engaged in two local " Derby " matches. On April 25th they visit Queen's Park Rangers, and to conclude the season they oppose Fulham at Craven Cottage on May 2nd.

BRENTFORD FOOTBALL AND SPORTS CLUB, LIMITED.

Registered Office :—GRIFFIN PARK, BRAEMAR ROAD, BRENTFORD.

President and Chairman :
MR. L. P. SIMON.

ALDERMAN W. FLEWITT, J.P.
MR. H. N. BLUNDELL.
MR. H. J. SAUNDERS.

MR. H. W. DODGE.
MR. C. L. SIMON.

Vice-Chairman :
MR. F. A. DAVIS.

MR. F. W. BARTON.
ALDERMAN H. F. DAVIS.
MR. J. R. HUGHES, J.P., C.C.

Hon. Treasurer :
ALDERMAN W. FLEWITT, J.P.
Club Medical Officer : DR. A. D. GOWANS.

Secretary-Manager :
MR. H. C. CURTIS,
" DORINCOURT," BOSTON GARDENS, BRENTFORD.

Telephones :
GROUND : EALING 1744.
PRIVATE HOUSE : EALING 1183.

Telegraphic Address :
CURTIS, FOOTBALL, BRENTFORD.
Ground : GRIFFIN PARK, EALING ROAD, BRENTFORD.

No. 21.   Saturday, April 25th, 1936.

Notes from the Hive.

LOVELY EASTER EGG

The Bees enjoyed a most successful Easter, in fact it might be said that their Easter Egg had a treble yoke, for all three games ended in victory for our boys.

This bright sequence was partially checked at Liverpool, where they had to be content with a division from a goalless contest.

Our reserves are making a brave fight for the London Combination championship. At the moment of writing Brentford, Arsenal and Portsmouth are bracketed at the top of the table with the same number of points and each club has two games to play. It looks like being a very exciting finish and if our boys get pipped on the post we shall still be able to say, " Well Done," with all the meaning in the world.

" DOUBLE " OVER EVERTON

The Easter holiday games commenced with a fine win over Everton, at Goodison Park, and in view of the fact that the Bees won the return game at Griffin Park by a 4-1 margin this double success of Brentford over their famous rivals kept Everton well down in the relegation zone. At Goodison Park, on Good Friday, Brentford won by the odd goal in three. McCulloch gave Brentford the lead sixteen minutes after the start. The home side equalised ten minutes later.

Brentford were on top during the second half, but only one goal came our way, McCulloch scoring mid-way through the second half.

HOME WIN OVER GRIMSBY

Next came a very good win over Grimsby Town, at Griffin Park, where the Bees won by three clear goals. Such a margin looks substantial enough but actually the Bees might have easily have won in even more convincing style for the visitors were overplayed almost from start to finish. The Grimsby goal had some remarkable escapes while on top of that the fine goal-keeping of Tweedy deserves special mention. This young goalkeeper has been well in the limelight this season and he certainly deserved all the applause he received in this game.

David McCulloch again found the net twice and Hopkins got the other goal, to which the visitors failed to reply.

NOTES FROM THE HIVE—*Continued.*

ANOTHER FINE HOME VICTORY

The Bees again touched the high spots in their home game with Everton and it can be truly said that the score of 4-1 in our favour in no way exaggerated the superiority of Brentford on the days play. Considering it was the third game in four days the play was both fast and interesting and spoke volumes for the physical fitness of the players.

It is worthy of note that our Scottish international centre forward did NOT score in this game. Evidently the fact that he scored both goals which gave the Bees victory three days previous had not been lost on the Everton players and David McCulloch was a well watched player in the game under review. But that fact only went to demonstrate that the Bees are in no way a one man scoring machine and while our centre forward was being carefully watched others were naturally being given more scope and they took advantage of the fact by collecting four goals. Hopkins (2), Holliday and Scott were the scorers.

DIVISION AT LIVERPOOL

After scoring eighteen goals in the previous seven League games our boys took an afternoon off in the penetrative business at Liverpool on Saturday last. As a spectacle the game was rather ruined by a strong wind which seemed to upset things in the matter of ball control, while the finishing on both sides left something to be desired. Yet, curiously enough, after having quite an equal share of the play the Bees might have easily suffered their first defeat for some weeks but for some smart work at times by Mathieson in our goal. Still, neither team really played well enough to deserve both points, so a division was a most equitable result.

Another point of interest about our drawn game at Liverpool was the debut of Cyril Smith, our local half back. It was his initial appearance in First Division football and he came through the test very well.

RESERVES' REVIEW

Two defeats in the last four games has rather pegged our reserves back in the quest for the championship of the London Combination once more. It may well mean that if one of these defeats had been avoided our boys may have been certain of finishing at the top, but as matters stand at the time of writing the honour may go to the Arsenal on goal average for they have to play Portsmouth at Highbury and visit Bristol City. Like Brentford, who have to visit Q.P. Rangers and Fulham, Portsmouth conclude the season with two away games—at Highbury and Southend.

Arsenal have easily the best goal average and by winning their two remaining games would be certain of the championship, but if Portsmouth should draw at Highbury, the Bees would have a chance to head the table by winning their two remaining games—not too easy, by the way.

MIDLAND VISITORS HERE TO-DAY

We have the pleasure of extending a cordial welcome to West Bromwich Albion this afternoon. At the moment the Albion are one of those clubs in danger of relegation, so they will be keen to gain some tangible reward at our expense. When the clubs met at the Hawthorns earlier in the season the Albion claimed the full spoils by virtue of scoring the only goal of the game, but we feel that with ground advantage our boys should at least reverse that verdict.

"BUSY BEE."

Jottings from the Board Room.

On Wednesday last, Bert Watson, Leslie Sullivan and Jim Raven were transferred to the Bristol Rovers F.C., and I am sure all followers of this club will join me in wishing them the best of good luck with their new club. Apart from these all other players have been placed on the " Retain List " for Season 1936-37.

The League team are to be heartily congratulated on their splendid record since Jan. 1st., 1936; of the 9 away games since then, 3 have been won and 6 drawn; also at home, of the 8 games, 6 have been won, 1 drawn, and only one defeat. Thus since Jan. 1st., 1936, the record to date is as follows :—Played 17, won 9, lost 1, drawn 7. G.F. 35; G.A. 17. Points 25.

The comparative records with last season are as follows :—

Football League—

	P.	W.	D.	L.	F.	A.	P.
This Season ...	40	16	11	13	73	58	43
Last ,, ...	40	25	9	6	90	45	59

London Combination—

	P.	W.	D.	L.	F.	A.	P.
This Season ...	44	28	5	11	93	52	61
Last ,, ...	44	24	7	13	80	52	55

Goal scorers to date are :—

Football League—McCulloch 22, Hopkins 15, Holliday 12, W. Scott 9, Fletcher 5, Robson 3, Reid 3, J. C. Burns 1, Dunn 1, Muttitt 1, McKenzie 1.—Total 73.

London Combination—Dunn 30, McAloon 16, Brown 15, Sullivan 11, Muttitt 8, Gibbons 5, Fenton 2, Smith (C.) 2, Fletcher 2, Smith (L.) 1, Dumbrell 1.—Total 93.

Supporters are asked to note that on Thursday next, April 30th, 1936, a full League team meet Brighton & Hove F.C. on this ground for the Brentford Hospital Cup; kick-off 6 p.m. The whole of the proceeds will be given to the funds of the Hospital who at the moment are badly in need of them owing to pending enlargement of the Hospital which necessitates the purchase of extra land for the enlarging and equipment and the new X-ray apparatus, the cost amounting to over £3,000.

Please endeavour to support the game

The Directors are entertaining the players and officials and wives at the Annual Dinner, Dance and Cabaret at the Wharncliffe Rooms, Great Central Hotel, on Monday next, April 27th, it is anticipated that the number to be present will be 250.

A Supporter writes to inform me that the League team have travelled 6,768 miles this season in away games, also he personally has travelled over 6,000 miles to witness most of the away games. I take this opportunity of thanking Mr. G. for his figures and to say that we are very proud to have such a valued and staunch supporter.

The Reserves are to-day away to Queens Park Rangers Reserves and for them to continue to have an interest in this season London Combination Championship they must obtain the points, here's wishing them the best of luck.

Tickets for numbered and reserved seats for our FINAL game this season on Saturday next, May 2nd, v Derby County can be purchased at 4/- each in Block " B " application by post must be accompanied by remittance and a stamped addressed envelope, otherwise they will not be considered.

Season Tickets for season 1936-37 will again be £3 10s. and £4 5s. (including tax). Application forms will be forwarded on application. Present Season Ticket Holders will greatly assist the Management by intimating their intentions of retaining their seats or not, as early as possible.

The FINAL of the London Challenge Cup, Arsenal v Brentford, takes place on the Fulham F.C. ground on Monday, May 4th, kick-off at 6.30 p.m.

The kick-off on Saturday next, May 2nd, v Derby County is at 3.15 p.m. NOT 3.30 p.m.

BRITISH LEGION THIRD ANNUAL DOG SHOW

This show will be held this year in conjunction with the Brentford Hospital Fete in Boston Manor Park, on Saturday, 27th June, 1936.

Full particulars as to entry and conditions of Show may be obtained at British Legion Headquarters, Inverness Lodge, Boston Manor Road, Brentford, on and after 1st May, 1936.

There are still a number of articles unclaimed which have been found on the ground after various games. These include keys, gloves, gaiters, a ladies raincoat, and an umbrella found in Block " C " of stand. Please apply at secretary's office.

Shots from the Spot.

It is interesting to note that if football had commenced at the beginning of the New Year, Brentford would have been at present at the top of the First Division.

* * *

As has been often written before, the Bees found First Division football quite different from that played in the Second Division with the result that they took time to " find their feet." The supporters who saw them at the beginning of the season will agree that there was not much fault to be found with the football the Bees played.

* * *

The Christmas games saw Brentford really settled down and since January the results have proved that is correct.

In fact, Brentford are " the champions of the League " since January and the following table shows what the positions of the clubs would be based on results since January.

	P.	W.	D.	L.	F.	A.	P.
BRENTFORD	17	9	7	1	35	17	25
Sunderland	17	9	4	4	40	32	22
Preston N.E.	17	8	5	3	25	17	21
Manchester C.	18	8	4	7	30	22	20
Derby	17	7	5	5	24	21	19
Aston Villa	17	7	5	5	36	31	19
Stoke	17	8	3	6	20	23	19
Everton	18	5	8	5	42	34	18
Leeds	18	8	2	8	29	25	18
Arsenal	17	5	7	5	24	18	17
Huddersfield	17	6	5	6	23	22	17
Bolton	18	5	7	6	28	28	17
Grimsby	17	7	3	7	26	27	17
Sheffield	17	6	5	6	24	32	17
Middlesbrough	17	6	4	6	32	28	16
Birmingham	17	6	4	7	23	23	16
Chelsea	17	5	6	6	23	27	16
Wolves	17	5	4	8	21	30	14
Portsmouth	17	6	2	9	18	28	14
West Brom.	17	5	3	9	37	43	13
Liverpool	17	3	7	7	17	29	13
Blackburn	17	1	6	10	11	38	10

* * *

There is a possibility that Brentford might have a tour for about ten days at the close of the season.

There are several continental countries that would like Brentford to pay them a visit but it is most probable that the Bees will go to Spain or France.

* * *

The annual dinner given by the Directors of the Club to the players and their wives will take place at the Wharncliffe Rooms, Marylebone, on Monday next. The company present will number about 250, and will include the Mayor and Mayoress of Brentford and Chiswick, Councillor and Mrs. G. R. Davidge, the Mayor of Ealing, Mr. S. F. Rous (secretary of the F.A.), and Mrs. Rous, Mr. W. W. Heard (F.A. councillors and secretary of the Middlesex F.A.), Mr. H. J. Huband (hon. treasurer of the F.A.), Mr. T. Kirkup (L.F.A. secretary).

* * *

Yet another London Club should be in the First Division next season. Charlton might even beat the Bees fine performance of coming from the Third Division through the Second Division to Division I in two seasons by doing it in one season. If they are successful they will create a record.

* * *

They have a great chance for they lead their nearest rivals, Manchester United by one point although the latter have a game in hand. Charlton's two remaining fixtures are at home so they have a great opportunity of obtaining four points.

* * *

Manchester United have two games away and one at home. In this Division two clubs gain promotion and there is still a chance of West Ham coming up with Charlton.

Should these two clubs do the trick, it will mean that in Division I there will be five London clubs.

OUR VISITORS TO-DAY.

HOW THEY MAY LINE UP.

One of the original members of the Football League, West Bromwich Albion's career dates back to 1879. They have been champions once (1919-20), but their greatest distinctions have been won in the Cup.

With Aston Villa and Blackburn Rovers they share the distinction of having reached the semi-final on 13 occasions (more than any other club). In three successive years—1886-7-8—they were finalists carrying off the trophy on the third occasion. They have won it three times altogether and been defeated five times.

Light, Norman (goalkeeper).— Born at Southampton. Height, 5ft. 11½in. Weight 12st. This much discussed goalkeeper cost the Throstles a big fee last month. Southampton was his first big club. Graduated with their " A " and reserve sides. Made a few appearances in the last two seasons, before establishing himself as first choice this season. Was apprenticed at the shipyards.

Shaw, George (right back).— Born at Swinton, Yorkshire. Height, 5ft. 10in. Weight, 10st. 10lb. After experience with Rossington Main joined Doncaster Rovers (which club his brother now assists). Went to Huddersfield in 1924 and made occasional first team appearances. It was not until transferred to West Bromwich in December, 1926, however, that he really came to the front. Is an English international v Scotland. Has queer hobbies for footballer—knitting and mat-making. Also good singer.

Trentham, Herbert Francis (left back).—Born at Chirbury, Salop. Height, 5ft. 9in. Weight, 10st. 11lb. Joined Albion from Hereford United in 1928-9 season and established himself the following campaign. While with Hereford had trial with Villa but was turned down. Always carries handkerchief in left hand. Was a junior international and has played for the Football League.

Sankey, Jack (right half).—Born at Winsford, Cheshire. Height, 5ft. 7in. Weight, 11st. 5lb. Was an inside-forward when he joined the Albion from Winsford United (Cheshire League) in November, 1930. Two years ago he developed into a sound half-back and has played regularly for the first team since.

Richardson, William (centre-half).—Born at Great Bridge, Staffs. Height, 5ft. 9¾in. Weight, 11st. 5½lb. This is his tenth season at the Hawthorns. Did not miss a match for something like three years following his first appearance, against Middlesbrough in December, 1928. Was previously with Greets Green School and Greets Green Prims.

Edwards, James (left half).—Born at Tipton, Staffs. Height 5ft. 8in. Weight 11st. 3lb. Was an inside forward when secured from Stourbridge in 1926-7. Soon settled down as a half-back and was member of side that won Cup promotion in 1930-1. Early experience with Tipton Park and Newport Foundry, where he was employed.

Mahon, John (outside-right).— Born at Gillingham. Height, 5ft. 9in. Weight, 10st. 13lb. Was secured at substantial fee from Leeds

BRENTFORD *v.* WES

BREN

Red an

1—MA

2—WILSON
Right Back

4—McKENZIE   5—
Right Half   Cer

7—HOPKINS 8—SCOTT 9—McC
Outside Right   Inside Right   Centre

Referee—Mr. G. C. DENTON (Northampton)

14—RICHA
Cent

12—WOOD   13—BOYES
Outside Left   Inside Left

17—EDWARDS   18—RICHA
Left Half   Ce

20—TRENTHAM
Left Back

22—

WEST BROM
Shirts, Navy Blue and W

THE LEAGUE—DIVISION I.

	P.	W.	D.	L.	F.	A.	P.
Sunderland	41	25	6	10	109	70	56
Derby County	40	17	12	11	57	46	46
Huddersfield T.	40	17	11	12	57	55	45
Stoke City	40	19	6	15	55	56	44
Arsenal	39	15	13	11	74	43	43
BRENTFORD	40	16	11	13	73	58	43
Preston N.E.	40	17	8	15	62	59	42
Manchester City	40	17	7	16	66	56	41
Birmingham	40	15	11	14	57	56	41
Leeds Utd.	40	15	10	15	64	64	40
Chelsea	39	14	11	15	56	67	39
Middlesbrough	40	15	9	16	84	66	39
Bolton W.	40	13	13	14	64	73	39
Portsmouth	40	15	8	17	49	64	38
Wolves	40	14	9	17	70	73	37
Liverpool	40	13	11	13	59	62	37
Grimsby T.	40	16	5	19	60	69	37
Sheffield W.	40	13	11	16	63	76	37
W.B. Albion	40	15	5	20	84	85	35
Everton	40	11	13	16	80	86	35
Aston Villa	41	13	9	19	79	106	35
Blackburn R.	40	11	9	20	50	89	31

BROMWICH ALBION

FORD
Stripes
ESON
per

3—BATEMAN
Left Back

IES   **6—RICHARDS**
alf   Left Half

LOCH **10—HOLLIDAY**   **11—REID**
ward   Inside Left   Outside Left

Linesmen—Mr. W. E. Wood (blue flag),
Mr. L. G. Aylett (red flag).

SON, W. G.
ward

15—JONES   **16—MAHON**
Inside Right   Outside Right

SON, W.   **19—SANKEY**
Half   Right Half

21—SHAW
Right Back

HT
per

CH ALBION
pes ; Knickers, White

LONDON COMBINATION

	P.	W.	D.	L.	Goals F.	A.	P.
Arsenal	45	29	5	11	115	51	63
Portsmouth	44	26	9	9	120	63	61
BRENTFORD	44	28	5	11	93	52	61
Swansea T.	45	20	10	15	75	65	50
Chelsea	44	20	9	15	93	80	49
Crystal Pal.	42	20	9	13	95	89	49
Queen s P.R.	45	20	8	17	81	68	48
Luton Town	44	21	6	17	115	104	48
Reading	44	21	6	17	92	92	48
West Ham Utd.	43	21	5	17	107	73	47
Northampton T.	44	18	10	16	91	75	46
Charlton Ath.	44	20	5	19	91	77	45
Tottenham H.	42	17	10	15	105	86	44
Millwall	43	18	6	19	61	75	42
Coventry City	44	17	7	20	76	87	41
Clapton Orient	44	14	13	17	64	91	41
Fulham	43	15	9	19	77	81	39
Bournemouth	45	15	9	21	70	97	39
Watford	45	16	4	25	87	121	36
Leicester City	43	15	5	23	72	94	35
Southend Utd.	44	12	11	21	78	100	35
Southampton	43	11	10	22	59	77	32
Brighton & H.A.	43	10	8	25	63	111	28
Bristol City	45	10	5	30	83	134	25

The Arsenal Arena, entirely reconstructed in six weeks.

3

famous grounds entirely re-constructed by

The White City Arena, entirely reconstructed in six weeks.

The West Ham Stadium Dog Track.

early this season. Is proving a worthy successor to Tommy Glidden. Was signed by the Elland-road club immediately on leaving Doncaster Grammar School. Plays on either left or right flank.

Jones, Harry Joseph (inside right)—Born at St. Helen's, Lancs. Height 5ft. 10in. Weight 10st. 12lb. Started with Haydock Juniors. Was spotted by Preston North End playing on a "coal tip." As centre forward he scored a crop of goals in their Reserves, but had to play second fiddle to Harper. Joined Albion at end of season 1932-3. Can fill all three inside positions and is a forceful attacker.

Richardson, William (" G ") (centre-forward).—Born at Framwellgate Moor, Co. Durham. Height, 5ft. 9in. Weight, 10st. 11lb. Slightly built for a centre-forward but is more than a handful for most defences. Very fast and elusive with a terrific shot. Once scored four goals in four and a half minutes (against West Ham, November 7th, 1931). Used to be a 'bus inspector and went to the Hawthorns from Hartlepools United. The " G " is added to distinguish him from the centre-half (no relation).

Boyes, Walter (inside left).—Born at Sheffield. Height 5ft. 5in. Weight 10st. 2lb. This diminutive fellow was originally a centre forward. His small stature told against him, however, and after joining Albion he played inside left, inside right and wing half. Developed into winger in season 1933-4 and was soon in the news. Played against Holland twelve months ago and for the League against the Irish League in 1935-6. Formerly with Woodhouse Mill (Sheffield), joining Albion in 1931.

Wood, Stanley (outside-left).—Born at Winsford, Cheshire. Height, 5ft. 8in. Weight, 11st. 9lb. Joined West Bromwich at a modest fee in April, 1928, from Winsford United. Soon began to make a name for himself, but lost his confidence following an injury in season 1933-4. Made only one League appearance last season, but is now back in his best form. Varies his tactics and is always willing to cut in and " have a go."

NAMES IN THE GAME.

William Bassett

William Bassett — popularly known as " Billy "—and West Bromwich Albion are synonymous.

You cannot write about one without bringing in the other. Billy Bassett was a great outside right for the Albion and England and played for his club 13 years. He played for England sixteen times and had an unbroken run of seven years against Scotland.

The Albion won all sorts of prizes in those days and Bassett was in the Cup Final three times; twice on the winning side. Though his playing days are far away, he is still a power in the game, for Billy Bassett is now chairman of West Bromwich Albion and a high official in Football Associaton and Football League.

Perhaps his greatest fame is that he has persisted in keeping his club, West Bromwich, on a consistently high level throughout all the years. How West Bromwich discover footballers is one of the great features of the game. There is no doubt Mr. Bassett has much to do with it. When a youngster is found he is taught on the Albion lines and if he has intelligence at all he cannot help succeeding. Football is the great secret of the club—not weird travesties of the game—and those who know Mr. Bassett know that he is behind all this.

A few years ago he had a serious illness and his doctor refused to let him watch football; he gets too excited. But in the end he was cured by being allowed to see the games again ! Football was never more in a man's blood.

DO YOU KNOW ?

The Wolves have done a lot of selling and player inter-changing this season, but in 1906 they created a record transfer deal when West Bromwich Albion signed eight of their players in one day.

* * *

Lancashire has had seven First Division clubs relegated in the last ten years.

* * *

It is four years since England last carried off the international championship.

* * *

Hughie Gallacher has not had a home goal since Boxing Day. But he has popped in five elsewhere.

* * *

Johnny Cochran, the Sunderland manager, never reads the paper when his team loses the day.

TOM LYNCH
Goalkeeper.

Born in South Wales, he has played for Barrow, Barnsley, Rochdale and Yeovil and Petters. He kept goal for the latter when they had that remarkable run in the English Cup competition reaching the third round.

He signed for Brentford during the close of last season and during the present season has made many appearances in the London Combination games.

He is 6ft. 2¼in. in height and weighs twelve stone.

FIXTURES, SEASON 1935-36.

FIRST TEAM

Date. 1935.	Opponents.	Ground.	Goals F	A
Aug. 31	Bolton Wanderers	A	2	0
Sept. 5	Blackburn Rovers	H	3	1
" 7	Huddersfield Town	H	1	2
" 14	Middlesbrough	A	0	0
" 18	Derby County	A	1	2
" 21	Aston Villa	H	1	2
" 28	Wolverhampton Wdrs.	A	2	3
Oct 5	Sheffield Wednesday	H	2	2
" 12	Portsmouth	A	3	1
" 19	Stoke City	H	0	0
" 26	Manchester City	A	0	2
Nov 2	Arsenal	H	2	1
" 9	Birmingham	A	1	2
" 16	Sunderland	H	1	5
" 23	Chelsea	A	1	2
" 30	Leeds United	H	2	2
Dec 7	Grimsby Town	A	1	6
" 14	Liverpool	H	1	2
" 21	West Bromwich Albion	A	0	1
" 25	Preston North End	H	5	2
" 26	Preston North End	A	4	2
" 28	Bolton Wanderers	H	4	0
1936.				
Jan. 1	Blackburn Rovers	A	0	1
" 4	Huddersfield Town	A	2	2
" 11	(3) Leicester City	A	0	1
" 18	Middlesbrough	H	1	0
" 25	(4) Aston Villa	A	2	2
Feb. 1	Wolverhampton Wdrs.	H	5	0
" 8	Sheffield Wednesday	A	3	3
" 15	(5)	...		
" 22	Stoke City	A	2	2
" 29	(6) Birmingham	H	0	1
Mar. 7	Leeds United	A	2	1
" 14	Manchester City	...	0	1
" 21	(S.-F.) Sunderland	...	3	1
" 25	Portsmouth	H	3	1
" 28	Chelsea	A	2	1
April 4	Arsenal	A	1	1
" 10	Everton	A	2	1
" 11	Grimsby Town	H	3	0
" 13	Everton	H	4	1
" 18	Liverpool	A	0	0
" 25	(F.) West Brom. Alb.	H		
May 2	Derby County	H		

SECOND TEAM

Date. 1935.	Opponents.	Ground.	Goals F	A
Aug. 31	Charlton Athletic	H	2	1
Sept. 4	Watford	A	1	1
" 7	Clapton Orient	A	0	0
" 12	Watford	H	2	1
" 14	Southend United	H	1	0
" 21	Northampton Town	A	1	0
" 25	Luton Town	A	1	4
" 28	Crystal Palace	H	4	3
Oct. 3	Luton Town	H	4	3
" 5	Reading	A	2	2
" 7	Met. Police—I..C. Cup	H	2	
" 12	Bournemouth & Bos. .	A	5	2
" 19	Tottenham Hotspur	H	3	1
" 19	Bristol City	A	3	1
" 21	C. Orient—L.C. Cup	H	3	
" 26	Millwall	H	4	0
Nov. 2	West Ham United	A	1	0
" 9	Swansea Town	H	0	0
" 11	Fulham (L.C.Cup.S.F.)	H	2	0
" 16	Leicester City	A	0	2
" 23	Coventry City	H	4	1
" 30	Arsenal	A	4	0
Dec. 7	Southampton	H	4	0
" 14	Brighton & Hove A.	A	0	1
" 21	Queen's Park Rgrs.	H	3	2
" 25	Chelsea	H	2	2
" 26	Chelsea	A	1	3
" 28	Charlton Athletic	A	5	0
Jan. 4	Clapton Orient	H	4	2
" 11	Fulham	H	4	2
" 18	Southend United	A	4	2
" 25	Northampton Town	H	5	1
Feb. 8	Crystal Palace	A	0	
" 22	Bristol City	H	3	0
" 29	Millwall	A	0	0
Mar 14	West Ham United	H	4	0
" 21	Leicester City	H	0	5
" 25	Bournemouth & Bos. .	A	1	1
" 28	Coventry City	A	3	1
April 1	Tottenham Hotspur	A	1	2
" 4	Arsenal	H	0	0
" 10	Portsmouth	H	4	
" 11	Southampton	A	1	4
" 13	Portsmouth	A	0	
" 18	Brighton & Hove A.	H	2	0
" 25	Queen's Park Rgrs.	A		
May 2	Fulham	A		

Half Time Scores.

	F.	A.			F	A
A—Arsenal v. Sheffield Un.	......	......	J—Sheffield W. v. Liverpool		......	......
B—Aston Villa v. Blackburn	......	......	K—Wolves v. Chelsea		......	......
C—Derby C. v. Sunderland	......	......	L—Charlton v. Bradford		......	......
D—Everton v. Birmingham	......	......	M—Fulham v. Swansea T.		......	......
E—Huddersfield v. Man C.	......	......	N—Port Vale v. West Ham		......	......
F—Middlesbrough v. Stoke C.	......	......	O—Tottenham v. Doncaster		......	......
G—Portsmouth v. Grimsby	......	......	P—Luton T. v. Coventry C.		......	......
H—Preston N.E. v. Leeds Un.	......	......	R—Southend Un. v. Q.P.R.		......	......

The Next Games.

Another home game next Saturday and then cheerio to football for a few months. At this stage for the past few seasons we have been able to write about how the next game or games might affect the Bees chance of promotion.

Now their first season in the highest grade of football is coming to a close and what will depend on the result of the games?

The gaining of the championship is out of the question just as there is any chance of relegation. But what are the Bees prospects of becoming the champions of London and also the runners up to Sunderland? There is little chance of the latter for Brentford are three points behind Derby County, and with only two matches to play can only gain a possible four points. At the same time Derby have two matches to play.

As regards being the highest of the three London Clubs in the League table they have bright prospects of doing so. Their only challengers for this are the Arsenal who are engaged in the Cup Final to-day. The Highbury men are level on points with Brentford but have a game in hand. Out of their remaining matches two are at home, and one away, this being Bolton. The Bees conclude their League fixtures at home.

Next Saturday, Derby County come to Griffin Park. This might be quite a needle game for there is every chance that Derby might need the points to place them as runners-up for the League championship. Brentford will go all out to further improve their fine record since the New Year and they should manage to do it.

The Reserves, who are still making a bold bid to regain the championship of the London Combination League, are away to-day to Queens Park Rangers Reserves, and on Saturday next visit Craven Cottage to oppose Fulham. These are two stiff matches. The better the opposition the better the Bees play so here's hoping that they will gain four points.

BRENTFORD FOOTBALL AND SPORTS CLUB, LIMITED.

Registered Office :—GRIFFIN PARK, BRAEMAR ROAD, BRENTFORD.

President and Chairman :
Mr. L. P. Simon.

Alderman W. Flewitt, J.P.
Mr. H. N. Blundell.
Mr. H. J. Saunders.

Mr. H. W. Dodge.
Mr. C. L. Simon.

Vice-Chairman:
Mr. F. A. Davis.

Mr. F. W. Barton.
Alderman H. F. Davis.
Mr. J. R. Hughes, J.P., C.C.

Hon. Treasurer:
Alderman W. Flewitt, J.P.

Club Medical Officer; Dr. A. D. Gowans.

Secretary-Manager:
Mr. H. C. Curtis,
"Dorincourt," Boston Gardens, Brentford.

Telephones:
Ground : Ealing 1744.
Private House : Ealing 1183.

Telegraphic Address:
Curtis, Football, Brentford.
Ground; Griffin Park, Ealing Road, Brentford.

No. 22.   Saturday, May 2nd, 1936.

Notes from the Hive.

RETROSPECT

The last day of the season is now with us and the opportunity is taken of having a look back on the doings of the Bees in their initial campaign in the First Division.

The general verdict will surely be that the Club has proved worthy of the company they have been in since last May.

The critical minded would no doubt point out that the Bees did not pull up any trees in the first half of the season and might go further and contend that when the half-way stage was reached Brentford were well in the danger zone. That is perfectly true and much might be accounted for in this connection by the fact that the Bees took an unduly long time to become acclimatised in the highest circle. Our boys naturally had to "feel their way," but it must not be forgotten that nearly every defeat sustained during the first half of the season was by the narrowest of margins—the odd goal. The Bees were playing quite good football and oftentimes enjoying the major share of the play, but just failing to get the goals which meant all the difference between victory and defeat.

Still, goals count for so much that something had to be done, and done quickly, for the lack of success was beginning to effect the standard of play.

NEW PLAYERS SECURED

Something was needed to restore the confidence of the team and the best and quickest means towards that end was the acquisition of new players. The directors went out boldly to improve the playing status by spending large sums on the acquisition of three new players. Dai Richards, the Welsh international half back, from Wolverhampton; David McCulloch, the Scottish international centre forward, from the Hearts; and Bobbie Reid, outside left, from Hamilton Academicals.

Very soon the fortunes of the Bees took an upward swing and the success of our boys has almost been of a non-stop character. So much so that the returns during the second half of the season have been amazingly good.

Look at the record since the turn of the year. Of the eighteen games played, nine have been won, eight drawn and only one defeat, an unexpected one against Birmingham at Griffin Park sustained. All will agree that this is extraordinary good going and deserving of heartiest congratulation to all concerned. It certainly makes us feel very opti-

mistic regarding the start of a new season.

Without actually stressing the fact too much, for team-work has been the plank on which the Bees have stepped forward so much on the League table, it is worth recording that David McCulloch has come out with a very fine average of a goal per game since he joined the club. That is a very good average in First Division football—or any other sphere for that matter.

But this is not a time to individualise and we want the congratulations to be equally distributed among the whole team for their excellent work, which has relieved the club of all anxiety and assured them of finishing in a high position on the League table. Well played everybody !

HOME POINT CONCEDED

A point was conceded to West Bromwich Albion, at Griffin Park, on Saturday last, which should never have happened on the actual play. The visitors were not certain of retaining their First Division status before this game was played, so they naturally played up in Cup tie style to get a point, or two if possible. An early goal, four minutes after the start, and another two minutes from the end, enabled the Albion to save a precious point which was certainly not deserved. This was a game which Brentford should have won in comfortable style, and the fact that they were denied the full spoils was largely due to the brilliance of Light in the visitor's goal.

He made some really excellent saves and his recent transfer from Southampton may have been a big factor in his new club retaining their place in the top class.

After the Albion had scored, Scott equalised and a goal by Reid enabled the Bees to lead at the halfway stage. Then came the late goal for the visitors, which robbed Brentford of the sweets of victory which their play had rightly earned.

LONDON COMBINATION CHAMPIONSHIP

The championship of the London Combination will not be decided until to-day. At the moment Arsenal, Portsmouth and Brentford are level in points at the top, with the Arsenal having completed their programme. After leading 2—0 they were beaten at Highbury last week-end in their vital game with Portsmouth by the odd goal in five. That places Portsmouth rather favourites for the honour, for if they win at Southend to-day they would secure the championship for the first time, for even if our boys win at Fulham, superior goal average would decide the honours in favour of Portsmouth. If Portsmouth drop a point and Brentford win, the honours would come our way, while if both Portsmouth and the Bees are beaten in their final games, the Arsenal would win the championship by virtue of superior goal average. The position is one of exciting possibilities. Brentford kept well in the running by beating Queen's Park Rangers, at Shepherds Bush, on Saturday last by five goals to three. McAloon (2), Muttitt, Brown and Dumbrell (penalty) scored our goals.

TO-DAY'S VISITORS

In the concluding game of the season we offer most attractive fare to our patrons, for Derby County, to whom we extend a very cordial welcome, stand as high as second on the League table. George Jobey's team, as their exalted position indicates, has done much better than usual during the campaign just ending. Derby County have often promised much, and the team looks a very good one on paper, but they have seldom got among the honours. Thus their

Continued on page 15

Jottings from the Board Room.

Our League team played Brighton and Hove League side at Brighton, on Wednesday last, for the benefit of the seasiders' captain, Potter Smith. Our boys won an enjoyable game by 2—1. Hopkins and McCulloch were the scorers.

On Thursday, the same teams met at Brentford, in a game for the Brentford Hospital Cup. The result was a win for Brentford by one goal to nil, our goal being scored by Holliday.

The following players have been retained for next season:

J. Mathieson, T. Lynch, J. Nichols. J. Wilson, A. Bateman, G. Poyser, W. Metcalf, G. Dumbrell.

J. James, D. Richards, D. McKenzie, A. Scott, H. Marley, S. Briddon, C. Smith.

I. Hopkins, W. Scott, D. McCulloch, J. Holliday, R. Reid, L. Smith, E. Muttitt, W. Dunn, J. Brown, G. McAloon, R. Gibbons, I. Fenton.

The Final of the London Challenge Cup takes place on the Fulham F.C. ground on Monday, kick-off at 6.30 p.m., between Brentford Reserves and Arsenal Reserves. A good game should complete the season's programme.

Comparative records with last season are as follows:

Football League—	P.	W.	D.	L.	F.	A.	P.
This season	41	16	12	13	75	60	44
Last season	41	25	9	7	90	47	59
London Combination—							
This season	45	29	5	11	98	55	63
Last Season	43	23	12	10	110	71	58

Goal scorers to date are:

Football League.—McCulloch 22, Hopkins 15, Holliday 12, W. Scott 10, Fletcher 5, Reid 4, Robson 3, Dunn 1, Muttitt 1, McKenzie 1, J. C. Burns 1.—Total 75.

London Combination.—Dunn 30, McAloon 18, Brown 16, Sullivan 11, Muttitt 9, Gibbons 5, Fenton 2, Smith (C.) 2, Fletcher 2, Dumbrell 2, Smith (L.) 1.—Total 98.

The team to win the London Combination championship this season will not be known until after to-day's games. At the moment Arsenal, Portsmouth and ourselves all have 63 points each. Arsenal have completed their programme, while Portsmouth are away to Southend Reserves and our Reserves are away to Fulham Reserves. Thus if both Portsmouth and our boys lose to-day Arsenal Reserves will be the champions on goal average, while if both Portsmouth and ourselves win to-day then Portsmouth would win the honours on goal average. We are hoping for our Reserves to win at Fulham and for Portsmouth to drop a point at Southend. Whatever happens, the Reserves are to be heartily congratulated on their fine fight.

Season Ticket holders are asked to notify the Secretary as soon as possible whether they intend to retain their seat for season 1936-37. Many new applications have been received, but cannot be considered until the present holders' decisions are known. Application forms can be obtained at the office.

BRITISH LEGION THIRD ANNUAL DOG SHOW

This show will be held this year in conjunction with the Brentford Hospital Fete in Boston Manor Park, on Saturday, 27th June, 1936.

Full particulars as to entry and conditions of Show may be obtained at the British Legion Headquarters, Inverness Lodge, Boston Manor Road, Brentford, on and after 1st May, 1936.

There are still a number of articles unclaimed which have been found on the ground after various games. These include keys, gloves, gaiters, a lady's raincoat, and an umbrella found in Block " C " of stand. Please apply at secretary's office.

Here's to thank all our supporters for their valued support during the season, with a sincere hope that same will continue during next season. On behalf of the Players, Management and Directors TO ONE AND ALL—MANY THANKS.

OUR VISITORS TO-DAY.

HOW THEY MAY LINE UP.

———◆———

The rise of Derby County to prominence was rapid, for when the League was founded in 1888 they were elected to one of the twelve places, though they had only been in existence four years. They have still to achieve the ambition of carrying off the First Division championship. In 1895-6 they were runners-up and seem almost certain to repeat that feat this season, though it may be only on goal average.

They have been finalists in the F.A. Cup three times, but on each occasion they have been defeated.

Kirby, John (goalkeeper).—Born at Overseal, near Burton-on-Trent. Height, 5ft. 11in. Weight 12st. 6lb. This well-built goalkeeper started with Newhall United, a Burton-on-Trent side. Was later with Gresley Rovers, Central Combination club. Joined the County in April, 1929. Got first team place in December, 1932. Played in the international trial a few weeks back.

Udall, Edward (right back).—Born at Atherstone. Height 5ft. 10in. Weight 11st. 7lb. A right back who was converted into an outside right and then moved back to his old berth. Went from Atherstone to Leicester City in 1931 as a full back. Became a wing forward but did not get a single First Division game. In 1934 Derby signed him as a deputy for Crooks, the fee being precisely nothing. Last season had not been in progress long before he returned to the defence and subsequently filled Cooper's shoes.

Howe, J. R. (left back).—This young back came to the fore with Hartlepools last season. This term has been much sought after by other clubs and Derby had to pay well for his transfer recently. Made his first team debut against Sunderland last Saturday and showed up quite well. Tackles cleanly and has a powerful kick.

Nicholas, Jack (right half).—Born at Derby. Height 5ft. 11in.. Weight 12st. 6lb. Son of a former Derby back, he was taken to Swansea as a youngster. Gained a Welsh schoolboy cap. Was at one time an amateur on Swansea's books but became a Derby professional as soon as he was old enough to sign a paid form. That was in 1927 and he got his first chance with the League side a season later. Dour tackler and neat in ball distribution.

Barker, John (centre half).—Born at Denaby, Yorks. Height 5ft. 11½in. Weight 12st. 10lb. Started with Denaby Rovers (Rawmarsh League). Moved to Denaby United and while playing in a Midland League match for that club against Scunthorpe, he was spotted by Manager George Jobey. At the baseball ground he has developed from practically a novice to England's first choice.

Keen, Errington (left half).—Born at Newcastle. Height, 5ft. 8in. Weight 10st. 6lb. Played with Newcastle United's nursery (Newcastle Swifts) as a youngster. In three years on the Tynesider's staff, however, he had only one first team outing—against his present club in October, 1930. It was soon after that he was snapped up by the County. Was capped for England against Austria in 1932, and has several times been reserve for representative matches.

OUR VISITORS TO-DAY.

HOW THEY MAY LINE UP.

———◆———

The rise of Derby County to prominence was rapid, for when the League was founded in **1888** they were elected to one of the twelve places, though they had only been in existence four years. They have still to achieve the ambition of carrying off the First Division championship. In **1895-6** they were runners-up and seem almost certain to repeat that feat this season, though it may be only on goal average.

They have been finalists in the F.A. Cup three times, but on each occasion they have been defeated.

Kirby, John (goalkeeper).—Born at Overseal, near Burton-on-Trent. Height, 5ft. 11in. Weight 12st. 6lb. This well-built goalkeeper started with Newhall United, a Burton-on-Trent side. Was later with Gresley Rovers, Central Combination club. Joined the County in April, 1929. Got first team place in December, 1932. Played in the international trial a few weeks back.

Udall, Edward (right back).—Born at Atherstone. Height 5ft. 10in. Weight 11st. 7lb. A right back who was converted into an outside right and then moved back to his old berth. Went from Atherstone to Leicester City in 1931 as a full back. Became a wing forward but did not get a single First Division game. In 1934 Derby signed him as a deputy for Crooks, the fee being precisely nothing. Last season had not been in progress long before he returned to the defence and subsequently filled Cooper's shoes.

Howe, J. R. (left back).—This young back came to the fore with Hartlepools last season. This term has been much sought after by other clubs and Derby had to pay well for his transfer recently. Made his first team debut against Sunderland last Saturday and showed up quite well. Tackles cleanly and has a powerful kick.

Nicholas, Jack (right half).—Born at Derby. Height 5ft. 11in.. Weight 12st. 6lb. Son of a former Derby back, he was taken to Swansea as a youngster. Gained a Welsh schoolboy cap. Was at one time an amateur on Swansea's books but became a Derby professional as soon as he was old enough to sign a paid form. That was in 1927 and he got his first chance with the League side a season later. Dour tackler and neat in ball distribution.

Barker, John (centre half).—Born at Denaby, Yorks. Height 5ft. 11½in. Weight 12st. 10lb. Started with Denaby Rovers (Rawmarsh League). Moved to Denaby United and while playing in a Midland League match for that club against Scunthorpe, he was spotted by Manager George Jobey. At the baseball ground he has developed from practically a novice to England's first choice.

Keen, Errington (left half).—Born at Newcastle. Height, 5ft. 8in. Weight 10st. 6lb. Played with Newcastle United's nursery (Newcastle Swifts) as a youngster. In three years on the Tynesider's staff, however, he had only one first team outing—against his present club in October, 1930. It was soon after that he was snapped up by the County. Was capped for England against Austria in 1932, and has several times been reserve for representative matches.

BRENTFORD *v.*

BREN

Red and

1—MA
G

2—WILSON
Right Back

4—McKENZIE   5—
Right Half   Cen

7—HOPKINS   8—SCOTT   9—Mc
Outside Right   Inside Right   Centre

Referee— Mr. P. SNAPE (Manchester)

12—HALFORD   13—STOCKILL   14—C
Outside Left   Inside Left   C

17—KEEN   18—
Left Half   Cen

20—HOWE
Left Back

22—
G

DERBY
Shirts, White

THE LEAGUE—DIVISION I.

	P.	W.	D.	L.	F.	A.	P.
Sunderland	42	25	6	11	100	74	56
Derby Cty.	41	18	12	11	61	46	46
Huddersfield	41	17	12	12	58	56	46
Stoke City	41	19	7	15	55	56	45
Arsenal	41	15	14	12	76	46	44
BRENTFORD	41	16	12	13	75	60	44
Preston N. E.	41	18	8	15	67	59	44
Manchester C.	41	17	8	16	67	57	42
Birmingham	41	15	11	15	60	60	41
Chelsea	41	14	13	14	60	71	41
Bolton W.	41	14	13	14	66	74	41
Middlesbrough	41	15	10	16	84	66	40
Leeds United	41	15	10	16	64	62	40
Portsmouth	41	16	8	17	52	66	40
Wolves	41	14	10	17	73	76	38
Liverpool	41	13	12	16	59	62	38
Sheffield Wed.	41	13	12	16	63	76	38
Everton	41	12	13	16	84	89	37
Grimsby T.	41	16	5	20	62	72	37
W.B. Albion	41	15	6	20	86	87	36
Aston Villa	42	13	9	20	81	110	35
Blackburn Rov.	41	12	9	20	54	91	33

ERBY COUNTY

FORD
Stripes

ESON
per

3—BATEMAN
Left Back

MES   **6—RICHARDS**
alf   Left Half

LOCH   **10—HOLLIDAY**   **11—REID**
ard   Inside Left   Outside Left

Linesmen— Messrs. A. Woolbridge (blue flag)
and S. McKenzie (red flag)

LACHER   **15—HAGAN**   **16—BOYD**
Forward   Inside Right   Outside Right

RKER   **19—NICHOLAS**
alf   Right Half

21—UDALL
Right Back

BY
per

OUNTY
rs, Black

LONDON COMBINATION

	P.	W.	L.	D.	F.	A.	P.
Arsenal	46	29	12	5	117	55	63
Portsmouth	45	27	9	9	123	65	63
BRENTFORD	45	29	11	5	98	55	63
Chelsea	46	22	15	9	100	81	53
West Ham U.	46	24	16	6	121	74	54
Swansea Town	46	21	15	10	77	66	52
Crystal Palace	45	21	15	9	100	96	51
Reading	46	22	18	6	96	96	50
Queen's Park R.	56	20	18	8	83	73	48
Luton Town	45	21	18	6	116	107	48
Tottenham Hots.	45	19	16	10	110	90	48
Northampton	45	18	17	10	91	79	46
Charlton Ath.	46	19	20	7	89	79	45
Millwall	45	19	19	7	65	78	45
Clapton Orient	45	14	18	13	64	97	41
Coventry City	45	18	20	7	83	88	43
Bournemouth	46	15	21	10	70	97	40
Fulham	45	15	21	9	78	82	39
Leicester City	45	16	23	6	75	96	38
Watford	46	16	25	5	87	121	37
Southend Utd.	45	12	22	11	81	104	35
Southampton	46	11	24	11	61	85	33
Brighton & Hove	45	11	26	8	65	115	30
Bristol City	45	10	30	5	63	134	25

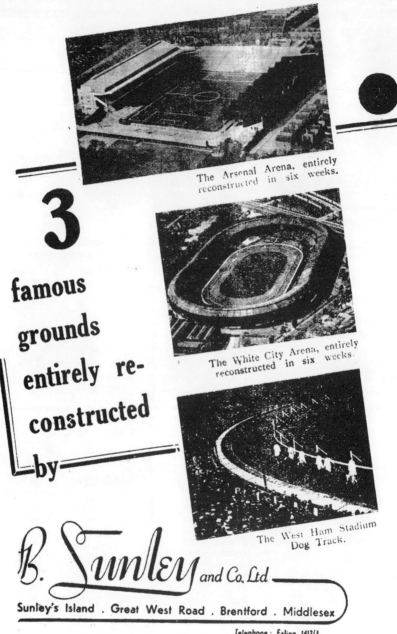

The Arsenal Arena, entirely reconstructed in six weeks.

The White City Arena, entirely reconstructed in six weeks.

The West Ham Stadium Dog Track.

3
famous grounds entirely re-constructed by

Boyd, James (outside right).— Born at Glasgow. Height 5ft. 9in. Weight 11st. One of the several ex-Newcastle players on the club's books. Went to St. James's Park after experience with St. Bernard's, a Scottish Second Division club. That was in May, 1925. Seven years later he won a Cup medal. Played for Scotland against Ireland before moving to Derby last year. Has proved capable deputy for Crooks.

Hagan, John (inside right)—Born at Newcastle. Height 5ft. 7½in. Weight 10st. 8lb. This young player has come into his own in recent months. Derby's search for thrust in the inside forward positions and the injury to Napier gave him his chance. Has shown plenty of clever touches and hard shooting power.

Gallacher, Hugh (centre forward) —Born at Belshill, Lanarkshire. Height, 5ft. 5½in. Weight 10st. 7lb. Was at school with Alex James. Started his first class career with Airdrieonians. Went to Newcastle United in 1925 at a fee of £6,500. Cost Chelsea £10,000 when he moved from Tyneside to Stamford Bridge, while last season Derby had to pay another four-figure fee. Has many Scottish caps and despite his lack of inches is still among the leading centre forwards.

Stockill, Reginald (inside forward).—Born at York. Height 5ft. 9in. Weight 11st. 3lb. A schoolboy international in 1928, he joined York City almost immediately afterwards, but was secured by Arsenal from Scarborough in the summer of 1931. Made several first team appearances before joining Derby in 1934. For some time was hampered by an injury, but has now fully recovered. Plays in any of the three inside forward positions.

Halford, David (outside left).— Born at York. Height 5ft. 10½in. Weight 10st. 10lb. Was schoolboy international for England against Scotland in 1930. Two years later he came into prominence with Scarborough, when that club did well in the F.A. Cup. Was signed by Derby and played his first games for the County's senior side in Germany in 1934. Recently he has proved a rival to Duncan for the left wing berth. Long-legged and elusive, with a powerful shot.

NAMES IN THE GAME.

GEORGE JOBEY

George Jobey, who is the manager of Derby County Football Club, was a famous half back and is now one of the best-known officials in the country.

He was on Newcastle's playing staff when they were at their zenith and he later assisted Woolwich Arsenal, Bradford, Hamilton Academicals and Leicester City before taking up his first official post. That was at Northampton, where he was player-manager of the Town. He later moved to Wolverhampton, where he built up the Wanderers' team that won the Northern Section championship in 1924.

His next move was to Derby, where he has specialised in developing budding players into first-rate stars. Steve Bloomer is one of his prime " spotters," and between them they have brought the County right to the front.

The football world still remembers the time when Derby almost secured Alex James, but the deal never came off. His biggest capture of recent years was Hughie Gallacher, who has done a lot for the County this past season.

NOTES FROM THE HIVE—*Contd.*

comparative success this season comes as a welcome relief to many disappointments occasioned in the past.

Derby have done very well in collecting no fewer than seventeen away points this season, as a result of five wins and seven drawn games.

It should be a fine game for a victory for the Bees would enable our boys to finish only two points less than the County, with a possibility, if not probability, of Brentford finishing as high as third on the list.

GOODBYE—TO ALL THAT

With the finish of another season the opportunity is taken of thanking the followers of the Club on their loyal and wholehearted support. It has been an exciting, if rather anxious at times, campaign, but the large attendances at Griffin Park have gone a long way towards solving the difficulties, because such solid support has heartened the directors in the enterprise they have shown and the heavy expenditure entailed. Thus we cordially thank our supporters for doing their bit, for without support no club can make any headway.

" BUSY BEE."

ERNEST MUTTITT
Inside Left.

Born in Middlesbrough, he first played as a professional with the Borough. He came to Brentford during the 1932-33 season and played in the team that gained promotion to Division II. He made regular appearances with the team in this Division and was in the side on 14 occasions during last season. This year he has played at outside left for the First Division side six times. He is a forceful player, revels in plenty of work and is a useful man for a club to have on its books. He is 5ft. 7in. in height and weighs 11st. 8lbs.

FIXTURES, SEASON 1935-36.

FIRST TEAM

Date. 1935.	Opponents.	Ground.	Goals F.	A.
Aug. 31	Bolton Wanderers ...	A	2	0
Sept. 5	Blackburn Rovers ...	H	3	1
,, 7	Huddersfield Town ...	H	1	2
,, 14	Middlesbrough ...	A	0	0
,, 18	Derby County ...	A	1	2
,, 21	Aston Villa	H	1	2
,, 28	Wolverhampton Wdrs.	A	2	3
Oct. 5	Sheffield Wednesday ..	H	2	2
,, 12	Portsmouth	A	3	1
,, 19	Stoke City	H	0	0
,, 26	Manchester City ...	A	1	2
Nov. 2	Arsenal	H	2	1
,, 9	Birmingham	A	1	2
,, 16	Sunderland	H	1	5
,, 23	Chelsea	A	1	2
,, 30	Leeds United ...	H	2	2
Dec 7	Grimsby Town ...	A	1	6
,, 14	Liverpool	H	1	2
,, 21	West Bromwich Albion	A	0	1
,, 25	Preston North End ...	H	5	2
,, 26	Preston North End ...	A	4	2
,, 28	Bolton Wanderers ...	H	4	0
Jan. 1 1936	Blackburn Rovers ...	A	0	1
,, 4	Huddersfield Town ...	A	2	2
,, 11	(3) Leicester City ...	A	0	1
,, 18	Middlesbrough ...	H	1	0
,, 25	(4) Aston Villa ...	A	2	2
Feb. 1	Wolverhampton Wdrs.	H	5	0
,, 8	Sheffield Wednesday ...	A	3	3
,, 15	(5)			
,, 22	Stoke City	A	2	2
,, 29	(6) Birmingham ...	H	0	1
Mar. 7	Leeds United ...	A	2	1
,, 14	Manchester City ...		0	1
,, 21	(S.-F.) Sunderland ...	A	3	1
,, 25	Portsmouth ...	H	3	
,, 28	Chelsea	H	2	1
April 4	Arsenal	A	1	1
,, 10	Everton	A	2	1
,, 11	Grimsby Town ...	H	3	0
,, 13	Everton	H	4	1
,, 18	Liverpool	A	0	0
,, 25	(F.) West Brom. Alb.	H	2	2
May 2	Derby County ...	H		

SECOND TEAM

Date. 1935.	Opponents.	Ground.	Goals F.	A.
Aug. 31	Charlton Athletic ...	H	2	1
Sept. 4	Watford	A	2	1
,, 7	Clapton Orient ...	A	0	3
,, 12	Watford	H	2	0
,, 14	Southend United ...	H	1	1
,, 21	Northampton Town ...	A	1	1
,, 25	Luton Town ...	A	1	4
,, 28	Crystal Palace ...	H	4	0
Oct. 3	Luton Town ...	H	4	3
,, 5	Reading	A	1	2
,, 7	Met. Police—L.C. Cup	H	2	2
,, 9	Bournemouth & Bos. .	A	5	2
,, 12	Tottenham Hotspur	H	2	1
,, 19	Bristol City ...	A	3	1
,, 21	C. Orient—L.C. Cup ...	H	3	1
,, 26	Millwall	H	4	0
Nov. 2	West Ham United ...	A	1	0
,, 9	Swansea Town ...	H	2	0
,, 11	Fulham (L.C.Cup,S.F.)	H	2	8
,, 16	Leicester City ...	A	3	2
,, 23	Coventry City ...	H	4	1
,, 30	Arsenal	A	0	1
Dec. 7	Southampton ...	H	4	0
,, 14	Brighton & Hove A. ...	H	1	0
,, 21	Queen's Park Rgrs. ..	H	3	1
,, 25	Chelsea	A	2	2
,, 26	Chelsea	H	1	1
,, 28	Charlton Athletic ...	A	2	3
Jan. 4	Clapton Orient ...	H	5	1
,, 11	Fulham	A	4	0
,, 18	Southend United ...	A	4	2
,, 25	Northampton Town ...	H	5	1
Feb. 1	Crystal Palace ...	A	1	
,, 8	Reading	H	0	1
,, 22	Bristol City ...	H	3	0
,, 29	Millwall	A	0	0
Mar 7	West Ham United ...	H	4	0
,, 14	Swansea Town ...	A	0	5
,, 21	Leicester City ...	H	1	0
,, 25	Bournemouth & Bos. .	A	1	1
,, 28	Coventry City ...	A	3	2
April 1	Tottenham Hotspur ...	A	1	0
,, 4	Arsenal	H	0	0
,, 10	Portsmouth ...	H	4	4
,, 11	Southampton ...	A	1	2
,, 13	Portsmouth ...	A	0	0
,, 18	Brighton & Hove A.	H	2	3
,, 25	Queen's Park Rgrs. ..	A	5	3
May 2	Fulham	A		

Half Time Scores.

	F.	A.		F	A
A—Arsenal v. Leeds...			J—Barnsley v. 'Spurs		
B—B'ham v. W. Brom.			K—Burnley v. Fulham		
C—Chelsea v. Blackburn R.			L—Charlton v. Port Vale		
D—Everton v. Preston N.E.			M—Hull v. Man. United		
E—Grimsby v. Man. City			N—Shef. U. v. West Ham		
F—Huddersfield v. Shef. W.			O—Coventry v. Torquay		
G—Portsmouth v. Bolton W.			P—Q.P.R. v. Luton Town		
H—Stoke v. Liverpool			R—Reading v. Southend		

UP IN THE HEIGHTS

" Well, I seem to have come a mighty long way in a very short time, but what a view to look back on!"

Messages to Supporters.

MR. L. P. SIMON

" We are determined to do our best for the welfare of the club in the future, as we have done in the past. I can only thank the supporters for the fine support they have given us during the season and compliment them on being such good sporting people. It is a pleasure to do anything for their comfort."

MR. H. C. CURTIS

" I extend my sincere thanks to our supporters for the wonderful way they have supported the Club during the season. Although we did not have too good a start our supporters continued to give us splendid support. We have done much better in the second half of the season and we feel that our first season in Division I has been highly satisfactory."

FINAL FOOTBALL LEAGUE TABLE
DIVISION ONE 1935-36

	P	W	D	L	F	A	W	D	L	F	A	Pts	G Avg
Sunderland	42	17	2	2	71	33	8	4	9	38	41	56	1.472
Derby County	42	13	5	3	43	23	5	7	9	18	29	48	1.173
Huddersfield Town	42	12	7	2	32	15	6	5	10	27	41	48	1.053
Stoke City	42	13	3	5	35	24	7	4	10	22	33	47	1.000
BRENTFORD	42	11	5	5	48	25	6	7	8	33	35	46	1.350
Arsenal	42	9	9	3	44	22	6	6	9	34	26	45	1.625
Preston North End	42	15	3	3	44	18	3	5	13	23	46	44	1.046
Chelsea	42	11	7	3	39	27	4	6	11	26	45	43	0.902
Man City	42	13	2	6	44	17	4	6	11	24	43	42	1.133
Portsmouth	42	14	4	3	39	22	3	4	14	15	45	42	0.805
Leeds United	42	11	5	5	41	23	4	6	11	25	41	41	1.031
Birmingham	42	10	6	5	38	31	5	5	11	23	32	41	0.968
Bolton W.	42	11	4	6	41	27	3	9	9	26	49	41	0.881
Middlesbrough	42	12	6	3	56	23	3	4	14	28	47	40	1.200
Wolves	42	13	7	1	59	28	2	3	16	18	48	40	1.013
Everton	42	12	5	4	61	31	1	8	12	28	58	39	1.000
Grimsby Town	42	13	4	4	44	20	4	1	16	21	53	39	0.890
West Brom Albion	42	12	3	6	54	31	4	3	14	35	57	38	1.011
Liverpool	42	11	4	6	43	23	2	8	11	17	41	38	0.937
Sheff Wed.	42	9	8	4	35	23	4	4	13	28	54	38	0.818
Aston Villa	42	7	6	8	47	56	6	3	12	34	54	35	0.736
Blackburn Rovers	42	10	6	5	32	24	2	3	16	23	72	33	0.572

Notes:

1) Final positions were decided by goal average and not goal difference. This was introduced in 1976.

2) Two points for a win only. The current system has been active since 1981.

BRENTFORD F.C.
PROGRAMME COLLECTORS CLUB

Founded 1990

Pre 1960 Programmes always wanted

Contact: Steve Hearne
c/o BRENTFORD F.C.
BRAEMAR ROAD
BRENTFORD
MIDDLESEX
TW8 ONT

Membership fee is £7.50 yearly. Meetings are held monthly.
Over £30,000 has been donated to the Football Club since foundation.

BRENTFORD

DIGITAL ARCHIVE

SAVING BRENTFORD'S PAST FOR BRENTFORD'S FUTURE

With the onset of digital archiving techniques, it is now possible to preserve digitally a whole treasure trove of newspapers, matchday programmes, photographs and memorabilia. This is why Brentford Football Club is undertaking the huge task of making a fully searchable digital archive, so that yesterday's heroes are remembered, not forgotten.

To complete this enormous task, The Club needs your help. We are particularly interested in all pre 1932 programmes, pre-war Official Handbooks, photographs, players contracts, old company information or anything of unique interest by either by loan or donation to digitally preserve these item for future generations to enjoy. We are also interested to hear of supporters that have kept records of past matches that Brentford played which can be considered of a non "first class" status ie: Friendlies, Testimonials, etc.

Please forward all enquiries to Mark Chapman via the club or please email: archive@oxygen3.tv

LIST OF SUBSCRIBERS

Mark Chapman
Gary Pain
David Ohl
Nick Smith
Richard Melmoth
SB Stapley
Graham Haynes
Geoff BuckIngham
Michael Cabble
Brian Jackson
Mr R Silver
Grahame Boosey
Paul Haines
John Edwards
John Hirdle
Paul Wood
Oavid Furlong
Andrew Cooper
Gary "Smudger" Smith
Fred Hermon
Leif Sorensen
David Robin Bates
Michael Burns
Tony Burns
John Boyce
Roy King
Arnold (Anthony John)
Raymond Smith
Gary & James Jenkins
Michael Wickham
Chris Wickham
Peter J Wickham
Dennis Smith
Brian Field

Ray Harrison
Ray Toms
Malcolm Pearce
John McConnell
Paul Fletcher
Ken Claxton
Jonathon Wiles
Doug Ensom
Mark Croxford
John McEnery
Paul R Hayward-Lynch
Richard Whaite
Gary Kentish
Alan Winter
lan Westbrook
Peter Gilham
Tony Ryan
Stanley Willis
Russell Wallman
Michael Cresdee
Jack Lahr
Gary Lahr
James Malcolm
George C Sansom
Frank Barry
Keith Sansom
Brett Gillingham
Ron Jeffery
Michael Page
Mike Coughlan
Tom Coughlan
Fred Hamilton
Paul Ansley
Dave Baxter